W9-ALX-181

Communism:

Its Rise and Fall in the 20th Century

Student demonstration in support of the students in Tiananmen Square held in Prague, Czechoslovakia, December, 1989.

Communism:

Its Rise and Fall in the 20th Century

From the pages of *The Christian Science Monitor*

Edited by Richard E. Ralston
With an Introduction by Earl W. Foell

Books from

THE CHRISTIAN SCIENCE MONITOR.

The articles in this book originally appeared in The Christian Science Monitor and World Monitor: The Christian Science Monitor monthly.

Cover Photo by Neal J. Menschel.

Book designed and produced by Good Graphics Group, Boston, MA. Designed by Stephen Goldstein.

Typeset in New Baskerville with Eurostyle Condensed & Helvetica Bold Compressed.

Color separations, signatures and jacket printed by The Nimrod Press Printers and Engravers, Boston, Massachusetts.
Bound by Horowitz/Rae Book Manufacturers, Inc., Fairfield, New Jersey.

Library of Congress Cataloging-in-Publication Data:
Communism: Its Rise and Fall in the Twentieth Century

1. Communism—History.
2. Communism—1945.
3. Communism—Europe, Eastern—History—20th century.
4. Europe, Eastern—Politics and government—1945-1989.
5. Europe, Eastern—Politics and government-1989.

I. Ralston, Richard E.   II. Christian Science Monitor.

HX44. C6427 1991   90-19535
ISBN 0-87510-218-2

Printed in the United States of America.

10 9 8 7 6 5 4 3 2 1

Dedicated to the journalists and all others who have labored every day to maintain the poise and perspective on events which have distinguished *The Christian Science Monitor* since 1908.

Any book which draws on editorial efforts spanning most of a century owes a lot to the work of thousands of people unknown to this editor. This book is dedicated to them.

More specific appreciation can fortunately be expressed to the following people:

Earl W. Foell, Editor-in-Chief of *World Monitor* magazine, and former Managing Editor, Editor, and Editor-in-Chief of the *Monitor* for writing the Introduction. Both his breadth and length of experience with the *Monitor* add greatly to this book.

Georgiana Hamm for managing the entire process of production for this volume, including the heroic effort to keep this Editor on schedule.

Marshall D. Wright for research in over 20,000 daily issues of *The Christian Science Monitor* to identify likely material for this book.

Jim Carlson for photo research.

Diane Ewart for keeping everything else going.

Casey Wright and David D. Hohle for their foundational work in establishing *Books from The Christian Science Monitor.*

Editor

Foreword

This is the history of a great journalistic enterprise as it relates to coverage of perhaps the major international story of the Twentieth Century: The birth, life, and death of Communism. It is not a detailed history of Communism or the Soviet Union. It is the story of the context and perspective which one great newspaper sought to bring to events which threatened the entire world with tyranny, terror, and destruction.

Rather than a year by year review of events, this book has concentrated on major journalistic efforts of some length which appeared in the paper during a number of intervals over the years. It therefore provides, in a sense, a history of the basic and underlying pattern of events. Material in this book is included in the chronological order in which it was published. Therefore, material on a particular period might appear in a retrospective analysis written a decade later.

The Christian Science Monitor has greatly benefited from a number of talented journalists who contributed extended series of articles. These series gave their writers the opportunity to convey a level of understanding to readers across a very broad subject that is not possible in shorter articles reporting on breaking news. This collection has necessarily emphasized selections from these longer treatments. Quantity was not the primary consideration in selecting these longer series, but quality. The quanlity in the series by Chamberlin, Stevens, Pisko, Wohl, Willis, and Temko was so consistent that it was extremely difficult to make the many cuts necessary for this volume. These correspondents achieved real break-throughs in conveying an understanding of essential issues that were both profound and timeless. Timeless in the sense that while editing them all—in itself a process of jumping back and forth frequently across the years—I found in those selections a freshness and depth of insight which made them almost interchangeable from one decade to another.

Other journalists not included in this selection made equally important contributions in giving readers a balanced insight into daily events in their regular reporting for the newspaper. I am greatful to Earl Foell for providing in his Introduction a complete history of the *Monitor* people involved in its coverage of the Soviet Union through the years.

Photographs make their own contribution—providing readers with understanding on a different level. The current staff of photographers at *The Christian Science Monitor* have provided the paper with some remarkable color images in the last two years which are the prominant visual features of this book. Unfortunately most of the original photographs from the early years of the newspaper have not been preserved and are reproduced here only in the form of reproductions of newspaper pages. We were fortunate to obtain rare archival prints from Sovfoto—in some cases the actual prints which were used in the *Monitor*. These are reproduced, frayed edges, bent corners and all—often as the only prints in existence. In one case even the frame of a news film is reproduced. Also represented are some of the color rotogravure covers of the weekly magazine section which was inserted in the newspaper in the 1930's and 1940's.

In more recent decades much of the noteworthy black and white photography of Gordon Converse and others was available and is included here. Color photography from the magazine *World Monitor* and even video tape images from the television program *World Monitor* complete the visual elements of the volume.

This book focuses almost entirely on the Soviet Union, which has been the nexus of Communism in this century, and through most of the century the only great power claiming Communism as a form of government. All Communist governments which came to power in this century through internal revolt or external force were not just Marxist but Leninist, and almost always Stalinist. Communist theory did not originate in the USSR. As a government in place it was born there and has now effectively died there.

At this writing Communist governments are still in power in Albania, China, Cuba, North Korea and Vietnam. Is it therefore premature to announce the death of Communism? Certainly no compassionate person can be comfortable while over a billion people are still imprisoned by such a system. The remarkable events of 1989 in Eastern Europe began to accelerate on June 4, the date of the Polish election which brought Solidarity to power. That same day students were massacred in Tiananmen Square in Beijing.

While the Chinese Communist government still hangs on to power, no one outside the reach of Beijing's troops is under any illusion that it is a government that can survive without the use of troops against its own citizens. In any case China is not a great power. Its huge population alone can claim to make it so, but that has been an empty claim for hundreds of years. With a GNP smaller than that of Italy or the United Kingdom, China is not a major power and has little prospect for becoming one. (Indeed tiny South Korea now has an economy about

40% the size of Communist China's. Because of such obvious economic problems, even this last large country with a Communist government has long since implemented reforms in the direction of a market economy—while trying to maintain all political power in its own hands.)

In light of these conditions, Communism is clearly dead as the government of a great power, dead as a role model for developing countries, dead as an option that the people of any nation might freely choose, dead as a living idea upon which government can be based anywhere.

Erwin D. Canham, Editor of *The Christian Science Monitor* for many years, titled his 1958 history of the newspaper *Commitment to Freedom*. It is my hope that these selections will convey both the spirit of the newspaper and that continuing commitment, supplemented in the last two years by the paper's monthly magazine *World Monitor*, as well as the nightly news program of the same name appearing on The Discovery Channel in the United States, and on additional networks in other countries.

The demise of Communism in no way allows for any reduction in the *Monitor*'s "commitment to freedom". Freedom is much more than the absence of Communism. It was challenged before Communism became a threat and will continue to be challenged. Alertness to any restrictions on the free action of men and women anywhere is required now as much as ever. To this task the *Monitor* will remain committed. We owe it to ourselves. We owe it to the millions whose unnecessary suffering in this century is recounted in this volume. We owe it to those who still strive for freedom and to all mankind now. This requires a vision of journalism which goes far beyond just giving people "news".

The Christian Science Monitor has never sought to be the first newspaper to scream a headline at its readers. It has sought to be a source of objective daily analysis in a manner which remains above the daily fray of events. In the face of the most alarming events it has always attempted to take a step back and look for the essentials. It has attracted readers who want to understand events in order to take action to effect events.

At its best it has brought enlightenment to its readers rather than just information. When this process has become a partnership with equally committed readers it has gone beyond enlightenment to the ennoblement of both readers and the read about.

Perhaps none of its readers has expressed it better than the late Alan Paton, author of *Cry the Beloved Country* who began reading the *Monitor* after a lifetime of fighting racial prejudice because, he said, "It gives no shrift to the idea of the irredeemable wickedness of man, or the futility of human endeavor. It is a newspaper of sober and responsible hope. Long may it live."

Richard E. Ralston
Editor
October, 1990

West Germans occupy the Berlin Wall at Brandenburg Gate in celebration of the opening of the wall, November, 1989.

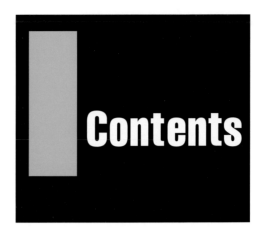

Contents

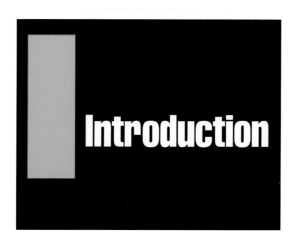

Introduction

This is a tale of an empire and smuggled chocolates.

It is a story of ruthless emperors caught up in the chess moves of power, self-deluded grand thinkers, a warm and philosophically inclined populace, and a small band of clear-eyed outsiders who saw through the emperor's clothes and catechism.

It is a selection of acute letters home from a series of writers who lived with the inconveniences of clanging purple steam pipes, one of the last traditional wooden houses in Moscow, extreme censorship, a stretch Volvo, and an interrupting rabbit.

It is, in short, the record of various writers' understanding of the 75-year span in which Communism, Leninism-Stalinism, scientific materialism, socialist realism, and the New Class triumphed and failed in Russia and its empire.

Please read these dispatches remembering that, when the reporters wrote, the leviathan they covered looked to much of the world unshakable, if not invincible. You may be surprised to find how prophetic are most of the assessments made by William Henry Chamberlin, who served in Moscow from the final Lenin years to the mid-1930s, or Edmund Stevens and Ernest Pisko in the 1940s and early 1950s. Much of what they wrote sounds uncannily fresh today. Much is echoed, point by point, by clear-eyed Russians like Andrei Sakharov, Roy Medvedev, and Dimitri Simes; and by the current wave of Western Sovietologists and foreign correspondents. But both these groups of more recent authorities write with half a century's added hindsight; and the Russian group enjoyed the further asset of native Slavic insight.

All in all, one has to marvel at the clear vision, perspective, and what must have been inner-driven persistence on the part of such omniverous viewers as Chamberlin and Stevens. They measure very well on the Tocqueville-Custine Scale of sharp insight into the psyche and machinery of a foreign society. (I've created the T-C scale from the names of those two 19th century French travelers, Alexis de Tocqueville and the Marquis de Custine, who achieved fame for their acute descriptions of life in, respectively, America and Russia.)

The best of the observers you will read on the following pages carry on Custine's mission of explaining life in the Muscovite empire after that empire went through a sea of change a century later.

The Union of Soviet Socialist Republics was, in the end, the greatest Potemkin village in history.

But, for a long time most of the world didn't realize it.

Prince Potemkin, you may remember, allegedly fooled his empress and onetime paramour, Catherine the Great, by ordering false building facades. He did so to disguise the weak points in his modernizing of the ramshackle southern towns she went out to review in 1787. The Communist emperors—Lenin, Stalin, and successors—managed a grander deception. They sought to convince the entire world they led the wave of the future. To do so they created Potemkin facades of happy, heroic art; the no-inflation, full-employment economy; bury-the-West industrial growth; Stakhanovite super-workers; a smooth alliance in Eastern Europe with outposts in all continents. In short, the new Socialist man breeding further generations of state-trained young pioneers. They had history by the tail.

For much of the 20th century the facade was overpoweringly successful. The proof: universal acceptance of the title "superpower," and widespread attempts to mimic the Soviet system, from China to Angola to the Andes. But success turned out to be shortlived, as ideology-driven empires go. The Soviet Union's lifespan—three quarters of a century as a monolithic communist empire—was brief compared to the long sway of the Ottoman empire, or the two centuries of the Holy Roman Empire.

Prime Minister and erstwhile newspaper reporter Winston Churchill described the USSR as "a riddle wrapped in a mystery inside an enigma." The aphorism was widely accepted. Most of the foreign correspondents doing their individual laps in the relay race of Moscow coverage felt challenged to prove they knew the answer to the riddle.

Few did.

It still seems to me remarkable that so many of those who did were in that thin line of *Christian Science Monitor* Moscow correspondents, many of whom appear in this collection.

Now I'd like to give you a glimpse of what is in store for you—and also of some of the reporters who don't appear in this anthology but who contributed to the continuity of sharp-eyed coverage. As we make this tour you'll find out where the chocolate, the purple pipes, the Volvo, and the rabbit fit in.

Foreign correspondents, like diplomats and spies, go abroad to be eyes and ears for others. Their success depends on their background, their shrewdness, their legwork, their instincts, and, above all, their judgment as to which local individuals they rely on for guidance. A great Pulitzer-winning correspondent for the late lamented Chicago Daily News once told me that a foreign culture is like an onion; most correspondents don't get beyond the dry outer layer. The writers included in this collection dug deep into the inner layers. To do so, they and their colleagues from other publications often had to use a great deal of ingenuity to slip out of the journalists' ghetto in which they lived and out of the control of "handlers" (often KGB) who accompanied them on their rounds.

The ghetto itself was relatively pleasant. Apartments were comfortable by Moscow standards. But they had their quirks. And, at times of official displeasure, life could be made tedious and uncomfortable for these guests at the pleasure of the state. To relieve that tedium for Chamberlin, his colleague Joseph C. Harsch recalls, anyone headed for Moscow was told to bring or smuggle in as many boxes of chocolates as possible to sustain the chocoholic Chamberlin. Sometimes the import supply ended quite thinned out after various customs inspectors had taken their commission.

Edmund Stevens started writing for the *Monitor* in 1939 as a steamship company clerk-turned-freelancer covering Moscow's takeover of the Baltic states and the start of the Finnish-Soviet war. He was soon elevated to staff status. After a daring war correspondent's career ranging from the Nazi invasion of Norway to Romania, North Africa, Ethiopia, and South Africa, he was sent back to cover the USSR. It was he and his Russian-born wife, Nina, who acquired the traditional dark wooden house within the city of Moscow. They became noted not only for Ed's superb reporting, which was eventually to win the *Monitor* its first Pulitzer Prize, but also for the dwelling itself, which was one of the very few private houses in the city (in contrast to the apartments in which most Muscovites, and reporters, live). The house, despite the inconveniences of an old-style structure, gave the Stevenses an advantage in terms of entertaining— and thus gaining access to more of the inside story of what was going on within the Enigma Capital. (It is worth noting that for about 70 years no one—no Kremlinologist, no CIA analyst, no Armand Hammer or Chip Bohlen, no Earl Browder or Mao Zedong for that matter—knew exactly what took place in the deliberations of the all-powerful Politburo.) In addition, the Stevens's daughter Anastasia ("Stasia") was later to become a dancer at the Bolshoi and a friend of the half-Establishment-half-iconoclast poet, Yev-tushenko. But before that time, the Stevenses were forced to close the bureau because of heavy censorship and other harrassment in the late Stalin years. That exile resulted in the *Monitor* series, "This is Russia—Uncensored," for which he won the Pulitzer.

During the post-Stevens diaspora, the newspaper had to use the listening-post approach to Soviet coverage, turning the writing over to two brilliant Sovietologists living in the US. One was Ernest Pisko, the noted Viennese editor who became assistant to the overseas news editor of the *Monitor*. Pisko had toured the USSR and written a cogent series titled "Stalin's Hoax" in the late 1940s. It exposed just how far the dictator's state had strayed from the Marxism it professed. Pisko then turned to analytical pieces using sources inside and outside the country at the end of the Stalin era and the beginning of the de-Stalinization period. Pisko had been an artillery captain in Emperor Franz Josef's army before becoming an editor. He and his wife, Risa, had to flee the Nazi takeover of Austria with little more than the clothes on their backs. They served as butler and cook in a British lake country manor before emigrating to America. There the always vigilant *Monitor* foreign editor, Charles Gratke, drafted Pisko to edit European copy—and to train two generations of future foreign correspondents, several destined for Moscow.

The second diaspora reporter was Paul Wohl, whose life was to be devoted to the patient analysis that became known as Sovietology. Another noted specialist on Soviet affairs, columnist Victor Zorza of *The Washington Post* and *The Guardian,* once said that a whole era of Sovietologists owed their inspiration and their methodology to what they learned from reading Wohl.

Paul's first prolonged contact with the USSR came when the Communist régime was still young. In the late 1920s he went there as a specialist on improving transportation systems, particularly railroads. He had been an official of the International Chamber of Commerce, very much a Capitalist bastion against Marxism. For that reason he worried about whether the Communists would receive him well—or at all. When he cautiously raised this point with a Moscow bureaucrat, the official replied: "Bring a top hat and wear it. We like to have visiting Capitalists dress for their role." Wohl wore the hat. It worked.

He also had another strike against him, if the Stalinist régime had ever discovered it. While living in Paris, he had once sheltered a noted Trotskyite for a night. Stalin was death—literally—on Trotsky and his followers.

Wohl started his work for the *Monitor* in 1941 but came into his own as a Sovietologist after Stevens departed Moscow. Wohl lived and did his research work in what was to become a famous garden apartment in New York's Greenwich village. The fame came in part from Sovietology, in part from turtles. *The New Yorker* magazine once did a profile on Paul's pre-Ninja turtlemania. Those who knew him recognized what they thought were good reasons for his unusual hobby: Paul bore a certain resemblance to a turtle, moving resolutely and blinking solemnly behind his researcher spectacles. To visit his apartment was to test one's peripheral vision. There, amid piles of provincial Soviet newspapers and obscure economic reports, various terra cotta and bronze replicas of turtles reposed on tables, desks, and the floor. Some served as paperweights, some as doorstops. Only gradually did the visitor become aware of subtle small motions. Some of the turtles weren't pottery; they were the real McCoy. The experience was eerie, like being part of a small universe in which the apparently fixed stars were all slowly revolving. Wohl tracked facts on Soviet oil production or meat shortages as painstakingly as he did his turtles. He was the first scholar to discover that Moscow was charging its allies more than its opponents for petroleum—a practice later reversed. (He also determined that two huge Galapagos turtles on the Atlantic island of St. Helena were not, as once thought, pets brought in to amuse the exiled Napoleon—merely their non-Methuselah offspring.) What he treasured in his herpetological friends, other Sovietologists treasured in him: patience, exactitude, unhurried judgment.

But back to Moscow and, oh yes, the Volvo and the rabbit.

Nikita Khrushchev had de-Stalinized the USSR and loosened the censorship reins to a considerable degree. Sovietology from New York, Vienna, and Helsinki no longer unraveled mysteries better than on-scene digging. It fell to Takashi Oka, previously a China/East Asia specialist and later to be perhaps the most-traveled of all the paper's foreign correspondents, to resume the *Monitor* presence in Moscow in 1966. The bureau space acquired was that of the just deceased *New York Herald Tribune.* It was a prime apartment, with good office equipment. And with it came the H-T's Ford, later to become a sore subject.

In 1968 Charlotte Saikowski succeeded the Okas. She was thoroughly prepared for the job, after years as second in command at Columbia University's "Current Digest of the Soviet Press." She and her successors, Leo Gruliow and Elizabeth (Beb) Pond, made a specialty of traveling widely and seeing a broad cross section of Soviet citizens as well as much of the vast territory of the USSR. Gruliow had had previous long service in Moscow in the 1930s before becoming the founder and longtime director of "Current Digest of the Soviet Press." Pond's book, "From the Yaroslavsky Station: Russia Perceived," examined the industrial, economic, and social problems of the nation in a colorful narrative growing out of the lives and observations of people met on a trans-Siberian train trip. Her book is still an assigned Russian history text on many college campuses.

Oh, yes, the car... Charlotte arranged to buy a Volvo, which came to be known as the stretch Volvo. That was not a reference to its length, which was normal, but to its longevity. Foreign editor after foreign editor, conscious that Moscow was his most expensive bureau (until the rising yen gave Tokyo the championship), insisted that the Volvo roll on through the years, much to the disgust of Sasha, the official — and still active — bureau driver. It was he who had to supervise a long series of ingenious repairs with spare parts brought in from Helsinki. Sasha, whose prestige sank as the car's age rose, was peeved when neither reporters nor home office showed any interest in acquiring a more fashionable chariot.

Pond's successor, Australian-American journalist David K. Willis, arrived at the end of the '70s to encounter the jarring purple pipes (created by some anonymous painter) and curling parquet floor in the *Monitor* flat. His tour of duty included the evolution of the country from the détente period of the mid-1970s back into the suspicion and frozen posturing of the final Brezhnev years. The Willises broke through some of the re-erected barriers facing the Western press for two reasons: David's indefatigable reporting, and contacts his wife Margaret made in the course of dancing at the Bolshoi ballet school. Willis's stint in Moscow also produced a book: "Klass: How Russians Really Live," a study of how a hierarchical, party-based class structure affected daily life. The Willis era also produced the rabbit, a pet which the three young children of the household could not bear to leave behind in America. Foreign desk editors in Boston soon got used to telex transmissions interrupted at a crucial point when Willis had to rescue the bunny from some predicament. Occasionally they heard the thump of rabbit feet across the uneven parquet in the background of phone conversations. The rabbit became as real a presence in the *Monitor* newsroom, 4,800 miles away, as the imaginary stage and movie rabbit Harvey was to his inventor. Willis also offered the coup de grace to driver Sasha's hopes when he (1) got rid of the limping Volvo but (2) bought a less reliable Soviet-made vehicle. There is a widespread hope in the press corps that Sasha will someday get to drive a BMW. But don't hold your breath.

Ned Temko, a versatile correspondent who spoke five languages and quickly added Russian, moved to Moscow from the Middle East. His addition to the repertory of Moscow coverage was to do something virtually unheard of at the time: seek interview appointments with high officials of the Central Committee of the party and of the government ministries. It's ironic that such a standard journalistic practice in other societies should have atrophied to the point where it had to be reinvented in late Brezhnev Moscow. The result for Temko: he often had to sit through long repetitions of official jargon; but, as he won the confidence of some of his interviewees, they opened up and told him what they really thought, gave him at least some glimpses of what was actually going on. You might call it Temko glasnost.

Candidness, even reckless frankness, is such a regular part of the Moscow scene in the last decade of the 20th century that it is hard to recall just how unusual these interviews were at the time. The political deck officers who manned the massive ship of state were beginning to question not just their captain but the naval architects and builders themselves — Marx, Lenin, Stalin.

Gary Thatcher, Paul Quinn-Judge, and Linda Feldmann were readers' eyes and ears during the 1980s — a decade that started with funereal inertia and ended with the acceleration of collapsing illusions and collapsing institutions. Quinn-Judge pursued the Temko approach of getting to know movers and shakers in the door-opening period of "glasnost." He and Feldmann also found it easier to talk to the new thinkers — economic and political — who were rapidly moving from publishing myth-shattering analyses to advising Kremlin leaders.

Linda gained unusual perspective by being one of the first American journalists to serve on a Moscow newspaper. She did so as part of a US-USSR exchange program. (The other end of which, incidentally, brought briefly to the *Monitor* Yelena Khanga, a black Russian, who covered the first Reagan-Gorbachev summit — and was herself covered extensively by the Washington press corps.) Linda's paper, "Moscow News," moved into the forefront of investigative reporting that challenged both dogma and old-line bureaucrats.

The final works in this anthology come from a scholar, a spy, a theologian, and a noted BBC commentator, all of them writing in the *Monitor*'s sister publication, the monthly *World Monitor* magazine.

The scholar, Professor Marshall Goldman, is associate director of Harvard's Russian Research Center. His analysis of Mikhail Gorbachev is particularly telling because it so accurately projected years ahead of time what was to happen to the leader's dizzyingly rapid, but never quite rapid enough, reforms. This first of many Goldman articles for *World Monitor* was written for a prototype issue of the magazine in March of 1988 — seven months before its formal launch. That issue never hit newsstands. But, by some alchemy, prominent members of Gorbachev's Central Committee heard details of the Goldman analysis and asked him to please send copies to the Kremlin.

KGB defector Victor Sheymov (cover name: Victor Orlov) came into WM's pages via a properly spy-like route. He phoned in unannounced from his CIA-arranged hideout somewhere in America to say he had seen the magazine, liked it, and wanted to write for it. One of his terms: he couldn't be contacted directly. Any editing or questions would have to get to him via an airline delivery service in a southern US airport. WM's editors, having no means of directly checking the accuracy of his KGB credentials — or even his existence — had to resort to a quiet conversation with a top CIA official to verify that this was a genuine, if lapsed, top KGB officer typing away on our manuscript. After two such articles, the spy who had served in Eastern Europe and China reached the point where he could come in from the cold war and go public at a Washington press conference. His article in this collection discloses the way in which each of the superpowers heard only its own version of the language they used to communicate with each other.

The BBC's global analyst, John Simpson, looks at both art and the unbroken roothold of Russian history in a profile of the colorful, freethinking painter, Ilya Glazunov. The artist's life provides a striking example of the strength of Russian traditions, which were often submerged only lip-service deep beneath the wordy creed of Marxism-Stalinism.

Theologian Harvey Cox, celebrated for such books as "The Secular City," traces the truly remarkable way in which that forbidden, supposedly outgrown explanation of life — religion — bloomed again, not just among old folk keeping the past alive but in young, state-trained technicians seeking to fill a void in their lives.

Now you have the cast of characters, most on-stage in this book, some off-stage. Before they begin to speak their lines, let me utter just two pieces of advice. First, don't get bogged down in the overture. The scene-setting short *Monitor* passages in the first chapter are there for the record and for context. Second, savor the work of Chamberlin and Stevens in particular. Remember that the Leninist-Stalinist world was new, virtually uncharted when Chamberlin began to assess it. John Reed, the journalist/enthusiast of the Russian Revolution, had told the world of the aspirations of the Bolsheviks to produce a new society and a new human. But the world needed to know how the experiment was going. The scene was Tolstoyan in breadth and complexity. But it was also obscured by slogans, the self-deception of true believers, purposeful deceit, closed lips, and difficulties placed in the way of the reporters. Imagine yourself facing such a broad canvas, so annoyingly confused and obscured. And then read, say, Chamberlin's 1935 summary of what he learned during 12 years of penetrating the enigma. It's a remarkable exercise in casting light on that huge confusing canvas.

Too often life is disorderly raw material for history; history is orderly but lifeless. In Chamberlin, Stevens & Company I hope you'll see both life and order — reality made clear.

Earl W. Foell

THE CHRISTIAN SCIENCE MONITOR

LAST EDITION — [Copyright 1917 By The Christian Science Publishing Society] — BOSTON, MASS., FRIDAY, MARCH 16, 1917—VOL. IX, NO. 92 — PRICE TWO CENTS

CABINET MAY ACT TO AVERT RAILWAY STRIKE

Brotherhoods and Managers Indicate Readiness to Take Up Further Discussion if President Should Express Desire

Special to The Christian Science Monitor from its Washington Bureau

WASHINGTON, D. C.—It was expected that President Wilson would make known today what steps he is to take in the effort to avoid a strike on the railroads but no announcement was forthcoming.

A meeting of the Cabinet was called for 2:30 o'clock and it is anticipated that the situation will be discussed at that meeting and a decision reached as to what means can be used to assure the uninterrupted continuance of traffic.

It was announced at the White House that a letter received from New York during the morning from both the brotherhood men and from the managers indicated that they are willing to take up further discussion and the feeling prevailed that both sides were waiting for the President to speak.

The fact was added strength to the generally prevailing conviction that the brotherhoods have taken advantage in the present national crisis to force their personal cause. Brotherhood members at the Union Station in Washington say they have received no strike order and that they were prepared to vote on the strike question. Furthermore they declare the strike order of last fall is not now in force.

In some quarters there is a feeling that if the President should speak at this moment firmly on the strike question and make the fact evident to the public that either side in the controversy that stands in the way of an amicable settlement of the question at issue will be held by the people of the country as morally guilty of treason, this juncture, a settlement would be reached, because neither side would desire to incur the feeling "that had placed.

This statement has been authorized by the White House, and all officials interested to be ignorant of what the President might intend to do. Some believed that having appealed again and again to both sides to adjust their differences, there was no step left for him to take. Others believed he can make some move before he can go on strike.

The President is known to regard a railroad strike is a menace to the safety of the country at this time, already entered an order prohibiting the interstate traffic of food. Apparently, however, he feels that he Administration is powerless unless it is absolutely necessary for him to adopt measures to keep the mails moving.

After a telephone conference with Secretary Wilson of the Labor Department it is understood the President is prepared to make no move during the night.

There is a disposition among some Administration officials to believe that unless something intervenes the progress of plans for the strike never will be permitted to conclusion. Before next Wednesday, the day by which it is proposed to make the walkout effective throughout the country, they believe a compromise will have been reached.

Precedents under which the Government might take a hand in the situation were being searched for last night.

Had the Sixty-fourth Congress, which adjourned early this month,

(Continued on page eight, column two)

OFFICIAL NEWS OF THE WAR FROM CAPITALS

The British have made further gains on the western front. London reports that the area of the German withdrawal has extended toward the south and that the German trenches on a front of 2½ miles, from south of St. Pierre-Vaast Wood to the north of the village Sailiisel. The French have also made gains east of Canny-sur-Matz, where they have penetrated the German positions to a depth of 300 meters.

Steadily increasing activity is reported from the Macedonian theater. The British have advanced their line southwest of Doiran, 1000 yards over a front of 3500 yards; whilst the Italian troops are advancing on Bulgarian and German positions between Lake Presba and Lake Malik.

BERLIN, Germany (Friday, by wireless to Sayville)—The official statement issued yesterday from army headquarters reads:

Western front: During the rainy weather the artillery fire in most sectors was limited.

In the Champagne French attacks on the northwest slope of Hill 185, south of Ripont, were developed, under our annihilating fire.

Reconnoitering advances took place in the Somme sector and on the west bank of the Meuse (Verdun front), where a post held by the French south of Cumieres was captured by

(Continued on page six, column seven)

GERMANS TO TAKE ACTION AGAINST SPANISH JOURNAL

El Liberal Claimed That Chilean and German Officials Were Implicated in Cartagena Plot

Special Cable to The Christian Science Monitor from the European Bureau

MADRID, Spain (Friday)—A new sensation is produced almost daily in connection with the discovery of explosives, etc., left at Cartagena by a German submarine. In connection with the matter, the Spanish Government is bringing four Germans and numerous Spaniards to trial.

It is now announced that finding the position difficult as a result of the piling up of new charges against German officials, proceedings are about to be taken against the newspaper El Liberal, at the instance of the German Ambassador who complains of articles published recently on German espionage in Spain. El Liberal, commenting on the threatened proceedings, states that part of the information in the article complained of appeared in the Conservative journal La Epoca, the previous day, and asks if the German Ambassador will dare take proceedings against the Conservative organ.

The new turn of events has created enormous interest and startling revelations are expected. For some two or three weeks El Liberal, which has just discovered that cases deposited by the submarine contained 1800 kilos of trinitrol, has been carrying on a vigorous campaign against German espionage in Spain, and admittedly its revelations have forced the Government to action against the Germans in the country. As a result, German diplomacy in Spain is in a difficult position, and it was evident Prince de Ratibor would be compelled to take some action.

In the issue, of which the German 'Ambassador' complains, 'El Liberal' indicated that, in some degree Chilean and German officials were implicated in the, Cartagena plot and that one of the chief Germans implicated, Herr Kallen, endeavored to escape in an automobile that had belonged to the Chilean Minister in Madrid. The latter immediately published a statement to the effect that he had sold the automobile the previous day. Herr Kallen was subsequently arrested and brought back to Madrid.

NOMINATIONS TO TARIFF BOARD ARE OPPOSED

Makeup of Commission Displeasing to Republican Senators — Ratification of Colombia Treaty Under Consideration

Special to The Christian Science Monitor from its Washington Bureau

WASHINGTON, D. C.—There is a question as to whether or not the Tariff Commission just named by the President will be confirmed at the present session. Strong Republican opposition will have to be faced, especially from the high profectionists, who view with displeasure the make-up of the commission as just nominated. It is intimated that committee opposition may keep the nominations from being reported at this session.

The Senate this afternoon appointed a committee to notify the President that unless he had further business for them, they were ready to adjourn until April 16, the date of the extra session.

Administration senators have given up hope of having the Colombian treaty ratified during the special session of the Senate and have consented to put it over until the extra session on April 16. In the meantime efforts will be made to have the State Department agree to "slight modifications" expected to make the treaty acceptable to the Republican opposition.

MONITOR INDEX FOR TODAY

MR. BONAR LAW TALKS ON THE IRISH QUESTION

Informs House of Commons Attitude of Nationalists May Cause Appeal to Country — Government Declaration Asked

Special Cable to The Christian Science Monitor from the European Bureau

LONDON, England (Friday)— Mr. Bonar Law, Chancellor of the Exchequer, in a statement on the Irish question in the House of Commons today said the attitude of the Nationalists in opposition might have the effect of compelling an appeal to the country. If the good will of the country could settle the question it would be done tomorrow.

John Dillon had asked whether there would be any one present to answer for Ireland. A rumor had reached him that orders had been issued to Dublin people to keep indoors tomorrow, St. Patrick's Day. Mr. Bonar Law said he knew nothing of the circumstances mentioned.

The Chief Secretary for Ireland had proceeded to Ireland so that there was no one to answer with authority for the department.

On the report stage of the vote of credit, Sir Henry Dalziel asked for an announcement of the Government's intentions regarding Ireland, and proposed the establishment of a powerful commission to deal with the matter. It was important in view of the grave state of affairs in Ireland and at a time when revolutions were in the air that they should have a frank declaration from the Government. His own information was not reassuring.

Friday—Mr. Bonar Law, in moving the vote of credit in the House of Commons yesterday, explained it was a very disagreeable surprise to him that he had to ask for an additional vote. In spite of every precaution that might have been taken it would have been impossible when estimating for £200,000,000 on Feb. 12 to anticipate the circumstances which now necessitated his occupying the House for two days with the question of further new money.

When examining the figures presented to him early in February he thought the margin rather fine and mentioned the matter to his advisers, and it occurred to him then that an additional £10,000,000 might wisely be added, but it was small satisfaction to feel even if he had taken the precaution that it would still not have avoided the present supplementary estimate.

The additional £40,000,000 asked for is made up as follows: Wheat from Australia £13,000,000; "advances to the allies and dominions £23,000,000; additional expenditure on munitions and expenditure by the Shipping Controller for increasing the supply of merchant ships £19,000,000.

In connection with figures covering the extra munitions and expenditure, the Chancellor said it should be a distinct satisfaction to the House, as it certainly is to the Government, to find they are getting these merchant ships more rapidly than they had reason to anticipate from the high profectionists, who view with displeasure the make-up of the commission as just nominated. The total amount of the credit voted during the present year would now be £301,000,000; excluding £250,000,000 voted for next year the aggregate vote of credit since the beginning of the war reaches the enormous total of £3,792,000,000.

ENEMY STEAMER CAPTURED

LONDON, England (Friday)— A small enemy steamer, attempting to cross the Tigris River, was set afire and ultimately captured, practically undamaged, today's official report from the Mesopotamian expeditionary force asserted. The capture occurred on Tuesday. The vessel carried 250 rifles and a quantity of ammunition.

CHANCELLOR TO VISIT VIENNA

AMSTERDAM, Holland (Friday)— It is announced that the German Chancellor is to visit Vienna at the end of the week to return Count Czernin's recent visit.

Nicholas II of Russia — Etching by W. Renison

BILL TO PERMIT CHALLENGING OF JUDGES FAVORED

Legislative Committee Makes a Report on Important Judiciary Measure, and House Passes It to Its First Reading

Legislation to permit either party in a suit in the Massachusetts Superior Court to challenge a judge on the ground of "personal bias or prejudice," is provided for in a bill favorably reported in the Massachusetts House today by the joint Committee on the Judiciary. Six of the 14 members of the committee dissented to the report, and it understood that a sharp contest will be waged when the measure comes up for its second reading early next week. It took its first reading today as a matter of course, as do most measures receiving a favorable committee report.

This bill is one of the most radical relating to the judiciary that has come out of committee with a favorable report in many years. If enacted, it would permit either party at a civil or criminal session of the Superior Court, who had reason to believe that the judge sitting on the case had personal bias or prejudice against him or in favor of any opposite party to the suit, to file with the clerk of the court an affidavit to that effect, in which event the judge would be automatically removed and another judge satisfactory to both parties would be appointed to the case by the Chief Justice.

The dissenting members of the committee are Senators Hobson of Palmer and Sanford of Boston and Representatives Kennard of Somerville, Abbott of Haverhill, Burr of Boston and Wolcott. The bill is a redraft of a bill introduced on petition of Representative Simon Swig of Boston.

A unanimous report of leave to withdraw was made by the Committee on Public Lighting, on Representative Sullivan's bill for repeal of the sliding scale gas act regulating the price of gas in Boston.

The same report was made unanimously by the same committee on the report of the Gas and Electric Light Commission, under a resolve of 1915, relative to the continuance, terms and extension of the sliding scale for the price of gas.

The Social Welfare Committee reported a bill that the Board of Parole may grant a special permit to be at liberty from the State prison to a prisoner who has served half his minimum term, if it appears that he is likely to lead an orderly life and not depend on charity.

The Committee on Public Institutions reported an appropriation of $11,450 for improvements at the Lyman school for boys, of which $5700 is for the purchase of the Batley place adjoining the school.

Leave to withdraw was reported by the Committee on Federal Relations on the petition of the Massachusetts Real Estate Exchange that a resolution be adopted asking Congress to investigate the subject of rare potentates.

Ought not to be adopted was re-

(Continued on page five, column six)

BRIEF SKETCH OF THE CAREER OF FORMER TSAR

Nicholas II Since 1894 Has Been One of Enigmas of Europe — How Duma Arose

Nicholas II, the Tsar of all the Russias, has, ever since he succeeded his father in the November of 1894, been one of the enigmas of Europe, at any rate to all except those few who had some grasp of the true facts. As is recalled by Mr. Gardiner in his able sketch of the Russian Emperor, written nearly 10 years ago, Mr. Heath, the Tsar's English tutor, relates how that one day he and his pupil were reading together "The Lady of the Lake," and when they came to the stirring passage which tells how the gates of Stirling Castle were flung wide open, and King James rode out amid the shouts of the populace, "Long live the Commons' King, King James!" the boy exclaimed eagerly, "The Commons' King, that is what I should like to be."

Mr. Gardiner goes on to make the cogent comment, that Nicholas II is one of those unhappy figures in whom "emotion is divorced from conduct, an idealist faithless to his ideals, a visionary doomed to violate his visions." This is, perhaps, as just a summary of the matter as could be made.

From his earliest childhood, Nicholas II has been the same. He received the ordinary education of all Russian

(Continued on page seven, column two)

BY-ELECTION FOR LIEBKNECHT'S SEAT

Special Cable to The Christian Science Monitor from its Southern Bureau

AMSTERDAM, Holland (Friday)— A Berlin telegram states that the by-election for Dr. Liebknecht's vacant Reichstag seat for the Spandau, Potsdam and Osthavelland constituency resulted in a victory for the Majority Socialists, whose candidate, Herr Emil Stahl, obtained 13,886 votes against 2859 secured by Dr. Franz Mehring, Socialist Minority candidate, who carried Dr. Liebknecht's Prussian Diet constituency by a large majority. Results have still to arrive from some districts, but Herr Stahl's election is certain.

Berlin papers state that Herr Stahl organized a great house-to-house canvass, while Conservatives gave him their support and workmen in the large factories in Spandau were given special leave to go to poll and civil servants took an active part in the election.

AIR RAID ON WESTGATE

LONDON, England (Friday)—A hostile aeroplane bombarded Westgate, a suburb of Margate in Kent, without casualties early today. A statement issued by Lord French, commander in chief of the home forces, declared the material damage was slight.

BRITISH DESTROYER SUNK

LONDON, England (Friday)—A British destroyer of an old type struck a mine in the English Channel yesterday and sank, the Admiralty announced today. One man was killed and 28 are missing.

LIBERAL PARTY SECURES SIGNAL VICTORY IN SPAIN

Special Cable to The Christian Science Monitor from its European Bureau

MADRID, Spain (Friday)—The elections of provincial assemblies have passed without incident resulting in an overwhelming victory for the Liberal Party, supported by the Conservatives, in the form of a monarchist coalition.

The returns show 150 members of 13th coalition have been returned, 20 Regionalists, 17 Carlists, 17 Republicans and 25 Maurists. The Socialists gave their entire support to the Republicans, but the latter were divided into several groups.

RUSSIAN ARMY TO HAVE FINAL SAY IN POLICY

New York Russoye Slavo Says if Army Stands With People Future of Russia Is Settled— Food Situation Brought Crisis

NEW YORK, N. Y.—Michel Znovolsky, Russoye Slavo, Russian daily paper of New York, said today:

"We expected a conflict between the pro-German and the anti-German parties," he said, "but hadn't looked forward to the tremendous success which seems to have attended the move of the Duma. Only a few days ago the pro-German party, of which Stürmer, Protopopoff and Rasputin were sturdy pillars, displayed its strength by exiling Amitcarrov, editor of the Petrograd Russkaya Volya.

"He had recently returned to Petrograd from exile under the promise that he would not be disturbed. Evidently those who made the promise were not strong enough to protect him. It was interpreted here as a sign of weakness on the part of the Liberals. The direct attempt of the Tsar to prorogue the Duma, too, made many believe that the pro-German influence was almost too strong. The success, then, of the anti-Germans came as a most welcome surprise.

"If the Army stands with the people, Russia's problem is settled. The people are overwhelmingly with the Duma. The need for change has been brought strikingly home to almost every one because of the apparent food shortage. The personal element in the problem assures the interest of all. They, too, have in mind that the Council of Empire at the opening of the Duma passed a resolution declaring that the food situation resulted from the failure of the administration to cooperate with the people.

"The army will have that say and hopes are high. The old units of soldiers such as defended the Czar and reactionaries in 1905 are gone—wiped out in the first big smashes of the war. Russia now has a citizen army. The rank and file is overwhelmingly anti-German and strong for a decision in the war. If the Petrograd garrison stands by the Government until the Duma permeates the empire it won't be long until Russia will have solved her problem."

The Russian newspaper Novy Mir says: "The people will not be satisfied. We may expect any day to see the temporary Government give way to a more radical one. If the radicals succeed, it is not likely to affect peace."

EXCLUSION OF CHINESE ONLY BY COURT ORDER

Federal Tribunal Holds Immigration Officials Can Act Only Under General Law

Special to The Christian Science Monitor from its Southern Bureau

NEW ORLEANS, La.—What is considered one of the most significant victories won by Chinese in their dealings with immigration officials, is a decision rendered by the United States Circuit Court of Appeals in New Orleans. The court ruled that immigration officials can deport only Chinese charged with violating the Immigration act, which applies to all aliens alike.

Where the charge is a violation of the Chinese Exclusion act of 1893, the court holds that the facts in the case must be determined by the judicial department of the Government, and not by the immigration branch.

The case decided was that of Lee Wong Him versus John P. Mayo, Commissioner of Immigration at New Orleans. The Court of Appeals made a distinction between the Chinese Exclusion Law, ruling that the immigration authorities are empowered to act only under the former. The immigration act gives the immigration officials power to exclude undesirable aliens, regardless of their nationality.

RUMANIA TO OBTAIN LOAN FROM BRITAIN

JASSY, Rumania (Friday)—At the Cabinet Council held on March 8 an announcement was made that England agreed to advance 1,000,000,000 francs at par to Rumania. This interest is to be at the rate of 5 per cent.

REVOLUTION IN RUSSIA BRINGS MANY CHANGES

Executive of Duma in Charge of Affairs in Capital—Reactionaries Arrested — Efficiency Aim of New Movement

Russia's popular assembly, the Duma, is undoubtedly in control of the situation in that country. As the details of the revolution of the past few days continue to come in, it is clear that the effect of the overturn is the virtual elimination of the reactionary and pro-German influences, and that the country has taken a long stride in the direction of popular liberty. While it is now stated that the abdication of the Tsar has not been actually effected, the revolution is regarded as indicating the end of autocracy in Russia and a more united and more effective action in the prosecution of the war.

All the leading members of the reactionary bureaucracy have been deposed from power, and are either imprisoned or in flight. These men were regarded as friendly to Germany in the present war situation, and the revolution which throws them out of power is regarded as a distinct triumph for the Allied cause.

Present reports indicate that the revolution was remarkable for the openness with which it was discussed in advance, and for the completeness with which it was carried out. It was also notable for the far-reaching results achieved with practically no bloodshed and comparatively little disturbance.

Special Cable to The Christian Science Monitor from its European Bureau

PETROGRAD, Russia (Friday)—The inevitable has happened. The people of Petrograd have risen against influences which they believe have sought after a separate peace; influences that for this purpose they believe have deliberately thrown out of gear the machinery of distribution, so that while grain rots in one part of the country there may be starvation only 100 miles distant; influences that for this purpose also have suspended the Duma.

The revolution has been carried through so far with ease and smoothness and any one's most sanguine hopes, although looking back it seems that one could scarcely have anticipated any other result. For it is the case that for months past in Petrograd, where, at one time to breathe the word revolution was to take instant departure for Siberia, revolution has been for every one's lips. It has been freely talked of in streets, in tramcars and wherever two or three persons are gathered together. It has been on the lips of soldiers, workmen and a congregation of common expression has been "when all is ready we will return and clear this matter up." This in strict faith they have done, and today Nicholas II is no longer Tsar of Russia.

His brother, the Grand Duke Michael, has been appointed regent. Nearly every Minister of State is in prison and the Duma is supreme.

The executive committee of the Duma, which is maintaining order, has published the following list of members of the new national Cabinet:

Prince Lvoff, president of the alliance of Zemstvos, is President of the Council, Premier and Minister of Interior.

M. Miliukoff is Foreign Minister.
A. Kerensky is Minister of Justice.
M. Nekrassoff, vice-president of the Duma, is Minister of Ways and Communications.

M. Konovaloff is Minister of Commerce and Industry.

Professor Manluiloff of Moscow University is Minister of Public Instruction.

M. Gutchkoff, who is a member of the Council of Empire and was formerly President of Third Duma and President of United Committees of Mobilised Industry becomes Minister of War and Marine ad interim.

M. Schingareff becomes Minister of Agriculture.

M. Terestchenko is Minister of Finance.

M. Godneff is Controller of State.

It was, of course, the food question which finally precipitated the revolution. The shortage of food and the lack of organization in a land of plenty had been generally attributed to the methods of M. Protopopoff, Minister of Interior, who was generally known shortly as the "Madman." On Friday the streets of Petrograd were full of slowly-moving crowds, including strikers from factories and the general public. Tramcars were stopped and bridges were closed by the authorities to prevent this movement as far as possible.

Through the crowds moved cavalry, Cossacks and infantry with fixed bayonets. Here and there cheering was to be heard, the people cheering the sol-

(Continued on page six, column one)

1. Origins And Revolution

B rief, even austere reports — usually without bylines were typical of these early years. In a way the reforms which began with the unrest of 1905 came to an end with the death of Stolypin. His imaginative efforts to create a rural, land-owning middle class through the distribution of land given time might have radically changed Russian society.

The end of his programs and the pressure of war beginning in 1914 destroyed the czarist system he had tried to reform.

Typical of the context and background which were eventually to become the hallmark of the Monitor is the history of the Russian Duma provided in the March 17, 1917 piece celebrating the democratic "February" Revolution — and the July 22, 1918 recollection of Nicholas II after he was shot.

Russian Premier Shot [9/15/11]

M. Stolypin, the Russian premier, was wounded Thursday night by shots fired at him while he was attending a performance at the opera. The Czar was present. In the afternoon a monument to Alexander II had been unveiled in the presence of 300,000 persons.

The shots were fired by a lawyer named Bogrof who was at once arrested.

Probably no one person other than the Czar himself has exercised greater strength or influence in the Russian empire in recent years than M. Stolypin, sometimes known as the "iron man" of the government, and he has been a special favorite of the Czar, who supported him in recent friction with the Duma.

After the shooting the audience, which was made up almost wholly of members of the aristocracy, sang the national anthem as a sign of loyalty to the Czar. Immediately after the first shot secret service men closed round the imperial box.

Stolypin Recovery Expected [9/16/11]

The recovery is expected of M. Stolypin, the Russian premier who was shot at Kiev while attending a performance at the opera in honor of the Czar. It is believed that the attack was made at the instance of revolutionaries. Bogrof, the man who fired the shots, is declared to have been present at the theater as an agent of the Russian police; he is supposed to have been formerly a revolutionary. The Czar visited M. Stolypin after the shooting.

Russian Premier Passes Away [9/18/11]

KIEV — Premier Stolypin, who was shot at the opera house here last Thursday by Dmitri Bogrof, passed away here today.

Stolypin resigned as premier and minister of the interior on March 20 of this year, but three days later reconsidered his action and consented to remain in office. It was learned that the Emperor had used his personal influence to retain Stolypin.

M. Stolypin as premier is the man who blocked a threatened revolution during the term of office of Count Witte.

His conduct in office has been very satisfactory to the Czar and his repressive measures are thought to have been responsible for his appointment as premier.

Kokovsoff May Be Premier [9/19/11]

In consequence of the passing away of Premier Stolypin from bullet wounds inflicted last Thursday at the opera in Kiev, troops are on guard throughout Russia and no disturbances have been reported. Vladimir Kokovsoff, minister of finance, is expected to be the new prime minister.

Assassination of Gregory Rasputin [1/3/17]

Information available regarding the monk, Gregory Rasputin, shows he was assassinated on Saturday morning in the garden of the Palace on Moika Canal, belonging to Prince Yusupolf. Prince Yusupolf is married to Princess Irene, second cousin of the Czar and eldest daughter of the Grand Duke Alexander.

While nothing is definitely known as to who was responsible, prominent names are freely mentioned, including that of a well-known deputy.

Commenting on the removal of "dark forces," often referred to in the Duma, the newspaper *Russkaya Volya*, which was founded by M. Protopopoff, Minister of Interior, but is believed to have severed its connection with him as it violently attacked him in its first issue, remarks there are moments when the contradiction between life and truth reaches a stage of extreme tension. At such critical moments public feeling is compelled to find an outlet to offer resistance to vile influences which undermine the honor of families, which foster in the less stable elements of the nation the vices of toadyism and sycophancy and make of politics a degrading game of secret intrigues marked by the eventuality of sale of public offices, purchase and sale of men's consciences; the choice of administrators from amongst the worst and least capable and the systematic poisoning of the whole Government organism by repulsive important service influences.

Dynasty of the Romanoffs at End [3/17/17]

Following upon the revolution in Russia and the reported abdication of Nicholas II, the latest developments show that the Romanoff dynasty has come to an end, and that the Government has been temporarily vested in the Executive Committee of the Duma and the Council of Ministers.

The policy of the new Cabinet, which aims at extensive reforms in the country, is outlined in a statement issued to all citizens of Russia. Recognition of the Provisional Government has been officially given by the United Kingdom, France and Italy. Meanwhile, conditions in the Empire are assuming their normal state.

The Provisional Government in Russia has issued to all Russian citizens a statement setting forth the basis of policy of the new Cabinet, composed it says, of men whose past political and public activity assures them the confidence of the country. These bases of policy number eight:

1. Immediate general amnesty for all political and religious offenses, including terrorist acts, military revolts and agrarian crimes.

2. Freedom of speech, of the press, of association and labor organizations and freedom to strike with extension of these liberties to officials and troops in so far as military and technical conditions permit.

3. Abolition of social, religious and national restrictions.

4. Immediate preparations for summoning a constituent assembly which, with universal suffrage as its basis, shall establish the governmental régime and the Constitution of the country.

5. Substitution for the police of a national militia with elective heads and subject to self-government bodies.

6. Communal elections to be carried out on a basis of universal suffrage.

7. Troops that have participated in the revolutionary movement shall not be disarmed but are not to leave Petrograd.

8. While severe military discipline must be maintained on active service, all restrictions upon soldiers in the enjoyment of social rights granted to other citizens are to be abolished.

In concluding this enunciation of its policy the Provisional Government adds that it has no intention of taking advantage of the existence of war conditions to delay the realization of the above mentioned measures of reform. This striking declaration has been arrived at only after considerable effort and considerable concession on the part of the various sections represented in the Government.

There is little to add to the news already cabled, but some details are interesting. Up to Thursday there was still a certain amount of sniping from the roofs and upper windows at soldiers and others. The snipers consisted of police and agents on whom M. Protopopoff is understood to have relied to crush the revolution which he had so long aimed at, provoking action on the assumption that if the revolution could be precipitated now he would be able to crush it more easily than later on and at the same time would have an excuse for withdrawing from the war.

Thousands of machine guns appear to have been posted all over Petrograd in all sorts of commanding positions, and the theory has been put forward that M. Protopopoff expected to have an opportunity to use these weapons at the recent opening of the Duma. It will be remembered that the workmen's representatives on the industrial committee were thrown into prison, and following this, agents' provocateurs went about among munition and other workers, urging them in the name of M. Miliukoff to make a demonstration at the opening of the Duma.

Some even endeavored to pass themselves off as M. Miliukoff, and the plot was only blasted by an urgent appeal by M. Miliukoff to all workers to continue at their work and not to play into the hands of their enemies. Several thousands of M. Protopopoff's agents are now under lock and key, and sniping is practically at an end.

As indicating the determination of the workers to win the war, certain factories, including the powder mills at Okhta, kept going throughout the whole course of the revolution, and by Wednesday the Putiloff and other munition works were again going. The question of transport has been facilitated by the commandeering of private and other motor cars in the early stages of the revolution. Some of the armored cars in the streets on Monday were originally brought to the city by M. Protopopoff for use in suppressing the rebellion, but were either seized by revolutionaries, or were used like the soldiers, to suppress the Government instead.

The Czar has definitely accepted the only course open to him. From the moment that the Executive Committee of the Duma decided that he must abdicate and that the Grand Duke Michael should act as regent it only remained to be seen whether the Czar would accept the position or resist. From that moment Emperor Nicholas was no longer Czar of Russia, because the Duma was clearly resolved that no concession could be made on this point. He has now abdicated in favor of his brother, the Grand Duke Michael, who, however, relinquishes his rights to the throne, and he has also transferred the supreme command of the Russian armies to the Grand Duke Nicholas.

Yesterday officers in Petrograd met at the invitation of the Executive Committee of the Duma and speeches were delivered on the text of the necessity, with a view to bringing the war to a victorious end, of establishing order as quickly as possible and carrying on the work in the rear of the army.

There was unanimous agreement to recognize the authority of the Executive Committee of the Duma in regard to the administration of the State until a constituent assembly had been convened.

A striking feature of the whole revolution is this rapidity with which attention is being turned at once to the question of restoring and maintaining order. It is the feature which characterizes the position not only in Petrograd, but elsewhere throughout the country, and the Zemstvos and municipalities are naturally playing a prominent part in this effort.

There may be a more rapid improvement in the food situation than might have been expected, and prices have already fallen considerably in Petrograd. Hundreds of formerly unused wagons have been hurried on to railway lines and throughout the whole of the revolution the train services have continued.

Throughout the revolution scenes of special impressiveness or interest such as the arrival of the Preobrajensky Régiment at the Duma; the adhesion of the Grand Duke Cyril, the surrender of M. Protopopoff and Pitirim and the enthusiasm shown for anyone and everything British. The Preobrajensky Régiment presented a spectacle drawn up four deep along the whole length of the huge Catherine Hall of Tauris Palace.

M. Rodzianko greeted them, according to the old soldiers' custom, by wishing them "good health," to which the soldiers shouted back, "We wish good health to your excellency." Then the President of the Duma in a short speech thanked them for coming there to help the Duma to establish order and to safeguard the honor and glory of the country. He referred to the fact that his own son had been serving in their ranks and then added: "To advance the cause undertaken by the Duma you must remain a disciplined force. Soldiers are helpless without their officers. I ask you to remain faithful to your officers and to have the same confidence in them that we have."

The soldiers then marched out, led by their officers, cordially cheering the Duma President.

A similar scene was enacted when other régiments came to the Duma for guidance, but the influence of the Preobrajensky Guards was very far-reaching.

The Grand Duke Cyril adhered to the revolution on Wednesday, proceeding to Catherine Hall with his staff and a deputation of sailors to place the services of the entire naval guard at the disposal of the Duma.

Another striking incident was the adhesion of all officers of the General Staff College.

M. Protopopoff actually surrendered late on Wednesday night. A student in front of the Duma was accosted by a man muffled up in a fur coat who said: "Lead me to the Duma committee. I am the former Minister, M. Protopopoff." M. Pitirim was hurried and bustled to the Duma by a crowd of unconcerned soldiers, but some supporters of the old régime who resisted were summarily dealt with.

When the history of the revolution is written in detail it will be found that the handling of the movement from its inner side was not the least difficult part. At one moment there was considerable danger that the extremists in their desire for a Socialist republic would bring the movement to ruin. That danger may not yet be over, but there is general alertness to avoid any risk of endangering the national cause against Germany by a refusal to make concessions to each other.

Hence an agreement was reached, both in regard to the formation of the Government, already cabled, and in regard to its proclamation. The moderate Socialists of the Plekhanoff party played a prominent part in bringing this about.

On Friday evening, M. Kerenski, Minister of Justice, addressed assembled soldiers and civilians from the gallery of the lobby of the Duma. He was given a great ovation, and stated that the new Government had taken office on the basis of an agreement with the workmen's and soldiers' delegates, who had approved of the agreement by several hundred votes to 15. He referred to the issue of the decree of full amnesty which would rescue their comrades of the second and fourth Dumas from the marshy wastes of tundras in the north of Asia where they were imprisoned.

He announced that the premiers and ministers of the old régime would answer before the law for all their crimes against the people, a declaration which was greeted with cries of "No mercy for them."

Replying, M. Kerenski said regenerated Russia would not resort to the shameful means utilized by the old

The front page of The Christian Science Monitor **for Saturday March 17, 1917 reporting the revolution and the fall of the Romanoff Dynasty.**

Views of St. Basils Cathedral [right] and one of the many Summer Palaces of the Czars [below] show the opulence in which they onced lived.

régime, and without trial nobody would be condemned. All measures taken by the new Government will be published.

He appealed for the cooperation of the soldiers, saying, "Free Russia is born and none will succeed in wresting liberty from the hands of the people." He warned them also not to listen to the promptings of agents of the old régime. "Listen to your officers," he said. "Long live free Russia."

The Labor leader, M. Cheidze, Minister without Portfolio, spoke of the marvelous spectacle of revolutionary soldiers hand in hand with revolutionary labor men. He warned them against the provocative efforts of the secret police who had launched proclamations as to the murder of officers by soldiers, and he urged the soldiers to regard their officers as citizens who had raised the revolutionary flag and as brothers in the cause of a great revolution for Russian liberty. Officers, soldiers and workmen shouldered the speaker and carried him through the crowd.

Russian Revolt Gives Greater Power to Army [3/17/17]

Prof. Alexander Petrunkvitch of Yale University, who has long prophesied the revolt against autocracy in his native land, said to a representative of *The Christian Science Monitor:*

"The Russian revolt is most opportune for the Allied cause, for now the Russian army will be unhampered in receiving its supplies. At the time of the first Russian retreat, in the summer of 1915, treason was discovered, both in the army and in the Government, but only lately has it been that this treason was due to German money and influence.

"So much indignation was aroused that several good men were put into office, and, for a little while, it looked as if matters would be better. But the pro-German influence was still so strong that it regained power. Stürmer was made Premier. With the aid of the Secretary of the Interior, Protopopoff, he managed to disorganize the munition and food supply, and even tried to make a separate treaty with Germany. It was this that caused their overthrow last November.

"When Rasputin, the power behind the throne and the tool of the pro-German party, was assassinated in January, the Secretary of the Interior became practically a dictator, and crippled the machinery of the Government and army in every way possible. The result was that although there were plenty of food supplies in the coun-

try, hunger was prevalent because of the inefficient food distribution. The inevitable result had been reached. The Government had to go.

"This revolt will be an uplift for the people. The army will now be able to accomplish something. The situation at the time of the French Revolution was similar. Unshackled, the army can now accomplish more against its foreign enemies, just as the French were able to."

Advices from Petrograd quote Prof. Paul Miliukoff, the new Foreign Minister, as declaring that the new régime was determined upon the abdication of Emperor Nicholas and the regency of Grand Duke Michael.

"The problems which we are going to solve consist of the reestablishment in Russia of a power capable of giving the people final victory over the enemy," said Professor Miliukoff, one of the most prominent Liberal leaders of Russia. "The great crime of the late Government consisted of throwing the country into complete disorganization and subjected it to the hardest trials. This state of affairs might even have had dangerous effects on the issue of the war. The increase of popular discontent was the cause of the turn which events have taken. The anger of the people was such that the Russian revolution was almost the shortest and most bloodless in history. The late Government was completely isolated, which confirms the fact that no one had confidence in it. The great events of the last few days make it possible for the people to gain fresh confidence. These events will increase popular enthusiasm and multiply the national forces, giving them, at last, power to win the war. During a few days the Duma attracted to itself the attention of the whole nation, and was the center of enormous moral force. Today it has material force also at its disposal, now that the army has taken its side. Every hour brings news bearing witness to the continual growth of power of the forces of national representation. The new Government considers it indispensable that the abdication of the Emperor be confirmed and the regency temporarily intrusted to Grand Duke Michael Alexandrovitch. Such is our decision. We consider it impossible to alter it. According to the latest news, the Emperor is at Pskov, 162 miles southwest of Petrograd. Contrary to certain rumors, His Majesty has not been arrested. The Empress remains at the Tsarskoe Selo, where she is in perfect safety."

The new Cabinet contains the names of men who led in the struggle against the old Government, and enjoy full confidence of the country. Professor Miliukoff and M. Shingaroff, the new Minister of Agriculture, have become especially prominent as champions of the rights of the people. It is due to Professor Miliukoff that revelations regarding the political intrigue and corruption of the old reactionary Government were brought before the public.

Michael Rodzianko, president of the Duma, a Liberal, was the visible head of the revolution in Petrograd, the logical head after his persistent work in the Duma towards the great object — free Russia, governed by a free people, according to domestic forms. Rodzianko is a large landholder in Ekaterinoslav, and has occupied the post of president of the Ekaterinoslav Government Council. When, in 1911, M. Alexeienko declined to stand for election as president of the Duma because some of the Octobrists charged him with excessive liberalism, the party decided to put forward M. Rodzianko, who, during M. Guchkoff's presidency, was nominally the Octobrist leader. M. Rodzianko was elected by 199 votes to 123.

The opening of the fourth Duma in November, 1912, gave rise to sensational developments. The Octobrists made common cause with the Opposition as a protest against Clerico-Bureaucratic interference with the elections and secured a majority for their candidate, M. Rodzianko, who was reelected president. In thanking the members for his reelection, he dwelt on the necessity for reforms, and said that the country would be called upon to make urgent provision for national defense. At a time when the public gaze was earnestly directed to the Balkans, he felt sure that the Duma would not stint money, and that Russians would not spare their efforts, and, if necessary, their life blood, in defense of interests so near to their heart. His words were prophetic. Though wealthy, he is a sympathizer with the peasantry of his native land.

He is a purely Russian character, boasting that he obtained his political education in the Zemstvos, the provincial assemblies, where the common people have a voice. Rodzianko and men like him have been strongly opposed to peace until the objects of the war were attained. Under his guidance the Duma, almost powerless in actual government, sprang at one leap to full control of the country. No popular champion achieved such a sudden triumph, even the French Revolutionists meeting opposition among numerous sections of their nation.

It was not perhaps without significance that when the Duma opened its first session the son of the Grand Duke Michael was the only member of the Imperial family who was present. In truth, the Grand Michael has all his life been in Russian politics, even before he could have been in them by any procurement of his own. It has long been common gossip in St. Petersburg that Michael was his mother's favorite over Nicholas, and that she much preferred the continuance of the heirdom-presumptive to the arrival of an heir-apparent. Moreover, the Grand Duke Michael is commonly esteemed to be a person of more capacity and force of character than his Imperial brother, as well as of much greater personal popularity. The history of revolutions, including that of the English Revolution of 1688, is full of admonitions that, when the actual holder of the "divine right" has become politically impossible, some possible person of the same descent may become eligible. The English "Act of Succession," under which the British throne is held more than 200 years afterward, is a compromise between the claims of "divine right" and the will of the people. It is true that the Duc d'Orleans, who got himself nicknamed "Egalite" and joined the National Assembly and voted for the death of his royal kinsman, did not make much by his motion, since he also, in due course, went to the guillotine. The Grand Duke Michael may make nothing by his motion, if the Russian Revolution, like the French Revolution, should extend beyond control. But if the Russian Revolution should be kept within bounds, and there seems no doubt it already is, the Grand Duke Michael may be taken as a serious factor in Russian politics.

Russia Enters Upon A New Path of Reform [3/19/17]

In his declaration from the throne on Friday, Grand Duke Michael Alexandrovitch said: "I am firmly resolved to accept the supreme power only if this should be the desire of our great people who must by means of a plebiscite through their representatives in constituent assembly establish a form of Government and new fundamental laws of the Russian State. Invoking God's blessing, I therefore request the citizens of Russia to obey the provisional Government set up on the initiative of the Duma and invested with plenary powers until within as short a time as possible a constituent assembly, elected on a basis of universal equal and secret suffrage, shall express the will of the nation regarding the form of Government to be adopted."

M. Miliukoff has addressed a telegram to the Russian representatives abroad in which he refers to the rallying of all elements to the revolution, enabling the national movement to obtain a decisive victory within eight days. This rapidity of realization, he says, has made it possible to reduce the number of victims to figures unprecedentedly small in the annals of upheavals of such extent and importance. He refers to the Czar's renunciation of the throne and Grand Duke Michael's subsequent renunciation of supreme power until the constituent assembly establishes the form of government and to the Grand Duke's invitation to Russians to submit to the authority, meantime, of the provisional government.

Russia's New Freedom
Finds Masses Ready   [3/19/17]

The dominant thought in connection with the revolution in Russia, as expressed by those familiar with affairs in the northeast of Europe, is that the events of last week clearly show another step in the unfoldment of democracy. That the coup executed in Petrograd was the inevitable result of forces, ambitions and yearnings that have been harbored in the breasts of the masses for ages, there seems a settled conviction.

Charles R. Crane, than whom there are very few more competent to speak of this people, gives the following candid view of the revolution at the request of *The Christian Science Monitor:*

"In the new Russia a formidable champion of democracy has stepped into the arena of the world. The heart of Russia has always been democratic, and the autocracy was only a shell inclosing the greatest mass of living democrats in the world. Over 80 per cent of the people of Russia are small landed proprietors, with a distinct genius for cooperative movements; and now, freed from vodka and a restrictive central government, we can count on some of the boldest and most thoroughly worked-out schemes of democratic life. Democracy with them is quite as much a matter of life as of faith.

"Sixty years ago, the Russians showed their enormous capacity for conceiving and working through great schemes of social reform, by the way in which they solved the problem of emancipating their millions of serfs, establishing them all as small landed proprietors, and giving them control of their local affairs, with the deliberate purpose of preparing them for the representative government in which they are now so well grounded. It was also a great and bloodless revolution, and required the cooperation, during long years, of all the progressive elements of the empire.

"The other bloodless revolution of last week shows the same genius for large affairs. It required the closest cooperation of all the elements of the Russian empire, and has behind it the confidence of the army, both in the field and throughout the country; the peasantry, the nobility, the working classes, the universities, and all the vast number of societies that are working together for the success of the war, including the Allies. It was a purely Russian revolution, managed by Russians, and in the Russian style.

"At this distance it seems to be antibureaucratic rather than antidynastic. The Emperor abdicates with a strong hold on the affections of the people, and will be remembered in history for conferring on his people the greatest boon that any autocrat has ever conferred on a people, the eliminating of vodka. He will also be remembered as the founder of the Duma, to whom he bequeaths the destinies of Russia.

"Although the Russian does not have much education in one sense, he has a great deal of education of his own kind. He does not read and write so much as he will later on but he has a great gift of talking, and talks very much more than western people, and he has a much larger vocabulary. They speak freely and easily in their small assemblies, and information travels very rapidly.

"During the long months of winter they occupy themselves with producing charming and useful things which show a very widespread sense of art.

"Their church music is the oldest and richest and easiest to follow and enjoy in the Christian world, and even today there are living eight or ten of the great composers of this wonderful music, any one of whom would be a great glory for any other country in the world. There is probably no place that is more democratic than the floor of the Russian church. On the floor of the Russian church the most important person in the Empire has not the slightest preference over the simplest Russian peasant, and the simplest Russian peasant has this feeling of proprietorship in everything that belongs to the church and its services. He is always a theologian, and the greatest reservoir of spiritual power in the world today. In spiritual power, art, literature and politics, the Russians are setting new standards."

No little comment has been heard in Washington on the significance of sentiments expressed in the Prussian Diet on Friday, indicating that democratic tendencies in Germany and Austria, especially in Hungary, may possibly have to be reckoned with before the war closes. It is the common view that hunger among the people that is leading them back to the primitive law of self-preservation is having its effects among the masses in helping them to see some advantages in popular government. The view is expressed that suffering and lack, such as is known to exist in Germany, may have its influence in leading to a change in the popular acceptance that the Emperor rules by divine right, or that a class may rightfully rule the mass.

Russian Soviet Sends Word Of New Revolution [11/8/17]

Reports of another revolution in Petrograd are arriving in this country from the official Petrograd telegraph agency, which was occupied yesterday by the forces of the Maximalist revolutionary committee.

As issued by Reuters, a message sent off at 9:50 p.m. yesterday, says toward 5 o'clock the Soviet military revolutionary committee published a proclamation, stating that Petrograd is in its hands, thanks to the garrison's assistance in enabling the coup d' état to be accomplished without bloodshed.

The proclamation declares that the new Government will propose an immediate and just peace, will hand land to the peasants, and will summon the constituent assembly.

Another message dispatched at 10 o'clock this morning says the delegates of three Cossack régiments yesterday declared they would not obey the Provisional Government and would not act against the Soviet, but were prepared to maintain public order with whatever means necessary.

The Petrograd Soviet held an extraordinary meeting, yesterday afternoon, during which Leon Trotsky, president of the Soviet, declared that the Provisional Government no longer existed, some of the ministers had been arrested, and the preliminary parliament had been dissolved. Mr. Lenine, who was greeted with prolonged cheers, outlined three problems now before Russian democracy. The three problems are as follows:

1. Immediate conclusion of the war, for which purpose the new Government must propose an armistice to the belligerents.

2. Handing over of land to the peasants.

3. Settlement of the economic crisis.

The assembly then adopted a resolution, expressing a wish that these problems should be solved as quickly as possible. At the close of the sitting, a declaration was read from representatives of the Social Democratic Maximalist Party of the Soviet, stating that party's disapproval of the coup d' état and its withdrawal from the Petrograd Soviet.

The Monitor *has often benefited from experts it has found on the scene. During the turmoil of the "October" Revolution the paper received reports from Professor Samuel N. Harper of the University of Chicago. In his history of Soviet-American relations, George F. Kennan noted that Professor Harper's articles in the* Monitor *played a major part in formulating American opinion on the Revolution. More importantly, it established at the time of the Revolution itself what was to become a consistent theme in the* Monitor's *coverage "one should not therefore lose faith in Russia, and judge all Russians by what is going on in Petrograd."*

Hold to Faith in Russia, Says Prof. Harper [11/10/17]

CHICAGO, ILL —At the date of writing (Friday night) we have only the news of what has taken place at Petrograd, sent from Petrograd, where the only telegraph lines to western Europe are controlled by the Bolsheviki or Maximalist leaders. We cannot therefore judge of the strength of the new revolution from the reports sent by its promoters. Assuming that Petrograd is completely in the power of the Bolsheviki, that the ministers have been arrested, with the exception of the Prime Minister, Kerensky, we must still wait for the news from the rest of Russia. One can, however, analyze somewhat the character and aims of the Bolsheviki, for they have been preaching and planning for some months the second revolution —what they claim is the real revolution. It is the last stage of the experiment, though the outcome of the experiment has been apparent for some time. Most Russians thought that the experiment was over, and that the results had been accepted. But a few fanatics saw the possibility of artificially prolonging the experiment, despite the dangers implied, and went ahead.

The Bolsheviki have been very clever. They have established the "dictatorship of the proletariat" and of the proletariat of Petrograd only, for they have had to admit that the workmen of Petrograd alone had become "conscious" and organized. But they emphasize first of all as one of the aims of the new revolution the transfer of all the land to the peasants. The test is of the common sense of the people of Russia, of the workmen of other cities, of the peasants and of the soldiers. For months the peasants have been told they have the right to all the land, and in many instances the peasants have gone ahead and exercised this right, provisionally and with violence. The workmen have been told that they must take over the factories, and in some instances they have done so, with disastrous consequences for the life of that particular factory. Attempts were made to organize a control by the workmen of the railways. But all this led to trouble, and the people were beginning to see that the doctrines which sounded good would not work.

It was on the basis of this change of psychology that Kerensky brought into his Cabinet a month ago, new forces, which would work to reestablish order and discipline. He took this step to save the country from the growing disintegration and at the same time, to save the army at the front, which could not continue to fight unless supported by a more or less orderly rear.

The appointment of the coalition Cabinet of Oct. 10 was bitterly opposed by the Bolsheviki, and they threatened to organize for its overthrow. This threat has been carried out to the extent that Kerensky has been forced to flee Petrograd. Again one must wait before one can say that the Provisional Government has been definitely overthrown.

All one can do for the moment is to ask oneself a few questions that will help one to understand the events of the next few days.

Can Petrograd be completely abandoned? All summer one felt that Russia would in many ways be stronger without Petrograd, and one often wished that Petrograd might be "cut out" in some manner or other. But Petrograd is still the administrative center of the country, and the machinery of Government is there. Petrograd is a big industrial center, and Russia is feeling particularly the shortage of manufactured articles. Some of the largest munition factories are in the Petrograd industrial district. The government mint is located at Petrograd, and, though they have been decreasing in value, the paper rubles are the medium of exchange. So Petrograd, with her Bolsheviki and her German agents, cannot be easily abandoned.

Will the present crisis lead to violence and bloodshed? It has been the aim of the leaders from the very beginning to avoid the use of force. Prince Lvoff would not resort to repression until the Extremists came into the streets armed and used force against the Provisional Government and the All-Russian Council of Workmen and Soldiers. Kerensky also has refused to resort to ruthless physical force. But the Bolsheviki announce that they will use "force without mercy" if persuasion fails. Perhaps those who have insisted that bloodshed cannot be avoided are right. Yet one of the most hopeful sides of the anarchy of these last months has been the absence of violence.

Are the Bolsheviki leaders honest, or are they German agents? Lenine and Trotsky have been charged with accepting German money, but the charges have never been substantiated. They are fanatics, cynical, intellectually dishonest — which is more dangerous than any German bribing. They say they are working for a general peace and a democratic peace, and for revolution in all countries; used against the capitalists of Germany as well as the capitalists of Russia or France or America. But they know that they are playing into the hands of Germany, where there are no signs of revolution of any kind.

Will a military dictatorship be established to combat and suppress the "dictatorship of the proletariat" established by Trotsky and Lenine? It is a possible issue. The expression was used very frequently these last months in Russia. But whenever one referred to the possible necessity of a dictatorship, one also added: "But that will not mean a return to the old régime. Autocracy has passed forever. The conquests of the Revolution are already consolidated. A military dictatorship would not mean a loss of all that has been won. Democracy and liberalism are secured to Russia, and the establishment of a military dictatorship would be only for the successful termination of the war." The demand for a "strong authority" has become more and more general. The Bolsheviki uprising can be dealt with only be a strong authority. Perhaps the "military dictator" loyal, however, to the Revolution of March, will come. But it will be a return to the ideas of the Revolution led by Prince Lvoff, Milyukoff, Gucknon and Kerensky, and not to the autocracy of Nicholas.

One serious complication may develop during the events of the next days. A very large percentage of the Bolsheviki leaders are Jews. This fact has served to start an anti-Semitic feeling among many classes of Russians, which may lead to pogroms. In fact many Russian Jews, Liberals, supporters of the first revolution, have frankly recognized this danger, and expressed their fears.

But the Petrograd uprising is in line with the experimenting of the extremists during these last months. The Bolsheviki have controlled the Petrograd workmens and garrison for some time and have attempted on previous occasions to impose the will of this small minority on the whole nation.

To date the new revolution is local to Petrograd. Without question German money and agents are playing a considerable role, perhaps with the knowledge of the Bolsheviki leaders, who have seemed to believe that the need justifies the means. One should not therefore lose faith in Russia, and judge all Russia by what is going on in Petrograd. Petrograd is not Russia. All news from Russia the last two days has come only from Petrograd.

Top, Stalin as he addressed a crowd gathered in Red Square on May Day, 1919. Left, the storming of the Winter Palace in Petrograd in winter 1917, in a frame from a film made of the event. Above, leaflets are handed out in Moscow during February 1917.

NEW YORK, NY — In an interview with a representative of this bureau, Alexandre I. Konovaloff, a member of the Kerensky Cabinet, said that upon the action which America and her allies decide to take with regard to Russia, depends not only the ultimate success of democracy in Russia, but, very likely, the question whether German militarism and *kultur* is to be decisively defeated within a reasonable length of time, or whether the economic and commercial and possibly the military resources of Russia are to help Germany prolong the war for something like an indefinite period.

Mr. Konovaloff, who generously consented to answer a series of written questions prepared by his interviewer, was the leader of the Progressive Party in Russia and the vice-president of the fourth Duma. After the March revolution, in which he took active part, he became Minister of Trade and Industry in the Provisional Government. He was a member of the first and second Cabinets, with Prince Lvoff as Premier, and later a member of the Kerensky Cabinet, where he held the position of Minister of Trade and Industry until the time of the Bolshevist revolt. He was also Vice-Prime Minister in the Kerensky Cabinet, and on many occasions, in Mr. Kerensky's absence, he acted as Prime Minister. After the Bolshevist revolt, Mr. Konovaloff was imprisoned in the Fortress of Peter and Paul. He left Russia in March.

"What is the best method," Mr. Konovaloff was first asked, "by which the United States, or the United States in conjunction with its allies, can extend the most effective help to Russia at this time?"

Mr. Konovaloff thinks this help should be both general and military, and that it should be extended without delay by all the Allies, after a declaration that the extension of that help is entirely friendly, with the aim of aiding Russia to restore her lost territories and to give her the opportunity for free political development. He believes an allied commission should be sent to Russia "to bring the country to normal conditions of life by rendering general economic assistance;" and at the same time a military expedition should be sent, by all the Allies, to help Russia restore her resistance against Germany.

Mr. Konovaloff believes that as soon as an allied army appears in Russia, the real Russian patriots will rally around that army, forming the nucleus of a Russian army which shall restore the eastern front. The allied task in this war, Mr. Konovaloff thinks, can never be fully accomplished until Russia returns to the lists as an active fighting power against Germany. It should not be forgotten that not long ago Russia had 8,000,000 men in the fighting ranks. To induce them and their officers to resume war on Germany, according to his view, an allied commission would be necessary, to extend such help as would form a kind of social program around which they could center; and both a commission and an allied army are needed to show them their proper enemy, Germany.

The next question was: "Can you state in detail how America and her allies could best send economic help to Russia?"

Mr. Konovaloff prefaced his answer by pointing out that the German economic penetration of Russia had already begun, but that the Allies could counteract it, if certain facts were remembered. It must be recognized, for instance, that individual business concerns could not accomplish much in Russia now, if they undertook their transactions at their own risk. The Germans are trying to establish their economic and financial control in Russia by buying up stock of the leading industrial, commercial and financial enterprises. This could be counteracted, not by individual effort, or by the effort of a single country, but by the establishment of a powerful financial organization controlled by all the allies, which should do everything in its power to prevent the further penetration of the Germans into Russian affairs.

In this connection, Mr. Konovaloff stated that the repudiation of the Russian debt to France, by the Bolsheviki, was not the last word on that subject. As soon as a stable democratic government is created it will recognize all of Russia's financial obligations and pay honestly all the debt and interest, although it was clear enough that present conditions made postponement of such payment imperative.

Mr. Konovaloff desired to emphasize especially that Germany's economic inroads in Russia necessitated not only prompt, but powerful action to offset and stop them, action by neither a single individual nor a single country, but by all the Allies.

To this end he proposed the organization of a special corporation (as a parallel on a smaller scale he mentioned the American Emergency Fleet Corporation) backed by all the Allies, with the United States, as he expressed it, in the center. This corporation, with plenty of money and organized talent, should undertake to build up Russia economically and financially, a reconstruction which would work for the interests of all the Allies as well as those of Russia. This corporation should devote its energies to providing Russia with the tools and machinery which would allow her to develop her natural resources. It should also aim to increase Russian exports, thus evening the balance of trade; and it should help to establish a stabilized system of currency, since the Bolsheviki had caused to be floated such an enormous amount of paper that energetic action in this respect was a great necessity.

Although Mr. Konovaloff recognized the need for immediate economic help, and the provision of food and clothing for the Russian people, he thought rolling stock, machinery and tools were even more essential for the reorganization of production. A general scheme by which such help could be brought to the nation was therefore of prime importance.

Mr. Konovaloff was then asked: "What is the feeling of the Russian people toward the Japanese, and how would that feeling affect the entrance into Russia of either a Japanese army, or an allied army including the Japanese?"

Although Mr. Konovaloff did not think this was a phase of the question which it was necessary to emphasize, he did believe it would be advisable to have the expedition into Russia consist of an allied army, of which Japanese soldiers would form a part. And he did not see any objection if the Japanese contingent should be increased, as the expedition developed, and the forces of the other allies increased along with it.

"In what condition," ran the next question, "is the Siberian Railway, and in what mood are the inhabitants of Siberia, with reference to the possible entrance of a Japanese or an allied army over that railway; and what force of men do you think would be necessary to hold that railway after the main force had swept on westward?"

The condition of the Siberian Railway, Mr. Konovaloff said, was not good, and therefore rolling stock and engineers must be sent at once to improve it. If proper help were received, it would be possible to improve it in a comparatively short time. As for holding the road after the forces moved westward, when order was reestablished in the rear of those forces, the normal number of police would be able to guard the road; therefore the number of military forces needed for this work could be placed at a minimum. For instance, some of the Tzecho-Slovak forces could probably hold the road as long as necessary.

Soviets Declared Foes of Russia [7/10/18]

NEW YORK, NY — In the second part of his interview with a representative of this bureau, Alexandre I. Konovaloff, formerly a member of the Kerensky Cabinet in Russia, told to what degree Russia had already disintegrated, and what are her chances of recovery within herself, if she does not receive outside aid.

Mr. Konovaloff said that if Russia did not face in Germany such a powerful foreign enemy, she would find herself in the proper time, without outside help. But as German domination in Russia was growing daily, and as the Russian democracy must fight two enemies, both this German domination and "the tyranny of the Bolsheviki," he could not imagine Russia being able to recover without immediate general and military help from all the Allies.

In answer to a question as to the real nature of Bolshevism, Mr. Konovaloff called attention to a statement he had just prepared for the American press, part of which is as follows:

"Nobody can be deceived longer as to the real nature of Bolshevism and as to the results of Bolshevist rule in Russia. The foreign policy of the Bolsheviki brought Russia to the Brest-Litovsk 'peace,' according to which Russia lost 780,000 square kilometers of territory, with 56,000,000 inhabitants, or over 30 percent of her entire population.

"The internal policy of the Bolsheviki resulted in the utmost disorganization of the country's industries, transportation, and finance. The terrorizing of the industrial class, and the 'workingmen's control' established in the factories, destroyed even the best established industrial enterprises. The output of raw materials and fuel steadily decreased, and this, together with the utmost disorganization of transportation, has stopped the work of even those industrial enterprises where the workingmen were anxious to continue working.

"What is left of the country after the Brest-Litovsk treaty is divided into ten separate states, isolated from one another. Hunger rages through entire provinces, epidemics are appearing here and there, menacing under the present conditions, the existence of millions."

The next question asked of Mr. Konovaloff was: "What is the real nature of the Soviets, and if the future of Russia does not rest in them or the Bolsheviki, in what does it rest, that is, in so far as any present political division within Russia can be accepted as a nucleus of political hope?"

Mr. Konovaloff here referred to the prepared statement again, and to that part of it which read as follows:

"After the real nature of Bolshevism has become clear to the entire world, the Bolsheviki themselves, naturally, do not insist upon the recognition of the Bolsheviki, but upon the recognition of the so-called government of the Soviets. Upon coming to America I found an active movement toward recognition of the Soviets. I wish to emphasize the extreme danger of this agitation, which is but a new camouflage for the Bolshevist propaganda in allied countries.

"The Soviet government not only does not represent the entire population of Russia, but it does not even represent the Russian laboring masses. The great masses of Russia's population never actually participated in the Soviet government. They participated in the municipalities and Zemstvos, which, after the March revolution, were elected on the basis of universal, direct, equal and secret suffrage. They participated in the Constituent Assembly, which was elected on the basis of the most democratic suffrage in the world. The Bolsheviki, supported by detachments of soldiers and sailors demoralized by Bolshevist propaganda, have dispersed with bayonets these democratic bodies, representing all the classes of Russia, and instead of a national democratic government, created what they call the government of the Soviets.

Former Czar Now Officially Slated To Have Been Shot   [7/22/18]

LONDON, ENGLAND — A Russian Government wireless message confirms the previous rumors of the shooting of the former Czar. "At the first session of the central executive committee elected by the fifth congress of councils," it states, "a message was made public, received by direct wire from the Ural regional council concerning the shooting of the former Czar, Nicholas Romanoff. Ekaterinburg being seriously threatened by the approach of the Tzecho-Slovak bands and a counter-revolutionary conspiracy having been simultaneously discovered, the presidium of the Ural regional council decided to shoot the former Czar and the decisionwas carried out on July 16.

"Romanoff's wife and son," it adds, "have been sent to a place of security and the documents concerning the conspiracy discovered to Moscow."

"Recently," the message states, "it was decided to try the former Czar for his crimes against the people and the trial was delayed only by later occurrences. The presidium of the central executive committee having discussed the Ural regional council's report, has accepted its decision as being regular, and announces it is now in possession of extremely important material and documents concerning the Nicholas Romanoff affair, including diaries he kept together with diaries of his wife and children and his correspondence which includes letters by Gregory Rasputin. "All this material," the message states, "will be examined and published."

Whatever may be the final estimate of Nicholas Romanoff, one time Czar of all the Russias, there can be no doubt that he was one of the most tragic figures of the war. It has been related of him by Mr. Charles Heath, who was one of his tutors as a boy, that one day they were reading together "The Lady of the Lake," and when they came to the vivid description of how, as King James rode out of the gates of Stirling Castle, the people outside raised a great huzza, and cried out, "Long live the Commons' King, King James," the young boy looked up at his tutor and said eagerly, "Why, that's what I would like to be, the Commons' King." In that little story lies the best key, as far as can be at present judged, to the life and experience of Nicholas II of Russia. He lived in two worlds, the world of lofty if somewhat fantastic idealism, and the world of a practice at all times its polar opposite. As a boy, he received the usual education of a Grand Duke of Russia, but he never took kindly to a military life, and when in 1894 he ascended the throne he already had a reputation for strongly pacifist views. It was Nicholas, of course, who sent out the famous invitation to the powers to the first Hague conference in 1898, and it was Nicholas II who, in 1904, plunged his country into the disastrous war with Japan, although largely, of course, as subsequent revelations have made clear, at the instance of the Kaiser. The Russo-Japanese War in many ways marked the beginning of the end, the beginning of that phase which reached such a definite period on Aug 1. 1914, and came to a final full stop on the 17th of March three years later. The story of the first 10 years of this period centers round the Duma, and indeed the story of the Duma and its struggles to maintain itself against the bureaucracy of Russia and the autocracy of the Czar constitute all or almost all that really matters is the reign of Nicholas II.

It was December, 1904, when the Russo-Japanese war was at its height, and the growing unrest throughout the country was obviously sweeping up toward something perilously like a revolution, when bodies of students were parading the streets of St. Petersburg shouting "Down with autocracy, stop the war," that the Czar issued his first decree to meet in any way the popular demand for reform. This decree was clearly only a tentative effort; it did not by any means meet the full demand of the people, who claimed and hoped for the immediate institution of some form of national assembly. The half measure, indeed, was bitterly resented. Feeling steadily

Left, from left, J.V. Stalin, V.I. Lenin &
M. Kalinin together in 1919. Below,
Lenin leaving the State Institute of
Pedagogies from a session of the first
All-Russian Congress on Education held
August 28, 1919.

deepened on the matter and the terrible incidents of Bloody Sunday in January, 1905, when workmen in immense numbers who had marched to the Winter Palace to lay their grievances before the Little Father were attacked by the Cossacks and many hundreds of them slain, were followed by immense strikes in all parts of Russia. A condition approaching anarchy obtained in many districts. Peasants burned the houses of nobles, mutinies in the army and navy were of frequent occurrence, and Russia as a whole reached a state of lawlessness approximating to the conditions rendered all too familiar by the events of the past year.

At last the Czar yielded, and in August, 1905, issued a manifesto in which he declared that, whilst preserving the fundamental law regarding the autocratic power, he had resolved to call, not later than January, 1906, a State Council or Duma consisting of elective representatives from the whole of Russia. The Czar's promise, however, still did not go far enough to satisfy the popular demand. The election of a national assembly was so hedged about with restrictions and safeguards as largely to eliminate its representative character. Feeling against the government was rather intensified indeed than otherwise by the move. There were more strikes and more disturbances, and after holding out for a time the Czar once more yielded. The suffrage for a new Duma was extended and finally in March and April, 1906, the elections for the new assembly were held. They resulted in their turn in an overwhelming majority of Constitutional Democrats, and the assembly thus constituted was formally opened by Nicholas II on May 10, 1906.

It was a short-lived effort, however Nicholas never liked it. He would be a Commons' King, but the Commons must be the Commons of the Little Father. Delegates from all parts of the vast empire came together fired with the tremendous enthusiasm for reform. Every measure was to be carried at once, and every reform must take effect at once. The members plainly demanded a new political millenium. No system was too firmly established for it to attack, and no distance was too great for it to go. The result was that within a few short months it had come to an end. The Czar hastily dissolved the assembly, declared himself "cruelly disappointed," and deplored the fact that the representatives of the nation, "instead of applying themselves to productive legislation, had attacked fundamental laws which could only be modified by Imperial will." He did not despair, however, a new assembly was called for the following July, and meanwhile all the efforts of the bureaucracy were directed toward taming the Duma.

The second Duma, however, although considerably tamed compared with the first, was by no means tamed sufficiently to find favor with the bureaucratic régime at St. Petersburg, and its life was even shorter than that of its predecessor. It was dissolved by Imperial ukase on June 16, 1907. Then Nicholas screwed his courage "to the sticking point," and took drastic action. He issued the famous Imperial manifesto and altered the electoral law in a most wholesale fashion. The right of choosing the majority of the members of the Duma was bestowed on about 130,000 land owners, and in reply to all protests the Czar asserted that the right of abrogating the law and replacing it with a new law belonged only to the power that gave the first law, the historic power of the Czar of Russia. The third Duma was thus at last thoroughly tamed and it sat out its full term of five years. All the time, however, the party of progress was steadily strengthening itself. The Duma had learned wisdom; it built on a firm foundation and advanced from point to point until at the outbreak of the war, and during the first year of the war, it was undoubtedly one of the great powers in the country. In its struggle with autocracy it had won and had overridden the indecision of the Czar.

During all this time rumors had been steadily flooding Europe as to the influences at St. Petersburg, which were being brought to bear upon the Czar and the Czaritza. What Father John of Kronstadt was to Nicholas' father, the monk Rasputin was to Nicholas himself, only the influence of Rasputin appears to have been much more decisive and mysterious than that of the famous wonder-worker of Kronstadt. In regard to all this it is clear enough that nothing like the whole truth is yet known, but sufficient information is known to show that the virtual ruler of Russia, for some years before the downfall of the Czar, was this ignorant, unlettered peasant from Siberia, and that his influence on the Czar and Czaritza was practically unlimited. The Czar in all his doings displayed an extraordinary vacillation, and although saved again and again from exposure due to the fact that he had an unlimited number of scapegoats at his disposal the true facts of the case, or at any rate a large number of them, were pretty accurately known. The end of the story is the story of yesterday. Events followed quickly upon one another. First came the shooting of Gregory Rasputin in Petrograd, then the sudden outbreak of the rebellion in March, 1917, then the abdication of the Czar and finally his banishment to the Siberian city of Tobolsk.

British Premier Calls Imperial Conference Study Genoa Crisis [4/18/22]

GENOA — In view of the critical situation brought about by the Russo-German Treaty, Mr. Lloyd George, The British Prime Minister, arrived unexpectedly at the Miramare Hotel early this morning and called the whole British Empire delegation together to discuss the situation before proceeding to a reunion of all the Allies. The signing of the compact provided the economic conference and probably the whole world with a first-class sensation.

While the general attention was centered on the Russo-allied conversations at the Villa di Albertis, the parties to the treaty, in seclusion at Bolshevist headquarters at Rapallo, calmly set their seals to a pact which, although undoubtedly a long step toward the restoration of pre-war conditions, nevertheless produced something in the nature of a political earthquake.

Briefly put, the accord, which was reached between the great Slav and Teuton nations settles the questions of claims and counter-claims, pre-war debts, indemnities, reparations, perquisitions and maintenance of prisoners by the simple process of wiping the slate clean. Germany and Russia are to mutually enjoy the most-favored nation treatment, but it is important to note that this does not extend to countries which were formerly part of Imperial Russia, and which are now hand in glove with the Soviet commonwealth. However, in this connection, it is worthy of note that Soviet Russia aims to maintain the integrity of the old empire and the treaty supports the theory more than once advanced in *The Christian Science Monitor* that the imperial ambitions of the republic closely approximate those of the late monarchy.

The real explanation probably is that the existing favorable opportunity was seized to complete the pourparlers and at the end the more subtle Slavs rushed the Teutons into signature. The existence of this treaty naturally strengthens the Russian position in some respects and the delight of M. Rakovsky is comprehensible enough.

Nothing was known of the completion of the affair in allied circles until one o'clock yesterday, when the Germans surprised the Italian delegation with the news. Mr. Lloyd George heard it on the way to his villa. In this connection, it was reported, the Germans insisted last night that the British and Italian governments were throughout isolated. On their part, the Russians may pride themselves on having stolen a march on the Allies, but in effect Germany is of little practical value to them

Monuments to Lenin. After more than 75 years he is still, with Marx and Engels, revered as the founder of the modern Russian State. Top, May Day parade in Red Square. Middle, Lenin's tomb. Bottom, poster of Lenin in Red Square.

in the present conditions. What they need, above all else, is credit for trade, and money for reconstruction and these are only obtainable from Great Britain and America.

Nikolai Lenine has Passed Away　　　　[1/22/24]

Nikolai Lenine passed away last evening at the village of Gorky, 20 miles from Moscow.

The general opinion here is that the immediate effect of the event will be to hush the echoes of party controversy. It is more difficult to predict the future, but as one official said: "The loss of Lenine is felt as a personal blow by every party member, but the experience of the last 18 months shows that the Soviet Government depends not on a single man, however great, but on a united disciplined party."

Nikolai Lenine, strong man of Russia and "Father of the Soviet," worked out, by his own dominance of leadership, the dream of revolutionary conquest which he, as a youth, first dreamed when his elder brother was executed by Czarist officials in the courtyard of the Schlüsselburg Bastile. His family, living in the Province of Simbirsk, in the Valley of the Volga, were members of the bourgeois class. His father, though he came from the peasantry, rose to the position of Councillor of State and Mr. Lenine's mother owned a small estate in the Province of Kazan. In that home Mr. Lenine's education was a matter of first importance for the father was an enthusiast for schools and everywhere was regarded as representative of the intellectual interests of the community.

Mr. Lenine, whose name in those days was Vladimir Ilyich Ulianoff, attended the Simbirsk Gymnasium, whose master was Feodor Kerensky, the father of Alexander Kerensky, from the wreck of whose Government, in 1917, Mr. Lenine built a Communist régime. Mr. Lenine's stormy career began shortly after his brother's execution. He graduated from the Simbirsk Gymnasium, apparently thoroughly imbued with the ideas of Karl Marx, and entered the University of Kazan. Revolutionary tactics in that institution, however, soon brought about his discharge. He then studied law, was admitted to the bar, pleaded one case and ended his professional career.

Although not a terrorist, as his brother had been, Nikolai Lenine plunged into the advocacy of socialism with such enthusiasm that he was quickly branded as dangerous by the Government, and hailed as a leader by socialists. He agitated strenuously — but not long —

The death of Lenin announced in The Christian Science Monitor. **The architect of the October Revolution had left his succession and the future of Communism in disarray.**

against the Czar's régime. The hand of the Government fell heavily upon him, and in 1897 he was sent out upon that long trail across the snow to exile in eastern Siberia. But he was young. His enthusiasm and determination were unbounded. He spent his months of exile in study and literary work, and emerged from that experience well qualified as the revolutionist he had determined to become.

From that time on his life was a succession of hegiras. He was the organizing genius back of the groups which advocated the overthrow of the Czar. International police were on his trail. He lived successively in Munich, Paris, Brussels, London, New York and Geneva. Then, at the second congress of the Russian Social-Democrat Party held in London in 1903, Mr. Lenine became the leader of the Bolsheviki (majority) faction. This party, in 1918, officially changed its name to Communist.

Since its establishment in 1917 up to a year ago Mr. Lenine has been the dominating figure in the Russian Soviet Government. He has had bitter fights with extremist factions in the Communist Party, opponents of the autocracy which he set up have been legion, but observers of the Russian situation have been uniform in their testimony that, during the most critical period, no substitute could be found for his leadership.

Doubtless, the most signal illustration of the brilliance of his leadership is revealed in the New Economic Policy which, because of the economic failure of Communism, he instituted in October, 1921. Collapse of the economic life of the Nation and growing discontent among the peasants forced Mr. Lenine to revise the measure of extreme Communism which had been rigidly applied in Russia when the Soviets came to power. A certain amount of private capital was countenanced, private property, in a measure, was restored, and, as a result, the Russian Government came under a rule more similar to that of State Socialism than Communism. The fact, however, of Mr. Lenine's ability to realize the necessity for this surrender of his Communist experiment, and his success in swinging his more radical colleagues to the new position, demonstrate the power which he has wielded.

For a year past, however, developments in Russia have gone forward by an evolutionary process, more and more distinct from the dominance of any particular leaders. Mr. Lenine's influence has been felt only indirectly. Conditions in Russia have gone far toward order.

Mr. Lenine served Russia when revolutionary leader seemed necessary. His death will not affect the normal progress which has followed his radical dictatorship.

Moscow Deciding Question Of Successor to Mr. Lenine [1/23/24]

The questions of appointing a successor to Nikolai Lenine has already been raised. The administrative functions of the Premier recently were divided between three men, Leo Kameneff, president of the Moscow Soviet, Mr. Rykoff, president of the Supreme Economic Council, and Mr. Tsurupa, former Food Minister, although important decisions really were adopted by the Communist Party's central committee.

No authoritative information is available as to whether the group system of administering the Premiership is to remain, or a definite successor is to be appointed. It is generally understood that this question, with other problems raised by the situation, will receive attention at the Union Soviet Congress meeting here next week. Closing a party conference, J.V. Stalin, in a speech yesterday, combined glowing praise of Mr. Lenine with a severe criticism of Leon Trotsky for disobeying and discrediting the central committee.

The following passages illustrate the tenor of the speech: "Of course, we students of Mr. Lenine understand that Mr. Lenine was the genius of geniuses, and such people are born only in centuries. We have only one leader, Mr. Lenine. That is why we often said that in the present condition of the absence of Mr. Lenine we must hold the course for a collegium."

In view of the crushing defeat of Mr. Trotsky's partisans at the party conference, it seems unlikely that any individual will inherit the authority of Mr. Lenine. The present group leading the majority of the central committee, including J.V. Stalin, Leo Kameneff, and F.C. Zinovieff, seems firmly entrenched in control of the party and the Government.

Moscow is absolutely quiet, with large crowds around the newspaper offices and news stands, and the public buildings are decorated with signs of mourning.

THE CHRISTIAN SCIENCE MONITOR
AN INTERNATIONAL DAILY NEWSPAPER

COPYRIGHT 1934 BY
THE CHRISTIAN SCIENCE PUBLISHING SOCIETY

BOSTON, MONDAY, MAY 28, 1934—VOL. XXVI, NO. 154

★ ATLANTIC EDITION | THREE CENTS IN GREATER BOSTON
FIVE CENTS ELSEWHERE

The March of the Nations
By Rufus Steele

Geneva Wrestles Arms Puzzle

French Airmen Cross Atlantic

Roosevelt Curbs Codes' Reach

Italy Lowers Standards to Arm

Club Women Fight Revolvers

U. S. Mints Get Old Gold Flood

GENEVA sees leading delegates try to save the Disarmament Conference from complete collapse. Sir John Simon and Capt. Anthony Eden of Britain hold a long conference with Norman Davis and Hugh Wilson of the United States, but announce no new possibilities. Mussolini's warlike speech in Rome adds to the general discouragement. Recent agitation in England, France, Germany and Poland of the dangers from air raids and poisonous gases undoubtedly hinders willingness to limit arms, but a Monitor investigation in these four countries shows the population not actually scared and that the basis of the agitation has been political and commercial. A military hope is advanced for the tottering Disarmament Conference—Some nation may yet discern and take the heroic action that alone could make it all mean something.

¶France is congratulated by the United States when Lieutenants Paul Codos and Maurice Rossi cross the Atlantic on their 6200-mile Paris-California flight. The huge silver monoplane Joseph le Brix is first sighted by Americans over Maine as it heads toward New York and on west. "Minor trouble," the aviators report by radio, which they hope to repair without coming down. Two nations hope with them. Paris immediately makes Rossi a captain, Codos a commander of the Legion of Honor—Honors should and do await men who shatter human limitations.

¶Washington sees steps taken that will have a far effect on industry and the stock market. President Roosevelt issues an executive order exempting the service industries—those that sell service rather than goods—from many of the fair trade practices of the NRA codes. This relieves NRA drastically and ends many prosecutions. Senate and House agree at last on their bills for bringing the stock exchange under rigid federal regulation by adopting the Glass compromise—The Senator from Virginia wins a long and spectacular fight for his way in Wall Street.

¶Rome hears Premier Mussolini draw a dark picture of the future in the Chamber of Deputies. He declares Italy will build its navy up to the full 70,000 tons permitted under the Washington treaty of 1921 and will spread the 1,000,000,000 lire cost over the years to 1940. The air fleet will be entirely renewed at an equal expense. He warns the people they will have to adapt themselves to a lower standard of living for years to come. He believes humanity is sturdy enough to stand the hardships he foresees—But how can any true leader advise by arguments at such a price?

¶America and the world thrill at the analysis of the future's industrial developments as disclosed by Alfred P. Sloan's survey among experts. Modern five-room homes, completely furnished, will cost only $2000. Clothing will be made of new, more enduring fabrics. Homes will have radio news teletype, television of new events, motion pictures by radio. Automobiles, safer, faster, will whisk along night-lighted trunk highways. Power from wind and sun, household drudgery swallowed by electricity—90 per cent better living standards, say the wisest, if we can only think it and accept it.

¶The General Federation of Women's Clubs repeats that its warfare on revolvers is to be relentless. Field and Stream magazine calls upon the Council before it adjourns at Hot Springs, Ark., to rescind its demand that pistols and revolvers be put back into the firearms bill now before Congress on the ground that the security of homes and families demands it. But the Council officers cry, No! no! and announce a slogan that defines the full intention—"We're out to disarm the gangster, not to arm the citizen."

¶Japan celebrates the twenty-ninth anniversary of the destruction by its navy of the grand fleet of Russia. But amid the festivities thousands pray outside a simple wooden house in Tokyo where Admiral Count Heihachiro Togo, who directed that annihilation, lies critically ill. This veteran sailor is more than a historic "Nelson of Japan"—Again and again he has inspired his people to heroic action.

¶The U. S. Treasury finds itself doing a huge business in old gold watches. Also gold chains, wedding rings, spectacle rims, dental scraps and gold medals pour into the stream that floods the melting pots. The Treasury's price of $35 an ounce, against the former price of $20.67, and its recent reduction of the purchase minimum from five ounces to one ounce explain the activity. A new domestic game develops—Many a household grows excited in digging up useless keepsakes to be turned into useful money.

NRA Abandons Efforts to Rule Service Trades

President's Order Affects Cleaners, Dyers, Hotels and Similar Lines

Special from Monitor Bureau

WASHINGTON, May 28—The Roosevelt Administration was today engaged in its first major retreat on the industrial regulation front. It involved abandonment of the NRA's efforts to enforce price-fixing and fair-trade practice regulations over service trades.

The order to fall back was given officially by President Roosevelt late yesterday. His action followed a recent intimation from ninth NRA quarters that enforcement of service trade codes had become a superhuman task due to widespread noncompliance which, in one of the trades, was said to reach as high as 90 per cent.

Brig.-Gen. Hugh S. Johnson, under the terms of the President's order, will specify the trades which are to be exempted. The list is expected to include dry cleaning, dyeing, pressing, hotels, barber shops, beauty parlors and similar trades consisting of numerous independent units. The dyeing and dry cleaning trades are considered the worst offenders against their code and the one most certainly to head the list for exemption.

Labor Provisions Retained

The retreat is strictly limited to price-fixing and fair competition practices. All wage and labor provisions of the codes are to remain in force. These include minimum wages, maximum hours of work, prohibition of child labor and the right of collective bargaining for employees.

As a concession to large numbers of enterprisers who have been protesting in advance against this step, the President's order grants to purely local groups within any one industry the right to set up local price and trade practice rules when such rules are agreed upon by 85 per cent of all members of the trade in the area. Such local agreements are subject, however, to the further limitation of approval by the national recovery Administration here.

The entire move is in the nature of a strategic retreat from exposed and dangerous positions to higher and more defensible ground. Not only has code enforcement in the service trades become a farce due to widespread noncompliance, but it has more than any one other thing made the NRA unpopular. And there is the third compelling reason of the doubtful constitutionality of federal interference in a trade which is almost purely intrastate in character.

Fewer Codes Indicated

Another phase of a general contraction of NRA activities now well under way is abandonment of efforts to draft separate codes for every small industry that comes along. General Johnson recently revealed that about 75 per cent of NRA's time was taken up by 15 per cent of the industries. Hereafter small industries are to be left under the President's unemployment agreement.

(Continued on Page 13, Column 1)

Flying Into the Sunset

9-10 Décembre 1930.
26-28 Janvier 1931   56°27 6739°
Mars 1931
Mai 1931   1876°
5I: ISTRES   900°
1939   150°

French Fliers on Way to California
Left—Capt. Maurice Rossi. Right—Lieut. Paul Codos.

French Fliers Tell New York They May Land

Imply 'Gas' Getting Low and Fields Make Ready— Exact Location Unknown

Goal Is San Diego

Longest Attempted Nonstop Flight—$66,000 Prize Is Possible—Weather Fine

NEW YORK, May 28 (P)—Safely over the Atlantic ocean, the French fliers, Lieut. Paul Codos and Capt. Maurice Rossi, raced down the New England coast early today while a flurry of conflicting reports accompanied their progress on the nonstop flight from Paris. San Diego, Calif., is their goal. They left Le Bourget Field, near Paris, at 11.10 p. m., E. S. T., May 26.

Observers throughout Maine checked a big silver monoplane tentatively identified as the Joseph Le Brix through Eastport, Rockland and Bar Harbor—the last named point at 10 a. m. E. S. T.

Meanwhile, every preparation for their landing was made at Floyd Bennett Field in Brooklyn on the strength of wireless reports from Chatham, Mass., that minor trouble had developed and a landing here would be necessary unless repairs could be made in the air.

A wireless message direct from the plane to the Chatham wireless operator of the Radio-Marine Corporation placed the time of their landing at 2 p. m., E. S. T., in event they find it necessary to come down at Floyd Bennett.

Field in Readiness

Officials had the field made ready to receive the ship as early as 9:30 a. m. on the strength of indirect wireless reports that the plane was in the vicinity of New York.

The nature of the "trouble" was not given in the brief exchange of messages with the Chatham station. Radio-marine operators estimated the plane was still north of the Massachusetts coast at 10 a. m., E. S. T., due to the strength of the wireless signals.

Observers along the route stated the big ship was evidently holding a leisurely pace down the coast.

Among the widely differing and conflicting reports covering Floyd Bennett and Roosevelt Fields was one stating that the Frenchmen would attempt to reach Cleveland, Ohio, for a landing if immediate repairs were found not to be necessary when they reached New York.

$66,000 Prize Possible

Although San Diego is their destination, there is a possibility that the fliers may choose to set their plane down at San Francisco. If they reach the Pacific ocean without a stop, a French Government prize of $66,000 is theirs.

Their plane is the same one in which they flew from New York to Rayak, Syria, to establish the present nonstop distance record of 5630 miles. The ship weighed more than nine tons when it climbed laboriously from the French flying field and started one of the most daring adventures of the air.

Seven hundred miles out from Southampton, the plane flew over the steamship Europa. Steamships kept in touch with the fliers by radio, giving them bearings.

Except for the fog and low clouds off Newfoundland, weather conditions were favorable. Dr. James H. Kimball, New York meteorologist, said after receiving new reports early today:

Have Good Conditions

He said Rossi and Codos have "even better conditions" than prevailed when Costa and Bellonte made their Paris-New York flight in 1930.

Rossi and Codos, in heading west across the Atlantic, dared an air current of

(Continued on Page 3, Column 3)

By a Staff Artist of THE CHRISTIAN SCIENCE MONITOR

Marx, Lenin, Stalin—Dreamer, Doer and Administrator of a New Russia

Soviet Russia Digging at Roots of Social System; Masses Are Dominated by Will of Ruling Few

More Autocratic Than, and as Ruthless as, Any of the Tsars, It Seeks to Fit Economic Life of People Into State-Controlled Supertrust

Still Remains Great World Influence

First of 18 Articles

By W. H. Chamberlin

There is something unmistakably impressive about the sheer bulk of the Union of Socialist Soviet Republics, as Russia has been renamed since the revolution. One is dealing here with the dimensions not of an ordinary country, but of a continent. The area of the Soviet Union is between one-sixth and one-seventh of the land surface of the globe.

From Russia's western frontier to the Pacific is a distance of over 5000 miles; from the ice-free port of Murmansk, which lies far to the north of the arctic circle, to the high plateaus and mountain ranges of the Pamir, in central Asia, is a journey of almost 3000 miles.

One can find within the Soviet Union all the climatic differences and contrasts that exist in the whole European Continent. Indeed there is less difference between Sweden and Italy than there is between the endless forests and the frozen tundra, or marsh land, of the Russian North and the hot deserts of Turkestan, where irrigation makes possible extensive cotton plantations and oases bloom out with rich fruit.

In population, the Soviet Union, with something over 160,000,000 inhabitants, is exceeded only by such Asiastic countries as India and China. In size and natural resources the Soviet Union ranks with the United States and with the British Empire, considered as a whole. China is another huge land mass, but lacks effective control of many regions which are still included within its geographical frontiers and is apparently much poorer than the Soviet Union in such vital sources of mineral wealth as coal, iron and oil.

Straddles Europe and Asia

Sprawled out over the eastern half of Europe and the northern third of Asia, Russia has always had a foot in each of these continents without belonging definitely to either. Its cultural forms and aspirations have led European, its governmental methods and its low living standards have suggested Asia.

This dualism has not been removed; in some respects it has been intensified by the revolution. As a result of the World War and the civil war the more westernized portions of the former Tsarist Empire, Finland, Finland and the Baltic provinces, split off and set up independent national states. The Soviet center of population and industrial gravity is very definitely being pushed toward the East.

It is in the Urals and in western Siberia that the Soviet Government is laying the foundation of a powerful industrial development.

Whether one is walking through the streets of Moscow or attending a Soviet Congress or waiting for a train at a station, one can scarcely fail to be impressed with the essentially Eurasian character of the Soviet Union. For along with tall, big-boned Russians one sees a great variety of faces and figures that belong to the East: slant-eyed Tartars from the Volga and the Crimea; yellow-skinned Mongols from eastern Siberia; tall, rangy, olive-skinned mountaineers from the Caucasus. Old racial and religious prejudices and antipathies have largely broken down among the younger generation which has grown up under the Soviet régime, with the result that intermarriage among members of the scores of various races which inhabit the Soviet Union is becoming more common and the considerable strain of eastern blood which could always be found in the Russians is being to some extent increased.

Disadvantages as Well

One should not be so carried away by the sheer vastness of the Soviet Union as to lose sight of some of its serious natural disadvantages. A considerable part of its area, especially the frozen stretches of northern Russia and Siberia, will never, in all probability, support any considerable population.

The Soviet Union today is landlocked, wit: a scanty ice-free seacoast and inadequate harbor facilities. Its great central plain is singularly poor in rock—which helps to explain the atrociously bad condition of almost all the country's roads. Such machine-building centers as Leningrad, such textile centers as Moscow and Ivanovo-Voznesensk, are located thousands of miles away from the main sources of cotton and iron, and are dependent on long hauls over a chronically overburdened and defective transportation system. There is no convincing evidence that Russia possesses exceptional reserves of gold, copper and some other nonferrous metals.

As against the fertility of the famous "blackearth" soil belt which runs through parts of central Russia, Ukrainia and the north Caucasus, one must set the shortness of the Russian agricultural year, the liability to famine through the offset of too-early winter or the lack of rain in regions which are extremely fertile in good years to severe droughts.

Yet, when one has made due allowance for all these negative physical factors in the Soviet Union, one cannot escape the conclusion that a country of Russia's vast size and population, with its proved and potential extensive resources in coal and iron, oil a.d timber, platinum and manganese, with its varied possibilities of agricultural development, is capable of very significant expansion, especially in its Asiatic regions, where there is much known mineral wealth awaiting efficient exploitation and considerable likelihood of new discoveries.

Hack at Vital Roots

Under any kind of strong government, under any social and economic system, apart from sheer chaos, the Soviet Union would be a force to be reckoned with in world politics and economics. But there is a stronger and deeper reason why the Soviet Union must be regarded as one of the most permanently significant and interesting countries in the world. This huge country, with its foothold on two continents, has been the scene of the most sweeping and thoroughgoing social upheaval of our time, perhaps of all history.

The present masters of the Soviet Union, the leaders of the Communist Party, smashing opposition to their will with all the ruthlessness of the most autocratic Tsar, are driving toward the goal of building up a kind of human society which will differ very substantially from anything that has hitherto been known.

They are laying the ax at the root of some very old and deep-rooted human impulses; the will to believe in something outside of and beyond the present material world, the peasant's instinct for personal owner-

(Continued on Page 3, Column 5)

Russia—Without Benefit of Censor

WILLIAM HENRY CHAMBERLIN, the author of these articles, has left Moscow, where he has spent 10 years as staff correspondent of The Christian Science Monitor, to become the Monitor's chief correspondent in the Far East. Two books on Russia have appeared from his pen and both have won a place among the outstanding contemporary works on that country. His first article is descriptive of the great sociological experimental laboratory. His second and subsequent articles will lift the curtain on the methods by which the inhabitants of the Union of Socialist Soviet Republics are molded by propaganda, terrorism and fanaticism.

At the same time, the articles will discuss some of the notable achievements of the Soviet régime since the revolution, which have merited the sincerest respect of unbiased observers.

W. H. Chamberlin

Mansfield Cuts His Budget $1,200,000 Under Last Year; Sunday Accident Toll Drops

New England Observer Remarks That Insurance Rates Are Tied Up With Property Loss and There's Still Plenty of That to Worry the Pocketbook

Mayor Mansfield today submitted to the city council his budget recommendations covering the departments directly under his control. The figures total $38,596,262.58.

This provides for city department allotments within the tax limit, city debt requirements, and revenue department allotments. The allowances recommended for city departments within the tax limit total $23,636,-007.26. This is $1,200,000 less than the appropriation recommendations submitted in 1933.

Cities

No Carnival

Carnivals, even though run by Elks, have no place on public playgrounds in Newton. So Newton children will not have calliopes, merry-go-rounds and other artificial fun devices crowding them off their play places this June. Opposition was on the grounds that the proposed use of the playground had aspects of immorality.

Police Joke

Newton police were unconscious providers of a surprise party to Mr. Benjamin Levine. When his doorbell rang, Mr. Levine found an officer on the steps.

"Your car has just been recovered," stated the officer.

Seeing his car standing at the curb where he had left it, Mr. Levine thought the officer was having a mere pleasantry. "Sure, officer. But since it hasn't yet been stolen, how could it be recovered. You are a great joker, eh?"

Led by the officer down to the curb, Mr. Levine found there was no joke, that his car had been stolen, wrecked at the foot of a steep embankment, dragged back by the police to his front door.

'Asset' Questionnaire

Reading, Mass., has long been noted for its forward looking planning. Its street layout data has been called for by even distant Tokyo. Much of this is unofficially credited to competent professors of civics and engineering who are residents.

Latest Reading promotional effort which smatters of wholesale inspiration is a tabulation of the town's assets and liabilities from the potential residential point of view.

"Why did you move to Reading?" will be the opening question by ERA investigators to every resident who

---

Motorists

Sunday Toll

Low-coat auto insurance is completely tied up with accident reduction. If last week's low figure of nine fatalities could be maintained, Massachusetts motorists could look forward to reduced rates. The total May week a year ago recorded 18 fatalities.

But fatal accidents are a small part of the motor toll which makes

(Continued on Page 7, Column 1)

has come into town within the last 20 years.

Transportation, aversion to apartment dwelling, opportunity to have a garden, living away from factory smoke, attractiveness of churches, schools and neighborhoods are some of the features sought by families seeking homes in the suburbs. Reading has all these, thinks there must be more and feels sure a list of assets would be imposing, with liabilities at the vanishing point.

Once recorded the information will be available to all town organizations, official, commercial, civic and social. Added point in improving present assets; letters are solicited offering suggestions that will improve Reading as a community of homes.

The Monitor Index

Arms Makers Mask Efforts In Air Scares

Monitor Survey Shows Only Apparent Menace Is Régime of Fear

'Peace Versus War'

Increase in Orders for Planes Throughout World Tells of Propaganda's Effect

By Press Wireless from Monitor Bureau

LONDON, May 28—LOST: an air scare.

Newspapers have been so full of the menace of air invasion, preparations and propaganda the last few weeks that the Monitor decided to search out the facts. Are the countries really alarmed? Are they making extensive preparations to withstand possible attacks from air? And in any case who is back of the business?

To this end inquiries were set on foot in London, Paris, Berlin and Warsaw to find out what the authorities in these countries feel about the matter.

With complete unanimity the answer to the question "Are you scared?" was "No."

Two Groups at Work

Here is the significant reply of the Monitor correspondent at Paris: There is as yet no air scare worthy the name in France, he says, but two groups with opposing motives are working hard to create one. One group is headed by peace organizations, working honestly for disarmament. The other—you will never guess it—is directed by the General Staff and armament manufacturers.

Strange to say, the same two diametrically opposed forces are busy in England. Thus on one side the Daily Herald, which advocates disarmament, published two scare stories last week.

The Daily Mail, which thinks Great Britain ought to have the world's biggest air fleet of 5000 planes (at present she has 1490 planes and is sixth), is equally active.

Returning to the continent, we find the Monitor representative saying that the people of Berlin do not believe in any air scare, though the authorities extensively exploited the air menace last autumn with the view to making Germany "air-minded."

A similar report comes from Poland. In that country there is a very active though unofficial League for Defense Against Air Attack and another for Defense Against Chemical Warfare.

Staged Shows

These leagues staged a number of effective dress rehearsals last year with the help of the authorities. One at Vilna filled the city with citizens wearing gas masks. Citizens without their masks were pounced on in streets and rushed spectacularly to the hospital as "casualties." It appears, however, that the services of most of those treated in this cavalier fashion had been specially enlisted by the league in pursuit of its campaign for "air-mindedness."

The Polish league for defense against air attack, which is known as "Ropp," is a profitable one too, for its members get 25 per cent reduction on fares when traveling by air.

These two leagues—and the sister organization, known as the League for Development of Internal War—are presided over, either by an ex-Prime Minister of Poland or a famous general.

So far the horrific propaganda put out by the parties concerned does not seemed to have been completely successful, though undoubtedly there is growing apprehension of possible danger of attacks from air. The Monitor correspondent at Paris reports the country as "vaguely apprehensive."

The Berlin correspondent says that generally populations "have never given 'scare' matter much thought."

Warsaw thinks Poland too sparsely inhabited to be open to serious danger from air.

In Britain experts are busy, including representatives connected with munition makers, discounting the danger of gas attacks. Air Commodore John Chamier, secretary of the Air League of the British Empire and former director of Vickers Aviation, Limited, pointed out that the press poison gas scares are based on laboratory experiments with small animals in inclosed spaces. This, he said, is a very different matter from developing a gas attack in the open air. Mustard gas, he added, is most suitable for this form of attack and mustard gas is not "lethal."

40 Tons of Mustard

The medical Journal The Lancet has declared London would be put out of action by 40 tons of mustard gas if left undisturbed for five days. Whereto someone made reply that if after the air raid London goes to sleep for five days and atmosphere fails to come to rescue, the city would wake up to find itself in the hospital.

A distinguished chemist on the staff of Imperial Chemical Industries has said one would be comparatively safe from gas in a bath.

London's press scares of last week included the bomb proof chamber the British Air Ministry is said to be planning for London. It would make for a substantial size to accommodate the whole population of the metropolis.

Another scare was attributed to Major Stuart Blackmore who was quoted as saying that poison gas ex-

(Continued on Page 5, Column 1)

2. Stalin Through The Thirties

William Henry Chamberlain was well disposed toward "the great experiment" of communism when he first traveled to Russia in 1922-1923. After a year this changed. He later wrote, "continued residence in the Soviet Union was a good cure for credulity."

He was a permanent correspondent for the Monitor in Moscow from 1923-1934. This indicates remarkable endurance at a time when there was no afternoon PAN AM flight to New York every day — not even an American Embassy until his last year there.

More important than his day to day coverage of events was the remarkable series of articles he wrote upon leaving the Soviet Union. The accounts of the million who died during the collectivisation of agriculture in the Ukraine and elsewhere were perhaps the first accounts receiving wide circulation which laid bare the face of Stalinism for the entire world.

His later articles throughout the 1930s, such as "Coddling Communism," brought a rigorous logic to the analysis of the Soviet Union, as well as a mature long-view on its historical evolution.

Much of the coverage of the late 1930s attempted to make sense of the tragic-comedy of the purges and show trials in the Soviet Union resulting from Stalin's paranoia.

Communism: The Faith Without God   [1/10/34]

By William Henry Chamberlin

It is in Russia, which officially rejects all the old forms of religion, that one finds one of the strongest organized faiths in the world today. For Russian Communism, as it has developed during the 15 years which have elapsed since the Revolution, displays in striking degree all the psychological traits if not of a new religion — and both Communists and members or recognized religious organizations would be equally inclined to protest against this definition — at any rate of a new crusading faith.

Communism has its body of doctrine in the works of Marx, Engels and Lenin; its creed and catechism in the *politgramota,* or course of instruction in Communist conceptions of government and economics which is drilled into every school child; its ecumenical councils to determine questions of faith and discipline in the Congresses of the Communist Party. Its insistence on the complete subordination of the individual to the requirements of the cause, its absolute intolerance of heresy and dissent, its conviction of a world Messianic mission — all these traits of fanatical believers in new dogmas are conspicuously characteristic of the Russian Communists.

Some years ago I was talking with a young woman, an ardent Communist, who was a member of the factory committee at a large electrical plant in Kharkov, the capital of Ukraina. A copy of Karl Marx's "Das Kapital" lay on the table. Pointing with reverence to this volume, my companion said: "Whenever we are confronted with any problem or difficulty in the factory management we look into that book and find the solution." A skeptic might cherish justifiable doubts about the efficacy of Marx's classical work as a panacea for leaky boilers or broken-down turbines and an older and more sophisticated Communist would probably not have attributed such magical powers to the book. But the remark of the young woman was typical of the attitude of unquestioning faith which has been instilled into a considerable part of the Soviet younger generation.

Present-day Russia can never be understood psychologically, except on the premise that its ruling group is dominated by an intense burning faith in the supreme rightness of their ultimate goal, which gives them a feeling of entire self-righteousness in applying any means, however ruthless, that may seem necessary in order to reach this goal. The disciplined Communist local official carries out a baby-saving campaign with one hand by pushing forward the establishment of nurseries in collective farms and with the other hand he drives through the so-called "liquidation of the kulaks as a class," that is, the expropriation and banishment of the richer peasants in his district, even though this latter measure does not increase the chances of longevity for the children of kulak families. The Party, which is the supreme authority, has ordered both measures, and it is the first duty of a Communist, as of a soldier, to obey orders regardless of what he may think of them. No one in Russia today would think of writing a moralistic denunciation of excessive drinking or loose living. The main criticism of such practices would always be based on the idea that overindulgence unfits a person to carry out the obligations of Party membership. This is not infrequently accompanied by sentences of expulsion from the Party or, in less serious cases, by public reprimand.

The basis of this kind of faith which has taken firm root in a population of more than 160,000,000 persons, inhabiting more than one-seventh of the surface of the globe, is the teaching of Karl Marx that human progress depends on the replacement of Capitalism by Socialism. Marx believed that the private profit system carried within itself the seeds of its own destruction by leading to periodic devastating crises of industrial stagnation and unemployment and to an ever-increasing concentration of more wealth in the hands of fewer people.

He advocated the revolutionary overthrow of the existing order and the substitution of a new society,

dominated at first by the industrial working class, in which private ownership of the means of production would be abolished. Ultimately this new society would become classless and would be guided by the theory: "From each according to his abilities; to each according to his needs."

In the softer atmosphere of western Europe Marx's ideas have scarcely emerged from the stage of parliamentary debate and academic discussion. In Russia, under the influence of the knout and Siberian exile, the Czarist means of repressing political opposition, they hardened into the philosophy, into the fanatical faith of the Bolshevik Party that emerged as the dominant power in Russia after the Revolution. Lenin, the unquestioned leader and founder of the Soviet régime, was a thoroughgoing Marxist in his philosophy and economic outlook. But by his elaborations of Marx's teaching and by his emphasis on certain phases of Marx's thought he gave a definite and distinctive character to Russian Bolshevism, as distinguished from prewar international Socialism.

Lenin's theory of the unequal development of Capitalism led him to the conclusion that a working-class revolution could be carried out successfully in one country, that the world Capitalist system could be broken at its weakest link. Marx and Engels had proceeded on the assumption that Socialist revolutions would occur simultaneously in the leading countries.

Lenin also put forward the conception that Capitalism had entered on its final stage of competitive imperialist systems, which would lead to international clashes, out of which would proceed in turn revolutions. Another point that received a good deal of emphasis in his teaching was the impossibility of a gradual peaceful transition from Capitalism to Socialism and the necessity for smashing the old state apparatus and building up an entirely new one.

While the bases of Communist doctrine are dogmatic, a certain amount of flexibility is shown as regards immediate objectives.

Like more than one fanatical group in the past, the All-Union Communist Party, seeking to give currency to these views, has built up two formidable machines: one of propaganda and one of repression. Complete state control of theater and motion picture, radio and school, press and pamphlet permit an organized system of mass propaganda that makes the wartime efforts of governments in the same direction seem very puny by comparison. Any speech by Stalin, any important new resolution or decree filters down to the population

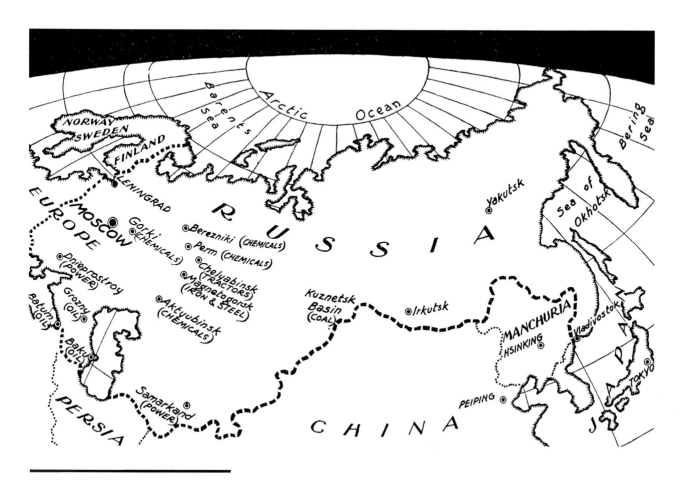

This map appeared in The Christian Science Monitor **in 1934 showing new centers of essential industry.**

through regular and systematic channels. The main ideas of the speech or decree are reiterated, hammered in, worked over and elaborated by Stalin's chief lieutenants at conferences of higher Party functionaries. These in turn pass on the message to the lower categories of the Party officialdom; and this process goes on until the lowest unit of the Party organization, the *yacheika*, or local branch, has been reached.

Side by side with the machinery of propaganda works the machinery of repression. The eyes and ears of the formidable Gay-Pay-Oo, or Political Police, are always alert, and this organization makes especially free use of its unlimited powers of summary arrest and of inflicting the penalties of exile, deportation or, in extreme cases, execution, in a period of strained class struggle such as the country is passing through. Not only the actions, but the thoughts of the Soviet citizen are carefully circumscribed. A watchful censorship is always quick to scent out "harmful ideological tendencies" in new books or plays or other artistic works and to see that the Soviet population is properly protected against the polluting influence of non-Communist ideas, whether they originate in the Soviet Union or abroad.

It is quite in keeping with the psychological character of Communism as a new faith that it should be thoroughly hostile to the older religions. The Communist attitude toward religion is summed up in Marx's phrase: "Religion is opium for the people"; and, while there is no prohibition of religious worship and the Soviet Constitution assures every citizen the right to "practice any or no religion," every effort is made to induce the citizen to choose "no" rather than "any" religion. The scales are weighted against religion in a variety of ways. Religious books are not published in Russia and the total circulation of the few tolerated religious journals would not exceed a few thousand, while every bookstore displays a plentiful assortment of anti-religious pamphlets and every facility is given for printing and circulating anti-religious magazines and newspapers. While one religious seminary has been dragging out a rather uncertain existences there are a multitude of courses for training anti-religious propagandists.

Every member of the Communist Party, numbering more than 3,000,000 and of the Union of Communist Youth, with about 5,000,000 members, must not only profess no religion, but must fight actively against all forms of religious faith. Membership in these organizations, of course, is voluntary, but members are expelled for failure to observe the code of Party ethics. In view of the fact, also, that many posts of authority and influence in Russia are actually, if not legally, barred to non-Communists, and because the Union of Communist Youth is the only mass organization of young people, the profession of religion has been much discouraged. Priests and ministers of religion are disfranchised, which means that they and their families are excluded from a number of social and educational benefits and that the priests and ministers are not allowed to hold food cards, so that they must either buy food at the inflated prices of the private market or rely on their congregations for support.

Teaching in the schools is definitely anti-religious and the country is covered with a network of anti-religious museums, which are often installed in former monasteries or cathedrals. A Soviet anti-religious museum gives a somewhat jumbled impression. Enlisted in a confused crusade against religion, one finds combined there the dogheaded gods of Egypt, charts showing incomes of medieval Russian monasteries, portraits of Rockefeller and other millionaires who support churchly ideals, and notices of "evolution" trials in the United States. A student of comparative religion or a person who did not feel that his faith depended on a miraculous explanation of natural phenomena would probably not be greatly impressed by the average Soviet anti-religious museum. But approximately two-thirds of the Russian population was illiterate before the war; and this fact alone explains the greater susceptibility of the masses to any new intensive propaganda. I remember the naïve remark of the wife of a factory worker in a small Russian city. In response to a question as to whether she went to church she replied:

"Before the Revolution I was taught that it was right to go to church, so I went. Now they tell me it isn't right, so I don't go."

Not all Russians, of course, are as passive as this woman. But post revolutionary developments have shown that the supposedly deep-rooted attachment of the majority of the Russian people to the Orthodox Church was little more than a myth, circulated by credulous and sentimental visitors to Russia in prewar days. One can still find individuals and groups passionately attached to some form of religion, and ready to undergo any kind of hardship or disability for their faith. But mass faith in the older religions in Russia is definitely crumbling. The new faith of Communism, by the sheer impact of its organized propaganda, is gradually pushing them out.

Communism: The Faith Without God

The Tractor Replaces the Icon, and the Russians of Today Accept the Gospel of Lenin and Marx Rather Than That of Their Fathers; They Turn Former Monasteries and Churches Into Anti-Religious Museums

By William Henry Chamberlin
Monitor Correspondent in Moscow, Author of "Soviet Russia," and other works

ANTI-RELIGIOUS MUSEUM

Pushkin Square in Moscow is Flanked on One Side by an Old Monastery, Which Has Been Converted Into an Anti-Religious Museum, One of Many in Russia.

NIKOLAI LENIN
Founder of Communist State

KARL MARX
Prophet of Communism

A LENIN CORNER

A Typical Peasant Cottage. The Old "Icon Corner" Has Been Strongly "Modernized" in That the Traditional Religious Oil Paintings Find Themselves in the Company of Revolutionary Placards and Pictures of Industrial Activities.

PILGRIMS TO THE TOMB OF LENIN

Within This Black Mausoleum in Moscow's Red Square Lies in State the Body of Nikolai Lenin, "Saint" of Modern Russia. A Line of "Reverent" Communists Move Almost Constantly Into This New-Style Religious Shrine.

NOT A RELIGIOUS PROCESSION!

The Ceremonial Processions With Banners Marking Religious Occasions in Pre-Revolutionary Russia Have Been Replaced by Processions Marking More Mundane Occasions. This Picture Shows Veterans of Russia's Civil War Carrying Banners in the Last Moscow May Day Celebration.

THE CHRISTIAN SCIENCE MONITOR   WEEKLY MAGAZINE SECTION, JANUARY 10, 1934.

Page Eight   Page Nine

Full page spread from The Christian Science Monitor **Weekly Magazine Section from January 10, 1934.**

No word among Communists is more abused than "mysticism." Yet it is ironically curious to see certain mystical tendencies of older religions reproducing themselves in the new faith of Communism. Pilgrimages to shrines and tombs of saints are rare in Russia today, although sometimes one may see an old peasant woman going through a monastery which is now used as an anti-religious museum, obviously regarding its icons and other religious decorations — which have been preserved for historical or artistic considerations — as objects of worship. But in these times there is a daily stream of pilgrims to the striking granite mausoleum on the Red Square, where lies in state the embalmed body of the founder of the Communist faith, Vladimir Ilyitch Lenin.

The "icon corner" with its gilt portraits of saints and Biblical scenes, sometimes garlanded with flowers, is going out of fashion in Russian homes. But in its place has come the Lenin corner, where portraits of scenes in the life of the Bolshevik leader are displayed, along with copies of his writings and texts from his works. At the formal opening of the Dnieprostroi hydroelectric power plant in 1932, when delegations of workers poured in, with their red banners and inscriptions, a spectator remarked: "How much this looks like an old-fashioned procession of the Cross, with the Communist slogans replacing the icons and texts from the Bible."

The attachment of the Russian masses to the creed of the Orthodox Church was an illusion. But the essential strain of fanaticism in the Russian character is not an illusion. The Russian has little feeling for moderation or relativity. The common sense, rule-of-thumb tradition of the Englishman and the easy skepticism of the Frenchman are alien to him. He thinks in terms of absolute values, which must be achieved at any cost. The industrialization of Russia, which at first sight might seem a prosaic, utilitarian process, in actual fact has been a demonstration of fanatical faith in a new god — the Machine — accompanied by the mixture of heroism, self-sacrifice, cruelty and suffering that explosions of fanatical faith usually generate. To the ardent Young Communist the tractor is not what it is to a Western farmer. It is not merely an implement to be used or discarded, according as it may or may not prove economic, but it is rather what an icon of Saint Nicholas the Wonder worker might have been to his grandfather: the symbol of his faith.

Most crusading beliefs have carried with them a conviction of a world mission; and Russian Communism is no exception to this rule. The Communist leaders

Wooden Russian Orthodox church, the Kizhi Church of the Transfiguration. Next page, clockwise from top left: Jewish synagogue in Trakai, Lithuania. The Cathedral of St. Dmitri in Vladimir constructed in the years 1193-1197. Gvari Chapel from the 6th century.

have always regarded the Russian Revolution as at once a prelude and a stimulus to similar revolutions in other countries. Failure of revolutions in other countries to materialize and absorption in problems of internal reconstruction may have appreciably diminished the belief of the Soviet leaders in the imminence of upheavals on the Russian model; but belief in the world significance of the Russian Revolutions remains an article of dogma to which at least lip service must be paid, and a missionary organization in the shape of the Communist International exists to spread the gospel of Marx and Lenin in infidel countries.

So far it cannot be said that the propaganda efforts of the Communist International, about which so much vague, exaggerated and irrational fear exists in foreign countries, have met with any conspicuous success.

What will be the future of Communism as a specifically Russian faith? It has already performed many historical fucntions; it has swept out of the country many archaic remnants and cobwebs of superstition; it has given Russia a powerful, if often clumsy and misdirected, shove toward industrialization; to the masses of the population today it is giving, along with many hardships and deprivations required as a sacrifice on the altar of the new god of industrial progress, far wider opportunities for education and advancement than they enjoyed in pre war times.

There is no reason to suppose that Russia's new materialistic faith will be more successful than some of its idealistic predecessors in realizing its own highest aspirations or in bringing the country to a Marxian millennium.

Every fanatical faith that maintains its power by dictatorial means inevitably generates, along with genuine devotees, a certain number of careerist hypocrites and an even larger number of adherents who cannot rise above stupid routine; and this in turn has a very marked effect on the character of the social order which broadens and develops on the basis of the new faith.

Whether the belief in the possibility of creating a "paradise in this world," to use a glowing phrase of Trotsky's, has permanently banished the more conventional forms of religious life in Russia, or whether the traditional questionings about a life beyond the grave will arise to perplex and occupy the minds of the children and grandchildren of today's ardently atheistic Young Communists is one of those fascinating speculative questions to which only the future can give the answer.

Soviet Russia Digging at Roots of Social System; Masses are Dominated By Will of Ruling Few [5/28/34]

There is something unmistakably impressive about the sheer bulk of the Union of Soviet Socialist Republics, as Russia has been renamed since the Revolution. One is dealing here with the dimensions not of an ordinary country, but of a continent. The area of the Soviet Union is between one-sixth and one-seventh the land surface of the globe.

From Russia's western frontier to the Pacific is a distance of over 5000 miles; from the ice-free port of Murmansk, which lies far to the north of the arctic circle, to the high plateaus and mountain ranges of the Pamir, in central Asia, is a journey of almost 3000 miles.

One can find within the Soviet Union all the climatic differences and contrasts that exist in the whole European Continent. Indeed there is less difference between Sweden and Italy than there is between the endless forests and the frozen tundra, or marsh lands, of the Russian North and the hot deserts of Turkestan, where irrigation makes possible extensive cotton plantations and oases bloom out with rich fruit.

In population, the Soviet Union, with something over 160,000,000 inhabitants, is exceeded only by such Asiatic countries as India and China. In size and natural resources the Soviet Union ranks with the United States and with the British Empire, considered as a whole. China is another huge land mass, but lacks effective control of many regions which are still included within its geographical frontiers and is apparently much poorer than the Soviet Union in such vital sources of mineral wealth as coal, iron and oil.

Sprawled out over the eastern half of Europe and the northern third of Asia, Russia has always had a foot in each of these continents without belonging definitely to either. Its cultural forms and aspirations have been European. Its governmental methods and its low living standards have suggested Asia.

This dualism has not been removed; in some respects it has been intensified by the Revolution. As a result of the World War and the civil war the more westernized portions of the former Czarist Empire, Poland, Finland and the Baltic provinces, split off and set up independent national states. Thus, it appears that the Soviet center of population and industrial gravity is very definitely being pushed toward the East, toward Asia.

It is in the Urals and in western Siberia that the Soviet Government is laying the foundation of a powerful industrial development.

Whether one is walking through the streets of Moscow or attending a Soviet Congress or waiting for a train at a station, one can scarcely fail to be impressed with the essentially Eurasian character of the Soviet Union. For along with tall, big-boned Russians one sees a great variety of faces and figures that belong to the East: slant-eyed Tartars from the Volga and Crimea; yellow-skinned Mongols from eastern Siberia; tall, rangy, olive-skinned mountaineers from the Caucasus. Old racial and religious prejudices and antipathies have largely broken down among the younger generation which has grown up under the Soviet régime, with the result that intermarriage among members of the scores of various races which inhabit the Soviet Union is today becoming more common and the considerable strain of eastern blood which could always be found in the Russians is being to some extent increased.

One should not be so carried away by the sheer vastness of the Soviet Union as to lose sight of some of its serious natural disadvantages. A considerable part of its area, especially the frozen stretches of northern Russia and Siberia, will never, in all probability, support any considerable population.

The Soviet Union today is landlocked, with a scanty ice-free seacoast and inadequate harbor facilities. Its great central plain is singularly poor in rock — which helps to explain the atrociously bad condition of almost all the country's roads. Such machine-building centers as Leningrad, such textile centers as Moscow and Ivanovo-Vosnesensk, are located thousands of miles away from the main sources of cotton and iron, and are dependent on long hauls over a chronically overburdened and defective transportation system. There is no convincing evidence that Russia possesses exceptional reserves of gold, copper and some other nonferrous metals.

As against the fertility of the famous "blackearth" soil belt which runs through parts of central Russia, Ukraina and the north Caucasus, one must set the shortness of the Russian agricultural year, the habitual extremes of heat and cold, and the liability of some regions which are extremely fertile in good years to severe droughts.

Yet, when one has made due allowance for all these negative physical factors in the Soviet Union, one cannot escape the conclusion that a country of Russia's vast size and population, with its proved and potential extensive resources in coal and iron, oil and timber, platinum and manganese, with its varied possibilities of agricultural development, in capable of very significant expansion, especially is its Asiatic regions, where there is much known mineral wealth awaiting efficient exploitation as well as considerable likelihood of new discoveries.

Under any kind of strong government, under any social and economic system, apart from sheer chaos, the Soviet Union would be a force to be reckoned with in world politics and economics. But there is a stronger and deeper reason why the Soviet Union must be regarded as one of the most permanently significant and interesting countries in the world. This huge country, with its foothold on two continents, has been the scene of the most sweeping and thoroughgoing social upheaval of our time, perhaps of all history.

The present masters of the Soviet Union, the leaders of the Communist Party, smashing opposition to their will with all the ruthlessness of the most autocratic Czar, are driving toward the goal of building up a kind of human society which will differ very substantially from anything that has hitherto been known.

They are laying the ax at the root of some very old and deep-rooted human impulses: the will to believe in something outside of and beyond the present material world, the peasant's instinct for personal ownership of the land which he tills, the home and family in the old-fashioned sense.

They are endeavoring to make the whole economic life of the country, industry and transport, agriculture and trade, fit into the scheme of an enormous state-controlled supertrust, from which every element of private ownership and accumulation of wealth is excluded.

The Soviet Union today is setting about somewhat the same task which the United States undertook after the Civil War: the tapping and opening up of vast undeveloped natural resources. Russia's East corresponds in some measure to America's West of the seventies and eighties of the last century.

Yet the differences between Soviet and American lines of development are surely more striking and significant than the similarities. America's appeal was to the initiative, the freedom, the hard work and good fortune of the individual. The typical American pioneer was the farmer, assured of his share of free land, the hunter and trapper, exploring the mountain vastnesses, the gold prospector, willing to risk certain hardship for a possible fortune.

Three generations of a peasant family listening to a government agent explain the Soviet goals. Below, young Soviets also try to understand the plans.

How different is the eastward push of the Soviet Union. America was built up by individuals; Russia is being built up by the state. Only a few of the present-day Soviet pioneers are going entirely of their own volition, or in search of personal fortune.

The young engineer who goes to Kuznetzk or Magnitogorsk or to some other hard and bleak post is fulfilling a semi-contractual obligation which he owes to the state organization which supported him during the period of his education. A large part of the labor that goes into the construction of the new plants in the Urals and Siberia is the forced labor of "kulaks" and other "class enemies." Two hemispheres, two mentalities, two methods of development.

And this sharply contrasted method of pioneering is only one of scores of fascinating problems which are raised by the vast sociological experimental laboratory into which Russia has been transformed by the Revolution. To indicate the nature of these problems, to suggest possible answers to some of them is the purpose of the following articles in this series.

Famine Proves Most Potent Weapon in Soviet Policy [5/29/34]

"The collective farmers this year have passed through a good school. For some, this school was quite ruthless."

This was how President Kalinin, in a speech delivered early last summer, referred to the food situation in Ukraina and the North Caucasus. When the prohibition on travel by foreign correspondents in the rural districts was relaxed in the autumn I had an opportunity to find out what this "ruthless school" had meant in practice.

I shall never forget a scene which I witnessed in a Ukrainian village named Zhuke, which lies some 15 miles to the north of Poltava. The president of the local collective farm and a state agronome, or agricultural expert, were accompanying me on visits to a number of peasant houses. So long as my companions chose the houses to be visited I found myself invariably meeting local Communists or *udarniki* (shock-brigade workers), with pictures of Lenin, Stalin and Kalinin on the walls and a fairly contented tale of their experiences.

I suddenly picked out a house at random and went into it with my companions. It was a typical Ukrainian peasant hut, with thatched roof, earth floor, benches running around the walls, an oven and a rickety-looking bed as the chief articles of furniture. The sole occupant was a girl of 15, huddled up on the bench. She answered a few simple questions briefly, in a flat, dull voice.

"Where is your mother?"

"She died of hunger last winter."

"Have you any brothers or sisters?"

"I had four. They all died, too."

"When?"

"Last winter and spring."

"And your father?"

"He is working in the fields."

"Does he belong to the collective farm?"

"No, he is an individual peasant."

So here was one man — his name was Savchenko — whose passive stubbornness defied even Kalinin's "ruthless school," who refused to go into a collective farm, even after almost all the members of his family had perished.

My companions, the president of the collective farm and the state agronome, had nothing to say. Smooth-tongued officials in Moscow might assure inquiring visitors that there had been no famine, only little food difficulties here and there, due to the wicked machinations of the kulaks. Here on the spot in Zhuke, as in a dozen other Ukrainian and North Caucasian villages which I visited, the evidence of large-scale famine was so overwhelming, was so unanimously confirmed by the peasants that the most "hard-boiled" local official could say nothing in denial.

Some idea of the scope of the famine, the very existence of which was stubbornly and not unsuccessfully concealed from the outside world by the Soviet authorities, may be gauged from the fact that in three widely separated regions of Ukraina and the North Caucasus, which I visited — Poltava and Byelaya Tserkov and Kropotkin in the North Caucasus — mortality, according to the estimates of such responsible local authorities as Soviet and collective farm presidents, ranged around 10 percent. Among individual peasants and in villages far away from the railroad it was often much higher.

I crossed Ukraina from the southeast to the northwest by train, and at every station where I made inquiries the peasants told the same story of major famine during the winter and spring of 1932-1933.

If one considers that the population of Ukraina is about 35,000,000 and that of the North Caucasus about 10,000,000, and that credible reports of similar famine came from parts of the country which I did not visit, some regions of the Middle and Lower Volga and Kazakstan, in Central Asia, it would seem highly probable that between 4,000,000 and 5,000,000 people, over and above the normal mortality rate, lost their lives from hunger and related causes. This is the reality behind the innocuous phrases, tolerated by the Soviet censorship, about food stringency, strained food situation, etc.

What lay behind this major human catastrophe? It was very definitely not a result of any natural disaster, such as exceptional drought or flood, because it was the general testimony of the peasants that the harvest of 1932, although not satisfactory, would have left them enough for nourishment, if the state had not swooped down on them with heavy requisitions.

Hidden stocks of grain which the despairing peasants had buried in the ground were dug up and confiscated; where resistance to the state measures was especially strong, as in some *stanitsas*, or Cossack towns, in the Western Kuban, whole communities were driven from their homes and exiled en masse to the frozen wastes of Siberia.

Unquestionably, the poor harvest of 1932 was attributable in some degree to the apathy and discouragement of the peasants, subjected, as they were at that time, to constant irregular requisitions, at inequitable fixed prices — the state was practically compelled, by the necessity for raising capital for its grandiose, new industrial enterprises, to squeeze out of the peasants a good deal more than it could give them in return — of their grain and other produce by the authorities, and driven against their will into an unfamiliar and distasteful system.

The Communists saw in this apathy and discouragement, sabotage and counterrevolution and, with the ruthlessness peculiar to self-righteous idealists, they decided to let the famine run its course with the idea that it would teach the peasants a lesson.

Relief was doled out to the collective farms, but on an inadequate scale and so late that many lives had already been lost. The individual peasants were left to shift for themselves; and the much higher mortality rate among the individual peasants proved a most potent argument in favor of joining collective farms.

The Soviet Government, along with the other powers which adhered to the Kellogg pact, has renounced war as an instrument of national policy. But there are no humanitarian restrictions in the ruthless class war which, in the name of Socialism, it has been waging on a considerable part of its own peasant population; and it has employed famine as an instrument of national policy on an unprecedented scale and in an unprecedented way.

At the moment it looks as if the famine method may have succeeded in finally breaking down the peasant resistance to collectivization. In 1921 the peasants were strong enough, acting no less effectively because they had no conscious union or organization, to force the Government to give up its requisitioning and to introduce the "Nep," or New Economic Policy, with its security of individual farming and freedom of private trade, by withholding their grain and bringing the towns close to starvation.

Now the tide of revolution has rolled beyond the "Nep" stage, and in 1933 the Soviet Government, quite conscious of what it was doing, was strong enough to wring out of the peasants enough foodstuffs to provide at least minimum rations for the towns and to turn the starvation weapon against the very peasants themselves.

Farmer Fits Poorly in Soviet Frame   [5/31/34]

The remaking of agriculture has been a far more difficult and complicated problem for the Soviet régime than the remaking of industry. This was because industrialization was largely a matter of mastering machines, whereas the collectivization of agriculture demanded, if it was to function with any degree of success, a far-reaching remolding of human psychology.

The first hints of an impending reorganization of agriculture could be heard in 1928, when Stalin was already sounding the warning that the country could not survive half-Capitalist and half-Socialist. At this time the towns, with the factories and the railroads, were "Socialist;" state ownership and operation were the rule. But the countryside was overwhelmingly "Capitalist" in the sense that the few state and collective farms were tiny islands in the vast sea represented by the private holdings of some 25,000,000 small proprietors.

The small peasant proprietor was objectionable to the Soviet rulers in the Kremlin for two reasons.

First, he was an individualist who did not fit into the huge state-regulated machine which was envisaged by the Five-Year Plan. His annual output could not be planned with any assurance that he would conform to the planning. He displayed an incorrigible tendency toward self-enrichment.

Second, the little peasant holdings, kept small because Soviet law forbade the passing of land from one hand to another through purchase and sale, were not efficient production units.

The Communists shut their eyes and dreamed of what a magnificent transformation could be brought about if the individualist muzhik peasant, tilling his little plot of land with a horse or a brace of oxen and stubbornly holding out his grain on the state if it did not give him the goods which he desired, could be transformed into an obedient disciplined worker on a large farm under some form of state control, equipped with tractors, harvesting combines and other modern machinery.

And, as the Communist leaders were not dreamers, but men of action, they proceeded to put their theories into practice. In the face of terrific difficulties, at a price in human suffering which can only be gauged by those who have actually seen freight cars packed with hapless peasants being deported from their homes or the desolate weed-grown waste into which considerable regions of the once fertile North Caucasus have been transformed, individual farming has been pretty thoroughly crushed out of existence in the Soviet Union.

This great change from individual to collective farming was brought about after a long and bitter struggle. As a general rule those peasants who had been most successful on their own farms were most reluctant to enter the collective farms and naturally used their influence to persuade their neighbors also to refrain from joining.

This measure went into effect in the winter of 1929-1930 and was ruthlessly carried out to the accompaniment of appalling suffering, especially on the part of old men, women and children.

The struggle did not end with the destruction of the kulaks. A good crop in 1930 was succeeded by a poor one in 1931. In 1932 the apathy and discouragement of the peasants, harassed by constant requisitions and uncertain how much of the crop they could keep for themselves, was reflected in very poor cultivation of the soil, with the result that some of the most fertile regions of the country became literally choked with weeds and the yield was very poor.

Disastrous famine followed when the state persisted in its requisitions and wrested the last reserves of grain from the hungry peasants.

The agricultural crisis, which reached its low point in the winter of 1932-1933, was somewhat mitigated in 1933 as a result of several factors. The Government changed its method of extracting grain and other produce from the peasants.

Instead of forcing them to sell, at nominal fixed prices, all their surplus grain, meat, milk and other more important products — and the peasants often disagreed with the government estimates of how much they required for their own sustenance and for that of their animals — a new law set fixed levies in grain, meat and milk, varying with different regions of the country.

Once the peasant fulfills these requirements, he is free to consume the remainder of his produce, or to sell it in any way he may prefer. The establishment throughout the countryside of so-called political departments, manned by Communists of administrative experience and intrusted with the function of stiffening morale and discipline in the collective farms, has also made the new system work more smoothly.

The harvest of 1933 represented distinct improvement over the preceding famine year, although I think there is grave reason to doubt the accuracy of the official figures, which claim a record grain crop of 89,800,000 tons. The head of the central statistical department, Mr. Ossinsky, himself admitted that this estimate was not confirmed by the results of the threshing, when these were measured, and that it rested on a flat deduction of 10 percent from the estimated "biological yield," i.e., the yield if it had reached the granaries without any losses.

Past estimates of losses in harvesting have always been greatly in excess of 10 percent. It would also be difficult, if not impossible, to understand why Russia, which fed itself comfortably between the years 1925 and 1928 on crops that ranged around 75,000,000 tons, is compelled to maintain a severe rationing régime after a "record" harvest of 90,000,000 tons.

The official belief in Russia is that the worst agricultural difficulties are over; and I am inclined to believe that this may be true, if the country does not become involved in war and if the Government does not attempt to change the present system under which the peasant, while he surrenders land, working animals and machinery to the collective farm, is allowed to keep his own cow and chickens, house and garden.

The machine-tractor stations which send out machinery to farm the land of neighboring collective farms will doubtless have an increasing number of tractors and other machines at their disposal from year to year; and this is a favorable factor in the situation.

Unfavorable, is the forcible elimination the kulaks, from the agricultural scene and the prodigious decline in livestock, which was partly destroyed by the peasants in rage and despair at being forced into collective farms and partly perished from bad management in the state and collective farms.

According to the most recent official figures, the Soviet Union now has 16,600,000 horses, as against 34,000,000 in 1929; 38,600,000 horned cattle, against

Front page of The Christian Science Monitor **from May 31, 1934**

68,100,000 in 1929; 50,600,000 sheep and goats, against 147,200,000 in 1929; 12,200,000 pigs, against 20,900,000 in 1929.

People Bend Slowly to Soviet Will   [6/1/34]

For more than five years the Soviet Union has been living under a régime of centralized planned economic life which has changed the physical appearance of the vast Russian land and affected the fate of its inhabitants with all the force of an elemental hurricane.

To the casual reader it might seem strange that four volumes of economic tables and statistics, of estimates of natural resources and means of developing them, the four volumes in which the first Five-Year Plan was published, could have such dynamic results.

But the adoption of the Five-Year Plan unmistakably did bring in its train a whole series of striking and fateful consequences. It erected great steel mills where there had been nothing but open steppe lands, browsed over by the cattle of Asiatic nomads. It set up a modern chemical works in the peaceful forests of the Urals. It tore vast numbers of hard-working peasants from their homes, stripped them of their property and sent them to hard labor in mines, in timber camps, at construction enterprises.

It hastened the process by which young Communists in far-away Muhammadan regions of the Soviet Union begin to forget the Koran and the Shariat and to think in terms of Marx and Lenin, of cotton mills and electrical power stations. It scattered tractors over the Soviet countryside, and denuded it of horses and livestock. It created great state "grain factories," in the shape of huge farms, and turned formerly fertile stretches of land in the neighborhood into weed-grown deserts, policed by terror and hunger.

It opened wide doors of opportunity for many young factory hands and peasants, now studying to be engineers and professional men. It ruthlessly destroyed — sometimes physically, more often psychologically — some of the finest representatives of Russia's old intelligentsia, convicted by Gay-Pay-Oo drumhead courts-martial of fantastic charges of "sabotage."

What was this Five-Year Plan, which brought so much change, so much growth in some fields, so much suffering in others? It was a stupendously ambitious effort to plot in advance the whole graph of national economic and social development, to decide, on the basis of the estimates of a central planning body, the Gosplan, or State Planning Commission, how much

coal should be mined, how many moving-picture performances should be given, how much each worker in the textile and metal industry should receive, how the state budget should be framed — to mention only a few of the numerous things which the plan endeavored to forecast in advance.

The first Five-Year Plan was officially declared ended at the end of 1932, after a period of four and a quarter years, and a second Five-Year Plan, the details of which have just been published, was put into operation and is supposed to run until the end of 1937.

The first Five-Year Plan aimed at an all-around expansion of industrial production, with special emphasis on the so-called heavy industries — iron and steel, chemicals and electricity, coal and oil and machine building — at the introduction of state and collective farming in agriculture, at a raising of the standard of living through increased per capita food consumption and higher real wages, at a wide increase in educational facilities.

It would be a grave mistake to look at the Five-Year Plan as an attempt to set up an athletic record, which would either totally succeed or totally fail. What was most important was not the five-year time period, not even the precise figures of output which the state industries were supposed to achieve, but rather the general success in building and operating the new plants which were designed for industry and in inducing the peasants to work efficiently under the new system of collective farming.

As the first plan slowly merged into the second it became evident that great changes had been brought about and that considerable progress had been achieved in some respects, but that the general level of achievement, as measured by the standards which the plan itself had set up, was extremely spotty and uneven.

Stalin, to be sure, made the claim that the plan had been fulfilled 93.7 percent and attributed the failure to achieve it entirely to the necessity of preparing for possible war emergencies.

But this estimate was based entirely on industrial output, where the results were far more favorable than in other branches of national economy. In agriculture the plan was underfulfilled by at least 30 percent, if one takes the yield of grain crops as a standard, by a good 50 percent or more, if one takes the condition of the country's live stock. Far from improving, real wages and the standard to living sharply declined, as a result of the acute shortage of foodstuffs and the adoption of a general rationing system.

The Five-Year Plan was perhaps most successful from the standpoint of military preparedness. Not only were the specific war industries, especially military aviation, greatly expanded, but many of the new plants which came into existence possess definite military potentialities. For instance the large factory for the manufacture of heavy tractors in Cheliabinsk could very easily be adapted to the making of tanks. A machine-building plant at Sverdlovsk, another of the industrial giants of the Five-Year Plan, is closely modeled on the Krupp works at Essen, which was one of Germany's main munition centers during the World War.

New large chemical works at Berezniki, in the Urals and at Bobriki, southeast of Moscow, are concentrating on the output of ammonium nitrate, which, as a foreign engineer once remarked, is "a mighty good fertilizer in time of peace, and a mighty good explosive in time of war."

The geographical placing of Russia's new industrial centers is also dictated obviously by strategic and economic considerations. New industrial building is being most energetically pushed in the Ural region and in western Siberia, 1500 to 3000 miles from the western frontier and, therefore, safely out of range of air attack.

There is a strip of hundreds of miles along the frontier where no new factories of any consequence are being built. The sole exception to this general rule is the city of Leningrad, which is very close to the border of Finland. Because of its prewar significance as an industrial center and because its population includes many skilled workers Leningrad has been developed as a machine-building center.

The big Dnieprostroi Dam, which makes the Dniper River navigable for seagoing ships and is linked up with a powerful hydroelectric power station which will supply operating energy for a group of steel, aluminum and metallurgical plants which are being built in the neighborhood would be within range of air attack. But most of the new Soviet industrial centers are almost impregnable, so far as the possibility of a hostile surprise assault is concerned.

Space limitation forbids a detailed analysis of all the results of this unprecedented effort to plan a nation's economic life. In brief summary one may say that the strained concentration of national effort on the physical development of the huge country has added appreciably to the Soviet Union's military and industrial equipment.

There has been no similar improvement in the supply of the population with goods of everyday consumption; this problem has been postponed for realization under the second plan, which promises, perhaps a little ambitiously, to double or triple the output of foodstuffs and manufactured goods.

The problem of poor quality remains the Achilles' heel of Soviet industry as a whole; passable standards in this connection have been reached, as a general rule, only in the war industries and in a few favored factories which work for export, although the new tractor and motor plants are showing some improvement, by comparison with their extremely poor showing in the first months of their existence.

Agriculture has made out much worse than industry under the new system; and this subject, because of its importance, is reserved for treatment in a separate article.

A dictatorial Government, wielding absolute power over the labor power, natural resources, finance, industry and agriculture of the country, has been able to put everyone to work. It has very definitely not been able, however, to create working and living conditions which would attract any influx of the unemployed from "Capitalist" countries. Hard as is the lot of the British or American unemployed, he has consideraably more to eat and a greater variety of food than the unemployed Russian worker in a provincial town, such as Poltava or Krasnodar.

Moreover, the Soviet system of "planned economy" has not proved feasible without far greater curtailments of individual liberty than any democratically governed people would be likely to accept.

As a matter of fact the successes and the failures of the Five-Year Plan proceed from a common source: the Soviet Government's ability and willingness to sacrifice the living standards of its citizens to its ambitious dreams of industrialization.

It soon became evident that the two goals of the Five-Year Plan, the improvement of everyday living conditions and the large scale extension of the nation's industrial plant, could not both be realized. Someone had to pay the bill for the enormous expenditure involved in the construction of gigantic new steel mills, chemical and machine-building plants, electric power stations, etc.

Because foreign capital was unavailable this new construction had to come, in a sense, out of the stomachs of the Russian people. This is why the most conspicuous achievements of the plan are in the sphere of new industrial construction, while its most obvious striking defects are in the field of everyday living conditions.

How far does a sweeping social upheaval, such as Russia has experienced, change human nature and daily living habits? In some ways very little, or not at all; in other ways, very much.

Under the Soviets, as under any other system, the ordinary citizen's main concern is to earn as good a living as he can. There are Communists old and young whose fanatical enthusiasm for their cause makes them work at any task to which they may be assigned without reckoning hours and without considering their wages or salaries. In other countries, also, such motives as patriotism, scientific curiosity, love of the work, may replace or very greatly supplement the motive of monetary reward.

Practical experience has convinced the Soviet leaders that in the majority of cases efficient productivity of labor demands the prosaic stimulus of a proper material reward. Several years ago a movement was initiated among factory and office workers to declare themselves *udarniki*, or, literally, shock-brigade workers, to fulfill and overfulfill the tasks which were assigned to them.

So, while a very great economic change has been brought about in the Soviet Union in the sense that no man today may employ another for the sake of making a profit, the present policy of the Soviet state toward its great army of employees is not to equalize their wages, but to differentiate as sharply as possible between the efficient and the inefficient.

The foreigner who has a vague idea that Communism means sharing everything equally, or paying everyone equal wages, would be more surprised perhaps, at this aspect of Soviet life than at any other.

If the piecework method of paying wages is practiced as zealously under the Soviet system as under Capitalism, there are some very real and striking differences between living conditions in Moscow and in almost any other world capital. One of the most fundamental of these differences is that, while most of the worry of statesmen and economists in other countries is concentrated on the problem of how to make demand catch up with superabundant supply, defective supply in Russia runs a futile race against insistent demand.

A key to an understanding of many features of Soviet life is the fact that there is not enough of anything, from butter to railroad transportation, to go around. Here is the origin of the endless lines which are

Front page of The Chrisian Science Monitor **Weekly Magazine Section from January 15, 1944. Next page: Present day collective farming much as it was more than fifty years ago.**

Front page of The Christian Science Monitor **from June 2, 1934.**

so characteristic of the Soviet Union. At various seasons of the year and on various occasions there are queues for almost every purpose: for bread; for kerosene; for the newspapers, of which there are never enough to satisfy readers; for buses; for public dining room meal tickets; for railroad tickets.

And some of the longest and most formidable queues are invisible ones. There are thousands of Communists, holding responsible positions, to say nothing of ordinary mortals, who are on the waiting list of the Moscow Soviet for apartments, whenever new ones will be built. Even a foreigner with *valuta* — the precious foreign currency which is most highly prized in the Soviet Union today — finds it no easy task to persuade a state organization to build him an apartment.

In this case the limiting factor is the shortage of building materials, large quantities of which are required for the new subway which is now actively under construction, as is evident from the huge piles of dirt and lumber and the frequent closing and blocking of streets in the neighborhood of the shafts.

Moscow today is probably the most overcrowded capital in the world. Its population is 3,500,000 as against 1,600,000 before the World War. There has been a certain amount of new housing construction, especially in the vicinity of new and enlarged factories on the outskirts of the city. But housing space has certainly not doubled, especially if one takes into account decay and depreciation of the old houses and the considerable number of buildings which have been converted to public use as a result of the establishment of the capital in Moscow.

The result is that the typical Moscow apartment-house — one excepts the dwellings occupied by higher Government officials and some cooperative apartment-houses built by groups of professional men — is a veritable rabbit warren, where every inch of space is occupied and corridors, kitchens and bathrooms are not infrequently pressed into service for living purposes.

Lucky indeed is the Muscovite who possesses an apartment; as a general rule a family occupies one, or at the most two, rooms, sharing kitchen and bathroom with a number of other tenants. Private houseowners, have, of course, gone the way of private factory owners; and rents, which in the main are low and are adjusted to earnings, are paid to the house committees which look after the upkeep of the houses or to the managers who are sometimes placed in charge of houses built by Government institutions for their employee's use.

This situation is reflected in a Russian joke which had considerable circulation a year or two ago, but which is beginning to be a little stale now, since rising prices are bringing about more equilibrium: "The Russians are the richest people in the world — because they don't know what to do with their money."

Throughout the period of the Five-Year Plan there has been an irregular and unacknowledged, yet unmistakable, devaluation of the Soviet ruble; and it would be a bold economist today who would endeavor to define just what that peculiar currency is worth.

Before the Five-Year plan was inaugurated the Soviet citizen bought his food where he chose without any restrictions except those imposed by his own pocketbook. Today the system of food supply and distribution has radically changed; people are obliged to buy in "closed shops" attached to their factories and offices and to eat in "closed dining rooms," also reserved for the workers or employees of a given factory or office.

The closed cooperative shop — Soviet cooperative stores are practically indistinguishable from state shops, inasmuch as both are cogs in the state machinery of distribution — gives its patrons, as a rule, very little at moderate fixed prices: two pounds of bread a day to a manual worker and one pound to an office worker; a minute monthly dole of two pounds, more or less, of sugar; occasional modest allotments of herring and cereal and of vegetables in season. A more substantial source of food supply can be found in the factory or office dining room; and children are given a hot meal in the schools.

Apart from the cooperative shops, there are so-called "commercial" shops, under state management, which sell foodstuffs without rationing restrictions, but at prices which are usually five or ten times higher than those which prevail in the cooperative shops. By far the best stocked and most attractive shops are those which display the sign: "Torgsin." Here only foreign currency, gold, silver or jewels are accepted in payment.

The Torgsin shops have proved a brilliant commercial invention, from the state standpoint, because they divert to the coffers of the state the remittances which Russians receive from relatives or friends abroad and also extract from the hungry population its last hidden stocks of gold and silver. It is not uncommon for a Soviet citizen to remove gold from his teeth and replace it with baser metal in order to have an opportunity to buy some of the tempting stocks of fruit, cold meats and dairy products which the Torgsin offers.

Yet it would be unfair and mistaken to paint Moscow life only in gloomy colors. By comparison with prewar times there has been a widespread development of outdoor exercise; skating, skiing and Association football are among the most popular sports, and a parade of *fizkulturniki* — as people who take part in organized sport and exercise are called — shows that a considerable part of the younger generation is keeping itself fit.

Opportunities for recreation and education, for attending school and going to the theater, for instance, are better for the masses than they were in pre war times. The majority of Russians care little for privacy and have a conspicuous capacity for enduring what might seem to a foreigner intolerable discomfort with nothing more than a shrug of the shoulders and a *"Nitchevo"* (Oh, nothing).

One compensating feature for the hardships sacrifices, and deprivations of Soviet life is the fact that there is little or no "keeping up with the Joneses." More than one Russian acquaintance who remembers prewar social conditions has spoken to me of the relief at not feeling an obligation to keep up to the living standards of neighbors and acquaintances. Where no one is well-dressed, no one is badly dressed; and, whatever other kinds of freedom may be lacking in the Soviet Union, sartorial freedom, right up to the point of being able to wear a collarless blouse in an opera box, is certainly undisputed.

Communism in the Cradle [6/4/34]

Propaganda and repression are the twin pillars of the Soviet régime. It is only by the skillful, unremitting combination of these two potent instruments of government — and Soviet propaganda can scarcely be matched for intensity, just as Soviet repression cannot be equaled in ruthlessness — that one can understand the ability of the Communist leaders to keep themselves firmly in the saddle during a period when great sacrifices and deprivations were being imposed on the whole population and when whole classes were being literally crushed out of existence.

Communist propaganda alone would not be so effective if there were any means of voicing counter-propaganda. Repression alone would also in the long run fail to achieve its objective. But when both weapons are used simultaneously in dealing with a population of which more than half was illiterate before the Revolution, of which 10 percent, at a liberal estimate, had any fixed or definite political convictions before the Soviets came into power, the effect, as one might reasonably expect, is very great.

The Soviet Government is in an unrivaled position, so far as possibilities of molding the minds of its population are concerned. In one way or another, it controls every agency of entertainment and instruction: the school, the theater, the press, the radio, the lecture platform. It is the sole newspaper publisher, the sole book publisher. It is well nigh impossible for a word of dissent to be uttered publicly, much less printed.

And the Soviet régime makes full use of its opportunities. From the time when a child can toddle, a red flag is pushed into its hand; it learns new Soviet songs; it is taught to lisp Soviet slogans. The continuous stream of propaganda, all directed to the purpose of making a new type of man and woman, entirely devoted to Soviet and Communist ideas, becomes intensified as the child grows older.

No one can visit a Soviet school without being impressed by the thorough manner in which the children are drilled in hatred of "Capitalism," and of the "bourgeoisie," and are brought up to regard the Soviet system as the best in the world. If one turns on the radio one is apt to hear, instead of a nonexistent Russian "Amos 'n' Andy," a dissertation on the glories of collective farming or the amazing strides of the Soviet nonferrous metal industry.

The theater repertory abounds in plays which, with slight variations, adhere to one plot formula: a new industrial plant built at record speed and triumphantly completed ahead of schedule, despite the machinations of a sabotaging engineer or a kulak who has sneaked in as a worker and plays the part of a wolf in sheep's clothing. Circus clowns have been ordered to give a proletarian twist to their jokes and their tumbling.

If one walks the streets by day one can hardly miss seeing red streamers calling on everyone to subscribe to the new state loan, or to perfect his technical education, or to give some voluntary labor to Moscow's new subway. The same edifying slogans are blazoned forth in electrical signs at night. If one goes to a gallery of modern French painting one finds placards about the development of French Capitalism foolishly and irrelevantly scattered among Gauguin's exotic paintings of the South Sea Islands.

If one goes to a concert one may hear an announcer interpret Mozart's music by saying that the composer could never make up his mind whether to cast in his lot with the decaying nobility or with the rising middle class of his time.

There has been an enormous expansion of newspaper reading in Russia since the Revolution. Before the War there were 859 newspapers in Russia with a total circulation of 2,700,000 copies. Today there are officially reported to be 5400 newspapers with about 38,000,000 readers. It must, of course, be borne in mind, that a very large number of the present-day newspapers are extremely sketchy affairs — district organs which appear perhaps twice a week and factory newspapers which appear even more irregularly. But, whatever one may think of the quantity and quality of the news which is supplied to Soviet readers, there can be no doubt that it does reach far more people than was the case in Czarist days.

The rules which govern Soviet journalism are in many ways the precise reverse of those which govern the conduct of newspapers in other countries which aim at mass circulation. Competition is, of course, nonexistent; and Soviet editors do not vie with each other in "scoops" and "beats." Ordinary crime and scandal are rigidly barred from the columns of Soviet newspapers. One would also look in vain for household hints, fashion and society articles, crossword puzzles or stock exchange quotations, which, indeed, do not exist in the Soviet Union.

On the other hand, there is a very full reporting of important speeches and decrees. A fair proportion of foreign news, with a distinctly tendencious coloring, appears in the large newspapers. The Soviet press suffers from the chronic shortage of paper; even such leading organs as *Izvestia*, official publication of the Government, and *Pravda*, the Communist Party newspaper, are restricted to four large pages; provincial newspapers are even more meager.

The Soviet press enjoys considerable freedom in exposing defects and shortcomings in the functioning of industrial plants and farms; in this respect it sometimes anticipates what the harshest foreign critics might say. But this freedom abruptly ceases as soon as any fundamental Communist idea or decision is touched upon by journalists.

One may, as a Soviet journalist, describe frankly a bad collective farm. But one may not even hint that collective farming is a bad system. Such things as the famine, the wholesale arrests carried out by the Gay-Pay-Oo, the sufferings of forcibly deported peasants are barred subjects for the Soviet newspapers, which are taught to repeat, in parrot fashion, such demonstrable untruths as that there is no forced labor in Russia, that there is no persecution of religion, that there is no poverty, until the editors, and possibly some of the readers, may come to believe them.

Soviet propaganda, while it is indubitably a powerful weapon, is not an invincible one. When the economic shoe is pinching too sharply it may well roll like water off a duck's back. A Ukrainian peasant who knows that his brother and some of his friends perished during the famine will not be impressed if he should read an eloquent journalistic description of how collectivization has improved his lot. Few workers probably are stupid enough to believe seriously the annual solemn farce when the Government announces that the workers of Leningrad, Tula or some other place have "requested" the levying of a new loan, subscriptions to which are virtually compulsory and are deducted from the wages and salaries of all workers and employees.

Generally speaking the "sales resistance" to the gigantic Soviet propaganda effort is greatest among the older and middle-aged peasants and among members of the educated classes who remember pre war conditions and who may in rare cases have access to foreign newspapers. The Soviet censorship organs see to it that very few non-Communist foreign newspapers find their way into the hands of Soviet citizens. The propaganda is most effective with young people who have no pre war standards of comparison, who have never traveled abroad and who have grown up entirely under Soviet influence.

When propaganda fails, the Soviet Government has other and harsher resources. These will be described in the next article.

Soviet Was Built on Ruthless Policy   [6/5/34]

It is credibly reported that when Lady Astor met Stalin in Moscow in 1931 she posed the blunt question: "How long will you go on killing people?" To which the Communist dictator retorted:

"As long as it is necessary."

Perhaps this retort revealed more of the underlying Soviet philosophy than Stalin would have desired. For there are no "inalienable human rights," such as "life, liberty and the pursuit of happiness" in the Soviet scheme of things. There is only the supreme right of the omnipotent state to arrest, banish and, in some cases, execute persons, with or without trial, often quite regardless of written law, "as long as it is necessary."

The main executive organ of the terrorist aspect of Soviet policy is the Gay-Pay-Oo, to use the familiar Russian abbreviation for an organization which bears as its full official title: United State Political Administration. The headquarters of the Gay-Pay-Oo are in a tall building in the center of Moscow which, by a remarkable accident, bears on its facade a bit of pre war decoration in the shape of the figures of the Parcae, the Greek Fates, cutting the threads of human life. The symbolism is none the less grim and effective for being quite unconscious.

The Gay-Pay-Oo has a great variety of functions. It guards the Soviet frontiers; keeps order on the railroad system; sends espionage agents into foreign countries. It even has a private army at its disposal, not unlike the Guard regiments of Czarist times; the special troops of the Gay-Pay-Oo are given the best of care and are reserved for use on occasions when the regular troops might falter.

The Gay-Pay-Oo officials are a caste within the "classless" Soviet State. They never lack for anything in the way of food and housing; ride about in the shiniest and newest automobiles, and an especially imposing new building in any town usually marks the headquarters of the Gay-Pay-Oo.

This organization possesses and exercises powers which make it far more similar to an emergency terrorist organization than to an ordinary secret political police. Indeed Stalin once likened it to the French Committee of Public Safety. It can arrest anyone and hold its prisoners indefinitely — in Russia there is no habeas corpus, only habeas cadaver; it can subject anyone administratively to several degrees of banishment, ranging from the mild "minus six," a prohibition to live in Moscow, to imprisonment at hard labor for a period up to 10 years in some grim concentration camp in the arctic wilds where insufficient food and clothing, hard labor and an unfavorable climate insure a high mortality rate.

More than that, it can inflict and carry out sentences of execution after a "trial" behind closed doors in which its collegium, or presiding body, combines the functions of accuser and judge.

It is difficult for the citizen of another country to imagine the feeling of hopeless despair with which the Soviet citizen who has been rounded up in the habitual nocturnal raids of the Gay-Pay-Oo enters its notorious prison on the former Lubyanka Square, now renamed Dzerzhinsky Square in honor of the organizer of this dreaded institution. He may be accused of "counterrevolution," of "sabotage," of hoarding gold or currency — the Gay-Pay-Oo performs such economic functions as torturing Soviet citizens who are suspected of possession of stocks of gold or foreign currency until they part with them and of administering forced labor camps where its prisoners are compelled to carry out such works as the digging of the Baltic-White Sea Canal or the felling of timber.

He is in the hands of an organization which not only has uncontrolled power of life and death over him, but can bring pressure through threats to members of his family — a fact which should not be forgotten in judging the credibility of the strange self-incriminating "confessions" which have been an unvarying feature of the few Soviet public trials.

On this point, we have the interesting testimony of the wife of Professor Tchernavin, a distinguished scientist who escaped from the Soviet Union, with his wife and son, in 1931.

"I learned afterward," she writes, in describing her own arrest, "that the examining officer had confronted him with the dilemma of either signing the statement that he was a 'wrecker' or of being the cause of my arrest... After my arrest my husband was presented with another alternative: either he must confess his 'guilt' or he would be shot, I would get 10 years penal servitude and our son would be sent to a colony for homeless children."

Professor Tchernavin's experience closely coincides with other illustrations of Gay-Pay-Oo judicial practice, one of which I shall cite. For obvious reasons, names are withheld. A man who was fairly well known in some circles abroad had made himself obnoxious to the Gay-Pay-Oo by his intercession on behalf of political prisoners. It was considered inexpedient to arrest him because of his age and because his arrest would have aroused attention abroad. So he was informed that, if he did not give up his intercession, his son would be arrested on some trumped-up charge and sent into exile.

Julius Rozinsky was a former employee in the Commissariat for Foreign Affairs. In the autumn of 1929 his father-in-law, an elderly man, who had been refused permission to join his family in Riga, made an unsuccessful attempt to cross the frontier illegally and was caught. Shortly after this Rozinsky himself was arrested; and in the spring of 1930 the old man who had wished to join his family and Rozinsky, who was perhaps suspected of knowing of his plan without informing the authorities, were both shot without any kind of open trial. It is noteworthy that Rozinsky was a man of distinctly Communist sympathies, the best proof of which was that he had frequently been assigned as interpreter to sympathetic radical visitors.

The orgy of arrests for "sabotage" of every conceivable kind among the intelligentsia, which was especially marked in 1930 and 1931, may be attributed partly to the abnormal mentality which unlimited power and the consciousness that their careers would be advanced if they could "discover" plots generated in many Gay-Pay-Oo officials, partly to the Government's desire to force engineers and specialists to work in difficult and inhospitable regions — it was easy to do this, once the engineers had the status of convicted criminals — partly to indiscreet talk and criticism on the part of some of the old intelligentsia. There were certainly very few, if any cases when their activity went beyond loose talk and indiscreet meetings with old friends among the émigrés when they went abroad; and great numbers of those who were arrested, banished and executed were in all probability guiltless even of such offenses.

At the time when I left Moscow there were strong rumors that the Gay-Pay-Oo would soon be reorganized, renamed and shorn of some of its more sweeping arbitrary powers. The truth of these rumors will be determined by the actual terms of the reorganization, if it takes place, and still more by subsequent practice, for there are few countries where written law and administrative practice differ so widely as in the Soviet Union.

Stalin Lets No One Stand in His Way [6/7/34]

At the apex of the Soviet pyramid of power stands Joseph Stalin, son of a Georgian shoemaker, whose olive skin proclaims his birth in the far-away romantic Caucasus, where Europe and Asia, Christianity and Muhammadanism meet in a bewildering medley of races, tribes and tongues.

Stalin towers above his colleagues in the Political Bureau as much as one of his native Caucasian peaks, Elbruz or Kazbek, would tower above the foothills in the distance.

Indeed, one of his methods of preserving his power has been to eliminate the men of greater force and independence of character in the governing circles of the party, from Trotsky down, and to surround himself with devoted henchmen whose political fortunes he has made and could unmake again overnight.

In Stalin, the autocratic idea which seems inseparable from Russian life, whatever may be the outward form of government, has found a new incarnation. His power is more absolute and far-reaching than that of any Czar, if only because it extends to every branch of national economic life.

With a stroke of the pen he can doom whole classes to extinction; he can decree the colonization of new regions and depopulate whole communities that are inhabited by recalcitrant peasants. By his decisions he can determine the lines of Russia's economic development and thereby influence, for good or for bad, the individual fortunes of more than 160,000,000 people. It would be strange if the possessor of such enormous power did not sometimes feel a sense of breath-taking giddiness.

Stalin is more and more surrounding himself with the attributes of an absolute ruler. It is an unwritten rule that no Communist leader may make a speech on any subject without paying a tribute to the wisdom, genius and unrivaled capacity for leadership of Comrade Stalin. Some of the outpourings on this subject at the recent Party Congress were so florid as to suggest a gathering of courtiers about a Byzantine Emperor, rather than a congress of revolutionaries.

Stalin's picture is seen far more often than Lenin's. The former list of the theoretical founders of Bolshevism, "Marx, Engels and Lenin," must now be enlarged by the addition of Stalin; indeed, Engels is sometimes forgotten and the new triumvirate reads: "Marx, Lenin and Stalin."

Stalin's rise to power and his subsequent maintenance of his position as leader of the Communist Party and master of the Soviet State is attributable to a combination of shrewdness and strength. A veteran Bolshevik, he must have realized, perhaps subconsciously, what immense power would lie in the hands of the man who could control the congresses and frame the decisions of a party which tolerated no dissent within its ranks.

The foundations of his future eminence were securely laid during the years immediately after the passing of Lenin, when, as general secretary of the Party, he assiduously built up a corps of Party officials who learned to look to him for promotion and who were in a position to assure the votes of their delegations at the Party congresses.

He then proceeded to the political destruction of his rivals by dividing them and picking them off in detail. Against Trotsky, he enlisted the support of Lenin's old lieutenants, Zinoviev and Kamenev, who then possessed great influence in the Party.

Once Trotsky was destroyed, the elimination, in their turn, of Zinoviev and Kamenev, was an easy matter; and Stalin also found little difficulty in disposing of three prominent leaders of the so-called "right opposition:" the former Premier, Rykoff; the former head of

Joseph Stalin, November 1936.

Front page of The Christian Science Monitor **from June 7, 1934.**

the trade unions, Tomsky; and the former editor of the Communist Party organ, Bukharin, when they began to protest against his mercilessly swift pace in industrialization and in the collectivization of agriculture.

It is highly significant that Stalin today is the sole member of the political bureau which existed at the time of Lenin's passing who still holds office in that body. He has rid himself of all the others.

As a ruler, Stalin exemplifies some principles of statecraft which might well have won the hearty applause of Nicolo Machiavelli. He can never be wrong personally; the Communist Party can never be wrong in its decisions. If a crisis arises which calls for swift remedial action guilty scapegoats are always found in "class enemies," such as kulaks, or sabotaging engineers, or, in some cases, in hapless local Communist and Soviet officials, who are summarily called to account and placed on trial as offerings on the altar of popular indignation.

Brought up in a little town in a remote mountainous country which scarcely knew modern industry, Stalin has unlimited admiration for the machine. He dreams of turning Russia into a "Socialist America," without perhaps fully recognizing the importance of the free play of individual initiative in building up America.

"When we put the Soviet Union on an automobile and the muzhik on a tractor," Stalin wrote on one occasion, "let the worthy Capitalists, who boast so loudly of their 'civilization,' try to overtake us."

This is a revealing sentence. For Stalin, "civilization" is "putting the Soviet Union on an automobile and the muzhik on the tractor." Wholesale executions, arrests, deportations and sentences of banishment without trial have nothing to do with the question of whether a country is to be regarded as civilized or not.

As any man in his position would inevitably be, Stalin is a prodigious worker, with an amazing capacity for attending to quite small matters which are brought to his personal attention. He finds his recreations in reading, in swift motor driving between his closely guarded country house on the Mozhaisk Road, west of Moscow, and his office in the Kremlin, in infrequent visits to the opera, in walking and bathing on the beautiful coast of the Black Sea between Sochi and Gagri, where he spends his summer vacation.

Stalin has a grown-up son by this first wife, who passed on many years ago. His second wife, Nadyezhda Alleluyeva, who passed on under somewhat mysterious circumstances — there were strong rumors of suicide — in November, 1932, left two children, a boy, Vassily,

Stalin and his henchmen: from left to right: Kalinin; Yaroslavsky; Rykoff; Voroshiloff; Stalin, with one of his infrequent smiles; and Gardiekko.

who is attending one of the best Moscow schools, and a daughter. Stalin has now contracted a union with the sister of one of his chief lieutenants, Kaganovitch.

Few foreigners have met Stalin, and none outside of a small circle of old Caucasian revolutionary associates enjoys his confidence to any extent. He has the double taciturnity of the mountaineer and of the revolutionary conspirator. Secure of a place among the great dictators who have molded human history, he has effectively veiled his inner personality from the gaze of a curious world.

The two outstanding figures, after Stalin, in the political bureau are Lazarus Kaganovitch and K. E. Voroshiloff. Kaganovitch, a man who has barely passed 40, has today reached the enviable point where he is habitually referred to as "Stalin's best collaborator." He is, the only one of dominant influence in Party councils today. Maxim Litvinoff, Foreign Commissar, is highly regarded as a clever and successful diplomat, but has no voice in internal policy.

Like his father, Kaganovitch followed the trade of a leather worker in the town of Gomel, in western Russia, and he has only two years of formal schooling — a deficiency which he has made up by extensive reading.

Kaganovitch for a time was Party Secretary in Ukraina; more recently he had been head of the party organization in Moscow; and much of the ambitious replanning and rebuilding of the old capital is attributed to his initiative. He is a man of immense energy, a good speaker and organizer; and he is undoubtedly Stalin's most prominent lieutenant at the present time. He has taken over much of the detail work of Party organization and also devotes a good deal of attention to the thorny agrarian problem.

Whether Kaganovitch would succeed Stalin in the event of the latter's disappearance from the political scene is an open question. His most formidable rival in such an eventuality might well prove to be K. E. Voroshiloff, the Soviet War Commissar. Voroshiloff is the son of a poor casual laborer and served an apprenticeship as a metal worker in South Russia until revolution and civil war brought him into prominence, first as a leader of partisan Red troops, then as political commissar attached to General Budenny's cavalry army.

It is largely attributable to Voroshiloff's watchfulness and firmness of character that this army, largely recruited from Cossacks and peasants, did not mutiny or disintegrate, like many similar forces, during the changing fortunes of the civil war. Voroshiloff has the reputation of a warm-hearted, hot-tempered man, with a gift for

horsemanship and is himself a crack rifle shot.

President Mikhail Kalinin is a typical peasant, with blue eyes and straw-colored beard, and he possesses a good measure of the proverbial peasant shrewdness. In his office he receives peasant complaints from all over the country; and sometimes he makes trips of inspection to the collective farms, where he can judge the quality of the seeds and the care of the cattle. Premier Vyacheslav Molotoff is a rather pale shadow of Stalin, a conscientious, hard-working, quite uninspired official, who stutters badly when he delivers a speech and would scarcely have reached his present post if it had not been for Stalin's potent patronage. Ordzhonikidze, another member of the Political Bureau, is, like Stalin, a Georgian, whose name has now been given to the town of Vladikavkaz, in the region where he distinguished himself during the civil war. The other members of the Political Bureau are routine Party and Soviet officials.

It is noteworthy that not one member of this highest governing organ knows any European language, apart from Russian. This is symbolic of the ousting from places of higher influence of the Communist intellectuals who had lived in emigration in Western Europe before the Revolution and of their replacing by men who, like Stalin himself, carried on their revolutionary activity exclusively in Russia.

Russians Take Pride in Their New Army [6/8/34]

Born in revolution, the Soviet Union has always lived under a real or imaginary shadow of war menace. Every Communist believes that in some more or less distant future the issue between Capitalism and Socialism will be fought out in a gigantic Armageddon.

Lenin and Stalin have always emphasized the view that, while rivalries and antagonisms between other states may delay the formation of a united front against the Soviet Union, the likelihood of an onslaught on the latter, as the standard bearer of world revolution, must always be borne in mind.

Since the autumn of 1931 the war threat, in the eyes of the Soviet leaders, has become more concrete. The Japanese seizure of Mukden and the inauguration of a forward policy in Manchuria tore down the buffer which semi-independent Manchuria had constituted between Russia and Japan. The former Soviet zone of political influences in North Manchuria disappeared when Japanese troops marched into Harbin and occupied the stations along the line of the Chinese Eastern Railroad.

Front page of The Christian Science Monitor **from June 8, 1934.**

The last two and a half years in Russia have been a period of strained military effort in the Soviet Union, primarily directed to the strengthening of the country's defensive position in the Far East. And, while a Japanese surprise attack in 1931 or 1932 might have encountered little effective resistance, the Soviet Union today is certainly in a position to put up a strong fight for its Far Eastern territory.

The double-tracking of the Trans-Siberian Railroad has been almost completed, with a liberal use of forced labor. A picked, well equipped Far Eastern Army, with a numerical strength that is reliably estimated in the neighborhood of 150,000 men, is stationed along the Manchurian and Korean frontiers. Steel and concrete fortifications have been erected at strategic points.

Japanese command of the sea is undisputed, as there is no serious Soviet naval force in Far Eastern waters. But the harbor of Vladivostok has been carefully mined and coast defense batteries have been erected along the shores in the vicinity. A few submarines have been transported to the Far East by train.

Experience has shown that the peacetime Red Army, carefully selected and intensively drilled in propaganda, as well as in rifle and bayonet practice, is a reliable bulwark of the existing régime. Large scale war would, of course, require an immensely enlarged army; and then the mood of the most discontented peasant elements might make itself felt. This is only one of several reasons why the Soviet Government is, I believe, unquestionably sincere in its desire to avoid a clash with Japan at the present moment.

Time works on the Soviet side in several ways. The building up of actual and potential munition centers in Siberia, and the colonization of sparsely populated eastern Siberia — a number of special benefits in the shape of reduced tax burdens for peasants and higher wages for workers and employees in Eastern Siberia have recently been granted — make progress from year to year.

The stakes in a Soviet-Japanese war would be tremendous. Crushing military defeat is the one conceivable factor which might bring the whole Soviet edifice tottering to its fall. Decisive victory would have equally portentious consequences for Asia and for the world. It might bring about revolution in Japan; it would certainly give a tremendous stimulus to Bolshevism in China, where the Chinese Communist Party claims over 400,000 members and large areas in south central China are under more or less permanent Soviet control. It is a question whether Great Britain could remain indifferent or inactive if Bolshevism knocked at the doors of Shanghai and Hong Kong, Calcutta and Singapore.

Two fierce, passionate enthusiasms, the traditional patriotic enthusiasm of Japan and the new, revolutionary enthusiasm of Russia face each other across the Siberian-Manchurian frontiers. Whether these enthusiasms will clash or will settle their differences peacefully is one of the major riddles if international politics.

Soviet Expects Much of US Recognition [6/9/34]

The establishment, after 16 years of nonrecognition, of diplomatic relations between the United States and the Soviet Union, two of the largest and most populous countries in the world, was an event of considerable significance not only for the two countries affected, but also for the entire international situation.

A few years ago, more specifically before the Japanese seizure of Mukden in the autumn of 1931, American recognition would have been regarded in Moscow as primarily economic in its significance. Today, although commercial possibilities are by no means ignored, Soviet emphasis is rather on the political aspects of recognition.

Soviet public opinion is inclined to be distinctly optimistic about America's attitude in the event of a Soviet clash with Japan. Every piece of news, however unimportant, that seems to point to strained relations between the United States and Japan is prominently displayed in the Soviet press. It is widely believed in Moscow that one of the purposes of American recognition was to ward off the threat of a Japanese attack on Siberia; and even non-Communist Russians are inclined to take it for granted that American support, in some form, will be forthcoming if the threatened conflict breaks out in the Far East.

So far as Soviet-American trade is concerned, it is reasonable to expect that one of the sequels of recognition will be some degree of recovery from the virtual stagnation which has prevailed in this field for the last two or three years. The establishment in America of a special bank, under Government auspices, for the financing of exports to and imports from the Soviet Union was the first concrete step looking toward a revival of Soviet-American trade.

Cold facts and figures, however, lend little support to the optimistic theorists who believe that the establishment of diplomatic relations with the Soviet Union will open up a market of inexhaustible wealth for the American businessman. The Soviet share in the enormously depleted world trade of 1932 was substantially less than 3 per cent.

So an enthusiastic Congressman who some time ago declared that the United States, by not recognizing the Soviet Union, was losing $500,000,000 worth of trade annually apparently overlooked the fact that the total receipts of the Soviet Government from exports — all of which obviously could not have been diverted to the purchase of goods in the United States — have been far short of $500,000,000 since 1930.

Mr. Maxim Litvinoff, foreign commissar, in his statement at the London Economic Congress, that the Soviet Union was prepared to place orders to a value of $1,000,000,000, over and above its planned purchases abroad, provided that credits were forthcoming, may be set down as a piece of window dressing. Assuming that the Soviet Government desires to preserve its credit, it is hard to see how it could afford to accept credits for $1,000,000,000, assuming that any country were willing to grant them, unless it were assured a corresponding expansion of its exports.

America's experiences with overlending to South America and to central Europe during the years which preceded the depression would seem to dictate a more sober and discreet credit policy in regard to the Soviet Union. Russia unquestionably needs large quantities of many American products: railroad and factory equipment, machine tools, excavating and dredging machinery, copper, cattle and cotton, to mention a few of the more obvious. America, on its side, can absorb a certain amount of Soviet timber, manganese, furs, bristles, platinum, matches and miscellaneous products.

If one studies the exchange of correspondence between President Roosevelt and Mr. Litvinoff which preceded the establishment of diplomatic relations, one finds only one Soviet concession to the American viewpoint which has no parallel in its negotiations with other countries. And this concession is of a "Pickwickian" character, i.e., it will obviously not be literally carried into effect. The Soviet Government undertakes "not to permit the formation or residence on its territory of any organization or group — and to prevent the activity on its territory of any organization or group, or of representatives or officials of any organization or group — which has as an aim the overthrow of, or bringing about by force of a change in, the political or social order of the whole or any part of the United States, its territories, or possessions."

Now, if words mean anything, this would seem to obligate the Soviet Government to expel from its territory the Communist International, which if one may trust the evidence of its numerous long winded resolutions, is certainly working for the overthrow of the United States Government, as of every other "Capitalist" government. But the Soviet Government obviously has no intention of doing any such thing; a Congress of the International will be held in Moscow this year.

Youth Rides High in Soviet Saddle [6/12/34]

The eternal conflict of viewpoint and psychology between the older and the younger generation in Russia, which found its highest artistic depiction in Turgenieff's famous novel, *Fathers and Sons,* is more in evidence now than ever before. The spiritual clash is more natural and inevitable now, because a middle-aged, prerevolutionary generation and a young Soviet generation stand face-to-face, with loyalties, tastes and ideals that are often in sharp contrast.

Whether a Soviet citizen takes an optimistic or a pessimistic view of his own living conditions and his country's future often depends upon whether he is under or over 30. Of course, it would be a gross and exaggerated oversimplification to set down all the Russians over 30 as pessimists and all those under 30 as optimists. There would be plenty of exceptions in both camps.

Yet there is something distinctive in the outlook of most of the young people who have grown up entirely under the Soviet régime, singing Soviet songs, studying in Soviet schools, getting their training in the expansive Soviet youth organizations. For every adult Communist there are several young people enrolled in a Communist organization. While there are about 2,700,000 members and candidates — applicants for admission on probation — in the Communist Party there are about 4,500,000 Komsomols, members of the Union of Communist Youth, between the ages of 14 and 23; there are almost 6,000,000 Young Pioneers, a body which enlists children above the age of eight, and there are about 2,000,000 Octobrists, still younger children who are being formed in the Communist mold.

As the Soviet child graduates from the Young Pioneers into the Union of Communist Youth and passes from elementary school to a higher school or to work in a factory or office he, or she, is put through a most intensive propagandist training.

He is taught that his two highest duties are to build up Socialism in the Soviet Union and to help the workers of other countries, who are depicted as cruelly oppressed and looking forward eagerly to the hour of victorious revolution. Stories, pictures, posters, cartoons, lectures hammer into his fresh impressionable mind the idea that religion is a fraud, conceived by Capitalists for the sake of holding the workers in subjection. He is taught to look on the kulak, or the formerly well-to-do peasant who is opposed to collectivization, as a monster of human villainy, for whom extinction is too good.

The Young Pioneer in his red kerchief, the Young Communist in his khaki uniform and Sam Browne belt are brought up to regard obedience to the orders which they receive from the Communist Party as their first duty, a duty which comes far ahead of any family ties or relations. Cases when children denounce their own parents are common and are always mentioned with approbation in the Soviet press.

Recently a Tartar schoolgirl named Olya Balikina reported to the authorities that her father and some other peasants were taking grain which belonged to the collective farm for their own use: an offense which, under the notorious law of August 7, would have exposed them to the infliction of the supreme penalty. Olya was held up as a model of young Soviet virtue and, as a reward, was transferred at state expense from her village school to a model school in the city of Kazan.

Communist leaders here employ a psychological appeal not unlike that of Tom Sawyer, when he induced the other boys to paint his back fence by assuring them that it was an honor and distinction to be allowed to do this work.

Another factor that tends to break up the old-fashioned family in Russia and to give the younger generation a sense of independence from an early age is the system under which students in technical schools and universities are supported, in the main, not by their parents, but by the state, in one form or another.

One of the most indisputable achievements of the Soviet régime during the last few years has been the expansion of the country's educational system. According to official figures, the number of pupils in elementary schools between 1929 and 1933 increased from 11,697,000 to 19,163,000; the number of students in middle schools from 2,453,000 to 6,674,000; the number of university students from 207,000 to 491,000.

Much of the stimulus to this expansion came from the grandiose industrial projects of the Five-Year Plan, which demanded a large number of new engineers and experts of all kinds and also a much larger force of skilled workers.

Quality is apt to lag appreciably behind quantity in every field of Soviet life; and many of the new high schools and specialized institutes which have taken the places of the old universities are not adequately equipped as regards teaching personnel, laboratory facilities, etc. Crowded dormitories and meager, unappetizing fare in student dining rooms also do not make for the best health and efficiency of the students.

Russian youth is not an absolutely compact mass. I know of one case when some young men who were studying secretly for the priesthood were banished to a place in Central Asia where, the general impression was, they would be very likely to contract a malignant form of malaria. On another occasion, when I met a group of Russian vacationists on a walking trip, one young man walked with me for some distance and poured out a stream of doubts and criticisms, ending with a fervent appeal not to mention his ideas to his companions, for, as he said: "Every Russian wants to eat, to live and not to sit."

"To sit" is a common Russian expression for being in prison.

But the dissenters among the youth are, I think, the minority; and they are certainly unorganized and unable to make their influence felt.

The Soviet leaders have succeeded in organizing and disciplining the younger generation, in giving it a liberal double dose of education and propaganda. Perhaps the real test of the permanent efficacy of this gigantic effort at remolding the mind of a people will come when and if the education imparted to the young people makes them begin to doubt and question the propaganda.

Above: Young farmer awarded the Order of Lenin for excellent work. Next page, clockwise from top left: Member of the Communist Youth Organization. Young shock brigade boiler maker. Foreman explaining tasks to his youthful work team.

Soviet Puts Its Best Foot Forward   [6/15/34]

It is regrettable, but probably inevitable, that the Soviet Union should be, among all the larger countries, the most imperfectly understood abroad. This is attributable partly to the very nature of the situation, partly to the naïveté of certain types of foreign visitors, partly to the instinct for concealing and suppressing unpleasant facts which the Soviet rulers of Russia have taken over, in somewhat intensified form, from their Czarist predecessors.

Pre war Russia to the average American or Englishman suggested a vague medley of sleighs careering over snowy steppes, church bells tolling for Easter, wolves pursuing benighted travelers, and dreary processions of exiles marching to Siberia clanking their chains.

A revolution of unprecedented sweep, led by men of whom few had ever heard, did not add to the popular understanding of Russia in foreign countries.

If one looks back to the years of civil war and intervention, one can easily realize that most news about Russia at that time was violent and intemperate, exaggerated and unreliable.

I think the Soviet régime today benefits indirectly by this first chilly blast of exaggerated hostile criticism. Because people are subconsciously ashamed of having believed, in 1918, that Russian women were "nationalized," which was quite false, they are reluctant to believe, in 1933, that vast numbers of Ukrainian and North Caucasian peasants perished from famine, which is just as definitely true.

During recent years there has been a growing stream of tourists, especially Americans, to the Soviet Union. This movement will doubtless grow as a result of the establishment of diplomatic relations between the two countries. Increasing familiarity with the physical appearance of modern Russia, with Soviet political and economic ideas and constructive achievements, with Russian literature, music and drama, is certainly desirable from every standpoint.

But some short-time visitors to the Soviet Union do not fully grasp the immense difference between the handling of a foreign tourist in the Soviet Union and in England, or, for that matter, in any West European country. In England, the foreign visitor goes where he pleases, meets whom he chooses, from the Fascist Sir Oswald Mosley to the leader of the British Communist Party, forms his impressions without the slightest official aid or interference.

The vast majority of tourists in the Soviet Union come under the auspices of Intourist, the Soviet State Tourist Agency. Indeed, under prevalent conditions of shortages of food and hotel accommodations and railroad travel facilities, it would be extremely difficult for the ordinary American, who knows no Russian, to get about in any other way.

Intourist does far more than similar agencies in other countries. It acts as a showman not only for places of scenic, historical and artistic interest, but also for the whole Soviet system. Its program includes visits to model factories, model crèches, model children's houses, model prisons, model collective farms.

The tourists are accompanied by guide-interpreters who have been put through a special training course in propaganda and who know that failure to create a favorable impression may have unpleasant consequences for themselves. They have been schooled not only in general Soviet ideas, but in how to explain such specific common Moscow sights as the demolition of a church or the queue outside a food shop.

There is a significant difference between what is and what is not shown to the foreign visitor. He is readily taken to the Sokolniki prison, where conditions for the prisoners, measured by Russian standards, are almost luxurious. Prince Kropotkin tells us in his reminiscences that the Czarist Government constructed a few model prisons for the edification of foreign visitors.

Our present-day tourist is not, however, given an inside view of the grim Butirki, which has an unsavory reputation for chronic overcrowding, bad physical conditions and frequent actual and attempted suicides among its inmates. He is conducted to the pleasantly located colony for reclaimed waifs which the Gay-Pay-Oo maintains in Bolshevo, near Moscow — an excellent institution of its kind.

He is not shown one of the numerous forced labor concentration camps, where conditions are very different from those in Bolshevo. If he wants to get an idea of Soviet agriculture, a model commune in Tambov Province, highly unrepresentative if only because it was founded not by native peasants but by returned emigrants who brought in a good deal of their own machinery, is at his disposal.

He is not encouraged to travel in the villages and collective farms of Ukraina where 10 percent and more of the population perished of famine and related causes during the winter and spring of 1932-1933.

The art of showmanship has ancient and distinguished antecedents in Russia. When the Empress Catherine II wished to take a boat trip on the Dnieper through newly annexed Ukraina, her favorite, Prince Potyemkin, hastily erected stage villages in the sparsely populated country through which the Empress would pass.

What is surprising in Russia today is not the persistence of the "Potyemkin villages" tradition, but the readiness with which some foreign visitors, not infrequently men and women with a reputation for scholarship and critical acumen in their respective fields at home, accept the Soviet conducted tour at full face value without apparently realizing that they are seeing only the bright side of a picture which has some decidedly dark sides.

Foreign journalists with fairly long terms of residence in Moscow are naturally less impressionable than the average short-time visitor. The Soviet authorities have worked out a number of regulations, to say nothing of methods of indirect pressure, for the purpose of keeping the less favorable facts of Soviet life out of the columns of the foreign press.

First of all, there is the preliminary censorship of all press telegrams, a system which does not exist in any other European country. Mail articles are free from censorship; but news developments of first hand importance, which cannot wait for the slower mails, can only be sent by telegraph in the phrasing which meets the censor's approval.

The scope of the censorship was considerably enhanced in the spring of 1933, when a new rule was established forbidding foreign correspondents to leave Moscow without submitting a precise itinerary of their route and obtaining the permission of the authorities. The obvious intention of this innovation was to prevent any first-hand reporting of the famine.

The prohibition of travel in the country districts went into effect in early spring; the first permits to travel were granted to some correspondents — there was conscious and calculated discrimination in the granting of the permits, and those correspondents who were regarded as too outspoken were penalized by being held in Moscow for a longer time than their colleagues — in September, when the new harvest was in and the raw visible traces of famine had been removed.

The rather humorless official explanation of the prohibition of the travel was that the presence of correspondents might hinder the reaping of the harvest. What was even more amusing than this explanation was that some foreigners were naïve enough to take it seriously.

Permits to remain in the country are granted to foreigners for only six months at a time and the foreigner who leaves the country even for a short time must reapply abroad for a return visa. This is a convenient Sword of Damocles to hold over the head of an unpopular correspondent; a delay in granting a return visa is a recognized way of warning a journalist that his writing is not regarded as satisfactory or "objective," to use a word of which the Soviet authorities are fond.

Mr. Paul Scheffer, distinguished correspondent for the *Berliner Tageblatt*, against whom no charge of factual inaccuracy or unfairness was brought, was kept out of the Soviet Union, when his views had become distasteful, by the simple device of refusing him a return visa. Direct expulsion is rarely practiced; it involves too much publicity and scandal. On the other hand, surreptitious

Front page of The Christian Science Monitor **Weekly Magazine Section from August 1, 1934.**

private efforts of Soviet agents abroad to undermine the position of unpopular correspondents with their home offices are quite frequent. Some of these efforts have been successful; in cases where the home office has vigorously supported its correspondent it has usually succeeded in keeping him in Moscow.

That this unusual régime of controlling press messages and imposing restrictions on the freedom of movement of correspondents clouds foreign understanding of Russia, and makes the task of the correspondent in Moscow more difficult than it is in many other capitals is obvious.

Personally, I am inclined to doubt whether this régime serves the best interests of the Soviet Government. The existence of censorship is known, at least to intelligent readers, and casts a shadow of inhibition over telegrams from Moscow. The maintenance of censorship furnishes the sole excuse for the periodic outbursts of scarehead alarmist rumors about Russia, emanating from the capitals of some border states.

Censorship implies that some things must be concealed. Its abolition would afford the most persuasive evidence of improvement in Soviet conditions, just as its tightening through the imposition of restrictions on travel in the spring of 1933 indicated to any well-informed reader that the Soviet countryside was experiencing a grave crisis, to which no foreign witnesses were desired.

Despite these considerations, it would be an agreeable surprise if censorship as a whole were lifted in Moscow, although the new, quite unprecedented ruling which forbids travel outside of Moscow without special permission, might conceivably be dropped. So it seems probable that the battle of wits between journalist and censor, the bartering of a vivid adjective for a qualifying phrase, of a mild verb for a strong noun, will continue. And readers who wish to get a full picture of the Russian situation from Moscow messages will be well advised to develop the art of reading between the lines.

Is Russia Prey of Perverted Idealism? [6/16/34]

I have a cordial antipathy to the "Me and Russia" type of book. For an outsider to come to a country which has lived through what is perhaps the biggest churning-up process in history and then to set down his reactions under some such title as "I Saw Russia" has always seemed to me to reveal a lack of sense of proportion that borders on impertinence.

At the same time, no one with sensitiveness and imagination could have lived for more than a decade in the Soviet Union without feeling some reaction, more probably several reactions, to the dramatic events which have played themselves out on this huge station. If the "Me and Russia" type of reporter seems out of place, I am also unable to share the viewpoint of a certain type of observer who looks on human beings, if they happen to be Russians, as on anesthetized guinea pigs or pawns on a chessboard and sees in the "liquidation" or wiping out of great numbers of them nothing but a perhaps unpleasant phase of an "interesting experiment,"

Now that new work is taking me away from Russia, in all probability, for a number of years, I think it may not be without interest and value to set down my personal feelings about the events and developments of which, for many years, I have endeavored to be a fair and objective reporter.

First of all, I must say that there are certain aspects of Russia which have nothing to do either with Czarism or with Bolshevism, which have for me the greatest charm and attraction. Few people are more gifted in many fields of art and culture.

Russian literature is little over a century old; yet there are not many authors of any nationality who can be compared with Turgenieff in rich, mellow, all-embracing human sympathy, with Tolstoy in epic breadth of scope, with Dostoevsky in fierce dramatic intensity, with Gogol in sharp and salty humor.

Equally striking have been the achievements of Russian music, and of many branches of Russian science. If one sometimes is tempted to think that the methods of Russia's rulers, past and present, place it among the backward Asiatic countries, one always returns to the thought that its thinkers, artists and natural scientists have won it a high place in European culture.

The pre war Russian educated class, I am convinced, is in many ways the most appealing in the world, perhaps, because it was younger, fresher, warmer in its appreciation of the cultural heritage which other countries take for granted.

Among the masses of the Soviet Union, among the peasants and workers and people of all occupations whom I have met in my trips throughout the country there are also qualities of hospitality, frankness, natural wit, friendliness to a foreign visitor that leave a favorable impression. Indeed, it sometimes happens that the simplest Russians are more entertaining conversational partners than are more sophisticated and educated people in other countries.

Certain aspects of Soviet life which are distasteful to some foreigners are rather attractive to me. I enjoy the absence of a showy and gaudy night life and the sartorial freedom which is perhaps the only kind of liberty that does indubitably exist in the Soviet Union.

For some of the achievements of the Soviet régime I have the sincerest respect. One cannot visit a workers' rest home or a workers' club, provided with library, reading room, games, reading circles, etc., and located in former slum districts, without realizing that a vast amount of useful social and educational work has been and is being done.

Industrialization in itself was a natural and reasonable goal for a country with the population and natural resources of the Soviet Union; and the Soviet leaders have displayed tireless drive and energy in setting up a network of steel and chemical plants, tractor and machine-building factories and electrical power stations. The industrial progress of the country is impressive in some ways, although one should bear in mind the fact, overlooked by some admirers of the Soviets, that pre-war Russia was developing its railroads and its industries very rapidly.

There is no reason to doubt that the Soviet leaders and the majority of the Communist Party members believe sincerely in their cause and are working hard for what they conceive to be the well-being of the country.

And yet, along with these constructive sides of the Soviet régime, there are the hard, undeniable, unpleasant facts of the régime of odious terrorism and espionage maintained by the Gay-Pay-Oo, of the decimation of the intelligentsia in weird sabotage trials and of the peasantry in wholesale deportation and in a régime of "military feudal exploitation" that reached its logical and terrible culmination in the great famine of 1932-1933.

How is one to reconcile these apparently contradictory sets of facts? It is my personal belief that the Bolshevik Revolution and the Soviet régime which grew out of it offer the world an example of historical tragedy of the deepest and truest type, a tragedy of cruelty and oppression inflicted not from wantonness and selfishness but from a kind of perverted, fanatical idealism — always the surest source of utter ruthlessness. And back of this tragedy lie several conceptions which are implicit in the Communist philosophy and which seem to me to be fundamental fallacies.

The first, the oldest and the most obvious of these fallacies is the belief that the end justifies the means.

Actually the overwhelming weight of historical evidence would seem to be to the effect that the means determine the end and that an idealistic goal, pursued by brutal methods, has a way of fading out of sight.

Such major atrocities as the liquidation of the kulaks as a class, the state-organized famine and the persecution of the intelligentsia have harmful results that go far beyond their immediate victims. They brutalize the society that is taught or forced to look on them with indifference or even with applause. More than once I have felt that there could be some very pointed applications, in present-day Russia, of the following passage from the introduction of Aleksei Tolstoy's novel of the times of Ivan the Terrible, *Prince Serebranny:*

"I throw down my pen in indignation not so much at the thought that Ivan the Terrible could exist, as at the thought that a society could exist which would look on him without indignation."

A second sentimental fallacy of Communism is its virtual ignoring of the problems involved in the concentration of enormous power in the hands of the few who must inevitably guide the political and economic life of the country during the period of the dictatorship of the proletariat.

Obsessed with the idea that "Capitalism," the private ownership of means of production, was the root of all human ills, Lenin never seems to have foreseen the abuses which might result when all power, political and economic, would be in the hands of the state.

There are certainly few peasants in the Soviet Union today who would not characterize the state as a harder taskmaster than the former landlord; and the possibility that a dictatorial state would exploit workers and peasants alike, not for the purpose of private enrichment, but as a result of blundering management, of grandiose ambition for quick industrial and military expansion is certainly vividly illustrated by Russia's experience.

Incidentally, it seems decidedly improbable that the Soviet state, after arrogating to itself the most absolute power over the lives of its citizens, will some day "wither away," as Lenin foresaw. Perhaps Lenin in his study could imagine as abstract conception, "the state," withering away.

It is very difficult for me, after seeing the privileges with which high Party, Soviet and Gay-Pay-Oo officials are surrounded, to imagine this new ruling class, or ruling caste, voluntarily "withering away."

The materialistic conception of history is another Communist dogma with which I am in vigorous disagreement. This effort to explain all human activity in terms of the play of economic forces seems narrow, inadequate and unconvincing.

Permanence of Soviet Lies in Peace [6/18/34]

The main outlines of the new Soviet political, economic and social order are fairly clearly marked out today. The era of ruthless, stormy, rapid change, which was ushered in by the adoption of the first Five-Year Plan, has been succeeded by a period of greater calm and stability. Barring the uncertain chances of war, the Soviet régime seems absolutely guaranteed against violent overthrow or subversion. Given peace-time conditions, its combined technique of intensive propaganda and terroristic repression is quite invincible.

At the same time, processes of change and development are inevitable and are already going on. One of the most significant present-day trends in Soviet life is the emphatically repeated official repudiation of the idea that complete material equality is or ever will be a Communist ideal. Stalin devoted some of his sharpest denunciation in a recent speech to those Communists who practice, favor or condone "uravnilovka," a Russian term which is much in use, but hard to translate, and may best be rendered as "equalization" or "leveling."

"Equalization in the field of consumption and personal life is reactionary petty-bourgeois nonsense, worthy of some primitive sect of ascetics, but not of a Socialist society," Stalin proclaimed on this occasion. As I read this denunciation of the idea of equal pay for all I recalled a talk with a village Communist, a former Red partisan, several years ago. "Liquidation of the kulaks as a class was just the first step toward complete equality," he declared. "The next step will be the abolition of all inequality in the pay of state employees."

"Do you think you will receive as much as Stalin?" I asked him, half jokingly. "Certainly that will come in time," he replied with conviction. This humble village Communist and others who think as he does will probably feel resentment and dismay at the spread of the official campaign for unequal pay for unequal work. It will go very hard against their psychological grain.

But so great is the power of the party leadership that there seems no reason to doubt its ability to repress any grumblings and mutterings of discontent from rank-and-file Communists who believed that the Revolution was made for the sake of making everyone eat the same kind of food out of the same kind of dishes with the same kind of spoons.

The very sweep of the industrial ambition of the Communist leaders has made them scrap the dream of material equality more quickly and decisively than otherwise might have been the case. One of the gravest mistakes of the original Five-Year Plan, and it abounded in mistakes, was its overrating of the machine and its underrating of the human element, both in industry and in agriculture.

It was rather naïvely assumed that a tractor in the hands of Russian peasants, with no previous experience in handling complicated machines, would run as smoothly as on a middle western farm, and that a modern coal-cutting machine would run just as well in the hands of an underfed, unskilled raw peasant laborer, as in the hands of a skilled mechanic in the Ruhr.

A number of disillusioning experiences showed the error of this neglect of the human factor in production; and, if the first Five-Year Plan emphasized the machine, the second plan is stressing the importance of placing the right men in the right places. And this, in turn, demands a rigid application of the new rule — unequal pay for unequal work.

A prominent slogan of the second Five-Year Plan is the creation of a classless society. At first sight this might seem to promise a sweeping increase in material equality. But in its actual application this slogan seems likely to be conservative rather than radical in its results. Once there are officially no more classes there is no justification for class struggle or class envy.

The unskilled laborer who in 1937, when classes are supposed to be abolished, may grumble when he compares his own Spartan fare and cramped living conditions with the more comfortable standards of Communist executives and engineers will be not a proletarian, justly indignant at his lowly lot, but a misguided comrade who must be gently but firmly instructed in the harmfulness of uravnilovka and the blessings of payment by piecework.

This is not to say that there is any likelihood or a reversion to private Capitalism, using that term in its proper sense, in Russia. There is not the slightest prospect of a reestablishment of private ownership of factories and mines, banks and railroads. The peasants will still be regimented in their collective farms. But inequality, within the framework of the system of universal state domination of the country's economic life, will tend to grow, rather than to diminish.

Another noteworthy trend in the Soviet Union today is toward nationalism and away from world revolution. If the Soviet Government enjoys a decade or so of

THE CHRISTIAN SCIENCE MONITOR

Weekly Magazine Section

A SURVEY OF WORLD AFFAIRS

BOOK REVIEWS   COPYRIGHT 1935 BY THE CHRISTIAN SCIENCE PUBLISHING SOCIETY   BOSTON, MARCH 27, 1935

THE KREMLIN, MOSCOW   Sovfoto

Postscript to Russia

By William Henry Chamberlin

ALMOST A YEAR HAS PASSED since I left Moscow and thereby brought to a close a period of almost 12 years of residence in the Soviet Union. The little charms and unconventionalities, the petty cares and annoyances, which are equally characteristic of daily life in the Soviet capital, have faded into the background. It is now possible to take stock of my years of personal contact with the most fundamental social upheaval of modern times with a fair degree of perspective.

The first point I should wish to make in discussing my attitude toward the impersonal entity called Russia, or the Soviet Union, is that I draw a definite line of distinction between the Russian people and the Soviet regime, and the Marxist-Leninist philosophy upon which the latter is based. There is in America an organization of admirers of every Soviet governmental policy and action, from summary executions to forced-labor camps, which calls itself The Friends of The Soviet Union. I have never applied for membership, but I strongly doubt whether, on the basis of my writings about Russia, I should be a welcome recruit. In the same way I don't think I should have been inclined, or been permitted, in pre-revolutionary

days to join a society called The Friends of Tsarist Russia, if this implied approval of such features of Tsarist policy as exiling of political opponents to Siberia, toleration of pogroms, ruthless repression of peasant and working-class disturbances without any effort to find out and remove their underlying causes.

But despite, or rather because of, the fact that I should certainly be blackballed as a professional "Friend of the Soviet Union," I do feel that I am an amateur friend of the Russian people. And if I hadn't felt such a strong sentiment of personal sympathy for individual Russians of various classes whom I met peace the idea that the Bolshevik upheaval in Russia was the prelude to similar upheavals in all other countries may simply evaporate.

Already one senses in the Soviet leaders a growing preoccupation with their own internal problems and in the Soviet masses a sentiment that is scarcely distinguishable from patriotism, even if it does still employ a Socialist and internationalist vocabulary: a conscious pride in the achievements of the Soviet Union.

The course of events in other parts of the world is certainly calculated to discourage the idea that Russian Bolshevism is a predestined form of evolution for other countries. To be sure, one sees almost everywhere tendencies that might loosely be called Socialist in the sense that governments are taking over more and more of the functions which were formerly reserved for private initiative.

But it is a far cry from these tendencies to Communist dictatorship on the Soviet model. Some features of Communist administration, notably the mixture of propaganda with repression, have found conscious or unconscious imitation in other lands; and the Soviet Union is not the only great country which today obeys the will of a dictator, ruling with the aid of a disciplined and organized party.

But this technique can be used just as easily to crush Communism as to promote it; and in Germany and Italy this is just what has happened. There is certainly no country in Europe or America today which reproduces the conditions that made possible Lenin's leap to power and his inauguration of the vast Bolshevik experiment: a middle class weak in numbers and politically inexperienced, a peasantry so eager to seize the big estates that it had lost the sense for private property, a working class far enough above the Asiatic level to be capable of conscious and disciplined revolutionary action and far enough below the European level to feel that it had little to lose in a general smashing of old economic and social ties.

Bolshevism is certainly not likely to triumph in other countries by force of the Russian example. Its planned economy, which has a magic sound to some economic theorists, has proved in practice just as fallible, just as liable to error as the unplanned economy of private Capitalism. And some of the mistakes of the Soviet planners, especially in the agricultural field, led to very terrible and ghastly results.

If one takes a long range backward view of Russian development since the Revolution one can easily distinguish three main periods: the first of which from 1917 until 1921 was marked by the struggle to establish the new régime and to crush the anti-Soviet forces; the second, from 1921 until 1928, by the relaxation and relative mildness that attended the freer scope for individual enterprise that marked the New Economic Policy; the third, from 1928 until 1933, by grandiose efforts to industrialize the country and to remake its agricultural system, accompanied by great physical hardship and ruthless terroristic repression of open or passive opposition.

Now the Soviet Union seems to be in the first stages of a new period, where the intense strain and cruelty of the first Five-Year Plan will quite conceivably be relaxed. Among various signs of a new spirit one may note the encouragement of the classics in literature and on the stage, the greater scope for amusement, the enunciation of the slogan that every collective farm peasant should become well-to-do.

That this, at the present moment, is an aspiration which is very far from reality does not alter its deeper significance. Hitherto one of the basic features of Communist policy in the village was the constant stirring up of the envy of the poorer peasants for their more well-to-do neighbors.

One cannot cast the horoscope of the Soviet Union for a long period of time without knowing whether the future will bring peace or war. Peace will mean essential stability and evolutionary development of the existing régime, some relaxation of the more extreme forms of terrorism, a gradual evaporation of the dream of world revolution, some increase of material inequality within the limits of a system which will never permit the accumulation of big private fortunes.

War would throw everything into a crucible of uncertainty, even the existence of the régime, if it should turn out disastrously.

Postscript to Russia [3/27/35]

Almost a year has passed since I left Moscow and thereby brought to a close a period of almost 12 years of residence in the Soviet Union. The little charms and unconventionalities, the petty cares and annoyances, which are equally characteristic of daily life in the Soviet capital, have faded into the background. It is now possible to take stock of my years of personal contact with the most fundamental social upheaval of modern times with a fair degree of perspective.

The first point I should wish to make in discussing my attitude toward the impersonal entity called Russia, or the Soviet Union, is that I draw a definite line of distinction between the Russian people and the Soviet régime, and the Marxist-Leninist philosophy upon which the latter is based. There is in America an organization of admirers of every Soviet governmental policy and action, from summary executions to forced-labor camps, which calls itself The Friends of The Soviet Union. I have never applied for membership, but I strongly doubt whether, on the basis of my writings about Russia, I should be a welcome recruit. In the same way I don't think I should have been inclined, or been permitted, in pre revolutionary days to join a society called The Friends of Czarist Russia, if this implied approval of such features of Czarist policy as exiling of political opponents to Siberia, toleration of pogroms, ruthless repression of peasant and working-class disturbances without any effort to find out and remove their underlying causes.

But despite, or rather because of, the fact that I should certainly be blackballed as a professional "Friend of the Soviet Union," I do feel that I am an amateur friend of the Russian people. And if I hadn't felt such a strong sentiment of personal sympathy for individual Russians of various classes whom I met during my Russian decade I might have been less strongly impelled to set down in unmistakable terms what I think of the system that has brought on the Russian people the uncounted sum of individual tragedies that is very vaguely and imperfectly conveyed by such phrases as "liquidation of the kulaks as a class," "sabotage trials," "famine," or "forced labor concentration camps." Sometimes these Russians were friends of many years' standing. Sometimes they were casual acquaintances whom I had never met before and shall never, in all probability, meet again.

One of the latter was a Ukrainian peasant woman with whom I talked in the village of Cherkass, which is about eight miles south of the town of Belaya Tserkov, immediately after the great famine of 1932-1933. In this village, which had been particularly hard hit, 600 of 2000 inhabitants had perished, according to the testimony of the secretary of the local Soviet. This woman whom I remember was a mere atom in an immense catastrophe of misery; but it is these atoms, these individuals who bring home the poignant realities that are lost when one speaks of anonymous millions of famine victims. The woman told me in her simple Ukrainian dialect how she had never enjoyed a chance for schooling herself, how she had three children in school, who, as she pathetically put it, were so *uchenie* (or "learned") —

and how all three had perished when food gave out in the famine.

Somehow those three children whom I never saw acted on me as the strongest argument for Democracy and against Dictatorship that I can well imagine. For they were only the symbol of the unnumbered victims of a famine that could easily have been averted, if the Soviet authorities had not decided to "teach the peasants a lesson," by letting several millions of them perish in a famine that was caused not by any natural disaster, but by ruthless requisitions and failure to give any adequate relief. Under democratic systems peoples have done many foolish things and some cruel ones. But nothing, I say with full confidence, remotely as bad as this state-organized famine.

And these Ukrainian peasant child victims of famine are only a small part of the host of individual existences that have been broken, warped, destroyed by the merciless application of Communist dogma, so logical in theory, so irrationally inhuman in practice. I think of the wretched wives and children of kulaks whom I saw at Magnitogorsk, dragging themselves home from forced labor tasks on rations far more meager than the food allowances of the British and American unemployed, of professors and scientists who were executed or sent into banishment on preposterous "sabotage" charges, or, in some cases, for refusing to bear false witness against their colleagues.

Say everything that can fairly be said about the constructive aspects of the Soviet régime. Recognize the industrial expansion of the country, the improved educational and recreational facilities for the masses, the absence of race discrimination, the sincere belief of many Communists that they are working for Russia's ultimate good. But to me personally the blast furnaces cannot roar loudly enough, the turbines cannot turn out electrical power fast enough to drown out the cries of the innumerable victims of this merciless sacrifice of large sections of the population on the altar of industrialization. The 4,000,000 lives deliberately lost in the famine, to me, outweigh the 10,000,000 tons of pig iron which Russia produced, for the first time in its history, in 1934.

If one introduces the element of comparison between Russia and the outside world, two circumstances should certainly not be overlooked. The Soviet Union, which boasts of having abolished unemployment, has attracted no rush of unemployed from other countries. Of the few thousand immigrants to Russia from America, mostly of Russian origin, who entered the Soviet

Front page of The Christian Science Monitor **from March 28, 1935.**

Union during recent years not a few are besieging the American Consulate, trying to get back to America. They would rather take their chance on going back to a country with a formidably large volume of unemployment than be employed in Russia — under Soviet conditions of food and housing. At the same time the Soviet Government has to maintain an extremely strict guard — with armed soldiers, barbed wire and specially trained police dogs — along its frontiers in order to prevent hundreds of thousands, if not millions, of its own desperate citizens from rushing out of Russia and throwing themselves on the mercies of an outside world that has not yet solved the problem of providing work for all.

The second point, which always comes to my mind, when I read in a Soviet newspaper of the alleged contrast between flourishing Russia and the collapsing world of Capitalism, is that tens of millions of dollars during recent years have flowed into Russia in the form, mainly, of food parcels sent to Soviet citizens by friends and relatives abroad. There has been no corresponding flow of money out of Russia to help victims of the crises in other countries.

Broadly speaking, my strongest feeling after living almost 12 years under a dictatorship is a very keen and lively enthusiasm for civil liberties and democratic methods of government. More than any other single cause, in my opinion, the dictatorial method has been responsible for what seems to me the utterly disproportionate cost of such progress as Russia has achieved under the Soviet system.

With my Russian experience in retrospect I find myself equally far removed from those impatient zealots who believe that the remedy for the failure of the democratic method to solve all social problems is to take a headlong plunge into Communist dictatorship, and from extremists of a different type whose instinct, figuratively at least, is to shoot every "Red" at sight. The man who is full of indignation at any violation of liberty anywhere except in Russia, but who has no word of condemnation for wholesale executions and large-scale peonage in the Soviet Union is morally and intellectually on a par with the man who is horrified at atrocities in Russia, but supports or fails to combat bad social conditions in America. The instinct to combat Communism by repressive laws may be emotionally understandable, but is fundamentally mistaken in its approach to the problem in my opinion.

I often think of the contrast between Czarist Russia and prewar England. The former was censored and policed beyond the wildest dreams of our professional "Red-hunters." The latter was about as free politically as is possible in an imperfect world. Czarist Russia now is only a memory. But England has remained pretty much the same England, after the terrific shock and ordeal of the World War.

Isn't the lesson here quite clear? Isn't it obvious that the unconscious makers of Bolshevism in Russia were the die-hard reactionaries of the Czarist regime, who kept the masses of the people poor, ignorant and brutalized, who fought the most moderate proposals of reform, who cherished a blind faith, so illusory in the end, that a huge standing army and a universal espionage system were sure guarantees against revolution?

And isn't it equally obvious that the greatest force for ordered progress in England were the men and women who worked, in spite of opposition and repression, to cure the evils of the first stage of the industrial revolution to raise the standard of living of the under-privileged classes, to give tangible proof that the masses can expect more through the method of Democracy, the method of free discussion and ultimate decision by the majority than through the fallacious shortcut of violent upheaval, followed by ironclad dictatorship, with no means of popular control.

My own feeling is that Democracy and Civilization are almost synonymous terms. Even if the method of dictatorship should produce a higher material standard of living (and Russia's experience up to the present time would emphatically suggest that this is not likely to be the case) I cannot conceive that it would be desirable to live in a society where every printed and spoken word was controlled, where one feared to talk freely, even to close friends, for fear that they might be Government spies; where social contact with a foreigner was positively physically dangerous, where some prying snooper was likely to read any incoming or outgoing letter, where one was never secure against arbitrary arrest and exile.

The foregoing description would apply to life in the Soviet Union as I have known it. It also applies, in greater or less degree, to every country that has thrown over Democracy for Dictatorship. My own feeling, in looking back at Russia, is that, if we want to prevent western civilization from breaking down, either in the Bolshevik way or in some other, possibly milder, but still unpleasant way, there is a very strong obligation to do two things: to work for peace and to work for social justice. Russia, on the basis of its present-day record, is not a challenge to any western country. But it is a very strong warning of what might happen to any country

under an irresistible double stress of war and of acute poverty and insecurity among large masses of the people.

Liberty is Test of Russia'a Future   [3/28/35]

It is far easier to get a bird's-eye view of Russia in retrospect than it is to cast the horoscope of the country's future. Whether we like it or not, we are unmistakably living in an age of ferment and of uncommonly rapid social and economic change. It would be a risky business to predict just how America will look in 1950, or even in 1940. How much more difficult, then, to draw up a blueprint of the future of a country where the processes of sweeping social revolution themselves represent such a huge x, or unknown quantity, where many new forces have been released and much that was fine and creative in the old Russian culture has been mercilessly destroyed.

However, there are a few trends in Soviet life that seem fairly clear. After a second spasm of fierce destruction onset on old habits, old economic relations, in which whole classes were decimated and swept out of existence, the Russian Revolution today shows definite signs of going the way of all revolutions in history and settling down.

One can find these signs both in Soviet foreign relations and in Soviet internal policy. Take, for instance, the entrance of the Soviet Union into the League of Nations last summer. For years the Communist leaders had vied with William Randolph Hearst and Senator Hiram Johnson of California in contemptuous abuse of the League and all its works. They had created for the Russian masses an image of the Geneva institution as a sinister Capitalist conspiracy, ready to pounce on the Soviet Union at the first convenient opportunity.

Then came the decision to enter the League of Nations and, by implication at least, to drop all the former charges against it. The moral of this will not be lost for Communist opinion in Russia and abroad. The stake on imminent world revolution, at least temporarily, has been abandoned. Taken in conjunction with the Soviet efforts to knit up an old-fashioned type of alliance with France, the decision to participate in the international forum at Geneva indicated Russia's readiness to play the diplomatic game along more or less conventional lines.

There have been some even more significant shifts in Soviet internal policy. Joseph Stalin's positively strident insistence on unequal pay for work of unequal quality is making for the emergence of new classes in Russia, of classes based not on private ownership of wealth, but on the rank which has been attained in the huge bureaucratic hierarchy which administers Soviet economic as well as political life.

The tightening of industrial discipline, the granting to the "Red director" of a Russian factory much the same status as the "boss" would enjoy in a "Capitalist" factory, the taking away from the factory committees of any rights of effective control over the management — these are all straws pointing in the same direction.

The Soviet régime is rapidly approaching, if it has not already reached, the point which the French Revolution attained after 1793, when Robespierre and his extremist associates had been guillotined and the new classes which had risen to power and wealth on the wreckage of the old began to solidify their position.

John Maynard Keynes once bitingly referred to the majority of the British Parliament which was elected immediately after the World War as "a group of hard-faced men who looked as if they had done extremely well out of the war."

There are many hard-faced men in Russia who have done quite well out of the Revolution: Gay-Pay-Oo officials who have won official favor by exploiting to the limit the unfortunate prisoners under their control in forced labor timber camps and construction enterprises; "hard-boiled" local Soviet officials who extracted the full quota of grain from the peasants without caring unduly as to how many lives might be lost in consequent famine; "Red directors" who drove through construction plans with rough-and-ready methods that would suggest the most ruthless pioneers of industrial expansion during America's period of large-scale opening up of new territory.

These types are the main visible and concrete beneficiaries of the Revolution that was made in the name of the workers and peasants. Under the present policy of officially sanctioned and encouraged inequality they are getting their reward in the shape of a standard of living that will set them off more and more from the masses.

The recent executions of Communists in Russia after a trial behind closed doors indicate that the Russian Thermidor, like its French predecessor, is not being carried out without victims. It is still difficult to ascertain how much opposition the present policy of "liquidating" the idea of general material equality, which was certainly a potent driving force in the early stages of the revolution, will elicit.

To say that the Russian revolution is settling down, destroying its own Left Wing, its own "troublemakers" (it is amusing to reflect that Bernard Shaw possesses a freedom to advocate complete equality of income in England which he certainly would not enjoy in Russia), is not for a moment to say that the immense changes wrought by the Revolution are being undone or that there is a "return to Capitalism," in the sense in which Capitalism is understood in America or England.

The classes which have been displaced by the revolution will remain displaced, scattered in the centers of Russian emigration all over the world, hounded and persecuted in Russia. The classes that have come on top will remain on top.

There is at present only a very faint and uncertain prospect that, if the trend toward moderation continues, some of the Russian émigrés, especially those of the younger generation, might find it safe or expedient to return to their native country. The system of state ownership and operation of the basic branches of national economic life will remain. But within this system there will be, unless all present-day symptoms are misleading, increasing inequality and more and more clearly marked class lines.

The Russian past is bound to cast its shadow over the Russian future. One of the most striking and also one of the most depressing aspects of Soviet life is the completeness with which the revolutionary régime has taken over, in somewhat more extreme form, one of the underlying points of the philosophy of the Czarist autocracy: that the individual has no rights which the state is bound to respect and that any sacrifice of individuals, or even of whole classes, in the supposed interests of the state, is justifiable.

The wholly avoidable famine of 1932-1933, the "liquidation of the kulaks as a class," the wholesale employment of forced labor under revoltingly inhuman conditions, the numerous shootings and banishments without any semblance of fair or open trial — these are practical applications of this particular aspect of "Old Russia in new masks."

That Russia will escape from this evil tradition under a regime which is second to none in the world in its denial of freedom of speech and press is unfortunately improbable. I think there is more chance of relative material improvement in Russia than of modification of arbitrary and ruthless practices of Government. The Soviet citizen will perhaps be able to count on a modest amount of butter and sugar long before he can feel safe against midnight arrest, cross-examination by a secret, irresponsible tribunal, followed by exile or "the highest measure of social defense," less prosaically, shooting.

The influence of national temperament makes itself felt in other ways. Despite the vast concentrated effort to make the Russians machine-minded, I doubt whether Russia within any predictable future will come within remote hailing distance of American standards of comfort and high-speed efficiency, simply because the elements of punctuality, practicality, sense for the little conveniences of life are so lacking in the Russian character.

On the other hand, I think it is quite probable that the education of the Russian masses, if it is accompanied by a gradual abandonment of the more stupid and extreme features of propaganda and censorship, will pave the way for a cultural renaissance and for a rich flowering of literature, drama and the arts, to which Russia has made such distinguished contributions in the past.

All predictions about Russia's future, of course, would tend to lose validity if the country should become involved in war. This would be the supreme ordeal of the Soviet system. Decisive defeat on the battlefield, in my opinion, is the one development which might bring the whole edifice crashing down in ruin.

What would succeed it is a vast enigma. Dictatorships of the modern style, with their combination of propaganda and frightfulness, have a disconcerting tendency to create a vacuum, so far as successors are concerned; and Russia is not the only country where military defeat might well bring about great and unforeseeable changes.

War would bring incalculable suffering to the Russian masses and would put a quick stop to that very modest process of recovery from famine and semi-starvation conditions which set in after the harvest of 1933.

Ruling out the possibility of war and reckoning with an evolutionary development of Soviet conditions, I am inclined to believe that both the hope and the fear which Russia today tends to inspire outside its frontiers will tend to wane. A revolution in retreat, a revolution that is repudiating or modifying its more extreme and utopian slogans, cannot indefinitely hold the allegiance of the apostles of discontent in other countries.

And the exaggerated fear which one sometimes finds in middle class circles in America and elsewhere that Moscow will by some mysterious means kindle the flame of social revolution in other countries will decrease as it becomes evident that the Soviet Union also has its rich and poor and that preoccupation with internal reconstruction is taking the edge off the propaganda for world revolution.

Religions Face Common Foe in Russia [3/29/35]

All forms of religion in Russia today are living through a major crisis. This crisis is no less severe and poignant because, as a result of the Soviet censorship and of the general conditions of life under the world's most sweeping and ruthless dictatorship, its details are largely hidden from the eyes of the outside world.

Russia is a land of many races and of many faiths; but the tragedy of its religious life affects equally the priests and ministers and devout adherents of all its various creeds. The Orthodox priest lives in great poverty and social obloquy. His children are excluded from the higher schools and from state employment (and almost all employment in the Soviet Union is state employment) unless they ostentatiously repudiate him and break off connection with him.

At any time his little church may be marked for demolition and he himself may be packed off in a freight car to forced labor in a bleak northern timber camp after a secret arrest and "trial" before a star-chamber tribunal on a vague and unspecified charge of "counter revolution."

The Baptist, the Evangelical Christian minister who believes in a different form of faith from the Orthodox priest, who teaches his simple peasant or working class parishioners that faith in the Bible and right living are more important than ritualistic observances, is in no better plight. A spokesman for the Union of Militant Atheists, the chief Soviet antireligious organization, told me that "the sectarians are our most dangerous enemies, because they do not uphold obvious superstitions;" and Soviet legislation in some respects bears harder on sectarians than on the Orthodox Church.

For instance, the Baptists and other evangelical groups had developed a far-flung network of charitable, educational, sport and recreation clubs and circles, and this had considerably strengthened their influence among the youth. The Soviet law on religious activity of 1929, which marked the transition from a policy of antireligious propaganda and discrimination to one of definite persecution, made all these organizations illegal with one stroke of the pen.

The seminary and general headquarters which the Baptists maintained in Moscow have been closed; they have no means of training ministers; and their present ministers, lay preachers and active members know very well that they are in constant danger of arbitrary arrest and banishment.

The Orthodox priest and the evangelical minister have their companion in the Jewish rabbi of the city or small town in Ukraina or Western Russia. Before the war the rabbi was the center of a close-knit Jewish community life, which held together with firmness and tenacity in the face of the systematic Czarist policy of racial discrimination, punctuated by occasional pogroms.

Today the rabbi perhaps finds satisfaction in the fact that there is no discrimination against Jews on racial grounds. But he sees the religious life which he has cherished, the specifically Jewish community spirit breaking up and disintegrating; the younger Jews will go to the Communist youth club, not to the synagogue, which, like the church, may be closed at any time.

And the Mohammedan mullah, accustomed to sound the call to prayer from the minaret of his mosque in the mountains of the Caucasus or the oases of Central Asia, discovers that the doctrine of Lenin is more powerful than the armies of the Czars, which once overran these Moslem lands, but did not break the faith of their inhabitants in Islam. In the Mohammedan parts of Russia also traditional religious institutions are crumbling.

This crisis of religion is in part attributable to the prodigious impact of the new ideas which were ushered in by the Revolution. But it is at least equally attributable to the ruthless persecution of religion which is an integral part of general Soviet policy. For the first time in history all the administrative and propaganda resources of an immensely powerful dictatorial state have been cast into the scale against all forms of religion.

While propaganda for atheism is lavishly encouraged, it is impossible to print or to import religious books or publications or to present the claims of religion in public addresses or debates. Teaching in the schools must be not only nonreligious, but definitely atheistic. Profession of religious faith may mark a student for dismissal from the university, an employee for loss of his post and subsequent blacklisting in the state service. The constitutional right of every Soviet citizen "to profess any or no form of religion," like many other features of that document, is systematically violated in practice.

I know of a case when some young men who had been guilty of nothing but studying for the priesthood were banished to an extremely hot and unpleasant place in Central Asia.

In traveling about the Russian country districts I repeatedly learned of instances when persons who had been selling candles or performing other minor offices in connection with the local church had been singled out for special victimization during the process that was euphemistically described as "the liquidation of the kulaks as a class." To be a priest or a minister is to be a member of the most dangerous profession in the Soviet Union today.

The circumstances of Russia's crisis of religion are very imperfectly known abroad. In this respect there is a noteworthy difference between the church controversy which has been proceeding in Germany for more than a year and the situation in Russia. There certainly has been, from time to time, state pressure against leaders of the German Church opposition; yet its leaders have succeeded in making their case pretty well known abroad through sermons, pamphlets and direct interview, granted to foreign correspondents.

The isolation which is imposed on Russian leaders of religious faith is infinitely greater. Any communication to the foreign press of concrete details of arrests, arbitrary closing of churches, conditions of priests and ministers in concentration camps would entail the sternest immediate reprisals not only against the individual who made it, but against anyone who was even remotely associated with him.

The course of the sole interview which the acting Patriarch of the Orthodox Church, Metropolitan Sergei, granted to foreign journalists confirmed very strongly instead of dispelling the impression of extreme repression. At a time when persecution of religion was especially intense, in the winter of 1929-1930, the Metropolitan was quoted in *Izvestia* (it was the first and last time within recent years that a Russian ecclesiastic was interviewed for the benefit of the Soviet official newspaper) to the effect that there was no persecution of religion in Russia.

Through the mediation of the Commissariat for Foreign Affairs, foreign newspapermen were permitted to put supplementary questions to him in writing and to meet him personally. However, this personal meeting was of extremely brief duration. The Metropolitan visibly took fright at the first concrete questions about the numbers of churches which had been closed and the numbers of priests who had been executed and banished, and rushed off with somewhat undignified haste, murmuring as he retreated from the room:

"Oh, I couldn't answer such questions. I must consult — the Holy Synod." The latter, according to the

THE CHRISTIAN SCIENCE MONITOR
Weekly Magazine Section
A SURVEY OF WORLD AFFAIRS

BOOK REVIEWS

COPYRIGHT 1935 BY THE CHRISTIAN SCIENCE PUBLISHING SOCIETY

BOSTON, AUGUST 21, 1935

Study in Inconsistency: Frowns for Direct Action in the United States, but Smiles for the Same in Communist Russia.

Coddling Communism
By William Henry Chamberlin

ONE OF THE MOST CURIOUS by-products of the Russian Revolution and the Soviet regime is the double standard of morals which has come to prevail, consciously or unconsciously, in the reactions of many American and British liberals and radicals to events in Russia and to developments in other parts of the world. The standards of judgment which are applied to other countries are harsh and severe; those which are applied to the Soviet Union are mild and indulgent to the last degree.

Some of the results of this double standard of morals are highly strange and confusing. It is no unusual experience to find people who are hotly indignant over the execution of Sacco and Vanzetti and over the continued imprisonment of Mooney who are simultaneously extravagant in their enthusiasm for a system in the Soviet Union which, both by virtue of its underlying philosophical belief that the end justifies the means and by virtue of its constant and unchanging administrative practice makes it inevitable that thousands of people should suffer the fate of Sacco and Vanzetti and that hundreds of thousands, in forced-labor concentration camps, should be condemned, without anything that could be called due process of law, to an existence rather less enviable than that of Mooney in San Quentin Prison.

Professions of ardent sympathy with the underdogs of the individualistic economic system, with the unemployed, with striking industrial workers or farm laborers, are combined with complete indifference to the more acute and extensive sufferings of the more numerous underdogs of the Soviet system: peasants who are herded in concentration camps or driven to despair and starvation as a result of merciless ex-general surmise of the correspondents, was a euphemism for the Gay-Pay-Oo.

In the present atmosphere of extreme repression and persecution, and with a wall of secrecy erected between the experiences of Russian religious bodies and the outside world, one can only hazard a conjecture as to the probable future course of developments. It seems probable that there will be a continued diminution in the number of openly self-confessed believers, partly because of the effect of the stream of antireligious propaganda, partly because of the likelihood of discrimination and persecution.

At the same time the faith of those groups which are prepared to stand by their convictions will become more intense. If religion is to survive at all in the unequal conditions of struggle which the Soviet régime has created for it, this result can only come about as a result of the exercise of exceptional faith and devotion.

Coddling Communism   [8/21/35]

One of the most curious by-products of the Russian Revolution and the Soviet régime is the double standard of morals which has come to prevail, consciously or unconsciously, in the reactions of many American and British liberals and radicals to events in Russia and to developments in other parts of the world. The standards of judgment which are applied to other countries are harsh and severe; those which are applied to the Soviet Union are mild and indulgent to the last degree.

Some of the results of this double standard of morals are confusing. It is no unusual experience to find people who are hotly indignant over the execution of Sacco and Vanzetti and over the continued imprisonment of Mooney who are simultaneously extravagant in their enthusiasm for a system in the Soviet Union, which, both by virtue of its underlying philosophical belief that the end justifies the means and by virtue of its constant and unchanging administrative practice makes it inevitable that thousands of people should suffer the fate of Sacco and Vanzetti and that hundreds of thousands, in forced-labor concentration camps, should be condemned, without anything that could be called due process of law, to an existence rather less enviable than that of Mooney in San Quentin Prison.

Professions of ardent sympathy with the underdogs of the individualistic economic system, with the unemployed, with striking industrial workers or farm laborers, are combined with complete indifference to the more acute and extensive sufferings of the more numerous underdogs of the Soviet system: peasants who are herded in concentration camps or driven to despair and starvation as a result of merciless exploitation at the hands of the state; engineers, agricultural experts and other non-Communist intellectuals who are consigned to prison and exile after star-chamber trials on fantastic charges of sabotage.

A keen critical sense in regard to social and economic evils which may be attributed to undue concentration of wealth in the hands of a small privileged class is habitually associated with complete shortsightedness when it is a question of the cruelties and injustices that naturally and inevitably arise when all power, political and economic alike, is concentrated in the hands of the small privileged class of rulers of the Soviet state, who are not restrained by the wholesome curbing and mitigating influence represented by freedom of speech, press and election.

One is sometimes tempted to wonder whether there is something about Russia that makes all sense of relativity fly out of the window when Soviet policies of repression are under consideration. I suppose that the anti-Semitic measures of the National Socialistic régime in Germany have excited about 100 times as much condemnation, at least in radical and liberal circles, as the so-called "liquidation of the kulaks as a class" in Russia. It is not my purpose to condone the race prejudice that has played a part in shaping German policies during the last two years. But there is such a thing as degree even in ruthlessness. In order to match the precedent set by the liquidation of the kulaks in Russia, Herr Hitler would have been obliged to drive every Jewish family in Germany from its home, to confiscate all their property, to send a large part of the Jewish population to forced-labor under revoltingly inhuman conditions. The fate of the German Jews has been hard enough in all conscience. But no one who is familiar with Russian and German circumstances would be likely to suggest that it has been as terrible as the fate of the Russian kulaks, who, with their families, were the victims of an artificially stimulated class hatred that was as inexorable in theory and much more ruthless in practice than the race hate that has led to the plight of the German Jews.

I have sometimes wondered what comments would have appeared in liberal and radical periodicals if Mussolini had issued a law establishing the death penalty for theft, if Hitler had decreed that no worker might be absent from work even for a day without being liable to summary dismissal, loss of his living quarters and of his food card. I imagine that phrases about "reversion to barbarism," "enslavement of labor," etc., would not have been wanting. But the Soviet Government did issue two such laws, the decree of August 7, 1932, establishing death penalty for theft of state property (which in Russia means almost all property), and a decree of November 1932, clamping down the above mentioned severe penalties for absentee labor without, apparently, exciting a ripple of protest on the part of its foreign admirers, who would certainly have burst out in unmeasured indignation if such laws had been promulgated in Fascist or democratic countries.

I think there are two main facts about Russian life on which practically all informed foreign observers would agree, although there is room for wide differences of opinion as to some of the details and as to the permanent significance of these two facts. First, Russia did make swift and undeniable progress in building up its heavy industries, its coal mines, its oil wells, its steel mills, its machine-making factories, and in starting new branches of industry which had been largely or entirely nonexistent before the war, in starting aviation, automobile, tractor, chemical plants, etc.

Secondly, this progress was purchased at a very great cost in human suffering and in human lives. If on the credit side of the Soviet balance sheet you would put the tall smokestacks of new factories, the contours of big new blast furnaces, the giant turbines of hydroelectric power works, on the negative side you would have to set down millions of victims of famine, enormous numbers of deported kulaks and other "class enemies" who were given the hard choice of starving or working for a subsistence minimum in timber camps and construction camps, a formidably long list of men of science and technical experts who were broken on the wheel of the sinister "sabotage" cases.

Now the liberal or radical has always been a man, who, in surveying American developments, has prided himself on placing human rights above property rights. He has argued eloquently and convincingly that mere material development is of small account, compared with the types of human beings that are being brought into existence. He has burned with righteous indignation whenever he has detected a grasping corporation squeezing out the small businessman, the farmer who stood in the way of its ruthless expansion. He has laughed with scorn at Mr. George F. Babbitt's speech at the Zenith Rotary Club, which incidentally, in some of its lyrical statistical passages, is highly suggestive of the speech which one of Stalin's first, second or third lieutenants might make at a Communist Party meeting in Moscow or Kharkov or Voronezh.

But on this question of human rights versus property rights, as in the issue of civil liberties and democratic methods of government, the liberal or radical, when he crosses the Soviet frontier, either literally or figuratively, all too often loses his philosophical bearings, strays into the wrong camp and strikes his own colors. America's own industrial development has been marked by plenty of unsavory incidents involved in the fierce competitive struggle for wealth and material goods, in the ruthless upbuilding of new industrial empires. But, after making full and due acknowledgment of this fact, it still remains true that at no time did the faults and weaknesses of the American system entail the death from starvation of millions of persons, or, after the abolition of slavery, the wholesale employment of industrial serfs — the sole correct definition for the unfortunate people who are working under armed guard and behind barbed-wire entanglements in the numerous Soviet concentration camps.

I was recently present at an interesting informal discussion of main trends in Soviet development at a gathering of people who had all spent some time in the Soviet Union and possessed first-hand knowledge of conditions there. The discussion gradually sharpened into something like a debate; and the point at issue narrowed down to whether the country's progress had been worth the human cost involved.

"I grant that the famine was terrible," said the spokesman who was more favorable to the Soviet viewpoint, "but why go on talking about it? The famine is like the war; it is over and done with, and Russia is going ahead. I think it is a great achievement for Russia to have produced 10,000,000 tons of pig iron last year, for the first time in its history."

"Suppose a country plunged into a war, lost several million lives and then turned out a big increase in iron and steel," retorted a representative of the critical opposition. "Would you say that the war was 'worthwhile'?"

It certainly seems safe to say that if the new régimes in Germany or in Italy had demanded such far-reaching immolation of their peoples on the altar of national industrial expansion the reaction of our typical radical would have been swift, uncompromising and negative. It is only in Russia that he is more interested in the number of famine victims, that production of pig iron and diesel engines seems more important than statistics about forced labor.

I am sometimes tempted to regard this infatuation with Russia, this naïve belief that Russia, or rather, its Soviet leaders can do no wrong and that any criticism, however mild, of the most obviously ruthless acts of the Soviet administration is somehow "bad form," as a kind of "Mississippi Bubble" of the intellectual world, an arbitrary socio-economic fashion that will sooner or later pass. Behind this bubble are several identifiable causes.

There is the emotional hangover from 1917 and 1918, when the Soviet régime could quite plausibly have been represented as a persecuted "underdog" in world relations. But 1935 is not 1918. The Soviet régime is today a firmly established and very "hardboiled" state, perfectly competent to defend its own interests. Emotional sympathy that might have taken the form of demanding a fair chance for the Soviets in the years of blockade and intervention from 1918 until 1920 might now be better expended in demanding a fair chance for their victims, the scientists and professors who have been crudely "framed up" in sabotage trials, the luckless peasants who have been sent in droves to chop wood on starvation rations in the timber and construction camps.

Then the word "experiment" has been, I think, decidedly overworked in connection with the Soviet Union. Of course the Soviet form of political and economic administration is an experiment. So is Fascism in Italy. So is National Socialism in Germany. So is Democracy in the United States and in those countries of northern and western Europe which, whether they are republics or constitutional monarchies, contrive to get along without the summary executions, the concentration camps, the gagged press and the other familiar attributes of dictatorship, whether of the Communist or Fascist model. The very people who are most anxious to excuse, to condone, to suspend judgment on the most outrageous acts of cruelty and violence in Russia, on the plea that an "experiment" is in progress, the issue of which must not be prejudged, are not sparing of harsh criticism of Hitler's or Mussolini's experiments or of the older American experiment in Democracy.

One would be foolhardy indeed to predict with dogmatic certainty what the future holds in store for Russia, or for any other country, for that matter. But the experimental quality of the Soviet régime would not seem to afford any valid reason for repressing a normal human instinct of sympathy and indignation in the face of such sweeping governmental atrocities as the "liquidation of the kulaks as a class," the great famine of 1932-1933, which the state could have prevented and did not, the widespread forced labor system and the recent wave of terrorist executions without anything that could plausibly be called a fair trial.

I was once asked after a speech whether it was not too soon to pronounce judgment on Russia's new system of collective farming. I replied that it would certainly be ill advised to predict with absolute assurance either what collective farming might bring to Russia or individual farming to other countries over a period of decades. But, I added, the judgment on the collective farming system of the millions of peasants who had perished during the famine which was directly associated with collective farming and with the ruthless methods which were employed to drive it through was certainly final and irrevocable.

Halos often are attributable to ignorance; and the halo around Russia is no exception to this rule. I recall how amazed I was a year or two ago when a man who has repeatedly visited Russia and conducted parties of foreigners there expressed bland ignorance of the fact that there were concentration camps in Russia. He had come to Moscow from Berlin and spoke of the hard conditions of the inmates of the Nazi concentration camps. When I remarked that Russians also did not regard such camps as desirable places of residence he asked: "Are there concentration camps in Russia?" When I recovered from my amazement at such a question I tried to assure him that all the inmates of Germany's concentration camps would scarcely muster one shift at some huge Soviet forced-labor enterprise, such as the Baltic-White Sea Canal. Whether I carried conviction or not I do not know; but such ignorance, not in a casual tourist, but in a man who wrote and spoke about Russia and enjoyed some reputation as an authority on the subject, seemed to be inexcusable.

Unfortunately, ignorance of this kind is by no means uncommon, just among people who profess the keenest interest in Russia and who would seem to owe it to themselves to be well informed on the subject. I recently picked up a copy of a well-known magazine which was formerly considered liberal but now repudiates that designation and might be described as generally anti-Capitalist, without adhering definitely to any political camp. In this magazine, along with a highly apologetic, almost eulogistic, article about the recent Russian executions, I found a listing of four reasons why a Fascist régime, as compared with a Socialist or Communist one, should be denounced. These reasons were "a belief in the brotherhood and inherent value of man, a belief in equality, a belief in objective reason and science, a belief in material welfare."

I mentally checked over these unexceptionable beliefs in the light of Russia as I had come to know it. "Brotherhood and inherent values of man" — in a country of mass executions, wholesale employment of forced labor under conditions which would make the worst cases of exploitation in a western country seem mild in comparison, and artificially stimulated class hatred. "Equality" — in a country where today any Communist who put out such a heretical slogan as equality of wages would be certainly expelled from the party and most probably put in prison. "Objective reason and science" — in a country where every printed word is censored, where art, literature, science, politics and economics are in the bonds of cast iron dogma, where anything Dictator Stalin might say, even though it should be the most palpable nonsense, would be treated as unquestioned and unquestionable truth. "Material welfare" — under a régime where, 17 years after the inauguration of the Soviet social and economic system, four fifths of the population, at a moderate estimate, have less to eat, less to wear and poorer housing than the average American or British unemployed.

Woodrow Wilson once referred to Russia as an "acid test" for the sincerity and good will of other countries. In a different sense I think Soviet Russia today might well be considered an "acid test" for liberals and radicals, for their ability to think logically, for the sincerity of their professions of humanitarianism.

The question might arise whether the attitude of a small group of people toward Russia is of any fundamental importance. If a certain type of liberal or radical (needles to say, in this article I am referring not to all liberals or radicals, but only to those who maintain the double standard of morals as regards Russia) gets an emotional stimulus out of believing that the Soviet Union is a kind of Mecca or Utopia, where all the world's problems have been or are being satisfactorily solved, why take it away from him?

It seems to me, however, that there are slight, but definitely harmful consequences of the Mississippi Bubble of infatuation with Russia. In the first place, it diverts the necessary thinking about how to meet America's problems into a wrong channel. If there is one certain thing about America's own future development, it is that the United States, with its pioneer individualist tradition and enormously widely distributed sense for property, is not going the way of Russia, where the course of pre war political, social and economic devel-

Front page of The Christian Science Monitor **Weekly Magazine Section from August 5, 1936.**

opment was about as different from that of America as it could be. Therefore, individuals who are preoccupied with Soviet political and economic formulas are virtually condemned to sterility, so far as exercising any practical influence on the trend of American development is concerned.

Secondly, while there is no "Red menace" in America, while it is fantastically improbable that Comrade Israel Amter or any other obscure local disciple of Moscow will rally the readers of *The New Masses* and hoist the Red Flag over the White House, an indirect menace of a different kind lurks in the present professions of contempt for political democracy, so fashionable in some left wing circles. In politics, as in physics, action produces reaction. Every outburst of left wing extremism simply plays into the hands of those forces, obscure but potentially powerful, which might, in the event of a severe future crisis, attempt to change the traditional American democratic form of government in a fascist direction.

In the light of what happened in Italy and in Germany, where the existence of a fairly strong Communist movement was of inestimable benefit to Mussolini and to Hitler, in rallying the frightened middle classes to the banner of dictatorship, it would seem that any American radical or liberal who deserts the platform of democracy and talks lightly of proletarian dictatorship is assuming a grave responsibility. For, given the American political and social setup, it would seem perfectly obvious that, once democracy were thrown overboard and a struggle of extremes set in, it would be the Fascist, not the Communist extreme that would emerge triumphant.

One may hope that the Mississippi Bubble of following the Russian will-o'-the-wisp will be pricked before it does too much harm. Perhaps Stalin will contribute to this end if he drives forward his present right wing policy with sufficient speed and vigor. Foreign admirers of the Russian Revolution who were willing to stomach any amount of violence when it was directed against individuals and classes which could be represented as "counterrevolutionary" may turn, like the proverbial worm, when opposition Communists are the preferred victims of the Soviet firing squads.

Apart from this consideration, it is to be hoped that one self-evident truth will finally make its way into the consciousness of those radicals and liberals who are not dogmatic Communists. This is that, just so far as they betray liberty in Russia by refusing to protest against Soviet acts of arbitrariness and violence, or even condoning or applauding them, they are betraying liberty all over the world and making more difficult the solution of present-day economic and social difficulties along lines which humane and rational people would regard as desirable.

Collectivism: A False Utopia? [8/5/36]

In what now seem to be the safe and tranquil days before the war the idea of a collectivist society was a popular debating theme between utopians and antiutopians. The former painted alluring pictures of a Socialist society where inequalities of wealth would be eliminated and all would work for the common good. The latter predicted that Socialism would be followed by a reign of idleness which, in turn, would be succeeded by a rule of despotism. Neither side in these arguments had any blueprints of actual experience to go by. The individualist method was taken for granted in the practical business of daily life.

Now the collectivist state is no longer a fancy. It is very much with us. The war that was to make the world safe for democracy has actually been the forerunner of the spread of an utterly different theory and practice of government. The three major postwar revolutions, which have led to the establishment of Sovietism in Russia, Fascism in Italy and National Socialism in Germany have all been definitely and wholeheartedly antidemocratic and anti-individualist. The collectivist utopia has come down to earth and assumed flesh-and-blood form.

Such a term as the collectivist state obviously calls for definition. And one may hope to build up such a definition by surveying the very large common denominator of identical administrative practice which can be found in the Soviet Union, Germany and Italy today.

First of all, the individual, in the name of the supposed higher good of the cause which the ruling régime represents, is required to forgo many of the rights which are taken for granted in democratic theory, such as freedom of speech, press, assembly and independent political organization. Power is monopolized by a single party, which is itself subordinated to a leader whose decisions are accepted as infallible. All checks, balances and safeguards for the individual are swept away. The collectivist state is omnipotent. It can enact and repeal laws of any description between breakfast and dinner. It can imprison, exile, execute any of its citizens without any "nonsense" of trial by a jury of one's peers.

The collectivist state undertakes to solve the problem of the conflict of interest between labor and capital (whether private capital or state capital) by setting itself up as a court of last resort in determining wages, hours and working conditions. In democratic countries wage earners' interests, insofar as they are organized, are represented by trade unions headed by officials who are elected by the rank-and-file membership. Under collectivism the state relieves the workers of the burden of defending their own interests.

The *Arbeitsfront* in Germany, the labor corporation in Italy, the trade unions in Russia are all controlled and dominated by representatives of the state and of the ruling party. No doubt such organizations transmit and reflect the demands of the workers when state exigencies permit. But the qualification is very important. When "state exigencies" call for higher living costs and lower real wages in Germany, for more intensive work in Russia, the Nazi or Communist labor organization not only fails to encourage strikes or other expressions of labor discontent, but plays the role of a policeman and a strikebreaker in checking any such manifestations.

The psychological basis of the collectivist state is an intensive application of the government monopoly of propaganda. At the present time the reaction of most Americans toward the "New Deal" seems to be hazy and spotty, full of "ifs," "buts" and reservations. But imagine what would happen if either Mr. Roosevelt or Mr. Hoover, backed by a dictatorial party, gained complete control of the press, the radio, the lecture platform, the schools and universities, all agencies of entertainment and instruction. Certainly far more people, their "sales resistance" crumbling before this massed onslaught of governmental advertising, would be brought to believe that the New Deal was either the best or the worst policy ever adopted in American history.

Another feature of the collectivist state is far-reaching interference in what would formerly have been regarded as the sphere of private initiative. Here, of course, the Soviet Union has gone much farther than Germany or Italy. It has wiped out even the smallest "Capitalists," such as the peasant with 20 acres and a cow, or the keeper of the dingy village teahouse. It has substituted a system under which the state, in one form or another, is not only the banker, manufacturer and common carrier, but also the baker, the butcher and the candlestick maker.

But Germany and Italy have gone a considerable distance along the same road to regimenting economic life, even in small details. An Italian businessman under the spreading shadow of Mussolini's totalitarian state has little more freedom in managing his own business than the state director of one of the large Soviet industrial trusts. He is heavily taxed; he is limited and directed as to what and how much he may produce and where he is to sell his products. This regimentation increased after the outbreak of war in Ethiopia.

The same tendency is visible in Germany, where foreign trade is as closely controlled by the Government as it is in Russia. When I was in Germany two years ago I wanted to sell a piece of jewelry, a small personal possession. I soon gave up the idea when I found that this apparently innocent transaction was probably illegal and meant, in any case, going through an incredible amount of bureaucratic red tape. I was vividly reminded of Russia, where the sale of one's typewriter was in a category with bootlegging operations in pre-repeal days.

So the contours of the collectivist state are made clear by the many common characteristics of the Soviet Union, Germany and Italy. It substitutes the single will of the dictator, supported by a strongly organized and disciplined party, for the interplay of contending interests that make themselves felt under a democratic system. Metaphorically and literally, it lines up and drills the population under its rule and disciplines those who are out of step. It sweeps away guarantees of personal liberty.

Now the collectivist state, whether of the Fascist or Communist model, is a powerful organization. Experience has shown that it can survive immense hardships without cracking. It is a far more active and formidable challenge and alternative to democracy than the old-fashioned type of despotism that maintained itself by grace of tradition, a well-paid army and numerous police. The number of individuals who feel a vested interest in the preservation of the existing régimes in the Soviet Union, Italy and Germany is considerable. There is the host of newly appointed party and state officials. There is the large part of the youth that naturally falls under the influence of the propaganda slogans of the ruling group when no adverse criticism is tolerated.

The fact that Communist and Fascist Party membership runs through all classes of the population is a tremendous advantage in the matter of keeping in touch with popular sentiment and spying out malcontents. There is little chance for an underground opposition movement to go far without detection.

Predictions of the fall of Bolshevism have been falsified by the event. And, barring the unpredictable results of unsuccessful war, the same fate will probably befall prophecies of the overthrow of National Socialism in Germany and Fascism in Italy.

The discrepancy between the ideals and the achievements of the Russian and German Revolutions has brought disillusionment to groups of individuals who were originally enlisted under the red flag and the *Hakenkreuz*. But neither of these facts is of great significance in assaying the future prospects of the existing régimes. In the modern collectivist state the cry of disillusionment is a very still small voice indeed. It is certain to be quickly and forcibly hushed.

So there is no reason to doubt the stability of the governments which base themselves on the method of propaganda and dictatorship. Moreover, such governments can at times achieve a greater concentration of national effort than is always attainable under a democracy. Russia's rapid industrialization and Germany's rearmament are cases in point. A dictator who can dispose at will of the lives and property of his subjects can sometimes achieve more spectacular immediate results than a democratic leader who must persuade before he can command. Some obvious evils of American democracy, such as gangsterism, could undoubtedly be got rid of more expeditiously by substituting *habeas cadaver* for *habeas corpus* as a rule of judicial procedure.

Yet one cannot dig far below the surface of any of the modern dictatorships without realizing that there is more mythology than reality in the idea that the collectivist state is a shortcut to Utopia. A highly significant fact in this connection is the merciless intolerance of adverse criticism that is characteristic of major dictatorships.

If the high-flown claims of national achievement and national regeneration so constantly and stridently voiced by Stalin, Hitler, Mussolini and their lieutenants and sub-lieutenants were justified, one might imagine that the dictators would positively welcome public criticism, merely for the pleasure of bowling it over by exposing its weaknesses. One could fancy the Soviet Government promoting coast-to-coast speaking tours by "counter revolutionaries" of as varied views as Grand Duke Cyril and Leon Trotsky, Mussolini inviting Professor Salvemini to debate economic issue with Fascist spokesmen, Hitler issuing similar invitations to German émigré Social Democrats and Communists. Alas, nothing of the kind is within the realm of remote possibility. And the extraordinary nervous care which every dictator takes to prevent any breath of criticism from reaching his subjects is strong ground for presumption that his achievements are not so persuasive.

The effect of the muzzle which every dictatorship clamps on its people was vividly brought home to me

Woman working on a collective farm, August 1936. Next page, clockwise from top left: Present day tractors harvesting a collective farm. Present day collective farm worker. Tractor drivers taking a break in a field camp, 1938.

when I left the Soviet Union for a trip in America in the winter of 1932-1933, returning to Moscow in the spring of 1933. Making the most liberal allowance for the historically higher American standard of living, there seemed to me not the slightest room for doubt that Russia at that time, relatively as well as absolutely, was in a vastly worse plight than the United States.

The American farm crisis was at its height. But farmers in Iowa and North Dakota were not dying in immense numbers of sheer starvation, like peasants in Ukraina and the north Caucasus. Unemployment in the United States had reached formidable and unprecedented figures. But when I read off to Russian friends a list of the foodstuffs that were given to the unemployed in Milwaukee as part of their relief they exclaimed in incredulity that this sounded like the ration of a highly placed Soviet official, not of a worker.

Yet I found many people in America convinced that the Soviet Union was forging ahead triumphantly, while America was sinking into some unpredictable catastrophe. The main reason for what seemed to me a complete lack of proportion in comparing the state of the two countries was that America's troubles stared from every newspaper and magazine headline, while Russia's were carefully concealed by an all-embracing censorship. There was plenty of publicity for the debt-ridden farmers of the Middle West, none for the starving peasants of southern and southeastern Russia. The sufferings of the unemployed in America were mirrored in scores of books and hundreds of articles. One could search the files of the Soviet press in vain for even one description of the sufferings of Russia's forcibly employed exiles in timber camps and new construction enterprises, living in foul barracks and dugouts under arctic conditions, receiving as "pay" barely enough food to make it physically possible for them to perform their allotted tasks.

Communist Chiefs at Moscow Renew Firm Grip on Military   [6/12/37]

Soviet Russia's Communist rulers are taking no risks that their powerful army and navy shall escape the firm control of the Communist Party's "general staff." After a lapse of 12 years, they have revived the rank of "war commissars," political officers attached to and ranking equally with every army and fleet commander. At the same time, they have instituted military councils, composed of both military and political officers, to convert Russia into "one vast army."

The device of war commissars was first conceived by Bolsheviks soon after they seized power; loyal Communists were attached to military officers to make sure they did not betray Bolshevik leadership. In 1925, war commissars were abolished with the explanation that the commanding staff had been sufficiently reorganized so that its members could be trusted.

Now the war commissars are restored. This action might be interpreted as an implication that the loyalty of military commanders is again suspected, and that political officers are needed to watch them. But if disloyalty is suspected now, suspicion is directed, not so much against former Czarist officers as against some Communists who do not fully agree with the Party leadership.

The Bolshevik system demands a degree of conformity unmatched in most countries. The recent conspiracy trials showed that many prominent Communists were not content to conform; denied the possibility of open opposition, they had resorted to secret opposition. The Communist "general staff" broke up incipient opposition groups by imprisoning or exiling thousands of those suspected of hostility to party leaders.

According to the published evidence, opposition leaders had entrenched themselves in state industry, agriculture and social organizations. It was logical to suspect they might also have penetrated military units; in fact, a few army officers were involved in alleged anti-Government conspiracies. The Communist "general staff" first reorganized the political police, one of the most powerful armed groups. Their commander, Henry Yagoda, was first removed to a lesser post, and then arrested and imprisoned.

The present action extends reorganization to the army and navy. The restoration of war commissars limits the power of military commanders over their men. The institution of military councils divides authority in military matters between military and political officers, with the latter selected by the Kremlin.

The new military councils, established in every military district and unit, are composed of three persons: the military commander and two other persons; how the latter will be appointed is not stated, but presumably they will be the direct agents of the Communist Political Bureau or "general staff." If the system is the same as that applied in 1919-1925, political officers will be more powerful than military commanders. They must countersign every military order.

Foreign military experts argued that this system weakened military discipline; division of authority, they believed, prevented the swift decisions necessary in times of emergency or war. But the Bolsheviks are firm believers in the power of political agitation, which has been proved to their satisfaction not only in Russia's civil wars, but in Communist wars in China and Germany and the civil war in Spain.

The present reorganization, in addition to strengthening the Communist leadership's hold on Soviet fighting forces, carries still further Bolshevik plans for militarizing the entire Soviet population. In this task, political officers share equally with military officers. In former wars, the Bolsheviks believe, the role of political agitation has not been sufficiently understood or appreciated.

The new military councils are entrusted not only with increasing the efficiency and strengthening the fighting morale of the army and navy, but also with organizing a complete "defense of the rear." New official regulations turn over to the council's direction of military training in Soviet schools, factories and collective farms. The councils are given authority over "defense and non-defense" construction in military districts, and "participation in civilian military organizations and defense of the rear." In a word, they are empowered and instructed to convert Soviet peoples into "one vast army," ready for mobilization in case of war.

Court Condemns Red Army Chiefs in One-Day Trial [6/12/37]

Eight of the Soviet Union's highest military leaders were sentenced to execution today for treasonable activity against the Red Army they headed.

No appeal remained from the sentences handed down by the military tribunal of the Supreme Court which stigmatized the army chiefs as traitors in the spy service of a foreign power.

The nation's highest tribunal announced the verdict at 2 A.M. (6 P.M. EST Friday), condemning Marshal Mikhail N. Tukhachevsky and seven generals, including important figures in the Soviet military hierarchy, to execution "immediately." Soviet custom dictates that such sentences must be carried out within twenty four hours.

The swift-moving military trial was deemed by foreign observers as probably the most important of the Soviet Union's treason trials, since it disclosed disaffection in the army's topmost ranks.

A communiqué said: "The Court has established that the accused were in the service of the military

Three judges hear evidence in the People's Court, 1935. Banner on the wall displays a statement from Stalin that the dictatorship is completely ready to deal with thievish activities.

service of a foreign state carrying on an unfriendly policy toward the USSR; that they have systematically supplied military circles of the country with spy information; carried on wrecking action in order to break the power of the Workers' and Peasants' Red Army, and in case of a military attack on the USSR, to prepare for the defeat of the USSR; that they aimed to aid the disorganization of the USSR and the restoration of landlords and capitalists in the USSR."

It was generally understood the unnamed foreign power was either Germany or Japan. Previous trials have accused the defendants of conspiring to deliver Soviet Russia into the hands of both those neighboring powers.

The court announced that all eight men confessed their guilt.

The Soviet press was filled with resolutions passed at mass meetings of workers calling for complete destruction of all oppositionists such as Tukhachevsky and the other army leaders condemned with him.

Details of the execution of the sentences will probably not be made known for the place, time and manner usually are kept secret.

News of the sentences themselves was published inconspicuously on the second pages of Moscow newspapers under the headline "The Supreme Court of the USSR."

In addition to Tukhachevsky, the officers convicted are:

Gen. Kazimirovitch V. Putna, former military attaché in London; Gen. A.Z. Kork, former commandant of the Frunze Military Academy, the Soviet West Point; Gen. I.E. Yakir, commander of the Leningrad district garrison; Gen. I.P. Uborevitch, commander of the Red Army in White Russia; Gen. Robert P. Fideman, former head of the training division for army reservists and civilians in aviation and gas defense; Gen. B.M. Feldman, chief of the personnel section of the general staff; Gen. V.M. Pranakoff.

Moscow Trial Gets Surprise; Defendant Shouts Innocence [3/2/38]

The latest in Moscow's series of "demonstration trials," which opened today, is certainly the most spectacular, both in the prominence of its defendants and in the nature of its accusations. No previous charges have been so implausible and fantastic, and no previous defendants have been so eminent as the 21 now charged with treason. Nor has any previous trial embraced such a sudden surprise as the fact that today one of the important defendants repudiated his alleged confession and claimed his innocence.

Among the accused are several close associates of Lenin who were far more powerful than Joseph Stalin in the conduct of the Soviet Government for years after the Revolution.

Alexis I. Rykoff was a former Premier; Genrikh G. Yagoda, a former Chief of the Political Police; Nicholas Bukharin was a foremost philosopher of the ruling Communist Party. The other defendants were Premiers in minority Republics until a few months ago, ruling over territories larger than most European countries.

Every Soviet mass trial has had its "theme" or number of themes. The 1936 trial emphasized the moral bankruptcy of the opposition to Stalin and their lack of any alternative program. The 1937 trial emphasized sabotage in industry. The 1938 trial apparently is intended to emphasize that the opposition was driven to madness by failure of their previous attempts to disturb Stalin's Government and became inhuman in their conduct.

Outwardly the Soviet trials are conducted with the utmost dignity. Photographers are not admitted to the small hall in Moscow's former Nobles Club where these trials are held. The audience is strictly limited and never permitted to make the least demonstration.

Judges and prosecutors are scrupulously polite to prisoners who are permitted to speak at length on their own behalf during and after testimony. It is necessary to understand, however, that hundreds of arrested persons are never tried publicly in Russia. Without exception in the past only those who confessed in advance to every charge against them have received public trials. It is therefore assumed that prisoners in public trials will invariably confess finally and any failure to confess would indicate that something had gone wrong. The chance that something might go wrong always lends a dramatic suspense to these trials.

The fact that the trial is held publicly is interpreted as evidence that the Soviet authorities are indifferent to foreign opinion and concerned primarily with the internal crisis. Moscow leaders certainly know that each such trial weakens their prestige and influence abroad and sinks even lower the strength of international Communism. But these trials are planned primarily for young children who apparently believe all the confessions, however fantastic. If they accomplish this result any loss of prestige abroad is considered comparatively unimportant.

Moscow Plot Trial Shakes European Balance of Power [3/14/38]

By Demaree Bess

Russia's first Communist conspiracy trial — which ended as expected with the sentences of execution for 18 chief defendants — assumes particular significance in view of this week's events in Europe.

The anti-Stalin conspiracy revealed in these trials has so weakened Russia that Europe's balance of power was completely upset. Germany, whose knowledge of Russian events is unparalleled, can plan its moves in Central and Eastern Europe with confidence that the Russians are in no position to interfere, probably for several years. France, having mistakenly based its plans upon the Russian alliance finds itself checkmated through Russia's internal weakness.

This third trial strengthens the arguments of those who believe that widespread Communist conspiracy existed in Russia. Observers must choose between this conclusion and the theory that Stalin somehow compelled his revolutionary associates falsely to confess in open court crimes which meant their execution.

This latter theory proves more acceptable to European Socialists because they cannot face the fact that a Socialist régime would breed such conspiracies. However, impartial observers realize that "proletarian dictatorships," like any other, breed conspiracies.

Despite the obviously impossible details in the testimony of the latest trials, it must be remembered that some false details in testimony or confessions do not invalidate the whole as in western courts of law. The fundamental testimony of the chief defendants in this trial sounded more convincing than in any previous trials. The testimony implicated additional prominent Communists, making additional open trials likely.

Meanwhile, hundreds are imprisoned awaiting disposal, including the former President of the Russian Federated Republic, and the former Chairman of the State Planning Commission. So many prominent Communists are involved that Stalin is still uncertain which of his remaining associates he can trust.

Execution for 18 Reds [3/14/38]

Eighteen of 21 defendants were sentenced to execution yesterday in Moscow's greatest treason trial.

Those who were spared, were: Christian Rakovsky, former Ambassador to France who was sentenced to 20 years imprisonment; S.A. Bessonoff, former member

Front page of The Christian Science Monitor **Weekly Magazine Section from February 17, 1937.**

of the Soviet trade delegation to Berlin, 15 years; and D.D. Pletnyeff, heart specialist, 25 years.

Those to be executed are former high-ranking Bolshevists accused of undertaking treason and murder at the behest of foreign powers.

Appeals for clemency, usually made immediately, heretofore have been rejected immediately in cases of such prominence as this, with a former Premier and five former Commissars or Cabinet members among the condemned. Three days will be given them for the judges to weigh their appeals and two more days must elapse before they are placed before the firing squad.

Among those sentenced to execution was Nicholas Bukharin, chronicler of the Red Revolution who electrified the last session of the long trial with an unexpected defense.

Among the other one-time high ranking Soviet leaders to be shot are Henry 0. Yagoda, former Chief of the Secret Police; Alexis I. Rykoff, Premier of the Soviet Union for 10 years who succeeded Lenin; N.N. Krestinsky, former First Assistant Foreign Commissar; and A.P. Rosenholtz, one-time Commissar of Foreign Trade.

All the defendants pleaded guilty to charges which included plotting to dismember the Soviet Union, overthrow the régime, restore Capitalism and murder Russian leaders.

Leon Trotsky, former Bolshevik leader now living in exile in Mexico, was named as one of the inspirers of the Anti-Soviet plotting.

The trial of the fallen leaders, by a military tribunal, marked the fourth Moscow trial staged before a worldwide audience. Previous trials, whose volumes of sensational testimony concerning plots against the Soviet Union, resulted in the execution of seven former high ranking Soviet leaders.

Power Balance Shaken by Reich-Soviet Move [8/22/39]

by William Henry Chamberlin

Important shifts in the European balance of power may follow the prospective conclusion of the Soviet-German nonaggression pact just at the moment when international tension over Danzig is reaching a high point.

Hitherto it was widely assumed in France and England that even if Russia took no active part in hostilities, its reserves of military supplies and raw materials would be at the disposal of the anti-German powers and would play a considerable part in strengthening the defenses of Poland and Rumania.

While it would be premature to be too positive in deductions until the pact is signed and its exact terms known, it may be that even this hope of limited Russian aid must now be revised.

Delays in the Anglo-Russian negotiations at Moscow are now seen in the new light of a Soviet effort to hold up to Germany a prospective alliance with France and England, but simultaneously to carry on secret negotiations with Reichsführer Hitler to ensure Soviet isolation from any prospective war.

The aims of Stalin's policy during the last month have been to ensure Soviet abstention from any European war, partly because of the purges which he has carried out in the army to make any mobilization dangerous for his personal dictatorship and partly because he wishes to have his hands free in the Far East.

Some observers believe a further Soviet objective has even been to promote an outbreak of war in Europe from which the Soviet Union could remain aloof. Such a war could be counted on to exhaust Germany's military strength. Reckoning that the forces of France, England, Poland, and the smaller allies would approximately equal those of Germany, Italy, and their satellites, a European war might be expected to be extremely long and to end in some form of a general social and economic breakdown.

Whether Mr. Stalin still thinks in terms of a world revolution or is only concerned with increasing Russia's national strength, those who feel he favors such a war believe its resultant breakdown could only be welcome to him.

Great Britain's guarantee to Poland and Rumania last spring vastly eased Mr. Stalin's position because his own western frontiers were automatically covered by French and British assurances of aid to Poland and Rumania.

In light of the present agreement with Germany, all the protracted talks, first political and then military, with the British and French representatives at Moscow, seem little more than an elaborate camouflage designed to strengthen British and French opposition to Germany in Eastern Europe by giving an illusion that Russia would co-operate with the western powers. German intransigence in face of what seemed formidable hostility may also be explained by the secret negotiations which preceded announcement of the nonagression pact. Its conclusion will certainly strengthen the hands of the Axis powers, whether for conference or for war.

3¢ Greater Boston Newsstands

THE CHRISTIAN SCIENCE MONITOR

AN INTERNATIONAL DAILY NEWSPAPER

3¢ Greater Boston Newsstands

BOSTON, MONDAY, SEPTEMBER 18, 1939—VOL. XXXI, NO. 249

**ATLANTIC EDITION | THREE CENTS Greater Boston Newsstands | FIVE CENTS Elsewhere

Nations Reach Accord In Amoy Controversy; Ship Bonus Trial Opens

The World's Day—At a Glance

Sept. 18, 1939

Japanese Agree to Amoy Settlement

AMOY, China (AP)—Settlement by compromise of the controversy over the Government of Amoy's International Settlement was announced today by Japanese authorities.

British, French, and United States forces were landed after Japanese blue jackets occupied the settlement which is ruled by the Kulangsu Municipal Council. French and British forces since have been withdrawn.

The announcement said the compromise provided for the Kulangsu Council to control anti-Japanese agitation, to co-operate with Japanese officials in maintaining law and order, and appoint one Japanese police inspector, now, and 10 Formosan police constables, subject to next year's meeting of taxpayers.

Effect on China of Tokyo-Soviet pact: Page 5.

Seamen Go on Trial in War Bonus Strike

NEW YORK (AP)—Sixty-one seamen, charged with disobeying sailing orders in a strike for a war bonus, went on trial today as seven United States vessels, scheduled to remove war-stranded Americans from Europe, remained tied up.

The trial by the Bureau of Marine Inspection and Navigation opened in confusion as Joseph Curran, President of the National Maritime Union, demanded that "all 500 seamen on the seven ships tied up in New York" be summoned for trial simultaneously.

Capt. Karl Nielsen, Chairman of the Trial Board, ruled that 61, all members of the crew of the United States liner American Trader, should be tried jointly. [Details: Page 17.]

War Stocks Slump in Selling Wave

NEW YORK (AP)—War stocks suffered a hard fall in Wall Street today, dropping for losses up to about $6 a share. United States Steel, Bethlehem, Anaconda Copper, Douglas Aircraft, Westinghouse Electric, and Union Carbide were down $2 to about $6 a share on the opening selling wave. Later the market stiffened, recapturing part of the initial losses.

Brokers attributed the decline to vulnerable technical position of the market after its almost straight-up war advance and week-end news from Europe, including the Russian move into Poland and the possibility that the Polish collapse might be followed by peace overtures from a totalitarian combination.

Wartime Rules Limit Trans-Atlantic Flying

NEW YORK (AP)—Pan American Airways today made public regulations which have been put into effect on its trans-Atlantic air passenger service because of the European war. Commercial cargo is restricted to air mail, and inauguration of air express service to and from Europe will be postponed indefinitely.

To avoid possibility of contraband being carried as personal effects, baggage of all passengers is subject to inspection at terminals—Baltimore, Md.; Port Washington, N. Y; Foynes, Ireland; Horta, Azores, and Lisbon, Portugal.

U. S. Envoy to Poland Ordered to France

WASHINGTON (AP)—Cordell Hull, Secretary of State, said today Anthony J. Drexel Biddle, American Ambassador to Poland, would make his headquarters in France for the time being. Mr. Hull said no decision had been reached as to whether the American Embassy to Poland would continue to function from France.

Japanese Good-Will Plane Reaches Miami

MIAMI, Fla. (AP)—The Japanese round-the-world good-will plane Nippon arrived here today from Washington. The twin-motored monoplane and its party of seven were welcomed by City and aviation officials.

The Nippon is scheduled to leave Sept. 19 for South America, later flying across the South Atlantic to Africa, thence back to Japan.

Air Vacation Travel Soaring in Volume

By a Staff Correspondent of The Christian Science Monitor

SAN FRANCISCO—Vacation travel by air is still "going up" in public esteem.

Continued popularity of vacation air travel during August aided in establishment of the sixth consecutive month of increased business for Transcontinental and Western Air, Inc., according to V. P. Conroy, Vice-President in charge of traffic and sales.

Mr. Conroy said there had been a gain of 58.1 per cent in passenger miles flown as compared with August, 1938, and that the passenger miles flown during August bettered those flown during July of this year by 3.07 per cent. This was a total of 10,231,358 revenue passenger miles.

"American tourists have established new recordings in airline patronage throughout the summer," said Mr. Conroy. "Following high August increases, the first day of September was the greatest single day for traffic in the 10-year history of TWA. On that day, preceeding Labor Day, a total of 520,000 seat miles was flown. The previous record was June 30 when 501,000 seat miles were flown."

N. E. Industries Prepare for Rush As Orders Pour In

With orders for 200 representative firms running 25 per cent ahead of a year ago, the story of New England's entry into the fall buying and producing season could today be written in bold strokes. Production is up, employment is up, many of the depressive factors that fettered New England industry all during the lean years have been corrected.

Most important of all, this improvement appears to result from domestic conditions with the war playing small part. As William M. Rand, leading manufacturer and president of the Associated Industries of Massachusetts, put it today: "Because of the instability of the European situation and the fog that surrounds it, many of our manufacturing concerns who have made extensive plans are waiting until they can see more clearly what is going to happen before they become committed to important changes."

Besides improvements noted in recent weeks in New England's historic cotton, woolen and shoe industries, the region, according to a broad range of reports, is enjoying general prosperity in most of its widely diversified products.

In addition to the index of or-

(Continued on Page 10, Column 7)

President Asks Unified Stand On Neutrality

Calls Landon and Knox, top G. O. P. leaders, to White House parley on policy.

By Erwin D. Canham

Staff Correspondent of The Christian Science Monitor

WASHINGTON, Sept. 18—President Roosevelt sought today to remove the partisan cleavage in the arms embargo struggle, which had been produced by a barrage of Republican isolationist statements, by inviting Alf M. Landon and Frank Knox, Republican Presidential and Vice-Presidential candidates in 1936, to the White House conference of leaders which will precede the extra session.

Both leaders were invited in telephonic calls by the President himself, and both accepted. Also present, in addition to the list announced a week ago, will be Representative Carl Mapes, (R) of Michigan, a close friend of isolationist Senator Arthur H. Vandenberg, (R) of Michigan. Representative Mapes is reported to be leaning now toward arms embargo repeal.

Sympathetic to Policy

Both former Governor Landon and Colonel Knox have been strongly sympathetic to President Roosevelt's foreign policy. The latter's Chicago Daily News has vigorously advocated repeal of the arms embargo, as well as of other neutrality legislation. Former Governor Landon, as far as can be determined, has made no public statement on the arms embargo, but he has firmly declared that politics should "stop at the water's edge." On several occasions, his declarations of support have helped the Administration in difficult foreign policy moments.

No single declared isolationist will be present at the important White House meeting, called for 3 p. m., on Sept. 20. The full roster includes the President, the Vice-President, the Secretary of State, Speaker William B. Bankhead, Senate Majority Leader Alben W. Barkley and his assistant, Senator Sherman Minton, Minority Leader Charles L. McNary and his assistant, Senator Warren R. Austin, Senators Key Pittman and James F. Byrnes, House Majority Leader Sam Rayburn, and Minority Leader Joseph W. Martin, Jr., Representative Sol Bloom, Chairman of the House Foreign Affairs Committee, and the three announced today.

The President is zealously seek-

(Continued on Page 17, Column 1)

Soviet Aids in Crushing Poles; Allies Hold Back War on Reds; Nazi Sub Sinks Plane Carrier

Republic apparently has ceased to exist as Government flees to Rumania.

By a Staff Correspondent of The Christian Science Monitor

LONDON, Sept. 18—After 18 days of struggle, the 21-year-old Polish Republic appears to have ceased to exist.

Crushed between the great mechanized armies of Germany and Soviet Russia, Poland has lost its President and most of its Government who have fled into Rumania. President Moscicki, Foreign Minister Joseph Beck and a Government party of 56 arrived last night at Cernauti, a Rumanian frontier town. About the same time the British and French diplomatic missions to Poland, including the British Ambassador, Sir Howard Kennard, arrived in Rumania, with diplomats of 35 other countries, being requested to go either to Bucharest or return home.

Poland's national archives and all its available gold had already been moved into Rumania. Some 135 Polish war planes landed at Cernauti and large numbers of infantry troops.

Government officials still remaining in Poland ordered the Polish Ambassador, Waclaw Grzybowski, to leave Moscow in protest against the Soviet march into Polish territory.

Fighting Continues

Divisions were reported still holding out east of Kutno and east of Lwow, but trapped between the Germans relentlessly driving eastward and the Russian forces moving en masse across the frontier at eight or ten points, to a depth of nearly 50 miles in two days, the defenders were carrying on a desperate resistance with nothing to defend save the soil they stood on and their indomitable national pride.

The amazing rapidity of events has overwhelmed the British and French Governments with new problems and immediate repercussions were impossible to obtain. There is no assurance even as to how long the position of

(Continued on Page 4, Column 2)

By a Staff Artist

Ignacy Moscicki
President of Poland

London attempts to discount importance of Stalin attack on eastern front—Warsaw protests to Britain and France on new aggression—Moscow's action seen as possible blow to Berlin.

By a Staff Correspondent of The Christian Science Monitor

LONDON, Sept. 18—The Soviet occupation of the strip of Eastern Poland has for some time been regarded by informed circles here as a probable step if the Polish armies were defeated. Consequently it is not accurate to assume at once that the Soviet invasion of Poland irrevocably throws the Russians into common cause with Germany.

In particular, it is considered improbable at present that the Soviet action will lead to an Anglo-French declaration of war on Russia.

Such a step, it is felt, would be merely to play into Germany's hands.

The Russians, in the note to the Poles and to Britain, declare they do not mean to depart from the position of neutrality they have maintained since the outbreak of the war.

However, the Polish Embassy has advised Britain that the entry of Soviet troops constitutes an "act of direct aggression." This notification is similar to that given by the Poles after Germany invaded Poland Sept. 1. It was on this notification that Great Britain began the steps which brought her into the war against Germany Sept. 3.

The British position was apparently awaiting further clarification of the exact situation. The British Government was understood to have requested its Ambassador to Moscow, Sir William Seeds, for additional explanation of the Soviet position.

Britain to Push Drive

It can also be stated definitely that there appears to be not the slightest weakening by Britain and France in their determination to prosecute the war to a victorious conclusion.

While the better informed section of British opinion had already braced itself for the jolt of a Soviet invasion of Poland, the news of the Russian attack proved a sharp and unexpected shock to the vast majority of the public, which certainly had not been given any reason to expect such an immediate development in the light of the almost complete absence of information about Soviet activities from the radio news bulletins.

The newspapers also had been discouraged by the Ministry of Information from playing up the news that the Russian shadow was looming over the retreating Poles.

Issue Is Defined

Taking a considered view, public opinion seems agreed on the "perfidy" of the Soviet action, but it is also convinced that although the path of the Allies looks immeasurably harder and twists and turns more unpredictable, the aim for which they are waging the war becomes correspondingly clearer. Democracy is now, in effect, fighting both the left and the right wings of the dictatorial menace, and therefore all sections of opinion have been closer united in the determination to bring the battle for freedom to a successful conclusion.

As viewed by competent authorities here, the collapse of Polish resistance meant that sooner or later the advancing German forces must meet the Russians and it is

(Continued on Page 4, Column 4)

Attack by Russia On Poles Arouses Paris Indignation

By William Henry Chamberlin

Staff Correspondent of The Christian Science Monitor

PARIS, Sept. 18—French opinion was thunderstruck by the news of the Soviet invasion of Poland. Russia's action unquestionably is the most important event since the beginning of the war, especially if it is considered in connection with the Soviet-Japanese rapprochement which immediately preceded it and which is evidently calculated to give the Soviet Union a free hand in Europe.

There is a unanimous outburst of indignation over what is considered the most treacherous and unprovoked Soviet aggression, with its violation of two existing treaties of nonaggression with Poland.

The newspaper headlines, from the conservative Figaro, which characterizes the Soviet invasion as a "dagger thrust in the back" to the socialist Le Populaire which calls it an "atrocious event," reflect this general indignation.

Blum Issues Appeal

The Socialist leader, Léon Blum, publishes an appeal to French Communist leaders to break with Moscow and "recognize that they have no duty or discipline except the common duty and discipline of French citizens."

What lends a peculiar quality to the perfidy of the Soviet action, according to French opinion, is that it occurred while the Poles were still gallantly fighting against overwhelming material odds. Neither Warsaw nor Lwow have yet been taken, despite the terrific German air bombing and frequent raids by motorized units on the Polish rear flanks. It is still premature to assess with certainty the full consequences of this Soviet intervention in the European war, and the French official attitude, which doubtless is closely co-ordinated with the British, is one of watchful waiting.

Guarantees in Poland

While theoretically the British and French guarantees to Poland would operate against Soviet as well as German aggression, it is most improbable, considering the extreme difficulties of any effective action in Eastern Europe against the combined German and Russian forces, that the Western Powers will take any initiative in attacking the Soviet Union.

Two facts on which French com-

(Continued on Page 4, Column 7)

Torpedoed British Carrier Had Reduced Load of Planes

LONDON, Sept. 18 (AP)—The British Admiralty announced officially today the loss of the aircraft carrier Courageous "by enemy submarine action"—the first warship casualty of the war reported by Britain.

An undetermined number of seamen and fliers aboard the 22,500-ton warship were saved.

The Ministry of Information in an authorized statement said the full complement of the Courageous, plus the personnel of the fleet air arm, was "about 1,200 officers and men. When sunk she had a reduced complement of aircraft and therefore presumably a somewhat smaller crew."

The Admiralty said the usual aircraft complement of 48 planes had been reduced since August.

The brief official announcement in reporting this blow to the fleet said the destroyers "heavily attacked" the submarine which torpedoed the Courageous and were believed to have sunk it in turn.

There was no indication of where the Courageous was sunk, but presumably it was attacked in sea lanes close to home waters either in the Atlantic or North Sea.

"Since the opening of hostilities it had been performing very good service in protecting ships of the mercantile marine against U-boat attacks," the Admiralty said.

Presumably this meant the Courageous had been a major factor both in convoying merchant ships and in launching aircraft to attack submarines from the air.

"Jane's Fighting Ships," authoritative work on world fleets, described the Courageous as a converted cruiser of 22,500 tons (26,500 tons full load). It originally was intended for Baltic service.

First built in February, 1916, Jane's figures showed it to be the oldest, but one of the largest of the six British warcraft used as aircraft carriers.

Jane's gave the Courageous' thickest armor plate as three inches on its sides and amidships.

It carried 16 4.7-inch guns, 4 three-pounders, and 17 smaller pieces.

British use convoys with merchant shipping: Page 17.

British Pamphlets Found on Germans

PARIS (AP)—Parisians were informed Sept. 18 that the first German soldiers captured in French action on the western front were carrying pamphlets strewn over Germany by British planes.

LONDON (AP)—The British Information Ministry has disclosed that Royal Air Force planes have dropped three different sets of leaflets over Germany.

The third set, as released by the Ministry, read:

"Germans . . . we hate war as much as we know you do but remember Britain never gives way. . . . We shall never give up."

The message, like the other, reiterated "despite the efforts of all men of good will to avert the catastrophe, the Nazi Government has plunged the world into war."

Eighteenth Day of the War:

By a Staff Correspondent of The Christian Science Monitor

Russia invaded Poland over the week end—the most surprising development since the outbreak of war Sept. 1. The Soviets declared they were "protecting" some 11,000,000 White Russians and Ukrainians in Poland.

London was inclined to give a measure of credence to the interpretation that Russia was protecting its part of a possible partition of Poland. Paris appeared the more surprised of the Allied capitals.

The question of an Allied declaration of war against Soviet Russia hung in the balance as Poland called the invasion an "act of direct aggression."

On the Polish-Russian front events moved with devastating rapidity. At 6 a. m. yesterday, the Soviet Government told Berlin it had decided to move into Poland. By night the Polish President, Foreign Minister, and other Government officials, allegedly also Marshal Smigly-Ridz, and large numbers of Polish troops had taken refuge in Rumania at Cernauti. The Russians had advanced on a 500-mile front, with practically no opposition, in some parts up to 50 miles, and within 50 miles of the advancing German forces. Vilna, Tarnopol and other cities are already reported to be occupied.

On the Polish-German front the Germans have continued their unremitting advance, driving part of the Polish army into the arms of the advancing Russians and encircling most of the rest west of Warsaw. After a first refusal, the commander in Warsaw was willing to receive an ultimatum for surrender with detailed instructions for the procedure. Although the ultimatum expired yesterday afternoon, no reply from the Poles had been received up to midnight. Germans reported the capture of Lublin, Kutno and other towns.

On the Western front, beyond the fact that the Germans, according to the French, were moving up reserves, there was little activity. Minor German attacks were reported east of the Moselle River and between the Saar and the Vosges Mountains, where the French have assumed strategic positions, but the situation remained unchanged.

At Sea a German submarine sank the British aircraft carrier Courageous. British mercantile losses were raised to a total of 22.

In the United States a new move toward repeal of the arms embargo was made by President Roosevelt in inviting former Gov. Alfred M. Landon and Col. Frank Knox, Republican nominees for President and Vice-President in 1936, to a White House conference Wednesday. Mr. Roosevelt thus hopes to prevent repeal from becoming a partisan issue.

Other war news: Pages 4, 5, 6 and 17.

This Changing World

Russo-Japanese Armistice — Another Twist in a Kaleidoscope in a World of Changing Alignments—Before the Hatchet Is Buried

By H. B. Elliston

Thirty-five years ago Lafcadio Hearn attempted his "Interpretation" of Japan after 14 years of residence in the country and of close study of its people and its institutions. In that book he confessed that "he could not understand the Japanese at all." There were those who thought of Hearn's conclusion when they read the news of the Russo-Japanese armistice on the Manchuria-Mongolian frontier and the manner in which the reporters treated it as the harbinger of a closer rapprochement.

For no country has less in common with the Soviet Union than Japan. It was fear of a Soviet threat that first put Japan on the warpath. When I was in Japan in the late twenties, the papers were full of the "menace coming from the direction of Urga." Urga is the old name for the capital of Mongolia. And even at that time it had been Sovietized—an example, the first example, of aggression which somehow escaped the attention of the Kellogg Pacters.

Now Mongolia adjoins Manchuria. The Japanese were just as much afraid that their legitimate interests in Manchuria might be upset by Soviet imperialism as by Chinese nationalism. Hence the Japanese action in Manchuria in 1931. This wasn't the start of the rash of world aggression, as I have often tried to show, but a riposte for Soviet aggression. To the Japanese, Manchuria was regarded as a "lifeline" just as much as the Mediterranean is so regarded by the British.

* * *

Back in 1931, militarists in Japan wanted to go as far as Siberia. The conquest of Siberia (and the Siberian fisheries) has been a Japanese dream ever since the Allied intervention in Siberia after the World War—when the military used to talk of "watering their horses at the Urals."

Tactically the situation was perfect. There hadn't been a good crop in the Soviet Union, morale was deficient, and Siberia then was ill served in communications, storage, and preparedness. But the militarists were deterred by the world reaction to the "Mukden incident" with the Chinese. Perhaps, also, they were a little afraid of their own grandiose dreams. At any rate, they stopped at the Siberian frontier, and then got bogged down in China proper.

Of course, ideology came to the aid of strategy in keeping civilian as well as military Japan turned against the Soviet Union. I mean that anti-communism was the servant in the military design against Russia. "Thought control" in Japan is strictly constitutional. "Dangerous thoughts" are a penal offense. And all manner of safe-guards are erected in keeping Japan safe from communism. To be sure, the young idea can't be prevented from indulging a yen for the isms. So trained teachers conduct courses in radical economies which end by convincing the unlearned that Marx was not worth studying in the beginning!

For adults, the Government acts as a policeman. For instance, special measures have been adopted to protect Japanese fishermen in Russian waters from contamination. This effort seems rather a work of supererogation. For the fisheries dispute with Soviet Russia is endemic, and many times in recent years, from lack of agreement, the Japanese fishermen have fished in Russian waters with Japanese gunboats around. Moreover, even the war in China flies under an anti-communist banner. Ideology, in short, is a red herring for the practitioners of power politics in Japan, no less than for those in other countries.

* * *

How far the Russo-Japanese armistice will go is a problem for the guessers. The world is in a state of flux, and the alignments that will form, disappear, and reform are just as impossible to estimate as the location of the lava that comes pouring out of a volcano. Nothing is impossible in a world which is operating without standards. I mean that a struggle for survival admits of no examination of the credentials of possible allies. In these circumstances one can offer only a few faint indirections, as Walt Whitman puts it, and leave the rest to the devil's dictionary.

The Russo-Japanese armistice, on its face, seems to bear out the interpretation which this column attached to the Russo-German agreement. That was Joseph Stalin's coup. The master of the Kremlin wants to keep the U. S. S. R. free from any commitments East or West during this period of world upheaval. For Soviet Russia, as the "purges" proved, is still lacking in unity. And a war in which the U. S. S. R. was involved would be an invitation to disturbance at home. Having made tolerably certain of freedom from a German descent upon the Ukraine, therefore, Stalin has made tolerably certain of a breathing spell from the Japanese. It is sometimes said that Mr. Stalin's object is to remain on the side lines so that when the world conflict is over he can pick up some juicy morsels for himself. Maybe. But I think he is intent first of all upon throwing up a Chinese wall around his dominions, lest the conflict break up the Pax Stalinica inside Soviet Russia itself.

* * *

In the Napoleonic wars, countries were constantly changing sides. Perhaps the present world war will bring the same changing realignments. But it is much too early as yet to say that Soviet Russia and Japan are bedfellows. So far only two conclusions may be drawn. First, that Mr. Stalin is no longer interested in getting out on a limb for the sake of oppressed China. Secondly, that the job in China appears to the Japanese to be big enough, now that Germany has left Japan out on a limb, to try to conciliate Soviet Russia.

The fortunes of the actual conflict between Britain and Germany will determine further developments. For, as Lord Grey's memoirs show, neutrals are apt to throw in their weight with the side that seems to be winning. This war, more than any other in history, may be decided by the neutrals. The Japanese, after all, aren't so difficult to understand as a power, no matter how many peculiarities they may have as a people.

'Detective' Hunts Meteor

Special to The Christian Science Monitor

Eugene, Ore.

The University of Oregon can boast that a member of the faculty is a new type of detective. He seeks things which are lost or elusive. Beyond that his quarry and methods are entirely foreign to the tricks of the modern sleuths

This detective is J. Hugh Pruitt, Professor of Astronomy. His quarry, generally, is a meteor, and he has found several.

Finding these elusive celestial visitants is probably the easiest part of Professor Pruitt's detective work. His more difficult assignment is locating where the meteor went after its fiery dash across the heavens on a dark night, or sometimes during the day.

The professor's efficiency in "running down" these fugitives from the heavens recently was demonstrated when he traced the approximate location of a meteor that streaked over northwestern Oregon and south central Washington on the morning of July 2. The meteor streaked across the country with a "roar," people reported, and its landing somewhere east of Portland was sufficient to produce the effects of an earthquake for miles around.

'Detective' Called

No individual was near the landing spot, so "Detective" Pruitt was called in. A Portland newspaper called him on the telephone a few moments after the "quake" for his impression of the visitor. Local residents had been calling him about the "thing" they had seen hurtling through the sky.

His first task was to garner reports from all sections of both Oregon and Washington from which the meteor had been seen. Each report had to include two points—where the observer first saw the object in the sky and, second, where it was last seen before disappearing from sight. Reports were received from 91 observers and all observations indicated on a map.

Lines were drawn from all points in the direction the meteor was first seen. Dotted lines were run from the same points toward the spot indicated as being last seen. Extension of these lines established two factors, first the direction the meteor took in its travels and over what territory it moved; secondly, dotted lines indicated approximately the territory where the meteor landed.

Spotted on Map

The completed map disclosed the fact that the meteor came from over the Pacific Ocean and was first sighted near Tillamook on the coast. From that point it traveled in a northeasterly direction, crossing over the northern part of Portland and the Columbia River, a short distance east of that City. Beyond Portland the dotted lines converged on a spot in Washington, just north of the Columbia River, about 15 miles east of Stevenson.

Although the meteor has not been found, evidence of how accurately Professor Pruitt estimated the location of the meteor has been produced. A young man in Washougal, Wash., about 45 miles west of where the meteor was indicated as landing, was picking blackberries when he heard explosions.

Next day he returned to the spot and traveled toward the spot from whence the explosives had come Within 200 yards he found a black, pear-shaped object, which he sent to Professor Pruitt, who identified it as a piece of the meteor.

Donald H. Black

A Literary Tour of New York
Page 2

The Monitor Index

Monday, Sept. 18, 1939

25 Cached Machine Guns Seized in Seattle Raid

SEATTLE, Wash. (AP)—Twenty-five machine guns, valued at $6,000, were seized by Federal Bureau of Investigation agents and City police today.

Witnesses at police headquarters said one package of guns contained a New York City newspaper dated April 15, 1925, described the weapons as of French make, and expressed belief they had been stored for a considerable time.

3. The Second World War

During the Second World War analysis of the Soviet System understandably was largely replaced by reports on an ally in a gigantic struggle for survival. The great conflict confused broader issues. Edmund Stevens—from whom we will read much in Chapter Four—extricated his bride from the Soviet Union in 1939, covered the Soviet invasion of Finland in 1939 from the Finnish point of view, and after much intervening war coverage from several theaters was covering the second Soviet invasion of Finland in 1943 from the Soviet point of view.

Soviet Aids in Crushing Poles; Allies Hold Back War on Reds   [9/18/39]

By William Henry Chamberlin

PARIS–French opinion was thunderstruck by the news of the Soviet invasion of Poland. Russia's action unquestionably is the most important event since the beginning of the war, especially if it is considered in connection with the Soviet-Japanese rapprochement which immediately preceded it and which is evidently calculated to give the Soviet Union a free hand in Europe.

There is a unanimous outburst of indignation over what is considered the most treacherous and unprovoked Soviet aggression, with its violation of two existing treaties of nonaggression with Poland.

The newspaper headlines, from the conservative *Le Figaro*, which characterizes the Soviet invasion as a "dagger thrust in the back" to the socialist *Le Populaire* which calls it an "atrocious event," reflect this general indignation.

The Socialist leader, Léon Blum, publishes an appeal to French Communist leaders to break with Moscow and "recognize that they have no duty or discipline except the common duty and discipline of French citizens."

What lends a peculiar quality to the perfidy of the Soviet action, according to French opinion, is that it occurred while the Poles were still gallantly fighting against overwhelming material odds. Neither Warsaw nor Lwow have yet been taken, despite the terrific German air bombing and frequent raids by motorized units on the Polish rear flanks. It is still premature to assess with certainty the full consequences of this Soviet intervention in the European war, and the French official attitude, which doubtless is closely coordinated with the British, is one of watchful waiting.

While theoretically the British and French guarantees to Poland would operate against Soviet as well as German aggression, it is most improbable, considering the extreme difficulties of any effective action in Eastern Europe against the combined German and Russian

Front page of The Christian Science Monitor **from December 1, 1939.**

forces, that the Western Powers will take any initiative in attacking the Soviet Union.

Two facts on which French commentators of various shades of opinion substantially agree are that as a result of the Soviet action the war will be much longer and more difficult than had originally been anticipated, and that the heroic Polish resistance is now doomed to collapse.

So far as is ascertainable, no direct Anglo-French help of any consequence has been given Poland. Any possibility of such aid is now excluded because the advance of the Soviet troops has already led to the occupation of the small section of Poland which borders on Rumania, thus closing the sole gateway through which munitions and supplies might reach Poland.

It is the general impression that some line of demarcation was agreed to between Germany and the Soviet Union regarding the advance of Soviet troops. The former housepainter, who is now Dictator of Germany, and the son of the Caucasian shoemaker, who is Dictator of Russia have proved worthy successors to their cynical imperial predecessors, Frederick the Great and Catherine the Second, who together systematically partitioned Poland in the eighteenth century.

It is considered probable that this line runs somewhere in the neighborhood of Vilna, Brest-Litovsk and Lwow, leaving the Soviet Union areas inhabited predominantly with the Ukrainian and White Russian minorities.

Germany would presumably reestablish its prewar eastern frontier, perhaps somewhat extended, and a buffer Polish State under a puppet government and under a joint German-Soviet protectorate would probably be established in the territory which neither state annexes directly.

The new German-Soviet "axis" seems certain to exert the strongest effect on the Balkans where political observers here anticipate that Rumania and Yugoslavia will feel obliged to make the maximum economic concessions to Germany for the purpose of averting military occupation.

The first reliable Anglo-French defense line in the Near East now seems to be the Dardanelles with Turkey apparently remaining unshaken. So long as Italy preserves its neutrality it will be easy to send Turkey the necessary supplies of munitions through the Mediterranean.

Regarding Italy's intentions there are many rumors but few facts. All suggestions of France either bribing or threatening Italy is denied in official circles here.

One puzzling feature of the Anglo-French military strategy in the first two weeks of the war was the inactivity of the Allied aircraft, while the German air force was mercilessly raiding Poland. Some bitterness in this connection is privately expressed in Polish circles here. In view of the extreme reserve by French and British military authorities, the reasons for this failure to launch mass air attacks against the German munitions center and airplane factories can be only conjectured. It is possible that France and England feel they have more to lose than gain through the extension of the scope of air warfare until they attain a position of decisive superiority.

What Hitler Paid Stalin for His Aid [12/1/39]

By Joseph C. Harsch

BERLIN–The heavy price Germany paid for the freedom to fight: a major war on only one front emerges graphically today as Russian penetration of the Baltic crystallizes in the new advance against Finland.

Estonia, Latvia and Lithuania have already gone, and with Finland now under the direct and dire threat of military invasion the old dreams of German domination of the Baltic, deriving from the legendary days of the Teutonic knights, seem vanishing in the northern mists of winter.

Nothing so sharply emphasizes the importance of Russian friendship, or at least tolerant neutrality, to Germany as the reaction to this latest Russian advance in the north which comes after Russia has already extended its shadow over the Balkans as well as over the Baltic littoral.

German officials of the Foreign Office and the Propaganda Ministry avoid all comment on the subject other than the facetious suggestion that since England has appointed itself guardian of all small European states it might observe consistency by extending the same comfort to Finland had it previously extended to Poland.

While the radio all day Nov. 30 was bringing in latest reports from Finland these officials insisted they had received no confirmation of a Russian military attack from Moscow and had no knowledge of such events.

That Germany can watch this extension of Russian power into the Baltic complacently is something no foreign observer can believe who has any knowledge of history or who recollects the days before the pact with Soviet Russia transformed the entire situation in Eastern Europe.

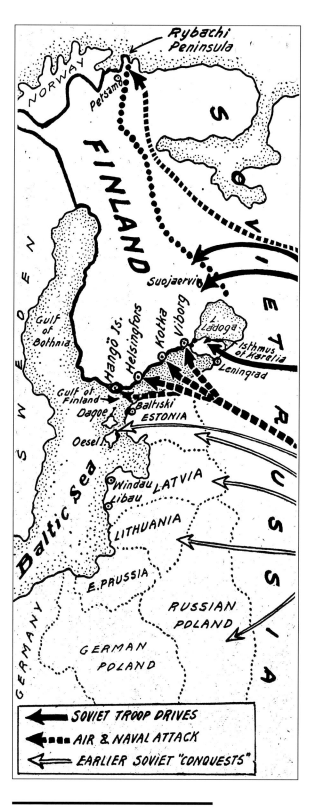

Map which appeared in The Christian Science Monitor **in 1939 showing the Russian advance westward on Finland.**

The fact is that for centuries there have been two main paths of expansion of German influence. One was the Drang nach Osten down the Danube and eastward. The other was along the Baltic Coast line—the dream of Teutonic knights.

Russia had had historic ambitions in the same directions in the persistent struggle of the Czars to carry their eagles towards Constantinople and into the Baltic—ambitions which seem to have been inherited and presently exercised by their Communist successors with the withdrawal of German opposition to such movements.

Certainly whatever unhappiness may exist behind the scenes, the greatest care is being exercised here to avoid any public appearance or expression of regret over the advance of Russian influence in the Baltic area. Indeed, emphasis is still being laid on the valuable contribution Russia is allegedly making towards supplying Germany with vital raw materials for prosecuting the war in the west. It would appear that no matter how high the price may seem here it is still not deemed too high a price for peace and economic cooperation with Russia in the east.

The press here gave only the scantiest notice to the Russian invasion of Finland while emphasizing the comfort which Russia's Premier Vyacheslaff Molotoff gave the German contention that the blame for this war rests on England.

No hint is available publicly to recall the fact that when Finland won its independence from Communist Russia it had strong German support, or that until the days of Russia's separate peace with Germany, the Reich had consistently supported the Baltic States against Russia.

Russia is quite clearly an indispensable friend to Germany today, an actuality which party leaders concede frankly in private, and therefore a friend which should not be alienated over Finland, no matter what damage Russia's attack may threaten to German interests in the Baltic.

Hope, of course, is held that Russia will limit its advance to the areas near the present border which were demanded in the unsuccessful negotiations. But, whether limited or not it seems altogether highly improbable that any protest will emanate from Berlin where the absorb-ing interest is the subject of the availability of Russian resources for the war in the west. without the needed resources the Allied blockade might turn out to be a far more serious danger that it yet has become.

Heroic Epic Written By Finnish People   [12/2/39]

By H.B. Elliston

HELSINGFORS–Helsingfors is today a deserted capital.

The story of the evacuation beneath the impact of Russian bombs and of the atmosphere here during the tense hours in which the Finnish cabinet resigned, can be seen as nothing short of a tribute to the Finnish people.

At the time Finland was busy changing governments, I chased the Diet around the countryside in the blackness of the night. The Diet was supposed to be meeting at Finland's imposing Parliament House. When I arrived the Mayor of Helsingfors himself was acting as guard. He stopped me, examined my passport, and would not let me go up the steps. I managed to persuade him that I was on journalism bent. Then he explained that the Diet was meeting in the country in secret session.

I begged to be told where, but he was grimly adamantine in his refusal. Through the gloom I saw busses loading the legislators for their new destination.

The streets were jammed with fleeing refugees. If the Russians had not missed the Saarinens railroad depot the congestion would have been unfortunate. Actually the evacuation has proceeded without too much confusion. The proof is the deserted condition of the streets this morning.

What is the damage of the previous days' frightfulness can still be estimated only in guesses. The Foreign Ministry has asked the correspondents not to indulge the Russians by revealing the main places hit. It is held that such data would provide good registration marks for the hostile aviators.

But I can say that houses, streets, some churches and schools, and one of Finland's prides, the Cooperative Centrals, are either in partial ruin or terribly scarred. Typical of the desolation is the story told by a temporary secretary I engaged early yesterday. She came to me after dinner last night and told me with tears in her eyes that her home was now a wreck and her mother lay wounded. She is now with the vast majority of the womenfolk. The center of the Capital is still intact, but last night when I filed my previous message I had to pick my way through streets filled with broken glass.

[Associated Press dispatches today said that roads outside Helsingfors were crowded with trucks, automobiles and wagons carrying women and children from the danger area. Railroad stations were jammed with refugees seeking less precarious residences inland. Business was reported almost at a standstill in Helsingfors. Only a few stores were operating.]

It is difficult to get comprehensive information, because all the departments in every Ministry have been dispersed to secret headquarters in or around Helsingfors. Communication is still uncertain. The correspondents who are getting news out regularly are those whose newspapers or European offices had the foresight to telephone to them in Helsingfors. For with the government clamping down on outgoing calls as well as intermittently on cables, the only sure way of communicating with the outside world is by incoming calls.

This correspondent, for instance, was called up all the way from Geneva and asked to give a broadcast to America. This I did at 2:00 A.M. Finnish time. It was to be picked up in Geneva and relayed to America. But I have learned since that Geneva was not successful even in picking it up.

The same misfortune happened to the former Foreign Minister, Eljas Erkko. All America has been waiting to hear him make a statement, several times he has spoken such a statement, but each time the Germans as their contribution to the campaign have drowned him out.

This is one of the consequences of Finland's unpreparedness. Last spring they ordered from Marconi in London a new radio installation for 50 kilowatt transmission. In the fall the firm said it could not make delivery because of urgent British needs.

Now Finland must be content with sending out hit or miss on the ether messages on two stations of one and two kilowatt power transmission—on the off chance that they will be picked up before they are drowned out.

It is the same story in every department: not enough bomb shelters, gas masks, airplanes, antiaircraft guns, hospital equipment. Finland wonders today whether it hasn't been more honorable than prudent in paying off 90 percent of its foreign debt in the last decade. If that money had been put into preparedness its plight today in everything save fortitude might not have been so serious.

How Finland Fell; A Final Tragic Day [3/14/40]

By Edmund Stevens
HELSINGFORS–Sometimes weeks and months of history are crowded into 24 hours. Such was the day when "peace" came to Finland.

The Finnish people arose in the morning thinking that they were at war.

Stenographers went to work with gasmasks across their shoulders. They had been told that there was peace in the air, but no one had paid much attention to it.

Then came the morning papers. Along with the usual war communiqué there was a headline that peace had been established with Russia, according to foreign radio reports, and that the treaty had been signed in Moscow. But no confirmation could be had from the government there.

Then at 12 o'clock came the radiocast of the tragic speech by the Foreign Minister, Vaeino Tanner, in which he said that Finland had been forced to accept peace on the Soviet terms. He placed the burden of Finland's capitulation on the shoulders of Norway and Sweden for refusing permission to Allied troops to cross their territory, a refusal which strangled Finland.

The detailed terms of the peace treaty signed in Moscow—known to the outside world—have as yet reached only official Helsingfors. But Mr. Tanner gave some of the points which were enlarged upon in bulletins. Thus Finland begins to grasp the important cession of territory in its southeast corner—the loss of the heroically defended Karelian Isthmus, the loss of the nation's second largest city, Viborg, and the important industrial center of Sortavala as well.

The magnitude of the Russian gains is not shown alone by the transforming of Lake Ladoga into a Russian pond and the transformation of the Hangoe Peninsula into a Soviet naval base. For the new boundary coincides roughly with that established in 1721 by the peace of Nystadt, concluded with Peter the Great after the northern war known in Finnish history as the "great wrath."

Hence it is evident that Joseph Stalin's recently awakened interest and admiration for Peter the Great and his policies have more than an academic importance.

The old Russian aspiration to reach the Atlantic across Scandinavia, which Peter initiated when he "opened a window on Europe" by founding the city of St. Petersburg, has found a new ardent champion. Mr. Stalin's Baltic policy is a combination of Peter's aspirations and designs with Adolf Hitler's methods.

The parallel between the present peace of Moscow which mutilated Finland and the Munich agreement which did the same for Czechoslovakia becomes obvious. Herr Hitler then sought to acquire those provinces which constituted Czechoslovakia's natural defensible frontiers. The Russians have done the same to Finland. Russia has grabbed all those areas along Finland's eastern border which with their impassable lakes and forests proved an effective barrier to the Red Army's heavy footed infantry and mechanized divisions.

It has left Finland with artificial boundaries, difficult to defend. But whereas with Czechoslovakia Germany had the Sudeten question as a tolerable excuse, Russia dispensed even with this figment. The districts it grabbed are purely Finnish in population and have been so for a thousand years.

It is predicted that practically all the inhabitants will leave with the withdrawing of Finnish troops who are abandoning everything they cannot carry rather than submit to the invaders.

And the Russians, just as hitherto in their few advances into Finnish territory, will find only emptiness to answer their boasted claim of being the "liberators" of Finland.

It was also revealed that Russia will not pay one cent of compensation for its damage to civilian property. The 200,000 evacuees from the areas ceded to Russia will only be allowed to take along their personal possessions. All else must be left behind.

This means that in Finland the problem of financial aid, both for destitute refugees and for the families of the fallen soldiers, becomes more serious now than ever. I know of one family who had a fine house in Viborg, a summer home at Terijoki, and a lodge at Lake Sortavala. These persons are now in Helsingfors with nothing to their name but their clothes on their backs, and they are typical of many other families.

Russia, which achieved its victory less by force of arms than by the cunning diplomatic connivance of its German partner, has adopted "woe to the vanquished" as its slogan, tossing its sword on the scales.

Little effort is made in the peace terms to respect even the dignity and feelings of the brave little people.

The preamble to the peace treaty begins by setting forth the purposes. They are given as follows, "One, to establish peaceful relations between Finland and the Soviet Union. Two, to secure the defenses of Leningrad and Murmansk."

No mention is made in the text of the defense or security of Finland. Although Finland blames only Russia for its plight, nevertheless, the failure of those whom it counted upon to help has compelled Finland for the moment to bow to its aggressor. Austria, Czechoslovakia, Poland, Estonia, Latvia, Lithuania and now Finland.

Such is the list of nations victimized for the crime of being weaker than their neighbor.

The first day of peace was not a day of rejoicing in Helsingfors. Everywhere the flags were out at half staff in sign of national mourning. Little knots of people collected in front of bulletins pasted on the boardings giving the terms of peace, but despite the highly charged atmosphere there was no suggestion of disorder anywhere. The people, like the government, bow to the inevitable.

But the shift from war to peace nevertheless requires a considerable period of adjustment. In front of my hotel window is a huge statue of Alexis Stenwall ("Kiwi"), celebrated Finnish writer. Yesterday some workmen were busy boxing the statue over with wood to protect it from possible bomb splinters.

This morning they were still on the job hoisting big two-by-fours into place and nailing them. Then after midday their work ceased. During the day here and there enterprising shopkeepers were pulling the protective boards off their show windows, but few persons seemed interested or to have much inclination for a "return to normalcy."

Under the conditions of such a peace you gather that most were longing for the healthy shrieking of an air-raid siren. Now for the first time since last November the air-raid precaution blackout regulations have been lifted. The electric clock on the railway station tower was lighted and here and there a shaft of light peered timidly from a house window into the gloom. But most persons failed to follow suit. Either the habit of months was too strong to break, or a naked light seemed somehow almost indecent and profane. At least such appeared to be the general sentiment.

The last surprise of the eventful day was provided by an announcement made by the Foreign Minister Tanner at a press interview at the Hotel Kaemp to the effect that a defensive alliance between Sweden, Norway, and Finland is likely to materialize in the near future. This, he said, had been attempted during the war but had not been proved practical then.

Now that the war was over it would probably be realized. One cannot avoid the feeling that this is somewhat like locking the stable door after the horse has been stolen. Many correspondents were surprised with the mild tone the Minister adopted in his evening speech regarding the Scandinavian countries, a considerable modification of the tone of the previous speech.

In all this tragedy there is one note of coming relief, and that is the end of the Kuusinen "Peoples' Demo-

Finns on their way to the homes they occupied prior to the Russian invasion in August 1941.

cratic Government of Finland" which the Soviets had expected to install in Helsingfors. When the Soviet Government agreed to treat with the Finns it ipso facto ceased to recognize its Kuusinen Government.

Yet even while Premier Risto Ryti and the other members of the Finnish delegation were negotiating in Moscow the Soviet radio continued cynically to acclaim this puppet outfit as the "only lawful Finnish Government."

However, the "traitor Kuusinen" will doubtless be consigned to the limbo which the Kremlin reserves for those tools who have outlived their usefulness.

Otto Kuusinen's "treason" had been partially redeemed by his two sons, who have fought bravely in the Finnish Army.

Another remarkable document issued is Field Marshal Baron Carl Gustaf Mannerheim's farewell to his troops. Among other things he gives the first figures on Finnish losses, which he places at 15,000 fatalities, without naming the number of wounded. He places the Russian losses at 200,000, and further reveals that in the course of hostilities the Finns have destroyed more than 1,500 Russian tanks and more than 700 aircraft.

Who Owns the Future? [8/2/41]

By William Henry Chamberlin

What the world is now experiencing is more than a war, although war news naturally bulks largest in public consciousness. It is more than a revolution, although the shocks and dislocations of the first World War ushered in an era that was remarkably productive of fundamental revolutions, of which the Russian, the German, the Italian, the Chinese and the Turkish are conspicuous examples. It could more accurately be described as a tangled mixture of war and revolution, as the third great crisis of modern civilization.

The first of these crises was associated with the Reformation, the second with the French Revolution. Every student of history knows how many conflicts, international and civil, were associated with these two great movements and how nationalist and dynastic ambitions and social economic changes were inextricably blended with the ideological challenges of the ideas of Luther and Calvin, and the ideal of "Liberty, Equality, Fraternity" which was proclaimed in theory, if not realized in practice, by the leaders of the French Revolution.

Three distinct ideologies are now in conflict: the Democratic, the Fascist and the Communist. The struggle between Democracy and Fascism is dramatized in the great war between the Axis powers and the British Empire and its allies, a war that is being waged on many fronts, from the deserts of Africa to the factories of the United States.

It would be a mistake, however, to overlook the Soviet Union, merely because it had long tried to avoid active participation in the war. In practice there is far more similarity between the Soviet Union and fascist powers than there is between either of them and the democratic countries. Both the communist and the fascist totalitarian states reveal such common features as the supposedly infallible leader, the single ruling party, the technique of government by a mixture of propaganda and terrorism.

But the Soviet Union, unlike Fascist Italy, was not a mere appendage of National Socialist Germany. Comment which represented Stalin as a helpless tool of Hitler after the Soviet-German Nonaggression Pact of 1939 overshot the mark. The best proof of this is that, while Germany took over Italy without firing a shot, Hitler's mechanized legions encountered some of the fiercest fighting in their career of conquest in the forests, swamps and steppes of Western Russia and Ukraina.

Stalin's policy between the signature of the pact with Hitler in August 1939, and the outbreak of war with Germany on June 22, 1941, could be summed up in the formula: "Peace for the Soviet Union, war for the rest of the world." Everything that Stalin has done from the beginning of the European war until the Germans struck at Russia is comprehensible in terms of this formula, and in terms of this formula alone. The Soviet dictator knew that his system, because of its relative military and industrial inefficiency, was badly prepared to stand the ordeal of large-scale war with such a formidable enemy as the Third Reich.

So he maneuvered, and maneuvered successfully, to canalize Hitler westward, against France and Great Britain. He hoped that there would be a long war of attrition and exhaustion, in which all the belligerents would thoroughly exhaust themselves. Then the day would come when he could step in with fresh and intact forces and spread his own power and Communism as an economic system all over Europe.

The swift fall of France was a shock and a disappointment to the Red dictator. He still hoped that England, with American help, would provide a counterweight to Germany. So he pursued a policy of outwardly appeasing Hitler, while secretly intriguing against him, not very effectively, in the Balkans. But the time came when Stalin's hope of winning the war by default, by

The Czechs Will Rise Again

By Ira E. Bennett

Former Editor-in-Chief of the Washington Post

THE GREATEST MISTAKE of the Allies and the United States during the World War was their failure to put down Austria-Hungary. That decayed empire was the Achilles heel of Germany. By shattering it the Allies and the United States could have shortened the war. But instead of striking the Central Powers in their weakest spot the Allies clung to the delusion that by dealing gently with Austria-Hungary they could induce her to leave Germany in the lurch. They believed that Austria-Hungary was an unwilling victim of Germany. This idea was fostered by Austrian and Hungarian intrigue, by the Vatican, and by influential pro-Austrians in allied countries, and the United States. Americans were taught to believe that Austria-Hungary was forced into the war by Germany.

Austria-Hungary played a double game for four years after the war began. She did not declare war against Italy, France, or Great Britain, but let them declare war against her. The Hapsburg emperor made a pretense of friction with Germany when he failed to break off diplomatic relations with the United States, following the break with Germany in February, 1917. This was merely a blind for carrying on intrigue in the United States in behalf of Germany.

As early as September, 1915, the Austro-Hungarian ambassador in Washington, Dr. Dumba, was exposed as an organizer of strikes in American factories for the purpose of blocking war exports to the Allies, and he was expelled. It was discovered that Austrians, financed by the German embassy in Washington, were engaged in treasonable peace plots in Paris. One of these agents, Bolo Pasha, was captured in October, 1916, and executed early in the following year.

For a long time, up to the summer of 1918, President Wilson was victimized by Austro-Hungarian wiles and immobilized by his own notion that he could split Austria-Hungary away from Germany. It was not until the Italian debacle at Caporetto, in October, 1917, that he saw the necessity of making war on the Hapsburgs as well as the Hohenzollerns. But even in his war message against the Hapsburgs he harped on the old fallacy that Austria-Hungary was an unwilling tool of Germany. "We owe it to ourselves," declared President Wilson, "to declare that we do not wish to weaken or to transform the Austro-Hungarian monarchy."

In January, 1918, in his Fourteen Points, Wilson said: "The peoples of Austria-Hungary, whose place among the nations we wish to see safeguarded and assured, should be accorded the freest opportunity of autonomous development." That is, they should be kept under Hapsburg rule. In the same month Prime Minister Lloyd George declared that Britain was not seeking the destruction of the Hapsburg empire.

It is little wonder that Thomas G. Masaryk, laboring in Washington in behalf of the Czechs and Slovaks of Austria-Hungary, failed to foresee the doom of that empire. His hopes may have been for independence, but his expectation and labors were centered upon autonomy under the Hapsburg crown.

I became acquainted with Dr. Masaryk soon after his arrival from Russia in May, 1918. The wonderful march of the Czechoslovak forces through Russia attracted worldwide attention some months later. It was directed in its early stages by Masaryk, as head of the national council, which held supreme command over Czech legions scattered in Russia, France, Italy and the United States. Masaryk's chief mission in the United States was to win sympathy and support for his people. They were at first unknown to Americans generally. Then they were confused with other "Austrians," and not until the brilliant feats of the Czech force in Russia became known were Americans aware of their identity and aspirations.

Dr. Masaryk solicited the friendly interest of the Washington Post. I was in frequent touch with him and his assistants and wrote many articles concerning the Czechs and their struggles, utilizing the information furnished by Masaryk. I continually urged more active military operations against Austria-Hungary. American naval officers were eager to make a sea attack upon Austrian positions in the Adriatic.

In May and June, 1918, the Allies expected another year of war, at least. Germany had failed to break through in March, but she was massing for a still heavier onslaught. The United States was increasing its forces in France, but apparently too slowly to turn the scale. No one looked for the downfall of Austria-Hungary.

Under the shadow of defeat the Allies finally composed their differences and placed Foch in supreme command. On Aug. 8 he delivered the counterstroke and Germany recoiled. Italy was turning the tide against Austria-Hungary. Bulgaria began to crumble.

About that time Dr. Masaryk showed me the draft of a declaration of autonomy which he had drawn up. I was surprised, as I had no other thought than that the Hapsburg dynasty was on the way out. His document was extremely long. It gave a detailed list of grievances, many of them seeming rather trivial in view of what I thought was coming. Masaryk dwelt upon restoration of the ancient kingdom of Bohemia, with a Hapsburg as king, under obligations to recognize the rights of Czechs as proclaimed when they voluntarily accepted a Hapsburg as their ruler, centuries before.

It was evident to me that our viewpoints were not at all in harmony, as I had supposed. The disparity led to more than one conversation, which I had reason to believe greatly changed Dr. Masaryk's opinions and plans. I began by asking him if he expected the United States to be defeated. He was astonished, and replied, "No, of course not!"

"The United States and Austria-Hungary are at war," I said. "One or the other must go. You know the United States was slow in going to war. It is impossible to defeat Germany without defeating Austria-Hungary also. Wilson tries to discriminate between enemies, but the war cannot discriminate. If the Allies and the United States win this war there will be neither Hohenzollerns nor Hapsburgs. If you believe that we will win, you must believe that there will be no Austria-Hungary to grant autonomy to you. Bohemia will be free. You should now declare your freedom. Change your declaration of autonomy and make it a declaration of independence."

This struck Dr. Masaryk with amazement. The color rose in his pale cheeks as he thought of it. I pursued the subject by drawing a parallel between his country and the United States. It was time, I said, to come out boldly, to sink or swim for independence. This would strike an inspiring note and encourage the Allies and the United States to beat down Austria-Hungary. Americans would be electrified and would understand what they were fighting for. I repeated phrases from the American Declaration of Independence, and urged him to recast his declaration along those lines.

Dr. Masaryk drew out a small notebook and began to make notes in his microscopic handwriting. This notebook perhaps may still be among his papers. "You are linked with the United States," I insisted. "Unless we perish you will triumph. Join your fortunes with ours. Throw off all thought of remaining under the Hapsburgs. Draft your declaration in terms that Americans will understand. You are appealing to the United States and the Allies. Don't make an appeal for autonomy. Americans know nothing of autonomy, but they know what independence means."

"Go on, go on!" exclaimed Dr. Masaryk, excitedly, as he made notes.

"The Rubicon was crossed when the United States declared war on Austria-Hungary," I continued. "Peace is impossible with the enemy unconquered. We are just beginning to fight—the enemy is nearly exhausted. Soon he will cry for mercy. He will offer you autonomy to save himself. What is autonomy worth? You cannot trust him. But why should America carry the war to the bitter end if the peoples of Austria-Hungary are satisfied to remain under Hapsburg rule? You owe it to Americans to respond to their efforts by striking off your own shackles. Make your declaration short and clear. Cast it in the mould of our Declaration of Independence and Americans will understand and fight your battle."

Both of us had in mind that his appeal would be submitted to President Wilson. Masaryk reminded me that Wilson had favored autonomy. I replied that Wilson was a stubborn fighter when aroused, and that his views were changing as the realities of the war bore down upon him. I believed that Wilson would be delighted if the Czechs would make a bold declaration of independence.

The enemy allies crumpled rapidly in September, 1918. Austria-Hungary asked for peace negotiations on Sept. 14. Bulgaria collapsed on Sept. 21. The German high command asked Berlin on Sept. 28 to appeal for an armistice, and on Oct. 5 this appeal was made. On the same day Austria-Hungary also sued for an armistice, stating its acceptance of Wilson's Point No. 10, relating to the autonomy of

(Continued on page 15)

DID THEY MISS AN OPPORTUNITY IN REGARD TO AUSTRIA-HUNGARY? Masaryk and Wilson and Masaryk and Beneš, Architects of a Free Czechoslovakia

THE CHRISTIAN SCIENCE MONITOR, AUGUST 2, 1941

Page Seven

Page seven from The Christian Science Monitor **Weekly Magazine Section August, 1941.**

remaining aloof, was shattered. Now he must do what he can to withstand the full weight of the German onslaught. Under this strain he still has perhaps one consolation and one hope. He remembers what luck Lenin enjoyed in 1918.

After ceding to Germany at Brest-Litovsk, Ukraina, the Baltic States and other regions, the richest parts of European Russia, Lenin saw the German Empire crumble under the blows of the Allied offensive in the west. Stalin's chance of survival, even of victory, is to hold on until Anglo-American pressure in the west becomes formidable enough to force Hitler to relax his grip on Russia.

One of the most striking symptoms of the profound crisis through which the world is passing is the breakdown of the unity of European and world civilization. Before 1914 nationalism was, of course, a divisive force and no effective means had been found to prevent the sovereign national state from resorting to war.

Yet there were certain generally recognized international rules of conduct and standards of value. There was a common profession of faith in the Christian religion. Individuals of all countries were able to meet at scientific and cultural and literary and labor and political international congresses and to exchange views as human beings. At such meetings there was no sense of compulsion to make propaganda for the views of their respective governments.

This situation has now radically changed. It is one of the most significant common features of Fascist and Communist philosophy that there are no binding imperative universally valid moral laws. Anything is considered good that advances the success of the movement. Anything that obstructs this success is bad.

Even before the beginning of the war a thoughtful observer could sense the schism in the unity of civilization. What had been possible for Russians, Germans, Italians, Frenchmen, Englishmen was no longer possible for Communists, Fascists, National Socialists, democrats, liberals.

So long as this schism continues there can be nothing in the nature of an international world order. Circumstances may bring about periods of truce, when some parts of the world will be recognized as totalitarian and others as democratic, but there can be no stable or enduring peace.

The question, Who owns the future, will obviously be determined to a large extent by the outcome of the war. At present there are three conceivable clear-cut endings of the war, apart from several possibilities of

Front page of The Christian Science Monitor **Weekly Magazine Section from August 2, 1941.**

exhaustion and compromise. One may list them briefly as follows:

1. A Hitler victory. The German land and air superiority may be too great. The British sea lines may be too thin. The American aid may be too little and too late. These are disquieting and distasteful possibilities to most Americans. But they must be faced.

In such an eventuality there would be a German domination of the European continent and of considerable adjacent areas in Asia and Africa. Whether the attempt to impose by brute force unity upon the diverse peoples of Europe would be permanently successful is doubtful.

2. A Stalin victory. This would be conceivable if the American aid had the effect of making it possible for England to defend itself, but not to reconquer the continent. If the war should turn into a long stalemate, a contest in mutual destruction, with England gradually acquiring the power to inflict on Germany devastation from the air comparable with the destruction which Germany has been inflicting on England, but lacking the strength to break Hitler's grip on the continent, the war might turn into a futile competition in long-range destruction which would create just those physical and psychological conditions which would be favorable to the spread of Communism.

A Europe gone Soviet under the strain of a prolonged war with modern implements of destruction which neither side was able to win decisively would not be as formidable and efficient a military-industrial machine as the kind of Europe that Herr Hitler might organize after a complete victory. But it would be a Europe where free trade and free thought would be equally absent.

3. An Anglo-American victory. The passing of the Lend-Lease Act and the implications of several of President Roosevelt's public addresses have pledged America to a total British victory. And it is certainly only on the assumption of an Anglo-American victory that the numerous books, magazine articles and roundtable symposiums on the kind of world that would be desirable after the war will have any validity.

Vindication and preservation of democracy in the United States and in the self-governing parts of the British Empire would of course do much to shape the future. Much more complex would be the organization of the rest of the world, and especially of those countries which have been indoctrinated with Fascist, semi-Fascist, and Communist outlooks on life.

What would add to the complexity is the fact that force, to a democratic country, is a last, not a first, resort.

Most probably world reconstruction will proceed most smoothly, in the event of an Anglo-American victory, if there is no attempt to impose a doctrinaire conception of democracy on the world, but if the emphasis is rather on preserving for every people, large and small, the right to preserve its own way of life free from external aggression. Much can also be gained by patient objective study of the causes of the first World War (among which unrestrained nationalism, unlimited state sovereignty, imperialism and competitive armaments certainly rank high) and of the failure of the peace that followed that war. Here, unwillingness either to take risks or to make sacrifices for a harmonious world order enters into the picture.

Perhaps the greatest tragedy of this age of strife and turmoil is that natural science, invention, and technology have made possible for the common man a standard of living that would have seemed fantastic a century ago. If the nations and the men of good will are to make a better job of the future, there must be bold exercises of imagination, a capacity to surmount narrow, restrictive nationalist influences and to realize that the good of all will be served only as domination and exploitation give way to cooperation.

Is there something "predestined" about the Fascist-Communist organization of society, or is it a mere throwback to outworn despotism? I doubt whether history will bear out either of these interpretations. Economic liberalism was declining even before 1914. A more positive conception of the role of the state was gaining ground in all countries and in all parties from the Right to the Left.

The effect of the first World War was to impart a brutal, violent, irrational turn to adjustments that would otherwise probably have come about in an orderly way. In defeated Germany and also in Russia and Italy, where the strain of war was too great for relatively weak political and social organisms, there was a violent swing to the leviathan-state, functioning without any checks and balances.

The future, assuming that the war does not end in the victory of one of the totalitarian systems, belongs neither to this leviathan-state nor to the laissez-faire liberalism of the nineteenth century, which, with the development of Capitalism, led to undue concentration of power in the hands of a few irresponsible magnates of banking and industry. It belongs, we may hope, to a society of free men working out by trial and order a political and social system which will combine a social-service conception of the state with those liberties of speech and press and election and association that were among the most precious achievements of the nineteenth century.

Success of a Parley: All Aid to Russia Now [10/2/41]

By Edmund Stevens

The Anglo-American-Soviet talks in Moscow have ended without a single apparent hitch two days ahead of schedule in complete unanimity.

It all seems so easy and simple — a group of important men sit at a baize-covered table, ably presided over by Foreign Commissar Vyacheslaff M. Molotoff, and agree to agree.

But to smooth the way for this meeting of opposites, two-thirds of Europe had to be devasted and 13 free Nations destroyed — not counting those who enjoy the doubtful privilege of figuring as Hitler's "allies." Rivers of human anguish whose levels are still rising — had to wash away the barriers of prejudice and mistrust before the present unity could be effected.

I recall another conference in Moscow, in the spring of 1939. Only two of the present three parties were then represented — delegates of the Chamberlain Government were negotiating in Moscow for a defensive alliance to meet the growing challenge of Hitlerism. America was in no way concerned or affected. Hitlerism was a purely European problem.

Unlike the recent conference where the British delegation was headed by Lord Beaverbrook, Minister of Supply, Prime Minister Neville Chamberlain sent to Moscow, to negotiate with the heads of the Soviet Government, a group of political nonentities headed by an obscure civil servant, William Strang.

Also unlike the present conference, instead of being brief and to the point, those 1939 negotiations took a long time to get nowhere. I was in Moscow at the time and recall the empty communiqués, the false hopes and disappointments as the parley dragged on week after week. The press and public in both Russia and Britain were optimistic at first and then gradually the realization dawned that somewhere, somehow, the negotiations were being sabotaged.

The inside story has never been disclosed, although after the final breakdown, when Russia signed on the Nazi dotted line, there was much mutual recrimination, with each side accusing the other of insincerity. The

Russians claimed with some evidence that Mr. Chamberlain was still hoping for another Munich, this time at their expense.

Whatever the circumstances, the fact remains that if Hitler had then faced the combined and determined forces that have now been aligned against him, he never would have marched. Then too, it could have all been arranged around a conference table.

As it is, the present agreement is only a beginning. It is one thing to promise supplies and another to produce and deliver them. It is one thing to make general high-sounding statements about war aims and another thing to live up to them, as President Wilson found out.

For years the Soviets have looked upon all foreign governments as basically their enemies. Efforts at rapprochment have invariably run into a hard stone wall of secrecy and suspicion. It foiled the attempt of President Roosevelt at closer relations following recognition of Soviet Russia in 1933. After vainly beating his head against it, Ambassador William C. Bullitt was forced to give up. It made a dead letter of the Franco-Soviet Mutual Assistance Pact of 1934 and contributed to the failure of the Anglo-Soviet negotiations of 1939.

On various occasions the other powers have indeed given Russia serious grounds for doubting their good faith. But the fundamental cause of the mistrust goes beyond political empiricism to the basic concepts of the Marxist system, which posits an underlying conflict of class interest.

The fact that they are in a tight corner induces the Soviet leaders to suspend some of these principles and reservations, just as circumstances impel the other countries to set aside their dislike of communism. But such expediency provides no basis for lasting peace and reconstruction.

The mutual sympathy and understanding of peoples rather than the formal declarations of Governments is needed if the victory of democracy is to be complete and not prove just the prelude to a new war.

Soviet troops marching from Moscow to the front in the winter of 1941.

Conference Closes
Two Days Ahead of Schedule [10/2/41]

By Edmund Stevens

The United States and Great Britain agreed to fill virtually every Soviet military need for war supplies in exchange for mountains of Russian raw materials at the concluding session last night of the three-power conference.

The rubble and ruin of Stalingrad in the winter of 1943.

The conference closed two days ahead of schedule after only three days of sessions—probably the shortest international council of such dimensions ever held. A communiqué issued by the British and American delegations and one by Russia announced its results.

For the United States and Great Britain, W. Averell Harriman and Lord Beaverbrook promised: "To place at the disposal of the Soviet Government practically every requirement for which the Soviet military and civil authorities have asked."

In return, said the communiqué issued by Mr. Harriman and Lord Beaverbrook, "the Soviet Government has supplied Great Britain and the US with large quantities of raw materials urgently required in those countries." Arrangements were said to have been made to "increase the volume of traffic in all directions."

The United States-British communiqué declared that Premier Joseph Stalin "expresses his thanks to the United States and Great Britain for their bountiful supplies of raw materials, machine tools and munitions of war," and acknowledged "the ample supply of Russian raw materials from the Soviet Government."

The communiqué ended with this statement: "In concluding its session the conference adheres to the resolution of the three Governments that after the final annihilation of Nazi tyranny, a peace will be established which will enable the whole world to live in security in its own territory in conditions free from fear or need."

The Soviet communiqué stressed the "atmosphere of perfect mutual understanding, confidence and good will" and said the delegates were "inspired by the eminence of the cause of delivering other nations from the Nazi threat of enslavement."

Premier Stalin, it said, "took an active part" in the conference which "manifested perfect unanimity and close cooperation of the three great powers in their common efforts to gain a victory over the mortal enemy of all freedom-loving nations."

The Russian communiqué did not specifically mention the agreement for exchange of weapons and raw materials.

In a speech to the closing session Foreign Commissar Molotoff said the conference has shown that "deliveries of arms of most important materials for the defense of the USSR, which were commenced previously, must and will become extensive and regular."

Mr. Molotoff added that "these deliveries of airplanes, tanks and other armaments and equipment and raw materials will be increased and will acquire growing importance in the future."

Britain and Soviet Hail America's Anti-Axis Role; US to Speed Ship Arming [10/2/41]

By Mallory Browne

LONDON–The United States now forms an integral— though so far unofficial—part of the three-power coalition against the Axis.

This is the interpretation that is beginning to emerge here from recent events culminating in the Moscow conference between representatives of Britain, America and Soviet Russia.

The speech of Secretary of the Navy Frank Knox, yesterday, virtually proposing a permanent Anglo-American partnership and linking Japan with Germany and Italy among the aggressors which the democracies must defeat, has come as a striking confirmation of the impression here that the United States is more nearly ready for decisive action.

Combined with Foreign Minister Vyacheslaff Molotoff's statement in Moscow at the conclusion of the supply conference there, it is taken as a sign that a new stage has now been reached in the war.

For the first time Italy and Germany, and potentially Japan, face a tripartite opposition prepared to act together and thus thwart Hitler's hitherto successful "one-by-one" strategy.

"There has at last emerged against Hitler a coalition of powers which will know how to find ways and means for the eradication of the Nazi poison in Europe," Mr. Molotoff declared.

Recalling the Axis aims of annihilating its enemies separately one after another, he continued, "the political significance of this conference lies in the fact that it shows how decisively these intentions of Hitler's are being frustrated as there now exists opposing them the powerful front of freedom-loving nations headed by Soviet Russia, Great Britain, and the United States."

There is a growing tendency here to feel that these remarks of Mr. Molotoff's summarize the situation which, if not quite fully crystallized, is rapidly taking definite shape.

Mr. Knox's speech is read in conjunction with reports from Washington that President Roosevelt is expected to have trouble in obtaining from Congress radical revision of the Neutrality Act, as well as the passage of the latest Lend-Lease appropriations.

In fact, it is probably no exaggeration to say that the presence of W. Averell as the representative of the United States Government at the Moscow conference has done a lot to convince opinion in Britain that

American sentiment is now emerging from a sort of isolationist slump that was causing so much concern over here up until a few weeks ago.

There had been serious doubts here whether American aid for Britain could successfully be extended to include American aid for the Soviets. The apparently successful conclusion of the Moscow conference has gone far to remove these apprehensions.

In fact, the press here today voices hope that the Anglo-American gains in the battle of the Atlantic — which are undoubtedly very far-reaching, though not conclusive, can be extended.

It also hopes that the same sort of Anglo-American cooperation can contribute substantially to another Nazi defeat in Russia.

Thus, as reports of snow in the Ukraine, as well as in Northern Russia, reach London, the conviction grows here that winter will find the Axis bloc of totalitarian aggressors facing a stronger coalition of democratic powers and that therefore Hitler's "one-by-one" strategy will have met its match.

Russian Advance: 50-Mile Gain Made; Nazi Supply Lines Cut [11/23/42]

By War Editor of *The Christian Science Monitor*

A formidable Russian Army force of infantry, tanks and guns pursued broken German divisions through the mine fields and fortifications on the frosty steppes northwest and southwest of Stalingrad today after smashing the enemy lines in the greatest Russian offensive of this year's campaign.

Already some 15,000 Germans have been killed and more than 18,000 captured since the Russians sprang their drive. German besiegers of Stalingrad have been placed in a perilous position, and German forces in the Caucasus are being held to a standstill as the severe Russian winter sets in.

The Stalingrad offensive stretched two arms around the Germans still holding positions in Stalingrad and placed the Russians astride two important railway lines used by the Germans to supply these forces.

The offensive began, dispatches said, with a one-hour artillery barrage so intense that when firing ceased only isolated enemy guns replied. Red Army infantry and tanks then piled through the German front line, driving the enemy from trenches into the open steppes.

The German front line was overwhelmed by the weight of the Russian offensive, dispatches said. Prisoners started to pour in and guns and mortars piled up as

the Russian Army carried the advance as far as 45 miles at some points.

"During the night of November 22-23 our troops in the Stalingrad area continued to carry out successful operations and continued to move forward," the Russian communiqué said.

The Russians announced that a Red Army force sweeping forward from northwest of Stalingrad had reached and occupied Kalach, 50 miles west of Stalingrad, while another column striking westward south of the city had occupied the railroad town of Abganerovo, 40 miles southwest of Stalingrad.

From positions northwest of Stalingrad, the Russians broke through the German lines on a front 18 miles wide and occupied Kalach, an important navigation port on the Don River and the railroad station of Krivomuzginskaya, a few miles southeast of Kalach.

The Russians still were sorting and assessing the material captured in the swift, three-day advance, but it was announced that 360 field guns and many machine guns, mortars, rifles, trucks and other equipment had been taken.

Seven enemy divisions, including one tank division, were reported "completely routed" and heavy losses were said to have been inflicted on 7 infantry divisions, 2 tank, and 2 motorized infantry divisions.

"This latest defeat of the German Army shows that the Red Army has the strength not only to thwart the enemy's plans but to destroy him completely," said *Pravda.*

Fighting still continued in a factory district of Stalingrad Sunday, the communiqué reported.

Dozens of inhabited localities were captured by the southern column of the advancing Soviet troops.

The costly struggle in the Caucasus continued and the Russians reported that three Axis counterattacks were repulsed. In another sector, the Russians advanced and occupied a factory.

The German High Command issued this communiqué: "Fighting activity in the Caucasus was restricted to local undertakings.

"Heavy defensive battles are taking place in the area south of Stalingrad and in the great Don River loop where German and Rumanian troops are collaborating with strong forces of close-range aircraft in order to ward off the Soviets.

"When the weather cleared temporarily in the central sector of the Eastern Front, bombers and dive bombers were engaged in raiding enemy artillery emplacements and troop barracks."

Soviet Encircling Axis at Stalingrad; German Casualties Grow in Russia To an Estimated 3,800,000 [11/24/42]

By Mallory Browne

A significant sidelight on present German difficulties in Russia is shed by new estimates of Nazi losses in the eastern campaign.

During the first year's fighting in the USSR—that is, not including the campaign in the south, which started last June—total German casualties amounted to 3,800,000. Of these 1,900,000 were fatalities.

These figures are not based on either Russian or German estimates. They are from an authoritative neutral source in the very best position to estimate the exact extent of German losses.

In the same quarter, German losses in the first four months of this summer's fighting in the south, including a major part of the battle for Stalingrad, are estimated to include at least 250,000 fatalities. This figure, however, it was emphasized, is tentative and based on incomplete information. Total casualties of all sorts are believed to have been much greater.

In any case, even taking total German losses in the Russian campaign at about 4,000,000, this represents a blow to the Nazi military machine the importance of which can hardly be exaggerated.

In the light of these exhausting casualties, most of which were inflicted on Hitler's very best shock troops, the full meaning of the present Russian counteroffensive becomes apparent.

A Russian communiqué today declared that these "successful offensive operations" continued last night. Both northwest and south of Stalingrad, the communiqué said, Soviet troops continued their advance, occupying several new places and capturing considerable booty as well as a number of prisoners.

The fact that the Russians are now taking prisoners in considerable numbers is interpreted here as an indication that the long strain has begun to show on the morale of German troops in the Stalingrad area. There are indications the Nazis were unprepared for these two powerful counter thrusts by Soviet armies, and that when cut off, large numbers of them surrendered instead of as continuing resistance until annihilated.

Russian successes in the Stalingrad area were admitted for the first time by the German-controlled Vichy Radio today.

The Vichy Radio quoted a German report of a "diversionary attack north and south of Stalingrad," in course of which the Russians gained "fairly considerable ground." The Germans admitted a Soviet breakthrough near Serafimovich, but claimed Russian forces had later been encircled by Rumanian troops.

Military observers here believe that at least 300,000 Axis troops are in serious peril of being cut off in front of Stalingrad if the Russians are able to make both ends of their pincer movement meet. So far there is still a gap about 40 miles wide and it remains to be seen whether the Russians will be able to close this gap before the Germans are able either to bring up fresh reserves and stem the twin Soviet drives or withdraw the main bulk of their forces through the gap.

Even if it fails to cut off Nazi armies in front of Stalingrad, the Russian pincer movement, it is felt here, is already an important victory. It shows that the Russians still have necessary reserves and equipment to hit the Germans hard. While the Russians remain able to launch such heavy and telling attacks, Hitler cannot hope to hold the Eastern Front with a mere fraction of his army while he transfers the other half to other theaters of operation, as he obviously has been intending to do.

But there are many signs that the Soviets have been assembling big reserves of fresh forces not only in the Stalingrad area but also on the Central Front near Moscow and in the north near Leningrad. It is believed here that Premier Stalin and his generals intend to profit by the coming month of relatively good weather, while the ground is hard but before big snows set in, to get a winter offensive well under way and thus continue to impose a heavy drain on Hitler's armies.

Russian Push On: Dual Drive Threatens to Trap Nazi Army [11/24/42]

By War Editor of *The Christian Science Monitor*

A double Russian offensive pushing west of the Don Bend was reported from Moscow to be closing steadily upon the Nazis' whole Stalingrad salient.

Despite desperate German resistance in an effort to keep open a corridor of reinforcement or escape to the long-besieged Volga bastion, the Russians reported new gains to maintain their average of 6 to 12 miles a day northwest of Stalingrad and 9 to 12 miles a day southwest of the city.

The deepest reported penetration was at Chernyshevskaya on the Chir River, 125 miles west of Stalingrad and 75 miles west of Kalach, the railroad town on the Don Bend which the Russians seized over the weekend.

The flag over Stalingrad, February 1943.
Bottom: [From left to right wearing hats]
Molotov, Churchill, and Harriman review
Russian troops on Churchill's arrival in
Moscow for discussions with Stalin and
Harriman in August 1942.

Chernyshevskaya is some 40 miles southwest of Kletskaya, the Don River citadel 100 miles northwest of Stalingrad which the Nazis overran in their fall drive toward the Volga. Now Germans holding positions at Kletskaya are menaced from two sides, since the Russians also are on the offensive in the Serafimovich area, 30 miles farther up the Don.

Southwest of Stalingrad, the Russians were pushing along the rail line which leads from Stalingrad across the bleak steppes into the northern Caucasus. They reported driving on after taking Aksai in a 10-mile advance from Abganerova, 40 miles southwest of Stalingrad.

The German High Command apparently regarded the turn of the tide on the Eastern European front as too great to conceal from its people, and a communiqué acknowledged that German defensive lines had been penetrated.

The communiqué said the Russians were attacking south of Stalingrad and in the Don Bend without regard to losses, and added that "counter measures are proceeding."

Front-line dispatches indicated the Germans were using reinforcements and battling desperately to hold the Stalingrad corridor.

German and other Axis divisions were reported entrenched and fortified in positions guarded by mine fields and tank traps and laid out in a defense system in some places five or six lines deep.

Details of the advances were not given, but many hundreds more Germans were reported killed, adding to the previous Russian estimates that the enemy lost 50,000 slain and captured through the first four days of the drive.

The regular midday communiqué did not name any of the towns captured through the night but said that "our units occupied a number of populated places" northwest of Stalingrad.

In local action at Tuapse within the Black Sea sector, the Russians said they repulsed a German counterattack on a recently acquired position and then dislodged the Hitlerites from a fortified point. Only light combat was reported in the Caucasus southeast of Nalchik.

To the northwest, near Leningrad, a Soviet detachment was credited with the capture of an enemy strong point and nowhere along the front lines was there any indication that Axis forces had made any gains.

While the Russians drove ahead in the offensive long columns of captives were reported moving east.

Many Germans and Rumanians marched with heads and bodies swathed in shawls and blankets.

Russians Mass on Oder River; Nazis Strive to Hold Flank [1/24/45]

By Joseph C. Harsch

The Russian offensive through western Poland has reached the stage where the issue, as in the German drive into the Ardennes, now hinges on the strength of the shoulders of the salient.

The scale of the two battles is enormously different. The Germans attacked in the Ardennes with about 20 divisions. The Russians are attacking with probably at least 200, and perhaps more. Yet the same basic principle of war applies—the principle that the safe depth of penetration on the front of a salient is governed by the width of the base.

The Russians have met little opposition at the point of the salient so far. The nose of the salient is pushing against the great Polish rail hub of Posen. But the Germans probably are no more basically concerned about this than the Western Allies were concerned in the Ardennes about the extreme point of penetration of the German attack there.

The Germans were frustrated in the Ardennes by the fact that the Allies held the shoulders of the salient at Stavelot and Malmedy on the north and Bastogne on the south. In Eastern Europe the issue now is the outcome of the battles being fought on the flanks of the Russian drive in East Prussia and Silesia.

These are developing into battles of the first magnitude. And it can be recorded as of today that the most strategically important of these, the Battle of East Prussia, is going well so far for the Russians. For the Germans to be able to hold the north flank of the salient effectively, they not only must be able to hold Königsberg, but also enough ground around Königsberg to have a sufficient field of maneuver for a counterattack. Their capabilities of doing this were much reduced when they lost Allenstein and Insterburg.

The Russians certainly have it within their possibilities to eliminate the East Prussia flank, except perhaps for the fortress of Königsberg itself which might become a "hold-out" port like St. Nazaire and L'Orient are on the Western Front.

It is axiomatic that the Germans must hold both flanks if they are to establish a holding front in the east.

If they were to lose Silesia, the Russians could sweep northwestward from southern Poland. If they lose

East Prussia, the Russians could drive due west from northern Poland. Thus in all reasonable possibility the loss by the Germans of either flank position—East Prussia or Silesia—would be fatal and would produce that quick conclusion of the war in Europe which is certainly a possibility, although by no means a probability.

The tone of extremity in the commentaries from Berlin indicate that the battle has reached the stage where everything hinges on these battles of the flanks which are opening. The German holding line without much doubt has been reached in Silesia where the Russians control the rail line from Breslau running southeast to Mährisch-Ostrau and on to Vienna.

The Russians are in control of the northern end of the Moravian gateway and can drive down on Vienna from the north for a junction with the armies driving up past Budapest.

Thus the battle of the southern flank already has reached its critical stage with everything depending on whether the Germans can hold the shoulder from Breslau to Mahrisch-Ostrau. If they succeed, they will have a strong flank position against the southern side of the Russian wedge.

From Breslau their natural line of defense would curve upwards logically to Posen (Poznan) and then up and east again toward the bend of the Vistula in the Bromberg (Bydgoszcz) sector. From around Bromberg—the city itself has already been taken—to the Baltic at Danzig, the Vistula is wide enough to offer a natural defense of some strength. This line, in theory, could be held even if East Prussia fell, although its strength would depend greatly on the amount of flank threat the Germans could maintain in East Prussia.

The Russian attack is sweeping up against these German base positions along the whole front. It is not premature to say that an issue has been joined which can bring the early end of the war in Europe. The decision will be reached along the lines which exist today.

Russian Eruption of War Power: How Mastery Surged from Within [2/3/45]

By Volney Hurd

A military spectacle not even approached in history sees Germany going down in flames today under the blows of the Red Army. For scale of battle and concept, for leadership, for sheer military power—nothing like it has been seen before.

It is a military spectacle that seems paradoxical. Thus it is a line of battle but not a battle line. Rather it is a series of great powerful armies working alongside one another. They are geared together for maximum effect, yet each one also operates freely within its own sphere of action. Thus a brilliant and full use of the advantages of overall attack combines with flexible individual operation.

Natural interest centers on the men leading these armies, operating this vast military machine with such intelligence and skill. There are eight main armies, under the following men, listed from north to south: Bagramian, Cherniakhovsky, Rokossovsky, Zhukov, Konev, Petrov, Tolbukhin and Malinovsky. They are different types of men.

That Russia, like the United States, is a melting pot is shown by the fact that of the eight men, Marshal Ivan Konev is a Serb; Marshal Konstantin K. Rokossovsky a Pole; Gen. Ivan Cherniakhovsky a Jew; and Gen. Ivan Bagramian an Armenian. Yet the job they are doing has such unformity of quality performance that we turn to their common denominators.

All of these officers are products of a strict Russian military training created since the Revolution. They stem from the Soviet's own West Point, the Frunze Military Academy. They come mainly from the plain common people who are the backbone of Russia. They are the product of a military literacy imposed upon a rugged stock which had centuries of illiterate serfdom behind it, practical proofs that ignorance is the product of environment and opportunity and not of heredity.

And in fact their being so close to the soil is an advantage. Self-reliance and the ability to improvise are fundamental to simple living. These men of the soil are very near to those phenomena of nature—river and wood, mist and rain, frost and snow. It is in just these elements that wars are fought and the Russian Generals' close relationship to them have provided invaluable allies.

For example, wars used to quiet down in winter. Yet the Red Army gained its first big victory over the Germans by opening up with a major offensive in winter. Instead of avoiding the elements, the Red Army leaders cooperated with them. Ski troops and sledges, fast-moving cavalry, white-clad soldiers who merged so perfectly with the blinding snow as to make superb camouflage, special lubricants to operate in below-zero weather—all these combined to catch the Germans unprepared for anything similar.

In fact, it is fitting that it should be in another winter offensive that the Russians are giving Germany its knockout blow. For this winter has eliminated the one natural hope the weakening Germans counted upon to defend Germany, the rivers. Frozen, these streams have become wide pathways for the fast-moving Russian tide, instead of barriers.

Night has been a time of rest in the military tradition except for occasional patrols. Yet the Russians have launched offensive after offensive at night. They have used double sets of troops, one lot fighting in daytime and hard-hitting cavalry troops keeping it up at night. The Germans got no rest and were worn and weakened by this use of the night.

Heavy blizzards used to see armies hovering around fires, and staying close to their tents or dugouts until it cleared. The Russians, however, have won victories and more military surprise by launching a major offensive in the midst of a blizzard. It is as though the peasant-originated Russian leaders said, "We belong to nature. Let us embrace her and use her."

Another advantage of the Russian military leadership has been both its ability and willingness to learn. In American schools, it is noted that children of immigrants, coming from homes where the advantages of education have been denied the parents, are often brilliant students. It is as though, freed from the shackles of ignorance, they turned all their energies in one direction. The Russian leadership expresses the same kind of eager desire to learn.

The Russians have added to their own military school knowledge and their new departures in exploiting nature as an ally—long, hard, and extensive lessons from the German Army. They have paid a terrific price—but they have learned.

One of the phases of the Russian war machine that has surprised people has been the ability to maneuver fast, to show great mobility and speed despite the fact that the Russian tradition always seemed to be the heavy steamroller. Again studying the background of the present leading Russian generals, one finds that five of the Big Eight—Zhukov, Konev, Rukossovsky, Tolbukhin and Malinovsky—were all former cavalrymen.

In other words, these leaders were trained in the one element of Russian military life which emphasized mobility over all other virtues. While later they were to take over the mass armies featuring what used to be less flexible branches, at the same time they took them over in an era of motorized warfare when tanks, airplanes, and motorized transports gave an entire army mobility,

speed, and maneuverability and therefore a continuous potential of surprise action. There are continuous signs of a cavalryman's thinking in the operations of the main Russian armies today.

With this cavalry thinking has been happily combined the valuable Russian quality of bigness of concept, of big armies, of heavy masses of men and matériel, of artillery to hit the heavy blows. And this artillery thinking has not only been in the way of numbers but weight as well. The Russians have artillery divisions whereas other armies only have artillery regiments.

Three hundred to five hundred guns to the mile smashed their way through the German defense line for the present drive to start. The Soviets designed and built huge self-propelled siege guns so that they could do as good a job on the German fortifications in Poland as the Anglo-American battleships did on the Atlantic Wall on D-Day.

The oldest military axiom is the concentration of forces. Russia took this literally, and the Red Army was built up to a size where it could have plenty of concentration at a number of places at the same time. Thus was exploited the one natural advantage of a country with twice the population of its western neighbors. The Russian generals have in addition used this vast force with mobility and skill.

They kept their artillery in step with this entire concept. All this has paid rich dividends in the past few weeks.

The Soviet strategy is not unorthodox. But the skill with which strategy is used is something else again. The operation of a vast line of battle with eight armies and with unbelievable problems of supply has only heightened the effectiveness of the Russian operations.

While western nations were criticizing the Russians for not breaking through at Warsaw last year after having been stopped there by heavy losses, and turning instead to the Baltic and Balkan flanks, the Red Army decision was vital military strategy. The Russians had to keep moving this vast line so it could not be outflanked. That movement had to overcome enemy resistance. It also had to be kept supplied with the vast amount of matériel needed to keep it moving and continue to overcome the enemy. That becomes very much a mathematical formula.

To move in further to the center with strong German forces on the flanks would be to invite disaster. So the Baltic states were conquered and then the Balkans. At the same time the center, at Warsaw, was being strengthened through the steady arrival of supplies.

THE CHRISTIAN SCIENCE MONITOR

Magazine Section

COPYRIGHT 1945 BY THE CHRISTIAN SCIENCE PUBLISHING SOCIETY

WORLD AFFAIRS • BOOK REVIEWS

BOSTON, SEPTEMBER 8, 1945

U. S. Signal Corps Army Pictorial Service

FIRST RADIO TRANSMISSION OF COLOR PHOTO FROM POTSDAM—Reading Left to Right Are Seen Prime Minister Clement R. Attlee, Great Britain; President Harry S. Truman, United States; and Generalissimo Joseph Stalin, Soviet Russia. Three Black and White Prints Were Made and Each Placed on a Cylinder Representing One of the Three Basic Colors—Red, Blue and Yellow—Then Transmitted by "Radiotelphoto" From Berlin Direct to Washington.

The Land of the Common Man   - - - - -   By R. H. Markham   - - - - -   Page Three

Front page of The Christian Science Monitor **from August 15, 1945.**

Just what colossal supplies must have been brought up is seen in the fact that the present Russian drive, which understandably could have stopped around Posen for a long breather, never even slowed down there. To plan for an all-out drive from Warsaw to Berlin with no rest calls for supplies and the ability to keep them moving in quantities never before envisioned. Yet it has been done.

The old pattern of moving up the center and then the wings and then the center again has roughly been followed. At least, the pattern was used as much as necessary to maintain safety, the main reason for the pattern in the first place. It has shaken the German defenses to pieces.

The Russian leaders have liquidated millions of Germans in their drives. That is not Soviet ruthlessness. Napoleon said, "I see only one thing—masses of enemy soldiers. I strive to annihilate them, confident that everything else will crash together with them." And Clausewitz, the classic German military strategist, said, "The armed forces of the enemy must be annihilated, that is, brought to a condition when they no longer can continue the war." That is exactly what the Russian leadership is doing.

One of the facts perhaps often overlooked as one considers the keeping of the peace in the days to come is that the Germans, through their unintentional but completely effective military education of the anxious-to-learn Russian, have lost their military mastery in Europe once and for all—that is, unless history brings about new twists which cannot now be foreseen.

For Russia will be three times the size of postwar Germany, it will have at least as complete and probably greater military skill and knowledge, and it will be able to so complete its industrialization in the next peaceful years so that an army three times as good as the Germans, can be kept in the field.

The Germans obviously could not have had the slightest knowledge of the full long-range mistake they made in attacking Russia in this particular direction, setting up a power three times as great in the one classification in which Germany was always sure it would excel, military power.

The Russians appreciate this great new advantage. Their plans for increasing military education, for setting up new types of military schools with orphans of present Russian officers starting the training from childhood on, all are aimed at ensuring the continuance of the Red Army leadership now tearing the vaunted Reichswehr to pieces.

Thousands of Muscovites packed the streets and bridges to watch the victory salute celebrating victory in Europe. Moscow, May 9, 1945.

THE CHRISTIAN SCIENCE MONITOR

AN INTERNATIONAL DAILY NEWSPAPER

Registered in U. S. Patent Office

VOLUME 41 NO. 274   COPYRIGHT 1949 BY THE CHRISTIAN SCIENCE PUBLISHING SOCIETY   BOSTON, TUESDAY, OCTOBER 18, 1949   CENTRAL EDITION   TWO SECTIONS   FIVE CENTS A COPY

This Is Russia
UNCENSORED

Exit of a Reporter: Suspicion Closes In

Fresh from more than a decade of close observation of Russian affairs from both sides of the Iron Curtain, Edmund Stevens today begins a series of uncensored, exclusive articles which will calmly but penetratingly reveal the Soviet Union as it is in 1949.

Though a native-born American, Mr. Stevens long has had a fluent and colloquial command of Russian and wide-ranging contacts among the Russian people and officialdom.

By Edmund Stevens
Staff Correspondent of The Christian Science Monitor

Berlin

An ever-widening gap divided us from Soviet soil as the good ship Byeloostrov cast off. While Leningrad slipped astern, our immediate feelings were of unrestrained relief.

After years of hope and frustration, our final memory of the U.S.S.R. was a three-hour bout with customs officials that left us angry and exhausted. Every carefully packed article was dragged out and scrutinized. A dydee doll of daughter's that squeaked when squeezed roused special suspicion.

Only at the end of a fruitless quest did we learn what they were looking for. At this point the chief inspector accused me of having sold our automobile illegally for gold to a Soviet citizen! I was able to furnish written refutation of this charge—the car in question had been legally transferred to a foreign diplomat—so the officials, looking somewhat crestfallen, permitted us to cram our effects back into trunks and go aboard.

This parting episode was final proof that our move was timely. Of late we had sensed imponderable walls closing in upon us. The air itself was clotted with hate and suspicion. The press attacks on everything American grew in violence and vituperation. Closer to home, no week passed without American correspondents being pilloried as spies.

The anti-American campaign penetrated even to the child world, Our son and daughter were taunted by their neighborhood playmates as "Amerikantsi," by now a term of opprobrium.

Soviet Contacts Disintegrate

Small wonder our last contacts with Soviet life around us disintegrated rapidly. Even the press department of the Foreign Ministry, through which all our official relations were funneled, now virtually ignored us. Our least request was ignored, our requests for appointments refused.

All this was bearable as long as it remained impersonal. But early last spring we suddenly discovered that we were constantly being spied upon. Whenever someone entered or left the garden gate in front of our one-story log house a curtain in a window opposite was raised slightly.

Young men, too well dressed for loiterers, lounged on nearby corners or strolled back and forth outside. Friends who dropped in were followed home, and in due course called in for questioning. Our next-door neighbors, too, were grilled, and though we had known them for years, they took to avoiding us utterly.

Soon we noted that not only was the house watched, but we ourselves were shadowed wherever we went. The number of persons assigned to keep tabs on us must have been considerable, and apparently they worked in several shifts.

If my wife and I left the house separately by car or taxi, each of us was tailed by a little black German BMW car with four men inside. They tried to be inconspicuous, ducking behind trucks or trolley busses, and whenever we halted, they, too, would pull up at a respectable distance, preferably just behind a corner.

Grim Game With Shadows

We soon learned their techniques, and one of our favorite sports was to lead them into a blind street and then make a "U" turn that brought us alongside. This seemed to embarrass them no end, and they would try to crouch down out of sight. The moment we got out of the car, they promptly deployed to strategic street corners or doorways, whence they could watch our moves.

They also followed us if we took the Metro or streetcar, and unless through a series of complex maneuvers we managed to shake them for a bit, they were on our trail from morning until we turned in.

It long has been commonly assumed that all telephones serving foreigners are connected to a central listening post—and on more than one occasion we had evidence that our line was carefully checked. However, there had not been, so we thought, any further penetration of the privacy of our home.

Then, one day, we caught Nastia rifling our personal desk drawers and collecting note pads and address books. Nastia had come to work for us back in 1946 as an apple-cheeked peasant girl fresh from the village. After one year, during which my wife trained her as a tolerable housemaid, she left to marry a policeman.

Servant Returns—to Spy

We next heard from her last spring, when she called up and asked for her job back. Since nobody wanted to work for Americans and servants were hard to get, my wife agreed to take her on. With the address-book incident, we realized that Nastia, no longer an apple-cheeked peasant girl, had been assigned to us. We also found that she was in the habit of cross-examining our daughter, age seven, who has that childish knack of total recall for grown-up conversations overheard—drawing her out with the gift of some trivial toy.

Before these troubles, we had lived in Moscow as peacefully and unmolested as anywhere else in the world. Though we saw few Russian friends, we took part in the social life of the closely knit foreign colony, which can provide a nightly party for those thus inclined.

We enjoyed to the full the splendid theaters, concerts, and other cultural advantages of Moscow. But we had trouble keeping art, music, and dancing teachers for the children. There were plenty available, well qualified and reasonable. But the moment they discovered we were Americans—usually after the second or third lesson, we could not keep daughter from coming out with it—they bowed out on some pretext.

At the same time, we were far better off, than most foreign residents who had no contacts with the Russians and who lived in drab flats or hotel rooms. We had a home of our own furnished and equipped like an American house, with everything including the kitchen sink and a small but attractive garden.

Timed to Gubichev Case

We could only guess as to why we suddenly had become the objects of so much organized interest. But the timing suggested that the Gubichev case might have had some bearing. The Soviets, who claimed diplomatic immunity for this Russian United Nations employee arrested for espionage, said plainly in print that reprisals might be expected against Americans in Moscow.

The number of candidates for such reprisals was uncomfortably small, and of these the correspondents were the likeliest. The Gubichev case had provided a new and dangerous precedent. Whereas the above-mentioned Americans had simply been shipped out of Russia, any future cases probably would be held for trial as long as Gubichev, perhaps even longer. The Russians believe in precedents.

These were the implications that made our intimate shadowing seem especially sinister and speeded our departure. A strange climax for an assignment undertaken with the conviction that the world's future depends on understanding and friendship between the United States and Russia.

But I hold that conviction now more than ever!

Mr. Stevens' next article will appear Thursday

Churchill Seems to Recoil at Further Cuts

Associated Press

Winston Churchill appears to be holding his hands up in horror at the thought of further cuts proposed by the Labor Party for Britain's standard of living. Actually he is telling photographers at a Conservative Party rally that he has had enough.

British Combine

Prime Minister Clement R. Attlee is mapping deeper cuts in the British economy in a new effort to put the country on a stronger economic footing. Here the leader of the Labor Party confers with his Foreign Secretary, Ernest Bevin (left).

Housewife's Purse Hit by Price Props

By Josephine Ripley
Staff Correspondent of The Christian Science Monitor

Washington

There is little prospect of the nation's food bill going down in coming months, with the government now spending more money than ever to keep food prices up.

Although surpluses are rolling which normally would mean a lower price level, the government is today spending billions to prevent it.

In effect, it is a case of the government competing with the housewife. If it were not in buying up eggs, for instance, the housewife in the East today would be paying perhaps 60 cents a dozen for eggs, instead of 80.

If the government were not buying up butter to support the price, the housewife might be paying 50 cents a pound instead of 70 cents or more.

$1,270,000,000 Spent

Price support today is big business. It is the biggest business it has ever been, and is due to be even bigger.

During the last fiscal year, the government spent $1,270,000,000 in price-support operations—a figure which broke all previous records. In the previous fiscal year, only $144,000,000 was paid out in price supports.

The inflated figure of today represents the effect of rapidly accumulating surpluses which the government is pledged to acquire in one way or another under present price-support legislation.

The government is still buying potatoes, though no longer at the 90 per cent support figure, but at the lower rate of 60 per cent.

So far this year, it has purchased some $37,000,000 worth of potatoes. That is not much in comparison with the $225,000,000 which was spent for the 1948 potato crop surplus, but it shows that the government is still supporting potato prices.

It is also buying eggs in large quantities, with 1948 and 1949 purchases totaling some $85,-000,000.

Dairy Products

Dairy products are now coming into the market in quantities, and the government is buying powdered milk, butter, and cheddar cheese to keep those prices from falling below the stipulated support level.

Some $80,000,000 or more has been spent in the purchase of these products. Last year it was necessary to spend only $416,000 in support of milk and milk products.

This contrast shows the extent to which production has increased and which would happen to prices if these foods were allowed to come into the market normally.

Turkeys Next

The government will soon be buying turkeys, too, and not for Thanksgiving. A big turkey crop is coming in, and to keep prices at the present support level, it will be necessary for the authorities to purchase large quantities of turkey—in competition with the housewife shopping for holiday birds.

So far hogs have not been supported, as supply and demand have combined to keep pork prices above the support level. But if prices should drop, the government is ready to step in there, too.

The basic grain crops—wheat, corn, oats, etc.—are coming in such abundance now that the government is accumulating huge stocks of grain under the loan program.

Bread Price Held

Crop loans for the fiscal year of 1948-49 amounted to $1,206,900,-000, as compared to loans of $138,-800,000 for the previous fiscal year.

With the government supporting grain prices at the 90 per cent of parity rate, grain prices are sustained at a higher figure than they would be otherwise, and this is reflected in the cost of bread and meat, and other things which depend upon grain for producing.

It is true that all the money which is being poured into price support does not represent a total loss to the government by any means. Much of it comes back as these crops and foods are resold sooner or later. The actual loss in spoilage usually is comparatively small when the final accounting is made.

Little Hope of Relief

But it is a fact that these expenditures prevent food prices from dropping to a lower level, as they would if they were not supported by the government, or if they were not supported at such a high rate of parity.

With Congress in its present tussle over the issue, there doesn't appear to be much prospect of relief.

Even if the Anderson bill were passed, with its provision for lower flexible supports, these would not go into effect for another year, with the high 90 per cent rate of parity prevailing in the meantime.

The House bill calls for indefinite continuation of the high 90 per cent scale.

The only hope for the consumer lies in the Aiken bill—that is, the present legislation—which will go into effect automatically the first of the year, if no other action is taken. Then food prices would undoubtedly come down under the 60 to 90 per cent price supports stipulated in that legislation.

Deeper Austerity Outlined To Hard-Hit British People

By Reuters

London

Britain probably will recognize the Chinese Communist government within the next three weeks, a usually reliable source said here.

By Peter Lyne
Parliamentary Correspondent of The Christian Science Monitor

London

Prime Minister Clement R. Attlee is to introduce yet another era of austerity for Britain.

Advance indications are that it will include a 25 per cent cut in dollar imports, affecting such items as cotton, tobacco, and timber.

The purpose is to bring Great Britain's economy into balance and to try to take advantage of the devaluation of the pound.

Parliament reassembles Oct. 18 and is expected to hear about the "unpleasant new cuts" as soon as they have been conveyed to a meeting of Mr. Attlee with the parliamentary Labor Party. This meeting is scheduled for Oct. 20 and is expected to include some very strong rank-and-file protests against further austerity.

New Turn Down

Mr. Attlee's political organizer in chief, Herbert Morrison, gave final warning of "cuts that will hurt" in a week-end speech at Doncaster. He described the new austerity as the "only alternative to a drift into economic chaos and unemployment."

The standard of living of the British people undoubtedly must take another downward turn. It is getting like a fairy tale:

"Once upon a time, there were people called the British. Again and again and again and again they had to lower their living standards. Some people living outside Britain wondered how it was they could go on this way, always taking more and more cuts. How could they live at all? Or in between times did they creep up?"

Yes, of course, they have from time to time taken a jump up the ladder, when austerity has been looking the other way.

Mr. Morrison explained the situation this way: "We in Britain are producing more and more wealth, but our trouble is that we keep on behaving as though we have more to distribute than in actually the case.

"Both as individuals and collectively as members of the community we keep on pressing for more tickets in the shareout than can be honored out of the amount we have all actually put into the kitty."

And he added: "We are like a man whose income rises a little each year, but who always is spending this year at a rate which he will not be earning until next year or the year after."

This appears to be a frank admission by the government of a part in the responsibility for Britain's being always slightly ahead of its pay check. But it cannot be denied that there has been considerable temptation and, in fact, good reason for giving the British people a little more jam from time to time with their bread.

Drastic Cuts

But now the government is appealing more earnestly than ever for restraint and sacrifice by the British people.

The Economic Committee of the Cabinet has been in almost constant session for the past few days. It is understood that cuts in what is known as capital investment, such as the building of schools, hospitals, and roads, will be more drastic than expected.

Truman Prepares To Make Hay From Congress Record

By Richard L. Strout
Staff Correspondent of The Christian Science Monitor

Washington

The odd thing about the record of the 81st Congress is that President Truman apparently hopes to make political capital not merely from the laws it passed but from the laws it rejected. There are evidences of this already as lawmakers are on the point of departure from the first session.

Not much remains to be done at this particular session except reach a decision on the pending form bill and get through a few remaining appropriations, of which the controversial armed services is the biggest.

Democratic Party leaders paid their last call at the White House Oct. 17 and said they wouldn't be back till Jan. 3, 1950, at the earliest.

Once more, Democrats took the opportunity of pointing with pride at the session's record—a pursuit, incidentally, which the Republican leaders regard with considerable disdain. On one thing, at any rate, they all agree, they will get out of Washington this week—and high time, too.

Issues—Both Ways

A review of the 10-month session shows that Mr. Truman has obtained about everything he asked in foreign affairs and a respectable amount in domestic affairs—a great deal more, indeed, than seemed likely after the Republicans joined conservative southern Democrats against him on a number of "Fair Deal" issues.

There seems every prospect that in the 1950 congressional election Mr. Truman will make an issue of his failures as well as his successes.

In particular, Mr. Truman will assail Republicans for blocking repeal of the Taft-Hartley Act and for aiding the Dixiecrats in the long Senate filibuster that occurred over the civil-rights issue. The Senate rule, it is alleged, makes civil-rights legislation next to impossible.

In the Truman camp, it is argued that the GOP has handed him two ready-made issues. Republicans naturally deny this.

DP Bill Snagged

The record of the administration in the first session would have looked a lot better if the liberalized bill to admit displaced persons had passed. Up to the last minute this was expected. On Oct. 15, however, it was postponed, 36 to 30.

This does not mean that the bill is killed. Thirty members of the Senate were absent or did not vote. The session has dragged on so long it is difficult to get a quorum. It does mean that Congress is in no mood to consider the controversy further till it has had a recess.

Efforts to get fast action on a revised price-support farm bill also have run into a snag.

But here the situation is different. If no new bill is passed, the Aiken law automatically will take effect next January. This calls for even lower flexible price supports than the Anderson substitute bill.

The row over the Anderson bill is because opponents say its flexible provisions are too flexible and do not give farmers the price support they need. Whatever the majority feels about the Anderson substitute, it is almost certain that it does oppose the Aiken law.

Truman Backs Brannan

Accordingly, initial failure of conferees of the two houses to reconcile versions of a new measure probably means little. Conferees went back to work again this afternoon.

James G. Patton, head of the

Citizen Committee Rallies to DP Bill

Washington

In deep disappointment at the shelving by the Senate of the displaced persons bill, the Citizens Committee on Displaced Persons has appealed to the Senate to pass the bill next January, "as it stands." The bill was put off until next January by a 36-to-30 vote Oct. 15.

The committee said the bill to bring additional thousands of displaced persons into the United States should not be mutilated beyond recognition, as it said the Senate opposition intends.

National Farmers' Union, after a White House call, declared that President Truman will make an issue of the Brannan Plan in 1950. Mr. Patton said the President is "certainly committed" to the production payment plan sponsored by Charles F. Brannan, Secretary of Agriculture, and will press for enactment next session.

The twin features of this plan are that farm products would be allowed to drop in price for consumers in accordance with supply and demand, and that farmers would receive a direct cash subsidy to bring their returns up to a specified level on respective crops. At present, crop prices are sustained by government purchases at a certain ratio with so-called "parity," an arithmetical ratio between farm prices and nonfarm prices.

A feature of the big farm debate has been the disclosure that Mr. Truman is committed to a high parity program as contrasted to Majority Leader Scott W. Lucas (D) of Illinois and Clinton P. Anderson (D) of New Mexico, former Secretary of Agriculture, who want lower, flexible farm price guarantees. Said speaker Rayburn today of the President:

"He's for a 90 per cent parity program. He made a campaign of it last year."

Farm Vote Analyzed

Those who accompanied Mr. Truman on his famous 1948 campaign tour do not recall that he made a sharp issue of the matter. His references on the topic were subordinated to other issues. The election, however, showed that farmers in normally Republican key states of the Midwest had turned away from the GOP and voted Democratic.

This generally was ascribed not to the 90 per cent parity issue, but to failure of the 80th Congress to provide federal storage facilities for wheat, failure to approve the international wheat agreement, and to certain GOP utterances indicating that the Republicans would let farm prices drop drastically after the election.

Faith in Education Termed U.S. Wall Against Communism

Special to The Christian Science Monitor

Claremont, Calif.

The world is governed by moral law "just as surely and immutably as it is by the so-called law of gravity," declared Ambassador Francis B. Sayre, addressing a Founders' Day Convocation at Pomona College.

Mr. Sayre, United States representative in the Trusteeship Council of the United Nations, emphasized America's faith in education as the greatest bulwark against communism. He said that the nation's educational system is an outgrowth of the Christian tradition, and is based upon the rock of moral law.

"The man or woman, the community or nation which flouts moral law will ultimately and surely go down to disaster," Mr. Sayre warned. "We are struggling today to defend a civilization based upon the rule of law and right of conscience as opposed to selfish greed and naked might."

Cause of Humanity

"Make no mistake about it, the forces of communism are bent upon wrecking those countries which uphold democratic western civilization," said Mr. Sayre. "What we invent today we cannot prevent our enemies from having tomorrow," he added. "The outcome will not hinge upon the possession of the deadliest and most powerful weapons.

"In the struggle for victory, Mr. Sayre said that those nations will emerge victorious which are committed, and by their statesmanship can convince the people of the world that they are committed, unswervingly to the cause of humanity rather than to their own selfish interests.

In discussing the place of the liberal college in the world of today, Mr. Sayre announced his conviction that the leaders of the country will come from the liberal arts colleges where they obtain "sufficient vision to sense the underlying moral issues."

Fundamental Moralities

"I venture the thought that in your generation the die will be cast which will either break or make western civilization," he told the Pomona College students.

"More intellectual power in this pending struggle will not be sufficient. Victory will inevitably depend upon leadership based upon fundamental moralities and conserved in the strengthening and protection of human rights. The function of the 'liberal college' is to train men and women to assume that kind of leadership," he concluded.

Mr. Sayre was the principal speaker at convocation exercises honoring the founding of Pomona College 62 years ago.

State of the Nation
Rajk Purge: Communist Camouflage?

By JOSEPH C. HARSCH, Chief, Washington News Bureau, The Christian Science Monitor

Washington

Laszlo Rajk is the name of a Communist who was hanged on a Communist scaffold in Hungary Oct. 15. Neither his name nor his case is familiar in the western world. The name does not come easy to a western tongue. Hungary is a long way off. And Communists always seem to be purging each other in that part of the world anyway.

Actually, it is an interesting case, and it is quite important to us of the West, primarily because the regime in Hungary tried so hard to make it appear Laszlo Rajk was a hired agent of the United States. He was sentenced on the ground of alleged services to the United States, which he purported to confess at his trial.

The record of that trial makes extremely interesting reading. There is obviously a great deal of fact in both the accusations and the confessions. There can't be any serious doubt that Rajk, who had at one time been the top Communist in Hungary, conspired or plotted against Matyas Rakosi, who is today the top Communist in Hungary.

Nor can there be much doubt that Rajk also had close relations with several top leaders of the Tito regime in neighboring Yugoslavia. It is even possible that he maintained to the end of his political career some connections with individual Americans.

But it would be one thing if Rajk did whatever he did because he was a political rival of Rakosi, and it would be a different thing if he did it for American gold or under American pressure of any variety. The difference between these two possible explanations is all-important. It is also a difference which involves motives. And you can't prove motives in a court or anywhere else except within the conscience of the individual.

You and I do not know what Laszlo Rajk's motives were. We never shall be able to find out. But we have before us two relevant facts: First, the Communist prosecutor at the Rajk trial obviously started with what he wanted to prove and then did his best to fit what facts he could find, or manufacture, to that pattern. And at many points it is an awkward fit. Second, the Hungarian Government, having induced Rajk to "confess" to the government's trial satisfaction, then proceeded to hang him even though capital punishment is supposed to have been abolished in the "people's democracies" of eastern Europe.

The haste with which Hungary put Laszlo Rajk away, coupled with the dubious relationship between fact and theory at the trial, points pretty strongly toward what really lies behind this case.

Rajk was a power in Hungary. He had led the Communist underground during the war. Stage-managed the breaking up of the first postwar non-Communist Hungarian Government, and he rigged the elections which let the Communists into power. In his own mind he undoubtedly deserved to be the Moscow cold warrior of offensive directed against the United States.

Add to this that as a Spanish Civil War veteran he had friends in all the other European countries which contributed contingents to the International Brigade in that war. Add finally that with the name Rajk, originally the German name Reich, he was a rallying ground for anti-Semitism which persists in Hungary and inside the Communist Party quite as much as outside it. Rakosi is a target of that anti-Semitism.

All these factors add up to the strong probability that Rajk had to be purged if the rule of Rakosi was to be consolidated. And we know that Rakosi was Moscow's chosen instrument in Hungary. In other words Laszlo Rajk is to-day a victim of Moscow's desire to make Hungary a dependable satellite. And the fact that it was necessary to hang him is further evidence that opposition to Moscow policy exists inside the Hungarian Communist Party, and on a very substantial scale.

Obviously, no satellite regime which upheld democratic western institutions is going to advertise to its public the existence of widespread opposition to its policies within the Communist Party. If they must purge a Rajk, they must think up some reason for doing it other than the true reason that he was a powerful political rival to Moscow's preferred agent. So they center the trial around the theme that Rajk was an agent of American "imperialism."

The trial, the verdict, and the sentence would all appear to be a Moscow cold war offensive directed against the United States.

It is much more probable that trial, verdict, and sentence are camouflage designed anxiously to conceal a serious weakness of the Communist regime in Hungary.

4. The Cold War

Edmund Stevens returned to the Soviet Union in 1947. Nearly three years later, when forced out by official harassment, he wrote a landmark account of Soviet society during the absolute depths of Stalinism and the real beginnings of the Cold War. "This is Russia Uncensored" won a Pulitzer Prize. The story presented a ghastly picture. Yet typical for the Monitor, he never lost sight of the long view. "While seeking a realistic modus vivendi with the Soviet Government, the United States should miss no opportunity to proffer the hand of friendship to the Russian people over the head of the Soviet Government. A splendid beginning along these lines by the Voice of America. Even today, what filters through the wall of interference is a far more powerful weapon than the atom bomb—a weapon for peace, that reaches men's minds and creates instead of destroying."

Other thoughtful perspectives are included here by Paul Wohl, William H. Stringer and Joseph C. Harsch. Ernest S. Pisko in 1952 wrote an extensive series titled "Stalin's Hoax on Communists" documenting the fact that while Communism itself was unworkable, Stalin's system no longer even remotely resembled anything that Karl Marx would recognize.

Shortly before the unexpected departure of Khrushchev, Paul Wohl wrote a series in 1964 titled "After Khrushchev—

What?" In many ways the course of events in the Soviet Union were frozen in the Brezhnev era which followed, as maintaining the status quo became the principle objective of the power structure.

Toward the end of the Cold War, David K. Willis continued the tradition of series published by Monitor correspondents leaving Moscow. Again, he touched on the essentials and undercurrents upon which the challenge of such a faulty system was based. "That challenge is materialism—the constant claim based that material force is what counts in the world.... The challenge needs to be faced rather than feared. It is the antithesis of the concept that ideas are mightier than military metal and brute force." In this series Willis provided both a perspective on the preceding Brezhnev years and a look ahead at the likely sources for the changes to come in the 1980s.

US to Double Berlin Air Freight; West Sees Least Risk in Firm Line [7/24/48]

By Joseph C. Harsch

One highly placed American official commented wryly this week that the handling of the Berlin crisis in the press has been much too much like the "he's up, he's down, he's up again" technique of the old school of sports reporters.

I note in the papers on my desk, as I write this, one lead announcing that peace prospects have improved and another that the Berlin situation has "worsened perceptibly." They stand side by side.

It hardly need be said that the Berlin crisis has put a strain on the poise of reporters. One explanation is that the slightest sign of a change in the matter becomes exaggerated when translated into a headline. Another may be that a good many picked up the story "cold" after several weeks of preoccupation with convention politics.

Obviously, it has been hard for both press and public to get the story in accurate perspective and maintain that perspective as minor developments occur.

Let it be reported here and now that the officials of government who have stayed with the Berlin crisis from the beginning have exhibited none of this kaleidoscopic variation from pessimism to optimism. When some headlines were screaming the loudest about the possibility of a "premature war," the men handling the matter were quite unruffled.

And when the headlines switched over to announcing excellent prospects for peace, the same responsible men were just as conscious of the grave nature of the situation as they have been for nearly a month.

The objective fact of the matter is that the situation today is just about what it was two weeks ago—no better and no worse, no more alarming and no less alarming, no more hopeful and no less hopeful.

The basic facts can be stated fairly simply:

The West intends to stay in Berlin.

The Russians want the West out of Berlin.

The West has opened a series of diplomatic exchanges which it is hoped will end in a resolution of the impasse.

The series in all reasonable probability will continue for some time—possibly for as long as two months.

At any time during this period of diplomatic exchanges, some ill-considered remark or impatient action could cause trouble.

Russia is estimated to be excessively sensitive and touchy in recent days due to serious troubles within the satellite fold. It is considered quite possible, in fact, very probable, that the Russians are more willing to take risks now than they would have been two months ago.

It seems likely that nothing has happened or can happen to relieve the situation of its danger until a resolution of the blockade is achieved.

But western strategy is just as determined to seek that resolution patiently as it is to remain in Berlin.

The chance that open hostilities might come out of this situation has never been rated very high, but has always been recognized as present.

The possible risks have been accepted calmly and with extraordinary unanimity for a basic reason.

There is almost complete agreement in high quarters in both Washington and London that capitulation to Russia over Berlin almost certainly would lead to even more extreme difficulties in the future.

In other words, the course of insistence on maintaining the western position in Berlin is believed to be the least dangerous course available to western strategy. It has its risks, but those risks are estimated much lower than the risks which would be involved in the alternative course of submission to Russian pressure.

These convictions and estimates have produced a truly extraordinary firmness of western action. There never has been a moment of deviation from the chosen course of a gesture of retreat.

The West is sitting tight, believing in the soundness of its position, confident that it has the bulk of western public opinion behind it, and strong in the knowledge that now is just as good a time as another to face it out. There are those who say that if the Russians want trouble, let it come now. Western prospects would be no worse, and conceivably better, at this stage than they might be a year or two later.

But it never has been reckoned more than a one out of ten chance that the Russians would choose to use force if even as much as one out of ten.

And the longer it goes on without the use of force, the less likely it is believed that it will lead to a military crisis.

The problem is conceived to be largely one of helping the Russians out of an impossible situation. They are overextended. Their thinking is clouded by the illusions of Communist ideology. Those illusions have got them into all kinds of trouble.

They failed to block the Marshall Plan and to weld the Communist satellite system into a viable empire. An iron curtain which rests in central Europe never has been impervious to western influences. Moscow presumably would like to nail it down along the Elbe for its own protection. But it doesn't nail down. Yugoslavia already is a dissident and unreliable element.

The power balance has been swinging steadily toward the West. The immediate task is to translate this into a settlement of Berlin, which presumably requires a settlement of the whole German problem. It may not come quickly or easily. There could be trouble.

But the men responsible for western strategy in this crisis are reasonably confident that the end result will be both peaceful and satisfactory. They have thought so from the beginning.

Big Three Weigh Talk with Stalin on Berlin Crisis [7/26/48]

By William H. Stringer

LONDON — Britain, France and the US reportedly are considering here the advisability of a direct personal approach to Prime Minister Joseph Stalin as a means of abating the East-West crisis over Berlin.

Certainly, whether the three western powers decide to authorize a personal approach to Stalin by one or more of their ambassadors at Moscow or decide to send new notes to the Kremlin, the present London meeting, which is determining the form and scope of a new allied démarche, is a most momentous move for world peace.

The addition of Walter Bedell Smith, American Ambassador to Moscow, and Charles E. Bohlen, top Russian expert of the United States State Department, to the three-power "Berlin team" of Lewis W. Douglas, Sir William Strang, and René Massigli gives welcome indication that the West's reply will be handled with greatest responsibility, that all available viewpoints will be marshaled, and that the critical alternatives available to the western Allies will be weighed carefully.

On all sides, there is hope that this indication will prove correct.

By personally contacting Stalin via their Moscow ambassadors, the western powers would be avoiding exaggerated publicity and its attendant problem of "face," which is bound to beset any dispatch of new notes to Moscow.

On the other hand, a note if carefully enough phrased— can state matters "for the record" with extreme exactness.

There even is some talk in London that the Americans have considered a proposal to invite Stalin to meet President Truman, Prime Minister Clement R. Attlee and France's premier designate, André Marie to discuss a new German settlement.

[No official proposal for a meeting with Stalin has been received by President Truman, an Associated Press dispatch from Washington quoted the White House as saying.

[According to same source, Charles G. Ross, secretary to the President, said Mr. Truman would welcome Stalin in Washington but had no intention of leaving the United States for such a talk.]

It is virtually certain that the western Allies will indicate their willingness to hold new Big Four discussions on the future of Germany. Any such talks, to have the remotest prospect of success, will require most careful preparation. This must include both clarification of the western viewpoints and greater western unity in support of those viewpoints.

It also is likely that the present London discussions are considering what steps the West can and will take in the event Soviet reaction to the new approach is hostile.

Concentration of western strategy-making at London ends a period of rather discursive deliberations during which Mr. Bevin was debating the "Western Union" at The Hague. Gen. Lucius D. Clay was discussing Berlin at Washington, and Ambassador Smith's expert advice was available only by doubtful wire or diplomatic pouch.

Meanwhile, western officials see their bargaining position distinctly improved by three separate developments.

The first is Mr. Truman's statement, featured prominently in London papers, that recent atomic tests in the Pacific showed the United States had "substantially" improved its position in atomic weapons.

A second reinforcing development is the statement by the United States Republican presidential candidate, Gov. Thomas E. Dewey, affirming his support of the nation's bipartisan foreign policy on Berlin—"No surrender under duress." Unless the Russians are unusually poorly informed on the state of American opinion, they must realize now that election-year politics will not weaken United States foreign policy.

Finally, there is increased optimism concerning the airlift to Berlin, particularly since General Clay's return from Washington with the promise of a substantial increase in Skymaster planes and the decision to build a big new airfield in Berlin.

There is growing belief that the western sectors of Berlin can be supplied with all necessities by air even during the winter, what with the use of war-developed flying aids.

The basic feeling here is that Russia would prefer not to risk hostilities at this time.

[The United States and Britain have banned movements of trains to and from the Russian zone of Germany, according to an Associated Press dispatch from Berlin. American officials said "technical difficulties" caused the stoppage.

[The joint American-British action appeared to be the most positive countermove yet taken by the western Allies to break the Russian blockade of Berlin, now a month old.

[Gen. Lucius D. Clay and Sir Brian Robertson, the American and British Military Governors, took the action at a conference in Frankfurt. The restrictions are effective at once. The prohibition is against the movement of all trains "originating or terminating" in the Soviet zone.]

But to believe that anything short of a patient effort to reach agreement with Russia — with simultaneously the swiftest implementation of a "Western Union" defense pact including the adherence of the United States and Canada will save the peace for very long is viewed here as pure folly.

Fresh from more than a decade of close observation of Russian affairs from both sides of the Iron Curtain, Edmund Stevens today begins a series of uncensored, exclusive articles which will calmly but penetratingly reveal the Soviet Union as it is in 1949.

Though a native-born American, Mr. Stevens long has had a fluent and colloquial command of Russian and wide-ranging contacts among the Russian people and officialdom.

Exit of a Reporter: Suspicion Closes In   [10/18/49]

By Edmund Stevens

An ever-widening gap divided us from Soviet soil as the good ship Byeloostrov cast off. While Leningrad slipped astern, our immediate feelings were of unrestrained relief.

After years of hope and frustration, our final memory of the USSR was a three-hour bout with customs officials that left us angry and exhausted. Every carefully packed article was dragged out and scrutinized. A dydee doll of daughter's that squeaked when squeezed roused special suspicion. Only at the end of a fruitless quest did we learn what they were looking for. At this point the chief inspector accused me of having sold our automobile illegally for gold to a Soviet citizen! I was able to furnish written refutation of this charge — the car in question had been legally transferred to a foreign diplomat — so the officials, looking somewhat crestfallen, permitted us to cram our effects back into trunks and go aboard.

This parting episode was final proof that our move was timely. Of late we had sensed imponderable walls closing in upon us. The air itself was clotted with hate and suspicion. The press attacks on everything American grew in violence and vituperation. Closer to home, not one week passed without American correspondents being pilloried as spies.

The anti-American campaign penetrated even to the child world. Our son and daughter were taunted by their neighborhood playmates as "Amerikantsi," by now a term of opprobrium.

Small wonder our last contacts with Soviet life around us disintegrated rapidly. Even the press department of the Foreign Ministry, through which all our official relations were funneled, now virtually ignored us. Our least request was ignored, our request for appointments refused.

All this was bearable as long as it remained impersonal. But early last spring we suddenly discovered that we were constantly being spied upon. Whenever someone entered or left the garden gate in front of our one-story log house, a curtain in a window opposite was raised slightly.

Young men, too well dressed for loiterers, lounged on nearby corners or strolled back and forth outside. Friends who dropped by were followed home, and in due course called in for questioning. Our next-door neighbors, too, were grilled, and though we had known them for years, they took to avoiding us utterly.

Soon, we noted that not only was the house watched, but we ourselves were shadowed wherever we went. The number of persons assigned to keep tabs on us must have been considerable, and apparently they worked in several shifts.

If my wife and I left the house separately by car or taxi, each of us was tailed by a little black German BMW car with four men inside. They tried to be inconspicuous, ducking behind trucks or trolley busses, and whenever we halted, they too, would pull up at a respectable distance, preferably just behind the corner.

We soon learned their techniques, and one of our favorite sports was to lead them into a blind street and then make a U-turn that brought us alongside their car. This seemed to embarrass them no end, and they would try to crouch down out of sight. The moment we got out of the car, they promptly deployed to strategic street corners or doorways, whence they could watch our moves.

They also followed us if we took the Metro or streetcar, and unless through a series of complex maneuvers we managed to shake them for a bit, they were on our trail from morning until we turned in.

It long has been commonly assumed that all telephones serving foreigners are connected to a central listening post—and on more than one occasion we had evidence that our line was carefully checked. However, there had not been, so we thought, any further penetration of the privacy of our home.

Then, one day, we caught Nastia rifling through our personal desk drawers and collecting note pads and address books. Nastia had come to work for us back in 1946 as an apple-cheeked peasant girl fresh from the village. After one year, during which my wife trained her as a tolerable housemaid, she left to marry a policeman.

We next heard from her last spring, when she called up and asked for her job back. Since nobody wanted to work for Americans and servants were hard to get, my wife agreed to take her on. With the addressbook incident, we realized that Nastia, no longer an apple-cheeked peasant girl, had been assigned to us. We also found that she was in the habit of cross-examining our daughter, age seven, who has that childish knack of total recall for grown-up conversations overheard—drawing her out with the gift of some trivial toy.

Before these troubles, we had lived in Moscow as peacefully and unmolested as anywhere else in the world. Though we saw few Russian friends, we took part in the social life of the closely knit foreign colony, which can provide a nightly party for those thus inclined.

We enjoyed to the full the splendid theaters, concerts, and other cultural advantages of Moscow. But we had trouble keeping art, music and dancing teachers for the children. There were plenty available, well qualified and reasonable. But the moment they discovered we were Americans—usually after the second or third lesson, we could not keep daughter from coming out with it—they bowed out on some pretext.

At the same time, we were far better off than most foreign residents who had no contacts with the Russians and who lived in drab flats or hotel rooms. We had a home of our own furnished and equipped like an American house, with everything including the kitchen sink and a small but attractive garden.

We could only guess as to why we suddenly had become the objects of so much organized interest. But the timing suggested that the Gubichev case might have had some bearing. The Soviets, who claimed diplomatic immunity for this Russian United Nations employee arrested for espionage, said plainly in print that reprisals might be expected against Americans in Moscow.

Guarded entrance to Kremlin tower.

The number of candidates for such reprisals was uncomfortably small, and of these the correspondents were the likeliest.

The Gubichev case had provided a new and dangerous precedent. Whereas the above-mentioned Americans had simply been shipped out of Russia, any future cases probably would be held for trial as long as Gubichev, perhaps even longer. The Russians believe in precedents.

These were the implications that made our intensive shadowing seem especially sinister and speeded our departure. It was a strange climax for an assignment undertaken with the conviction that the world's future depends on understanding and friendship between the United States and Russia.

I hold this conviction now more than ever!

'Forbidden Zone': Red Elite Live Here [10/20/49]

A sudden hush has settled on Moscow's busy Arbat Street. The sleek asphalt roadway, emptied of its traffic, threads between two lines of white-uniformed, white-gloved police spaced at 10-meter intervals along either curb.

The police are on tenterhooks, their eyes strained toward the far end of the street. One of them darts out, bodily lifts up an old peasant woman who has strayed into the road, and deposits her back on the sidewalk. The tension rises to its climax.

With a sudden swoosh a shiny black sedan flashes down the fairway, then an open car full of bodyguards follows in close pursuit. The tension is over in a trice, and the Arbat returns to noisy normal.

Bystanders exchange knowing nods: "Hozyain proyekhal" (There went the boss).

But the black sedan was curtained too heavily and went by too fast for anyone to identify the rear-seat passengers. And the bosses who thus speed between their offices and *dachas* (country houses) twice daily during the summer are not one but numerous.

In a matter of minutes they are rolling along the smooth Uspenskoye Chaussee highway through the charming countryside. It is like an enchanted land out of a Russian fairy tale. The log-built peasant *izbas* (cottages) are trim, with brightly painted roofs and pretty flowerbeds behind neat fences. The borders of the highway are carefully landscaped, and even the side roads are tarmacked. Immaculate policemen just like those along the Arbat stand at every intersection diligently patrolling traffic.

The dachas, too, have an air of enchantment. White walls and shining gabled roofs glisten through the dark evergreen foliage along the side of the Moskva River. But woe to the person who treads too nigh these magic dwellings without the proper MVD (secret police) credentials. He finds himself in major trouble.

Once, while out for a drive the summer before last we took a wrong turn and ended up at a tall green gate. There was nobody in sight, but realizing our mistake, we made a quick turnabout.

A figure in an MVD blue cap suddenly materialized from the bushes, waving his arms, red-faced and furious. As I pulled up he demanded to know where we were going. Having heard our explanation and apparently impressed by our car, he warned, "Don't let me ever see your around here again."

This whole area along the Moskva River west of the capital is officially designated as the "Forbidden Zone." Only persons with special MVD clearance may reside there—and no foreigners, under any circumstances!

Last year we still could drive along the main roads, and the diplomatic corps often picnicked and bathed in the area. Now, however, all foreign cars are turned back at the city limits.

Many of the Soviet great and near-great, from Prime Minister Joseph Stalin down, have their dachas in the Forbidden Zone. Besides top government and party chiefs, cabinet ministers, and leaders of the armed services, they include factory directors, members of the Academy of Sciences, prominent authors, artists and stage celebrities.

These privileged groups comprise the cream of Soviet society. Not that the Russians have even a remote counterpart of western social life. There are no country clubs in the Forbidden Zone. Neighbors seldom call—in fact, they usually do not even know one another unless their work brings them into contact.

There are two main factors tending to discourage free social contact within Soviet high officialdom. The first is fear. Such contact is frowned on by the ever-suspicious, ever-vigilant MVD. Moreover, personal friends are potentially dangerous. If they know too much, they may denounce you—or if they get into trouble, your ties with them may incriminate you. During the great purges many persons were undone by their own family relationships. A prudent Russian today hesitates to confide in even his wife too fully.

The second factor that circumscribes the cultural as well as social life of the high Soviet official is work. Few persons work harder and longer hours than those in responsible Soviet positions. The average workday of a Soviet official begins around 11 o'clock in the morning when, after a hasty breakfast, he heads for his office. There he works through steadily until after midnight, with brief time out at 4 and again at 9 o'clock for a bite in the buffet or dining room.

"Reception hours" in most government offices and ministries run from 11 P.M. to 1 A.M., and during this time the official must be on deck just in case the Kremlin telephones or one of his superiors drops by with a query. He arrives home at about 2 in the morning, when his faithful wife has dinner ready—and so off to bed.

After a week of this routine, when Sunday rolls around, rare is the husband with strength or inclination for anything beyond a brief round of shopping. Nor does the wife of such a Soviet functionary have much independent existence of her own. With rare exceptions, such as Mme Molotova, wife of Vyacheslav M. Molotov and twice a commissar in her own right under her maiden name, the ordinary Soviet official's wife is not a career woman. Though she be married to a member of the mighty Politburo, the public probably has never seen her picture or even her name in print. The Soviet press does not go in for either society or gossip columns.

The official's wife goes to the ballet, the theater or a concert only on those rare occasions when her husband can get off to escort her, though she may take in a motion picture from time to time unescorted.

Ordinarily, the Soviet official's dacha, town flat and automobile all go with his job, so if demoted or dismissed he stands to lose much. At the same time, the charges he pays for these facilities are almost nominal. His salary, with allowances, may range up to 8,000 or 10,000 rubles monthly (about $1,940).

Academy members, who are in a class by themselves, draw a total of 25,000 rubles a month (about $4,800). In addition, their regular incomes are supplemented from time to time by cash bonuses, especially in the case of factory directors.

Such is life among the upper Soviet official and managerial classes at or near the apex of the Soviet social pyramid.

Essentially they belong to the same social category and live by the same book of party rules. For leading citizens of a revolutionary new society, their behavior patterns are surprisingly conservative and conventional. Indeed, they are more restricted and inhibited than their counterparts in western "bourgeois" countries.

Peasant Is Squeezed 'Twixt Quota and Cow [10/25/49]

"Auntie" Dasha's problems are discussed in detail—a clear sketch of a peasant life behind the Iron Curtain emerges from the experienced pen of a veteran Moscow correspondent, now in Germany.

Ever since her husband went off to war, never to return, Auntie Dasha's whole economy revolved around her cow. Each morning at 4 she milked the patient animal, trudged two miles to the railway station with her two cans of milk, and caught the 5:30.

Arriving in Moscow at 6:15, she delivered by streetcar to her five steady customers, caught the 7:15 back from town, hurried home with her empty cans, helped herself to some boiled-potato mash from a big black pot on the cold stove, and after some hasty instructions to son Grisha, age eight, was out of the house in time to report at 9 o'clock for the day's field work on the collective farm.

At 1 o'clock Auntie Dasha came home, lit the samovar, and built just enough fire in the stove to warm the pot. After that she and Grisha had their main meal of the day, consisting of warmed-up boiled-potato mash and generous chunks of black rye bread, washed down with a hot drink brewed from dried raspberry leaves.

By 3 o'clock she was back in the field, where she worked until 6, getting home just as the cows, back from grazing, ambled through the village, mooing lustily, while the little cowherd brought up the rear, cracking his long rope whip.

Each cow, including Auntie Dasha's, turned in at its own yard without prompting. While the cow waited for her in the shed, Auntie Dasha went off to inspect her large potato patch, just to check up on Grisha's hoeing. When Sunday come she would tend it herself. After the evening milking, followed by a supper of cold potato mash and black bread, Auntie Dasha would sit down to do her sums. She could neither read not write, but necessity had taught her figures.

Laboriously she multiplied the day's yield of milk in liters by the day's market price in rubles. Next she subtracted her train fare, then her streetcar fare, then the cost of a kilo of black bread and any incidental purchases, such as matches, a candle, or some salt. She checked the remainder against the cash knotted in her kerchief before she deposited it in her mattress.

With the market price of milk fluctuating seasonally between 3 and 7 rubles (60 cents to $1.40) a quart and her cow giving about 800 quarts a year, Auntie

Dasha grossed around 3,500 rubles ($760) a year. She spent about 500 rubles ($100) on black bread (at 1 ruble 75 kopeks a kilo), and other incidentals. Transportation, with the new fare increases, added up to more than 600 rubles ($120). This left a balance of something under 2,700 rubles ($540).

At this point, the figuring became more involved. As the owner of a private cow and with half a hectare of land for her private use, Auntie Dasha had obligations to the state. She had a state delivery quota of 30 kilos of butter a year, but in lieu of butter she was permitted to pay a cash equivalent of 1,500 rubles ($300). Though she kept no chickens, she had an annual delivery quota of 500 eggs annually. In place of these, she paid a cash equivalent of 500 rubles.

After meeting all these obligations last year, she still had more than 600 rubles left with which to buy fodder for the winter.

Auntie Dasha met her remaining obligations to the state in kind. She filled her meat quota by slaughtering the calf which her cow bore each January. Her private potato patch yielded her 600 kilograms of potatoes. After delivering her quota of 300 kilos to the state, this left her with 300 kilos, which was just enough to take care of herself and Grisha through the coming year.

In the fall, she received a load of hay and a large bag of turnips from the collective farm as payment for her workdays. The collective farm chairman, whose house had a new tin roof, had explained at a members' meeting just why that year the collective farm was in no position to pay off in grain or cash. But his arithmetic was way over Auntie Dasha's head, and anyway she was thankful for the hay.

All in all, it had been a fairly good year. She had rented the front part of her *izba* (cottage) to my family for the summer for 800 rubles. Even after paying the 50 percent tax on "unearned" revenue, this would give her money for shoes for the winter.

That was in 1948. When we saw Auntie Dasha again this spring, she had just been notified that under the newly decreed scale, all her delivery quotas had been raised. Sadly, she had about decided to sell the cow and buy chickens with the proceeds. She still would have to fill her egg, meat and potato quotas, but with no cow her butter quota would be cut. With no calf to slaughter, she would discharge her meat quota with cash. But with fresh eggs bringing as high as 15 or 16 rubles (about $3) for 10 on the open market, she thought she still might do better if she shifted from a dairy to a poultry economy.

Leon Trotsky once loftily described the peasant as the pack animal of civilization. He wanted to express his appreciation of the peasant's economic role, in addition to his contempt for the docility with which the peasant allowed himself to be exploited under the old régime.

Since then the whole structure of society has been transformed. But the new régime has evolved techniques for squeezing the peasant far more thoroughly than those of the old-time landlords. Save in certain pampered areas, like the Georgian citrus groves or the rich wheatland of the Kuban Cossack country, the peasant has yet to reap most of the benefits enjoyed by the urban intellectual and working classes.

The money the peasantry collected from high food prices in wartime was canceled by the currency reform. Their obligations to the state in kind and money have been upped from year to year. Consumer goods, abundant in the cities, have yet to reach most rural areas, and prices to the peasant are higher.

It is hard to generalize about living standards of the peasantry in such an enormous country. Conditions vary with the texture of the soil and the resourcefulness of the people. Economic changes, too, including changes for the better, can take place in the Soviet Union with dramatic suddenness. One day the government may unexpectedly relax the pressure on the peasantry. Until then there will be millions of Auntie Dashas pondering whether to trade their cows for chickens or vice versa.

Graft Grafts Itself to Roots of Business   [11/1/49]

The shortcomings of Soviet trade are a favorite target for Soviet "self-criticism." Nothing conveys to the average Soviet citizen-consumer the impression the government really has his interests at heart more than these frequent and candid ribbings of corruption and inefficiency in the wholesale and retail distribution systems. Seldom, however, does censorship permit their transmission abroad.

In publishing such unsavory material, the Soviet press invariably absolves the Soviet system of any blame or responsibility. The abuses involved are pictured as "capitalist survivals," the inference being that they presently will be outlived.

This picture is correct in the sense that government trade organizations have tended to attract persons who once were in private trade, either before the Revolution or during the NEP (New Economic Policy) period when private trade was legalized for a time. Many of

Peasant women today around the USSR
engaging in free enterprise—selling
fruits along the roadside.

these persons, having endured severe personal hardship through confiscation and expropriation, are secretly antagonistic to the Soviet system—and privately bent on recouping some part of their losses.

At the same time, much of the waste and inefficiency the papers inveigh against stems directly from absence in the government trade system of the commercial competitive element which operated as a powerful corrective to incompetence under a free economy.

No Soviet Government trade organization can go bankrupt no matter how mismanaged—unless the government as a whole goes bankrupt. Moreover, by eliminating the profit motive from trade, the Soviet trade system tends to deprive management and sales personnel of the main incentive toward greater effort and efficiency.

This is no hypothetical argument. One may see the results on every side, in the prevailing slovenly nature of window displays, in the indifference of sales clerks toward customers (model stores excepted), in buying stock without reference to consumer demand.

One roving reporter, for example, calculated that it would take the local toy stores in the town of Baku 3,000 years to dispose of their present supply of jack-in-the-boxes. He also told how the local pharmacy trust, unable to dispose of its stocks of tooth powder, finally sold the lot as ceiling whitewash.

Another story dealt with the leading Kiev art shop, which, instead of supplying the public demand for busts of Lenin, Stalin, and other Soviet leaders, gluttted its shelves with plaster cherubs and cupids. When the "apolitical" bourgeois character of these exhibits was called to the manager's attention, he merely chopped the wings off the cherubs and cupids, tied red kerchiefs around their necks, and tried to palm them off as statues of "young pioneers."

Besides bad management, petty grafting is fairly common in Soviet retail trade. One of the favorite practices, judging by press reports, is for a store manager to mark up certain highly salable items just a fraction above the authorized retail price. He then splits the difference with his bookkeeper and sales force. Such cases are small stuff compared to the full-dress public scandals that are aired from time to time.

Several months ago, the Moscow newspaper, *Trud*, broke the story of a large ring of speculators operating in and around the state jewelry merchandising organization known as "Yuvelirtorg." It began with a raid by the antispeculation squad on a big jewelry store on the Petrovka, sometimes called Moscow's Fifth Avenue. The police arrested 17 persons and seized 2,000,000 rubles' worth of valuables in this first haul.

The technique employed by the speculators was simplicity itself. They stationed contact men outside the various Yuvelirtorg shops. Private citizens who came to sell their valuables to the store would then be approached with offers to buy their watches, jewelry or gold coins, privately. If they agreed, the articles thus acquired would be either resold directly to private customers or else turned in to Yuvelirtorg. In either instance, the ring made a handsome profit.

One trick was to buy broken watches at a low price and sell them to the government organization at the price authorized for watches in good repair. *Trud* reported that more than 2,000 defective watches were thus foisted onto the government at a profit of more than 1,000,000 rubles for the ring. All this was possible because of the complicity of the manager of the Moscow division of Yuvelirtorg and of his head bookkeeper.

Trud sharply rebuked the Minister of Trade for failing to take corrective action and even reprimanded the Moscow Chief Prosecutor for the "extremely sluggish tempo" of his investigation—and demanded that the case be followed through regardless of who got stepped on. No other paper touched the story.

One sequel of the raid on Yuvelirtorg, I learned from different sources, concerned a man whose phone number was found by the police in the possession of one of those arrested. The party in question was picked up one night and released five days later—but only after his wife had gathered up all the family valuables, including jewels and silverware saved from before the Revolution, and delivered them to the police officer in charge of the case. Thereupon the man was let out and all record of his arrest destroyed. The use of a government store front for private speculation is fairly common not only in the case of jewelry but also in the so-called commission shops, which sell clothing, furniture, musical instruments, and objets d'art of every description for private owners, deducting a 15 percent commission. In such cases the appraiser either will refuse to accept the article for sale on commission, or else will name an unacceptably low figure.

As the chagrined owner reaches the door, he is accosted by someone who offers him a better price privately. The owner's mood by then usually is such that he jumps at an offer even though he is not getting the price to which he is entitled.

Other instances of "underground capitalism" dug up by the Moscow press have centered around such fabulous figures as the "button king," who cornered the button supply, short-circuiting the legitimate state channels, and the "mouse king," who built up a million-ruble private business breeding white mice which he sold to state laboratories.

All this suggests that some private enterprise—even although it is of an underground nature—persists in Soviet Russia at this present stage of development toward "full Communism."

The 'Thing' Stalks: Its Initials Are MVD [11/8/49]

During our last weeks in Moscow we obtained an unusual, close-up view of how the Soviet police state operates. The protocol and decorum that ordinarily shield foreigners from too-near contact with this Frankenstein—which we came to call the "Thing"—were suspended.

No longer content with peeking through the window, the "Thing" invaded the privacy of our home, peered over our shoulders, breathed down our backs. We suddenly realized that, despite our American passports, we had no more legal rights vis-a-vis the "Thing" than tens of millions of Soviet citizens all around us.

Lenin, in has famed essay "The State and Revolution," reduced the state apparatus to a common denominator of naked, unchecked coercive power—army plus police force plus prisons—in the hands of the few who impose their will on the helpless multitude. Though Lenin had in mind the czarist state which he was out to destroy, the Soviet police state he established was a carbon copy of this concept.

The Soviet system took over the apparatus of czarist absolutism—the army, police, and, in particular, the prisons and penal settlements. It expanded and refined this heritage to the point where Nicholas I and his gendarmerie or Nicholas II and his *Okhrana* (secret police) would seem like easy-going amateurs.

Czarist absolutism in its heyday never succeeded in fully silencing the defiant voice of freedom. The Russian intellectual giants of the 19th century feuded with the government all their lives, and, though subject to various reprisals, never abandoned the field. The present régime never would suffer a Pushkin, a Gogol, a Belinsky, a Staltykov-Schedrin or even a Tolstoy to denounce its tyranny, criticize its injustices, puncture its self-inflation, lampoon its hypocrisy.

It knows how to nip in the bud effectively the least indication of disaffection or rebellion. The difference between czarist absolutism and the Soviet police state is

that when Lenin was sentenced to Siberian exile he was allowed to take his library with him and pursue his revolutionary writings.

Under czarism, the individual still enjoyed some legal defenses from the whim of absolutism. Soviet state practice recognizes no inalienable human rights or other limitations to its total monopoly of power.

Reversing the order of the social contract, the Soviet state does not derive its powers by delegation from the citizenry, nor is it their creation. The citizens are the creatures of the state, enjoying only such rights and liberties as the state affords them—and these the state is free to abrogate whenever it wishes.

Paradoxically, the Soviet "Stalin" Constitution guarantees a whole list of civil rights—including freedom of press, speech, assembly, fair trial and independence of the courts. But this, like the Soviet "free" elections and the Soviet Parliament, is unreal window dressing.

The essence of power is vested in the Ministry of Internal Affairs, whose three Russian initials, MVD, cast a dread spell the length and breadth of the Soviet Union and even far beyond its borders.

The MVD need answer for its action to none but the topmost Kremlin hierarchy. No other ministry or government agency dares gainsay it, and I have seen high officials quake at the mere mention of the letters.

Just as the Soviet Constitution formally guarantees personal liberties which are denied in application, so the whole terminology of democratic society has been taken over and each word endowed with peculiar connotation closer to the opposite of their original meanings.

Thus, for "democracy" read "dictatorship," for "voluntary" read "compulsory," for "free elections" read "rigged one-party ballots," for "peace-loving" read "truculent"—and you can't go far wrong.

Under the Soviet system the people have become the property of the state along with land, industry, and other forms of national wealth. Hence the state's right to dictate what the individual reads and thinks and deny him access to all sources of unauthorized information.

Hence the right of the state to tell the citizen where he must live and work, to tie him to his job or place of residence more firmly than his serf ancestors ever were.

Hence the right of the state to specify whom he can or cannot marry, to reward or penalize him for the number of children he has or has not.

Hence the right of the state to invade his privacy by opening his mail, calling him in for third-degree questioning, or searching his home without pretext or explanation.

Finally, hence the right of the state to withdraw whatever limited freedom of movement it has accorded him any time it so desires by the simple expedient of arrest, unhampered by *habeas corpus*.

In the Soviet Union nobody ever tries to sue the government or contest the legality of its actions. Against the overwhelming weight of absolute power the individual has no legal protection or redress whatever; he is at the mercy of the merciless.

I recall once how *Krokodil*, the Soviet humorous weekly, picked up the story of a life prisoner in an American penitentiary who sued a publisher for damages—and won the case. It was over the publication of his story which the publisher presumably had distorted.

The idea of a man serving a life-term sentence winning a court case appealed to *Krokodil's* sense of humor as absurd. Whoever heard of a convict in the Soviet Union winning a court case? The fact that under American law even a lifer still might have legal rights was beyond *Krokodil's* understanding.

This view of the citizen as state property explains, among other things, the Soviet attitude toward displaced persons of Soviet nationality. The Soviet state demands the right to reclaim its citizens—regardless of whether they themselves wish to be reclaimed.

The Soviets, along with denial of other individual rights, do not recognize for their citizens the right of expatriation. The methods of the police state are nowhere so revealed as in the treatment of Soviet citizens who apply for permission to go abroad.

The Great Red Purge: Password — Torture! [11/28/49]

The great purge began with a bullet in the back of Stalin's heir apparent, Sergei Kirov, in the drafty second-floor corridor of Leningrad's Smolny Institute on December. 4, 1934.

A few days later sharp-eyed readers of *Izvestia* could trace the letters "Stalin" faintly etched onto a published photograph of Kirov lying in state. More than three years afterward *Izvestia's* chief editor, Nikolai Bukharin, was executed as a self-confessed traitor after the last of the notorious "model" trials.

By then the purge had almost run its course. The number of victims never will be known unless some day the archives of the Soviet Ministry of the Interior are opened to historians. But Russians who did not suffer close personal hurt in the purge are as rare as Russians unaffected by the war.

I recall the case of a German Communist we knew who held a responsible job. One night the NKVD (secret police) took him away. It was rumored that he had belonged to the Trotskyites. His Russian wife, a long-standing party member, promptly added her own accusations. She cited domestic trivia, such as the circumstance that he always kept one drawer of his desk carefully locked and never permitted her to touch it, as evidence that he had guilty secrets to conceal.

This display of "vigilance" not only allayed suspicion, but so commended her to the favorable notice of the authorities that two years later she was sent to Washington as personal secretary of the Soviet Ambassador, a supreme expression of party trust.

She returned to Moscow at the war's end to find that her ex-husband (one of her first acts after his arrest had been to secure a divorce), like other German émigrés for whom the Kremlin now had use, had been totally exonerated and was earmarked for an important post in eastern Germany. Her offer to go back to him was spurned.

Foreigners who had taken out Soviet citizenship were among those hit hardest by the purge.

Joe Fineberg had given the best years of his life to translating the works of Lenin and Stalin. At the end of 1937 he disappeared. Six months later he was released, looking 20 years older and minus his front teeth. The investigators had "removed" them while trying to determine his guilt or innocence.

Albert Troyer was a citrus fruit specialist from southern Alabama. Soviet talent scouts, looking for someone to help develop varieties of lemons suited to the Black Sea coast, persuaded Mr. Troyer to sign a lucrative "valuta" contract—salary in dollars deposited abroad, ruble expenses paid while in the Soviet Union.

When the Troyers reached Sukhumi in the summer of 1932 everything was better even than the contract provided. They had a cozy bungalow in a lovely garden on the rim of a turquoise sea. Mr. Troyer's Soviet employers eagerly provided him with every experimental facility he requested. For the first time in his career he could cross and graft lemons to his heart's content. For nearly five years the Troyers were very happy in their subtropical paradise. The lemons grew bigger and better, and Troyer, completely dedicated, had no time or interest left for political developments.

Then, one day in the spring of 1936, his immediate superior at the botanical station told Mr. Troyer an order had come from Moscow that foreigners no longer could be employed, and that he, Mr. Troyer, must either quit or become a Soviet citizen. He was given three days to decide.

Mr. Troyer's wife was determined to keep her American passport, but he could not bear to give up his lemons. To him the question of passports seemed trivial compared to his research. Accordingly, he filled in the forms and turned in his American passport.

One week later he was arrested while at work. His wife was not permitted to see him. Packages of food and clothing which she took to the local NKVD were accepted for three days, but on the fourth day the package was returned with the explanation that it could not be delivered as her husband had been transferred to an undisclosed destination.

Soon the authorities made trouble for Mrs. Troyer, refusing to extend her residence permit. After fruitless efforts to learn something of her husband's fate, she left for Moscow. Sympathetic American Embassy officials who heard her story told her they could do nothing since her husband had signed away his American birthright.

Today, back home in the United States, Mrs. Troyer still awaits word of her husband.

We saw the purge at close quarters in those years. We occupied one room in a communal flat, and we lost several shifts of neighbors. Our room was next to the outer door, and when the squads rang the bell at 2 o'clock in the morning I would jump out of bed and let them in.

They were blue-capped youngsters, scarcely out of their teens. When the man they were after happened to be away overnight, one of them dialed a phone number and asked instructions from a "comrade colonel." The speaker identified himself as "This is Kursant number so-and-so." (A *kursant* is a trainee in special security troop officer schools.)

My most vivid recollection is that of a young mother. Across the years I still can hear her screams as they took her two-month-old baby from her and she and her husband were led off to the "Black Crow"—Russian equivalent of the "Black Maria," or police wagon. Only three weeks previously her husband had returned from an assignment to Japan with all sorts of lovely presents for his wife and child.

The brakes were applied to the tumbrels in the summer of 1938, and soon the purge rolled into reverse. Nikolai Yezhov, H.G. Yagoda's accuser and his successor as head of the NKVD, vanished without trace. Minor purge abuses were investigated and denounced. The provincial papers were full of proceedings against ogrelike NKVD officials who had rounded up school children as counterrevolutionaries. By then the Kremlin realized that in its zeal to eliminate possible opponents it had undermined public morale and impaired the country's economic and military strength through the wholesale destruction of intellect and talent.

The purge disclosed, among other things, the utter physical dependence of the all-powerful Kremlin rulers on their NKVD bodyguard.

Stalin and his retinue no longer appeared in public unless all within gunshot had been carefully checked for security. The Kremlin itself was an armed camp, bristling with tommy gunners, ever on the alert to repel sudden attack.

These extraordinary precautions themselves were a source of gravest danger, for anyone who controlled this praetorian guard might easily have staged a palace revolution.

Such intentions, in fact, were imputed to Yagoda, and in the course of the purge the Kremlin security setup was cleaned out more than once.

Accordingly, in 1939, Stalin brought his fellow Georgian and old-time comrade, Lavrenty Beria, to Moscow to succeed the fanatical, unbalanced Yezhov. Thereafter he doubtless rested easier.

Stalin Sits as Legend: Malenkov Sits Tight [11/29/49]

"Stalin is the Lenin of today."

This recent formula, which Soviet editorial writers use with recurring frequency, sums up the postwar apotheosis of the Kremlin leader.

At one time, Stalin claimed to be no more than the humble apprentice of Lenin, the great revolutionary master. The very term "Stalinism" was coined as a derogatory epithet.

Seldom in history has a man become a legend in his own lifetime. Yet Stalin the man already has been totally replaced by Stalin the legend where the Russian public is concerned.

The legendary Stalin is a mellow, unclelike character, who loves to accept bouquets of flowers from little girls in token of thanks for their "happy childhood." He radiates gentle patience and benevolent wisdom.

All this bears little resemblance to the sharp, ruthless politician who gained control of the party machinery as Lenin's hand faltered and who, by a series of deft moves, not only consolidated his own position but outmaneuvered the entire group of Lenin's close associates, who finally were disposed of during the purges of 1934-1938.

Chief promoter of the Stalin legend is Stalin himself. His mode of life, his every public act or utterance, is calculated to fit this role. Having divorced himself largely from the everyday business of government, he descends from the Olympian remoteness of his semi-retirement only at rare intervals to make history with a few well-chosen words, usually in the form of a press release.

Stalin has not made a public speech since February 1946, when he addressed his constituents during the Supreme Soviet election campaign. From year to year, he lengthens his vacations at his Sukhumi villa on the Black Sea shore, leaving Moscow in August and returning only just in time for the May Day parade.

Meanwhile, responsibility for running the state gravitates increasingly to Stalin's lieutenants, the members of the Politburo. This is the level at which the struggle for personal power takes place.

The order of ascendancy at a given time always can be ascertained from the alignment of portraits displayed on Soviet holidays. When Andrei A. Zhadnov was alive, Stalin, in the center, was flanked invariably by Vyacheslav M. Molotov on the right and Zhdanov on the left.

Next to Molotov came Georgi M. Malenkov and next to Zhdanov, Laurenty P. Beria, but at one time Beria was alongside Molotov.

The demise of Zhdanov disarranged the pattern and for a time Beria and Malenkov appeared to be running neck and neck while Molotov continued to hold first place.

The race was so close that I recall how, during the November 7, 1947, festivities, the positions of Malenkov and Beria portraits were shifted twice in the course of a single day.

Stalin and Kirov together in 1926. Eight years later, Kirov would be assasinated during the Great Red Purge.

Soviets Pen History with Blot on West   [12/10/49]

"The capitulationist Trotskyite-Zinovievite bloc was unmasked as an anti-Soviet bloc, and the capitulators of the Right as agents of the kulak... The capitulationist Troskyite..."

By now I was wide awake. Though my watch said only 6:30 A.M., the bright May early morning sunshine already flooded the room.

The voice of our 11-year-old son droned on through the open door:

"The capitulationist..."

"Hey, there," I shouted, "why don't you turn over the record, or, better still, turn it off?"

"But, Pa, we have party history first thing in the morning today, and unless I can repeat the text the teacher will be terribly angry. The capitulationist Trotskyite . . ."

"Party history" is a required subject in the Soviet Union, from the fourth grade onward. And everyone in the Soviet Union, from child to graybeard, uses the same textbook: "The History of the Communist Party (Bolsheviks) of the USSR—Shorter Course," commonly known as "Shorter Course" for short.

More than 15,000,000 copies of this have been printed, in every language of the Soviet Union and in all important world languages.

The "Shorter Course" appeared first in 1938. The flyleaf carried no author's name, but simply the note that it was prepared by a special commission of the Communist Party Central Committee and was approved by the latter.

Last year, hailing the 10th anniversary of the publication of this momentous work, the Soviet press let it be known that it, like so many other remarkable things, was the product of Stalin's genius.

The "Shorter Course" is the official, authoritative history of the Bolshevik movement. Its every phrase, word, and punctuation mark have been literally weighed on an apothecary's scale and scrutinized under a microscope, and are guaranteed 100 percent duration-proof. For party members and Soviet citizens this is the distilled essence of wisdom beyond all question or debate.

The "Shorter Course" purports to trace the development of the Russian Revolutionary movement from its inception. The pictures it presents are highly unflattering to Stalin's political rivals; it gives the impression that most of Lenin's chief lieutenants were traitors and agents provocateurs, the main villain of the piece being Leon Trotsky. Stalin, by contrast, emerges as Lenin's closest and most trusted disciple.

The "Shorter Course" is so universally studied by young and old because it is the only authoritative textbook on party history. Writers of lesser weight than Stalin are in constant danger of deviation.

Since the war the "Shorter Course" has been supplemented by the appearance of Stalin's "Collected Works," of which 12 volumes have been published so far, with more to come. Here the reader will find the materials of the "Shorter Course" amplified and documented.

The third volume, covering the revolutionary period of 1917, makes Stalin's contribution to the Bolshevik triumph appear hardly less than that of Lenin. The two men emerge as virtually equal partners, and Stalin as the one who actually planned and prepared the October 1917, uprising that carried the Bolsheviks to power while Lenin was in hiding. The biographical chronology at the back of the book contains the following illuminating entries:

"October 24—Lenin arrives at Smolny in the evening. Stalin briefs him on the course of political events."

"October 24-25—Lenin and Stalin lead the October armed uprising."

All this is a far cry from the days when Stalin claimed to be nothing more than the humble pupil of the great revolutionary teacher Lenin.

Rewriting of history in the interest of the party line is not confined to the "Shorter Course." The whole of Russia's past, among other things, is being realigned to back up Kremlin policy.

The entire expansionist policy of czarism, the subjugation of non-Russian peoples in Asia and Europe by an empire which Lenin described as a "prison of peoples," is approved now as a "progressive" development. Some current authors even write nostalgically about the Russian colonization of Alaska.

By far the most astonishing revision of history relates to the recent world war, astonishing because the events revised still are fresh in the memory of millions. Yet a man from Mars, landing today in Russia with no foreknowledge of earthly affairs, would gain the impression from much of the current Soviet literature that the Soviet Union, fighting singlehanded, defeated a Capitalist coalition of Germany, Japan and Italy, backed by the United States and Britain.

The outcome of the war is now invariably acclaimed as a Communist victory over world Capitalism. The role of the western powers in the defeat of Germany is completely discounted. The West is portrayed as deliberately stalling on the opening of a second front while secretly aiding the Nazis.

For example, Colonel Chistov, writing in the army paper *Red Star*, describes the effects of Anglo-American bombing on the German war potential as nil, and concludes:

"Only the heroic struggle of the Soviet armed forces, which fought Fascist Germany singlehanded and were able by themselves without any outside help to completely smash the Hitler war machine and liberate

Europe from the German Fascist invaders, compelled the ruling circles of the West to hasten the debarkation of forces in France."

The further inference is drawn that the main objective of the landings was less to defeat the Germans than to forestall this complete "liberation" of western Europe by the Soviets.

In a *Literary Gazette* piece titled "General Bradley— Warmonger," Boris Lavrenyev writes:

"After breaching the mythical 'Atlantic Wall.' Bradley's troops raced ahead, opposed only by meager German units which had no hope of reinforcement because the Germans, routed by the Soviet offensive in the East, were in no position to send reserves to the West.

Another writer on military matters, Major Gernal Zamyatin, in a lecture on the Soviet offensive of January 1945, ascribes the German breakthrough in the Ardennes to the inactivity of the Anglo-American forces, who were in no hurry to wind up the war. He implies that had it not been for the launching of the Soviet offensive, the Germans would have reached Antwerp.

Revision of the war's history proceeds by stages.

Having written off the part of the western powers in defeating Germany, Soviet historians are building up the Soviet Union's brief participation in the Pacific war as the decisive factor in beating Japan.

Far from agreeing that the atom bomb hastened Japanese surrender, the Soviets belittle the military effects of the Hiroshima and Nagasaki blasts, while playing them up as "atrocities."

According to one *Pravda* explanation, the atom-bomb blasts were intended mainly to frighten the USSR. The western powers, says the author, were impelled to this step by rage and chagrin over the swift Soviet victory over Germany.

Soviet Moral Code: How Wrong is Right [12/13/49]

The Soviet practice of doctoring facts to fit the party line is not confined to history. Truth, falsehood, good and evil, right and wrong, theories, beliefs and personalities—in all spheres, climes or ages—are judged solely by whether they serve or hinder the Communist purpose.

A year ago, the newspaper *Evening Moscow*, reviewing a Russian edition of one of Upton Sinclair's recent novels, wrote:

"We know Upton Sinclair as one of the most honest, righteous, and scrupulous of writers."

Six months later, the *Literary Gazette*, also published in Moscow, declared:

"Upton Sinclair has long been known as a careerist and literary racketeer."

The total turnabout in the Soviet estimate of Mr. Sinclair's literary integrity was caused not by any new book of his, but by his support of the Atlantic Pact. Had he instead chosen to support one of the various Soviet-sponsored "peace congresses," he still would be hailed as "scrupulous." Such examples are legion.

This overall party-line approach to everything was prescribed for his followers long ago by Lenin. Deriding the belief in absolute standards of good and evil as a capitalist "humbug," the founder of the Soviet state declared that every human society devised its own moral code.

He told the youthful delegates to the Third Congress of the Soviet Young Communist League (Komsomol), for their guidance: "Morality is all that promotes the destruction of the old exploiter society and the unification of all laborers round the proletariat which is creating the new society of Communists."

Lenin's attitude on morals follows from the premises of his materialist philosophy, set forth in his treatise "Materialism and Empiriocriticism," in which he stated:

"Materialism admits in general the existence of objective reality [matter] independent of consciousness, sensations, experience...Consciousness...is solely the reflection of being, at best a reflection that is approximately correct."

Further, he added: "Matter is the thing that, acting on our sensory organs, produces sensations; matter is objective reality...Matter, nature, being, are the prior data, while spirit, consciousness, sensation, the psychic, are the secondary data."

From this it logically follows that human consciousness, being derived from and dependent upon inanimate matter, cannot establish any independent, absolute spiritual values or moral code.

Stalin, who has a knack for oversimplifying Lenin's philosophical abstractions in practical terms, wrote in "Problems of Leninism:" "Whatever the nature of society, whatever its material conditions, such are its ideas, theories, political views."

Paradoxically, Lenin, for all his materialism and denial of moral standards, had a boundless idealistic faith in the perfectability of man and human institutions and endowed his unthinking material universe with an essentially rational character. Therein lies the

ПОМНИ, ШКОЛЬНИК, ТВЕРДО ЗНАЙ:
КАЖДЫЙ КОЛОС В УРОЖАЙ,

ЧТОБ ДЕВЧОНКИ И МАЛЬЧИШКИ ЕЛИ БУЛКИ И КОВРИЖКИ.

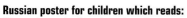

Russian poster for children which reads:
"Remember, schoolboy, know it well:
Each must do his share
at harvest time,
so little girls and little boys
can eat rolls and gingerbread."
**Right, Young Pioneers induction
ceremony near Red Square.**

major philosophic contradiction of the whole Communist position.

Lenin believed not only in a matter that "moved" but also in one that was able to "think."

In this picture, which Marx and Engels first developed and Lenin elaborated, matter — or nature — including human society, moves from lower toward higher forms of organization. This is essentially the 19th-century concept of progress — motion forward toward something better, as opposed to reaction — motion back-ward toward something worse. Neither Marx nor Lenin troubled with the following question: How, without fixed standards of good and bad, is one to judge what is better and what is worse regardless of whether the motion is forward or backward?

In explaining how this progressive motion operated, Marx and Lenin also borrowed from 19th-century idealism, adapting to their system the "dialectic" process of thesis-antithesis-synthesis developed by the German philosopher Hegel. With Hegel, the process was consciously directed toward the perfection of an absolute idea that was also supreme reality.

Lenin, too, had his goal of perfection. Applied to human society, the law of development from a lower to a higher form was construed as meaning that in the current stage Capitalism must of historic necessity be replaced by Communism.

Commenting on this "discovery" in the party history "Shorter Course," Stalin writes: "Socialism [Communism], from being a dream of a better future for mankind, became a science."

This ingenious combination of philosophy and wishful thinking is a decisive factor in shaping Kremlin policy today. The concept of "historic necessity" accounts for such statements as the Molotov assertion that today "all roads lead to Communism."

A more analytical approach to their philosophic assumptions might help Soviet leaders realize that Communism has no monopoly claim on "historic necessity." Thirty years ago Oswald Spengler invoked the same concept to justify the expansionist dreams of the Kaiser.

More recently, it cloaked Hitler's dream of world conquest and prompted his boast that the history of Europe had been decided for the next thousand years. Even Mussolini proclaimed his "century of fascism." And dictators and conquerors from Alexander to Napoleon have identified themselves with destiny.

As for Lenin's statement that everything that promotes Communism is moral, the present Soviet lead-

Above, Larissa Arkadeyvna Kaleendariova, Director of an experimental school in Moscow that teaches the basics as well as vocational skills. Right, Students in geography class in an experimental school in Moscow.

ership has used it as carte blanche to justify everything in the name of the cause. Hence the right to withhold or distort the truth; hence the right to make or break agreements, to subject its own and alien peoples to the most absolute and ruthless rule the world has yet seen.

In the final analysis, this materialist denial of intrinsic moral standards and spiritual values does away with everything save the formula that "might makes right" and save naked power, exalted as an end in itself. The clearest illustration of this outcome is the present Soviet police state.

This is a far cry from Lenin's belief in Marx's prediction that under Communism the state would "wither away."

The Children's Hour: US is Big Bad Villain [12/22/49]

"We must create for Soviet children works that will wrathfully expose the beastly countenance of the Anglo-American imperialists, those warmongers, slave traders ..."

Thus spoke shy, mild-mannered Sergei Mikhailov, favorite children's author, to the 11th Congress of the Komsomol last spring. By that time Mikhailov, like so many other former friends, blushed with embarrassment and pretended not to see us if we chanced to run across him.

A few days after this speech our son, practically in tears, came home from a visit to his best friend, a Russian boy named Valya. Valya's big sister had been home. Our son had told her that we had promised him that if he behaved well and got good marks we would send him to America for the summer.

"H'm," sniffed Big Sister, "America indeed! You should be sent there as punishment if you're naughty, not for being good. Did you hear what Mikhailov had to say about America?"

"I'm afraid I wasn't very polite after that," our son told us ruefully. "I told her she didn't know anything about America and to keep her fool mouth shut ... and a lot more besides."

Thus ended a beautiful friendship. Our son's contacts, like ours, were diminishing rapidly—and for similar reasons.

Grownups in the Communist Party Propaganda and Agitation Department were consciously beaming the anti-American campaign toward the children. *Pioneer Pravda* and other publications for the young described American Boy Scouts as trained spies; said American

children from the cradle upward played with toys patterned on the atom bomb and were trained as little warmongers.

We saw the practical fruits of this when neighborhood youngsters hurled insults at us over the fence, sometimes accompanied by harder millings.

Denouncing America has become the surest key to literary, stage and political success, the quickest way for a writer, including a children's writer, to fill his pockets and prove his party loyalty.

No Soviet play or novel nowadays is complete without American diplomats, newspapermen, engineers or businessmen who are at the same time spies and provocateurs, either in the lead or in auxiliary parts. No comedy review is complete without several anti-American numbers.

Constantine Simonov, first to hit the jackpot with an anti-American play ("The Russian Question"), declared in a recent burst of self-criticism that instead of spending so much time on the "split personality" of Hearst reporters he should have concentrated more on "their actual daily anti-Soviet activities."

Certainly as time goes on the anti-American activities of Soviet writers tend to get rougher.

Roughest anti-American quickie to date is a play by party playwright Anatoly Surov titled "The Mad Haberdasher." The chief character is a haberdashery salesman from Kansas City, Mo., who has a strong physical resemblance to Hitler. The Pendergast machine politicians hit upon the idea of proclaiming that he is indeed der Führer, secretly saved from the Chancery bunker, and plugging him for President on an American Nazi platform.

Apparently some of the Party Propaganda and Agitation Department gagged over this, for announced openings of the play have been canceled several times.

The party line on America runs thus: The United States is the center of world Capitalism and the rallying point of all forces hostile to the Soviet Union, which is the leader of "progressive mankind" in this current period of worldwide polarization. The United States Government, which is the agent of American monopoly capital, is intent on achieving world hegemony, and in this connection is planning an aggressive war on the Soviet Union.

As customary in Communist practice, once the line is formulated the Propaganda and Agitation Department chooses the facts to support it.

Anything tending to show that American policy is not directed primarily toward war with the Soviet Union

Thoughts of children are reflected on the sidewalks of Russia in Leningrad.

is suppressed. Nor are the Soviets prepared to admit the sincerity of any American who wants friendly relations between the two countries on a basis of mutual respect and fairness. The Russians do not admit such reciprocity. The price of Soviet friendship is to be a fellow traveler and play the Soviet game.

It should be added that in making its case sound convincing the Department of Propaganda and Agitation is greatly assisted from time to time by the irresponsible statements of certain United States public figures, including members of Congress, urging immediate armed action against the Soviet Union, including the use of atom bombs. To the Soviet public this sounds like corroboration of *Pravda*.

The traditional feeling of friendliness and respect for America of the Russia people is the most serious home obstacle which the anti-American campaign must reckon with. These feelings were enhanced by the wartime alliance and by American aid to the Soviet war effort.

Not only is everything being done now to erase America's part in the war, but there is constant effort to discredit the American contributions in all fields of culture and natural science.

Writer Peter Pavlenko, for example, declared on his return from the New York "peace" conference that all music in America was imported, that Americans had no music of their own worth mentioning. Similar sweeping negations may be read almost any day in the Soviet press about American literature, art, architecture, techniques.

The fantastic purge of "passportless cosmopolites" last winter was designed to wipe out all influence of non-Communist western culture and ideas, together with the last sparks of intellectual integrity and critical faculty. Thereafter, the Propaganda and Agitation Department hoped, there would be none left to scoff, openly or secretly, at the crude efforts to credit Russian with most of the world's major inventions, discoveries and cultural achievements. In literature, the field would be cleared for the party hack who would write to order what the department wanted.

An outstanding example of what the department expects from a Soviet writer is playwright Nikolai Virta.

Virta has completely adapted his considerable literary gifts to the writer's proscribed role of party propagandist. In 1946, when the party was busy jacking up collective farm discipline after wartime laxity, Virta wrote "Our Daily Bread," a play about jacking up collective farm discipline.

In 1948, when the Communist coup was justified as "rescuing" Czechoslovakia from the West, Virta wrote "Conspiracy of the Doomed," a play about how a Communist coup in an eastern European Slav country barely forestalled an American plot to seize the country.

Virta's latest, just completed, is a play portraying the struggle of Yugoslav "patriots" against the Tito "renegades." It is a safe conjecture that at least one of the villains in this piece will turn out to be an American spy.

Noted Composers Are "Out of Tune"   [12/29/49]

When we left for Moscow on long-term assignment back in 1946, Dr. Serge Alexandrovich Koussevitzky, now distinguished and beloved director emeritus of the Boston Symphony Orchestra, gave us a consignment of clothing and other gifts for his old friends among Soviet musicians.

His instructions were, if possible, to turn everything over to R.M. Glier, a minor composer and one of his classmates at the Moscow Conservatory, requesting Glier to make the distribution.

Having secured Glier's home address, one evening, by appointment, my wife and I drove to his house with our largest suitcase. The Gliers proved to be a pleasant elderly couple. They had just moved into a new flat, but water had spoiled the living room ceiling and fixing it would prove quite expensive.

Our host rummaged inside an old secretary, and produced a yellowed group photograph, where, along the rows of earnest young faces staring into the camera shutter, he picked out himself and Serge Alexandrovich. Glier glowed at the recollection of their old friendship, and when we told him the Dr. Koussevitzky was hoping to give some concerts in Russia and had offered to the Soviet authorities to pay the entire expenses for himself and his orchestra, Glier was enthusiastic. As a member of the Composers Union, he declared he would do his utmost to promote the trip.

As for the clothes and gifts, Glier readily agreed to make the distribution and promised to send us word of how he had arranged it when he returned our suitcase.

Dr. Koussevitzky's proposal to bring over his orchestra at his own expense and give the box-office receipts to aid war orphans elicited no response whatever, although it was made repeatedly through several channels. It was the same with all other American moves to develop cultural relations with the Soviet Union. Any such plan, including musical relations, was definitely out of tune with the party line.

This became graphically and publicly apparent two years later when the Communist Party, under the aegis of the late Andrei Zhdanov, initiated the first musical purge in human history.

The musical purge began in a rather offhand manner. The Bolshoi Theater offering in honor of the 30th anniversary of the Revolution in November 1947, was the brand-new opera "Great Friendship," by the Georgian composer Vano Muradeli.

From almost any party angle the choice seemed a safe one. The opera dealt with the Revolution and civil war in the Caucasus, culminating in the victory of the Bolsheviks. The composer was Stalin's fellow countryman. The Bolshoi, however, had reckoned without Zhdanov, himself an amateur musician of considerable accomplishment and with definite ideas on the subject of music.

So after the first highly laudatory press notices, there came a party decree which lashed the score as full of dissonances and declared it showed the influence of western bourgeois-decadent music. Not content with this, like charges were leveled against a whole galaxy of leading Soviet composers, including Serge Prokofiev and Dmitri Shostakovitch.

In standard purge fashion, there followed "self-critical" meetings of the Composers Union, at which the smaller fry took turns sniping at the fallen idols (in the Soviet Union the only time you can hit a man is when he is down) and the composers under fire "confessed" their mistakes.

Shostakovitch proved most adroit at this and earned commendation for his "sincerity." Though most of the music that won him world acclaim has now been scrapped as far as the Soviets are concerned, his theme music for the filming of Fadeyev's novel *The Young Guard* was lauded as "showing promise." Since then he has completed his comeback with his "Cantata of Forest," written in praise of the party reforestation program.

Unlike Shostakovitch, Prokofiev refused to do public penance. He stayed away from the inquisitorial meetings on the grounds of ill health, but furnished the required written recantations, together with assurances that he was making every effort to compose what the party wanted.

Prokofiev had returned to Russia from voluntary exile in the early 1930s at the invitation of the Soviet Government. With him came his charming Spanish-French wife, Linette, who for his sake became a Soviet citizen. They had two sons. We had known the family many years. In 1939, when my Russian-born wife was

Dmitri Shostakovich and his five year old son, Maxim outside the cottage (furnished by the Soviet government) where the composer wrote his Eighth Symphony.

rather appalled at the prospect of going to America for the first time, Prokofiev had humorously reassured her as to conditions in New York and how she would like it there.

Came the war. Prokofiev, apparently anxious to disassociate himself completely from his émigré past and go native, jettisoned his family. He must have reasoned that Linette, as a foreigner, was a social and political liability.

For a time Linette sought to appeal to her husband's affections. But when this failed she devoted her efforts to getting out of Russia, where she no longer had friends or roots, and rejoining her mother in Paris. Whenever we saw her she assured us that exit visas would soon be issued to herself and the two boys, that she had talked to a very important person who had promised to assist her, and that her husband, anxious to get rid of her, would help.

One day, having not seen Linette for months, we phoned her. A frightened voice on the other end told us she no longer lived there. Soon we had confirmation the Linette had been arrested and the boys were in the care of the state.

By then Prokofiev was completely immersed in his own troubles. His opera "Tale of a Real Man," about a Soviet war hero, on which he had pinned his hopes of a comeback, had been given in Leningrad in concert form.

The party press had howled condemnation: "A typical recurrence of formalism." Even the hapless conductor who had played the score on his own responsibility was criticized. Croaked the *Literary Gazette*: "Evidently the composer [Prokofiev] has not drawn his own conclusions from the historic party decree and continues to advocated modernistic dissonant music incapable of expressing the spiritual world of a Soviet man and merely botching a big patriotic subject."

After this compounded failure, Prokofiev virtually withdrew from the world. The gay, witty, gregarious, and perennially boyish Prokofiev we once had known became a morose, sulky, frustrated and broken man. He virtually gave up composing in the realization that he was temperamentally unsuited to piping the party line and, unlike the younger Shostakovich, too set in his ways to readapt himself.

Glier, in the meantime, prospered. With the musical giants in temporary or permanent eclipse, there was room at the top for mediocrity. And when next the Stalin Prizes in music were handed out, one came his way. Perhaps this enabled him to fix the ceiling of the living room, though we do not know for sure. When we left Moscow after more than three years we were still waiting for him to call and return our suitcase.

Laws of Nature Rigged by Reds [1/5/50]

The natural sciences in the Soviet Union have been spliced to the Communist Party line as tightly as the arts and literature.

Today the biologist or physicist, like the writer or composer, is completely under the thumb of party ideology. The Communist Party Central Committee, not the laboratory, determines whether the findings of research are true or false. The laws of nature are established by party fiat.

Once a given theory or hypothesis in any field has official party backing, it no longer is open to question or criticism. Natural scientists who disagree are invited to jettison their doubts or else "get out of Soviet science." The vast majority conform. Here, as in other spheres of Soviet life, the social and economic compulsions are overwhelming. This was strikingly shown by the recent Soviet "biological purge."

For more than 14 years an agronomist named Trofim Denisovich Lysenko, who had some practical success in producing new varieties of drought- and frost-resisting wheat but little natural scientific schooling, had been campaigning against the generally accepted views of heredity.

Lysenko, regarded as something of a quack by serious biologists, denounced the chromosome theory, rejected the findings of Mendel and Morgan, and proclaimed himself the follower of Ivan Michurin, a sort of home-grown Russian Burbank, who produced new varieties of apples and believed in the transmission of acquired characteristics.

Apart from his professional merits, during the purge of the 1930s Lysenko won a formidable reputation as a man with strong Kremlin connections and dangerous to cross. He fared even better in the postwar period, when, in line with the general trend of repudiating foreign influences and exalting home-grown talent, his "Michurin biology" found increasing official favor.

By comparison, those biologists who still held with Mendel and Morgan were sitting targets for the now fashionable accusation of "groveling to the bourgeois West."

Lysenko was named president of the Lenin Academy of Agricultural Sciences. His moment of supreme triumph came on August 8, 1948, when he announced at a special session of the academy that his views had been officially approved by the Communist Party Central Committee.

Thereupon Lysenko's humbled opponents, one by one, came trooping to the podium with declarations of recantation. Heading the procession of penitents was Academician Pyotr Mikhailovich Zhukovsky, who only two days previously, while the session was still "debating," had strongly attacked Lysenko's views and defended the theory of the chromosome. Now Zhukovsky quavered: "My speech of two days ago before the Central Committee was a watershed dividing the two currents in biology, and was unworthy of a member of the Communist Party and a Soviet scientist. I admit I held a false position."

Hinting indirectly at the motives that prompted his recantation, the graybeard pleaded: "I am a responsible person, for I work in the Committee for Awarding Stalin Prizes and in the Commission of Experts for the Conferment of Scholarly Degrees. I therefore consider it my moral duty to become an honest Michurinite, an honest Soviet biologist. Comrade Michurinites! If I declare that I cross over to the ranks of the Michurinites and shall defend them, I do so honestly … Let the past that divided me from Trofim Denisovich Lysenko be forgotten. Believe me that today I act and speak as a true party member—that is, honestly [applause]."

The above is quoted from the published stenogram of the session. Others followed in Zhukovsky's train with almost identical recantations. The stenogram does not record if any of them emulated the famous example attributed to the great Italian astronomer Galileo Galilei, who, forced to disavow his assertion that the earth revolves around the sun, is nevertheless said to have muttered under his breath, "Yet it does indeed move."

The session then moved on to the next order of business, the adoption of a resolution that said in part: "The Michurinite trend, headed by Academician Lysenko, has performed important and fruitful work in unmasking and smashing the theoretical positions of Morganism-Mendelism."

Then, before closing, the session unanimously approved a letter of greeting to Stalin, concluding with the words: "Long live foremost biological Michurinite science! Glory to great Stalin, leader of the people and guiding star of foremost science!" This, the stenogram records, was followed by "stormy, long-sustained applause, developing into ovation."

Only a few diehards refused to recant, and were dealt with accordingly.

Academician Nemchinov, director of the Timiryazev Agricultural Academy, was loudly heckled when he asserted: "The chromosome theory of heredity belongs to the golden fund of human knowledge." When he added that as long as he headed the academy this theory "would not be concealed from the students," the claque stamped and shouted: "You should resign."

The noise and interruptions grew even louder when Nemchinov ventured to defend one of his faculty members, Professor Zhebrak, who had committed the cardinal sin of publishing an article in an American periodical, *Science*. While deploring this "unpatriotic action," Nemchinov insisted Zhebrak was still a distinguished natural scientist, and refused to discharge him from the faculty or liquidate his experimental project.

Soon after the session Nemchinov was removed as director, and Zhebrak's project was liquidated.

Even before the session got under way the press warm-up had indicated that Lysenko's critics would be thrown to the party lions. Describing the atmosphere, Academician Boris Zavadovsky, a distinguished senior biologist, forced to interrupt his vacation in the Caucasus and hurry to Moscow to defend his views, complained: "The conditions under which this session was called were not quite normal. Insufficient opportunity was given to those who, either justly or unjustly, are listed among the Weissman-Morganists to prepare themselves and to enable them to speak out frankly."

After subjecting many of Lysenko's views to searching criticism, Zavadovsky further declared: "I see a profound contradiction between the line our party follows in favor of raising the authority of our Soviet science and the manner in which, in the *Literary Gazette* and elsewhere, all Soviet scientists who do not join in the chorus are condemned wholesale." He added: "There are other methods and approaches which must not be sacrificed and denied in science and in practice merely because they are not included in Lysenko's field of vision."

This warning went unheeded.

Collective Slavery is Seed for Revolt [1/28/50]

The serflike bondage of the "free" Soviet citizen to his job is one element of an unrelaxing economic stranglehold upon the masses. Equally important is the total state control of the production of food and consumer goods, a control constantly used to coerce and cajole, reward and punish, in the interests of the Communist party line.

In the past, the government deliberately starved the refractory peasantry into submission to collectivization. Today the Soviets are vigorously wooing the loyalty of urban workers and intellectuals by making more and better foodstuffs available to them at lower prices. This is made possible by the substantial gains in postwar production, plus the economic benefits reaped through control of eastern Europe.

Soviet postwar economic progress is a tribute not only to the country's recuperative powers, but also to the effectiveness of large-scale economic planning. This principle, which the Soviets pioneered, has now been accepted and adopted in some measure throughout the civilized world, on a national and even international scale. Perhaps the crowning expression is the Economic Cooperation Administration.

In meeting the Communist challenge, the democratic West now seeks to demonstrate that economic planning can succeed in a free society, without the physical and mental compulsions on which the Soviets rely so heavily. This is vital, for one of the greatest dangers to democracy is lest the West, in opposing Communism, resort to the same methods the Communists employ, and lest human liberty succumb to some equally odious brand of totalitarianism.

One saw this happen in Germany, where Naziism largely began and developed as an anti-Communist crusade. Historians long will study the similar methods of the two antithetical systems. Hitler used economic pressure for political ends in the same way Stalin does. He, too, wooed the working class with improved living standards. Ironically, the wealth of eastern Europe, now flowing into the Soviet Union to raise the Russian workers' living standards, 10 years back was pouring into Germany, where it helped convince the German workers and intellectuals that it paid to belong to the *Herrenvolk* (master race).

The common denominator of Naziism and Communism is in the appeal to materialism, in the conviction that violence and coercion can settle any issue, in the belief that power justifies any means. Above all, both inherit, from a common philosophic source, the rejection of fixed standards of right and wrong, true and false. Without these moral compass points to steer by, no nation can cleave to the course of progress. Technology and organizing efficiency, instead of benefiting mankind, then operate for evil. In the Nazi Weltanschauung (philosophy), it accounts for concentra-

tion camps, lethal gas chambers, and dreams of "tomorrow the world."

In the Soviet Weltanschauung it has led to forced labor camps, mass purges, police terror and dreams of world Communism—and the end not yet in sight.

Yet people in the West, who, from mental laziness, lapse of memory, or sheer exasperation advocate a preventive war as the only way out, at present should be reminded that the recent war generated problems fully as serious as those it solved, plus the tremendous senseless destruction. Even in vanquished Germany, final victory over Naziism still hinges on whether the German people can be won over to democratic ideals.

The notion that Communism can be disposed of effectively by military means is even more absurd. Not only is such a war likely to result in universal ruin, visited on victors and vanquished alike, but the decisive battle would still remain to be fought in the realm of ideas—and for the possession not of territory but of men's minds.

In the coming years, the strongest, most determined foes of the police state are likely to develop east of the Iron Curtain, where not even forcible indoctrination can neutralize the lessons of immediate knowledge and experience. There are in Russia today legions of thinking, intelligent people who chafe under the omnipotent police state and long with their whole beings for freedom.

The Russians as a race are neither domineering nor aggressive nor xenophobic. They are warmly human, gregarious and endowed with an avid and friendly curiosity about other peoples. All these qualities tend instinctively to alienate them, if not from the Soviet system, at least from its present policies at home and abroad.

Moreover, thousands upon thousands of people in all walks of life have at some time sustained some deep personal hurt from the police régime. Each new purge or "ideological campaign" adds new contingents of malcontents. While all open criticism of the régime is effectively prevented and the ears and eyes of the MVD (secret police) are omnipresent, such is human nature that every individual has at least one person he fully trusts, and thus an endless chain extends, even though it lacks organized form.

The mental outlook of the average Soviet citizen passes through three main stages, according to age groups:

1. Below 25 years of age, most susceptible to intense indoctrination—the glowing visions conjured by

propaganda appeal to the youthful imagination, unsullied as yet by worldly experience.

2. From 25 to 35, gradual frustration of hopes destroyed by contact with daily life and conditions.

3. After 35, final disillusionment. This breeds hard, selfish cynicism, resigned routine-conditioned apathy, or intense inner rebellion, depending on the status and makeup of the individual. The men who staff the party and state apparatus come under the first category (cynicism). The majority of citizenry fall in the second (apathy). But many, at the least sign of hope, would gravitate toward the third (rebellion).

The opening months of the Nazi invasion disclosed how deeply disaffection had eaten into the fabric of Soviet society—before Hitler's political blunders and cruelties repelled even those who at first looked upon the Kremlin as the greater evil.

It is essential that the West learn to distinguish between the police state and the Soviet people, for if the former are implacable foes, the latter, unless stupidly antagonized, are potential friends and allies.

And it is they who eventually will decide their country's destiny.

US 'Voice' Haunts Red War Planners [1/31/50]

The triple wrapper of mystery, riddle and enigma which, paraphrasing Churchill, cloaked Soviet intentions some years ago has evaporated since the war. Today the Soviet policy pattern no longer is concealed, but publicly advertised in such classic boasts as Molotov's: "All roads lead to Communism."

The mantle of inscrutability did yeoman service during the war years, when it was politic to hoodwink the western Allies as to Kremlin plans. When Stalin reassured the West early in 1944 that he wanted a "free and democratic" Poland, the West eagerly took him at his word, little realizing that Stalin was giving the familiar, reliable adjectives in a highly specialized Communist content.

This marked the beginning of the cat-and-mouse game of "people's democracy" now in its final stage. The Communists acclaimed "people's democracy"—and the democratic elements took them at their word—as a brand new kind of state wherein Socialist and Capitalist elements were happily blended, combining the best features of East and West.

Since then the world has watched while the Communists swallowed the democratic parties, including Socialists, piecemeal, and—having achieved

monopoly of power—put forward a purely Communist program. "People's democracy" was redefined as nothing more nor less than the old "dictatorship of the proletariat"—that is, Communist dictatorship. The process of assimilation now has reached a point where little remains to be done short of outright incorporation of the satellite states into Russia.

Not only has Soviet policy in eastern Europe been laid bare. The aims and methods of Communism everywhere are out in the open. Moreover, the relationship of the various Communist parties to the Kremlin, once tangled in a maze of double talk, has been fully exposed, largely as a consequence of the Cold War and the European Recovery Program.

Today, with Soviet aims plain to all who care to see, the foremost question in many persons' thoughts is: Are the Soviet leaders, who now have an atom bomb, bent on war?

The best answer to this query is: No—and yes. The contradiction in this answer is resolved by the time element. For the immediate, even the foreseeable, future the answer is: No. The Kremlin, for one thing, is convinced that time is on its side, and that with every passing day the ratio of world power shifts in its favor. The long-term answer is: Yes. The Communists believe that though a given conflict may be averted, an eventual clash between the two antagonistic world systems is inevitable and will result necessarily in the triumph of Communism.

Accordingly, the Soviets, while expecting to avoid war at present, give military preparation top priority in all their economic planning. They also run certain calculated war risks for immediate objectives, as in the case of the Berlin blockade. Nevertheless, the Kremlin realizes it would be hard to sell the Soviet people on a war of aggression, and that knowledge counsels caution at many a turn.

Therein lies the most substantial margin of hope for peace and avoidance of a war. The West, by putting its own house in economic order, can destroy the roots of Communism in its own dooryard and refute Soviet propaganda in practice.

Meanwhile, avoiding appeasement, the West should continue patiently to explore every possibility for genuine agreement with the Soviets on vital issues.

It should remember that, despite doctrinaire aims and outlook, the Soviet leaders are fully capable of changing their minds. Stalin himself, in an empirical mood, once proclaimed: "The logic of things is the strongest of all logic."

The stakes in this game are enough to justify any expenditure of effort and patience. Western statesmen driven to exasperation in their dealings with the Soviets might derive solace from the following commentary by the historian Vladimir Klyuchevsky on 17th century Russian diplomacy: "The diplomatic methods of the Moscow Boyars [Russian aristocrats under the czars] were often the despair of foreign ambassadors, especially those who wished to deal straightforwardly and honestly. The foreign ambassadors complained bitterly of the duplicity and abruptness of Moscow diplomats, of their inconstancy, and of the levity with which they made and broke promises. To avoid their snares, it was not enough to discover that they were lying. One also had to ascertain the purpose of the lie, how to evaluate it.

"When detected lying they did not blush, but answered reproofs with a sneer [a tactic used today by Vishinksy]. No matter how precisely and positively the point of negotiation was defined and agreed, whenever necessary they always found ways, by means of various intricate interpretations, to weaken its force or even present it in another, unexpected form."

Compare this last with Gen. Lucius D. Clay's observation during the Berlin blockade: "The Soviet Government seems able to find technical reasons at will to justify the violation of understandings."

Yet General Clay, by his resoluteness and patience in dealing with the Berlin blockade, set a historic precedent on how to deal with the Soviets successfully — and short of war.

While seeking a realistic *modus vivendi* with the Soviet government, the United States in particular should miss no opportunity to proffer the hand of friendship to the Russian people over the head of the Soviet Government, and to refute Communist propaganda to the effect that America is scheming to attack the Soviet Union.

A splendid beginning along these lines has been made by the "Voice of America" Russian-language broadcast programs.

The best tribute to the broadcast's effectiveness is the all-out scale of the Soviet jamming effort of these programs. Before the jamming, we had many direct indications that the programs commanded a wide and eager audience.

Even today, what filters through the wall of interference is a far more powerful weapon than the atom bomb — a weapon for peace, that reaches men's minds and creates instead of destroying.

Workers in the Soviet Union. Top, Woman on scaffolding renovating building, 1979. Above, worker in a shipyard, 1974.

Clockwise from top left: Statue of Lenin in Azerbaijan beckoning workers to their tasks. Worker on street in Moscow. Farm laborers in the Ukraine.

THE CHRISTIAN SCIENCE MONITOR

AN INTERNATIONAL DAILY NEWSPAPER

BOSTON, TUESDAY, MAY 2, 1950

FIVE CENTS A COPY

SCAP Bids Japan Ban Communism

Pulitzer Prize Winner

This Is Russia

Edmund Stevens, Winner of Pulitzer Prize

Writer of Russian Series In Monitor Wins Honor

Lattimore Turns Guns On Accuser

CIO President

Communist CIO Chiefs Under Fire

Paris Eyes U. S. Arms For Bao Dai

U.S. Prods West: Accept Germany Or Lose Key Ally

State of the Nation

Truman Phones—And World Wonders

Extension of Draft Hits Snag in House Committee

The Christian Science Monitor **from May 2, 1950.**

This is a grave day in the history of the world. This is the day when the race for the hydrogen bomb officially began. It began with heavy hearts freely admitted by all responsible leaders in Washington. President Truman, who announced the decision to authorize construction of the hydrogen bomb, did so in the manner of one unable to avoid a fearful duty. The leaders of Congress, most of whom approved the step, did so with equal gravity and foreboding. And all of them emphasized the necessity of trying again and again to reach agreement with Soviet Russia which would prevent use of any of the new engines of mass destruction.

By happy circumstance, *The Christian Science Monitor* today publishes the last in the remarkable series of articles about Russia and its policies by Edmund Stevens. In this article, Mr. Stevens—who has observed Russian policy in Moscow for over a decade—asks the question we all are asking today: Are the Soviet leaders bent on war? He answers: "No—and yes." For the immediate, foreseeable future, he says the Kremlin will not make war—atomic bomb or no. He says Russia is convinced that time is on its side and that with every passing day the ratio of world power shifts in its favor. Of course, Mr. Stevens wrote that before he knew of the hydrogen bomb announcement. And the big question now is whether the men in the Kremlin will be impelled into or deterred from mad adventure.

If the reason they have not precipitated war before is because they believe time is on their side and their strength is increasing, perhaps the hydrogen bomb would throw the balance the other way. Or the hydrogen bomb—if they are unable to posses it themselves—might be a powerful deterrent against war.

But these are all speculations about which nobody has the facts—not President Truman, not Marshal Stalin. Taking the longer–range view, Mr. Stevens goes on to point out that the Communists believe that a clash between two antagonistic world systems is inevitable. In that sense he answers the question: "Yes."

Mr. Stevens says other very significant things, based on his own recent observation. He says the Kremlin would find it hard to sell the Russian people on a war of aggression today, and he emphasizes that such support would be necessary. That, he says, is the most substantial margin of hope for peace. And he urges the West to put its own house in order, destroy the roots of Communism in its own dooryard, and refute Soviet propaganda in practice.

This is the policy which the United States has already adopted. Our determination to remain strong has been supplemented by the decision to make the most fearful weapon ever seriously projected. But we must be equally determined to seize every opportunity to reach agreement with the Russians. So perhaps the time will soon come when President Truman can begin a peace offensive as dramatic and significant as the arms race to which he committed us today.

This does not mean that there need be any rabbits in the hat. It does mean that we must persuade the peoples and governments of the world that our intentions in beginning the hydrogen bomb are in no sense aggressive but entirely defensive.

We must persuade people and governments that the United States wishes to break with all speed the vicious spiral of the armaments race; that we wish peace and the protection of our people and of all free peoples. If the United States Government and the American people behind it speak out tomorrow with a mighty and a convincing voice saying: Yes, and we have had to start the hydrogen bomb, but we wish peace and freedom and genuine agreement above all else — even if two inimical systems must exist side by side — then this day in history may be justified.

What obstacles lie in the way of a satisfactory plan for the control of atomic energy? First of all, the Soviet Union and its satellites alone held out against the Baruch Plan before the United Nations. Should we stand pat on that plan, or present some revised proposals?

Obviously nothing is to be gained merely by standing pat. Just as obviously, any plan must have one ingredient: effective international inspection and control of what nations may do with these new weapons. That is a tall order. It calls, as an inescapable minimum, for the contribution of a considerable part of national sovereignty.

The United States, by making the Baruch offer, pledged itself to blend with others this minimum amount of national sovereignty. Congress never passed on the offer, but by many comments indicated its support. Now the problem is to persuade Russia to make a like contribution.

In any event we are now seeking to lead from strength, rather than from weakness. Strength, we have learned, is necessary in today's world. But it is not all. It is not enough. There must also be moral purpose and integrity and good will. When once we persuade the people of other nations that we possess these essential elements of policy, we will be on the road to agreement.

Stalin's Hoax on the Communists [7/28/52]

By Ernest S. Pisko

In an attempt to refute Abraham Lincoln and "fool all the people all the time," Soviet Prime Minister Joseph Stalin has played a gigantic hoax not only on the 25,000,000 card-bearing members of the various Communist Parties and the Soviet people but on the world in general and the western democracies in particular. And he almost carried it off unnoticed.

The purpose of his hoax was to make people within and without the Soviet sphere believe that the Bolshevik system is identical with Communism.

This does not mean that Communism is better than Bolshevism. It means that the two have little in common. Communism, as will become abundantly clear in the course of this series, is an outmoded and unworkable socioeconomic theory. It reflects conditions as they were a hundred years ago, and it was unworkable even then on account of its inner contradiction between total freedom and total organization.

Stalin apparently recognized this fact earlier than any other of the leading Bolsheviks. Indeed, there may be ample justification to ascribe his personal triumph as well as his successful stewardship of the Soviet Union to his insight into the fundamental defects of Marxist Communism and to his decision — reached some time between 1925 and 1928 — to revise the blueprints and change the structure of the Soviet state while in the midst of the building process.

How complete a reversal of the Marxist doctrine Stalin has brought about during the past 25 years can be seen by comparing Karl Marx's key tenets with their present counterparts in the Soviet Union.

To start with the economic features, since these probably are the first ones everybody thinks of when Communism is discussed:

In the Communist state, as designed by Marx and Engels, all private property, inheritance rights, taxation, and profit were to be abolished.

In the Soviet Union toay, however, people may own property. They own their clothing — whether it be one threadbare and patched suit or a wardrobe full of the finest wearing apparel. Soviet citizens own their furniture, their books, their stamp collections, their automobiles, motorcycles or bicycles. If they belong to the upper classes, they may own their house or even several houses.

As radically as in the case of the economic tenets, Stalin either has done away with most of the other key features of Marxism or has distorted them beyond recognition.

The Communist society which Marx envisaged was to be classless; it was to express the will of its overwhelming majority, and this will was to be ascertained by strictly democratic means; it was to be impervious to such "bourgeois" emotions as nationalism or such "bourgeois vices" as imperialism.

The Soviet Union today is a super Capitalistic, militaristic, hierarchical, and tyrannical state.

It has taken over from capitalism the profit motive and such features, obsolete in Western countries, as the piecework system and restrictions on labor's freedom of movement.

It is militaristic in nature because of its preferential treatment accorded to members of the armed forces, the militarization of youth and the government's ever-present will to use military pressure for foreign political ends.

It is a hierarchy modeled on the pattern of ancient Egypt. Every Soviet citizen's standing in society is determined by rigid rules. Worst of all, it is tyranny since the Constitution provides for no checks on the government or redress against government actions.

The reason Stalin took this course is not difficult to understand. It was the only way to keep the Bolshevik Party, which never represented more than a fraction of the Russian people, in power. What may seem puzzling, however, is that the Communists—Russian as well as foreign—have not turned against Stalin. The puzzle's solution is that Stalin, whenever he took a step away from the Communist program, explained the shift as a step on a detour toward Communism.

He used Marx's utopian promises of freedom, abundance, leisure and equality for all to lure the people into his gigantic labor camp.

In springing his hoax on the Communists, Stalin has received unexpected help from the free world. By blaming the detestable methods of his régime on communism, the free world actually has been playing into Stalin's hands.

Stalin has retained hardly anything of Communism except the name and the dubious promise of the "glorious future" to which it would lead. But the free world's failure to distinguish between Communism which Stalin threw out because it would not work and Sovietism which he put into the saddle, has allowed him to represent any attack on the Soviet system as an attack on the ideals for which the Soviet masses have been paying so heavily.

Lenin 'Equality' Scrapped By Hierarchy in Kremlin [7/30/52]

The hoax which Stalin has played upon the Communists can nowhere be seen more clearly than in the Soviet concepts of state, of the value of the individual and of equality. They are the very opposite of the original Marxist views on these issues.

On all three points the "Communist Manifesto" of 1848 was quite definite. And later writings by Karl Marx and Friedrich Engels show that the founders of Communism never saw any reason to modify their opinions.

Their utopian aim was the formation of a free association of people—not a "state"—and this aim was to be achieved by the so-called "emancipation of the proletariat."

The "proletariat," according to their terminology, comprised all the oppressed and exploited classes. Marx and Engels contended however, that the proletariat could not "attain its emancipation without at the same time, and once and for all, emancipating society from all exploitation, oppression, class distinctions and class struggles."

In 1917, when Lenin began mapping his plans for a Bolshevik seizure of power, he reiterated Marx's and Engels' utopian promise of total and universal freedom and professed his belief in their doctrine of the state. He promised to do away with the state which he called "an organ of class rule...legalizing and perpetuating the oppression of one class by another."

In addition to freedom for all, Marx and Engels also insisted on equality for all. Fulfillment of both demands was promised by the Bolsheviks.

Lenin stipulated that there would be only one scale of income for all citizens of the new state—working-men wages. Nobody, and specifically no member of the government, was to receive higher pay, he announced, adding that governmental functions must be stripped "of every shadow of privileges, of every appearance of official grandeur."

Stalin, some 20 years after that announcement, called the idea of eliminating the distinction between intellectual and manual labor an idea that could be conceived only by "windbags."

Today, inequality is one of the hallmarks of the Soviet régime. Wages of industrial workers average $125 monthly, but reach up to $500 for top specialists and to $1,000 and $2,000 in the case of widely propagandized shock workers.

Managerial salaries average $12,000 to $20,000 a year, and top annual incomes of professional people and artists easily reach the $25,000 to $50,000 bracket.

Hand in hand with gradations in income go fantastic differences in housing, clothing, access to higher education, and so on.

The right to inherit was reintroduced in 1923, limited to an estate value of 10,000 rubles. In 1926, this limitation was removed and a stiff inheritance tax was instituted. In 1943 the tax was abolished.

The technical and managerial staff in Soviet factories has its own dining rooms where better quality food is served. The same goes for upper grade officers of the Soviet Army.

Special privileges are accorded to the MVD (secret police). They have their own food, clothing and furniture stores, where choice merchandise is sold at bargain basement prices. Their children—at least in Moscow—attend separate model schools in which the best available instruction is provided.

Thus it can be said without exaggeration that the system of graded class privileges and discrimination which flourished in Czarist Russia and which the Bolshevik Revolution promised to wipe out, has come back with a vengeance.

In western countries, instances and trends of discrimination can be and have been attacked. There, as a result of these attacks, discrimination often has been halted or lessened. In the Soviet Union no disclosure or criticism is permissible, no remedy is possible because perpetuation of inequality is one of the chief instruments of government. The masses, downgraded on the scale of human values, instead of being freed and lifted up, have to keep silent.

Soviet Toots Nationalism In Switch to New Anthem [8/1/52]

"It is not national culture which is written on our banner, but international."   —Vladimir Lenin

"A real internationalist is one who brings his sympathy and recognition up to the point of practical and maximal help to the USSR in support and defense of the USSR by every means and in every possible form."
          —P.E. Vyshinsky, 1948

"Soviet patriotism is indissolubly connected with hatred toward the enemies of the Socialist Fatherland. It is impossible to conquer an enemy without having learned to hate him with all the might of one's soul."
          —Joseph Stalin, 1946

When Vyacheslav M. Molotov visited Washington as Soviet Foreign Minister during the war, a military band greeted him at the airfield with the playing of "The Internationale."

Inside the Soviet Union, whenever officials gathered for some festive occasion, proceedings either were opened or closed with the playing of "The Internationale."

"The Internationale," the flaming appeal to a worldwide proletarian revolution, was the anthem of the Soviet Union and the battle hymn of Communists everywhere.

Today, all this has changed. "The Internationale" has lost its place of honor. It has been crowded out by "The Hymn of the Soviet Union" which was performed for the first time on January 1, 1944, and which glorifies the "one and mighty Soviet Union," the "safe bulwark of the friendship of peoples."

This change of anthems has its deeper meaning. On the surface, it fitted into the sequence of measures by which the Kremlin, after June 1941, mobilized a general and nonpolitical feeling of patriotism in the fight against the German invaders. But on a deeper level, the adoption of a new and plainly nationalistic anthem signified that Stalin apparently thought the time had come to tear down the pillar of internationalism, one of the last Marxist pillars left in the remodeled edifice of Sovietism.

Marx and Engels, the two founders of Communism, and co-authors of *The Communist Manifesto,* saw in internationalism the ideal for mankind.

Lenin followed their lead. In 1913 he wrote that "Marxism cannot be reconciled with any nationalism;" and in 1917 he declared that true internationalism "is characterized mainly…by its relentless war against its own imperialist bourgeoise."

In 1921 at the 10th Party Congress, attacked those comrades who had "deviated" from Communism toward what he reproved as "the colonizing spirit, the spirit of Great Russian chauvinism."

In 1931 he told the German writer Emil Ludwig: "The task to which I have dedicated my life…is not to strengthen any national state, but to strengthen a socialist state—and that means an international state."

In 1934 he denounced any "deviation toward nationalism" as an attempt "to undermine the Soviet system and to restore Capitalism." He demanded that this deviation was to be fought "regardless of whether it went in the direction of local nationalism or toward Great Russian nationalism."

The new trend, which so strikingly contradicts the Marxist-Leninist doctrine, gradually rose to the surface during the war. The first faint ripples of its current could be noticed in 1941, when Stalin, in a conversation with the Polish Premier Gen. Wladyslaw Sikorski, made the amazing statement that the Slavs as children of "a young and still vigorous race" are "the best and bravest airmen of the world." Such a remark, without any doubt, would have been scorned by Marx, Engels and Lenin not only as nonsense but also as rankest chauvinism. But even more startling changes were soon to come.

At a victory celebration on May 24, 1945, Stalin in a special toast to the Russian people — who amount to about 50 percent of the Soviet population — called this group "the most outstanding nation of all the nations forming the Soviet Union."

Since then the two themes dominant in Soviet domestic propaganda have been the virtue of national pride and the Russian "nation's" claim to leadership in the Soviet empire, including the satellite countries.

The journal *Voprosy Filosofii* stated flatly that no nation has a history of culture as rich as the Russians and that "all the other countries of the world have drawn upon it and continue to draw upon it."

Clearly, the new trend is a full reversal of the Marxist doctrine. It seems equally evident that Stalin never took internationalism seriously. He merely used it as a bait to hold the loyalty of Communists abroad during those years when Soviet power was not yet sufficiently consolidated.

Darkness Shackles People [8/20/52]

"There can be no genuine stability in any system which is based on the evil and weakness in man's nature — which attempts to live by man's degradation, feeding like a vulture on his anxieties, his capacity for hatred, his susceptibility to error and his vulnerability to psychological manipulation." —From "America and the Russian Future" by George Kennan, (*Foreign Affairs*, April, 1951, p. 336.)

"I believe that the elemental traits of the Russian character are not compatible with the aims and methods of the present Soviet leaders." —From *The Strange Alliance* by John R. Deane. (The Viking Press, New York, 1947, p. 325.)

Revolutions start with people sharing their thoughts. That is why the Soviet people cannot rise against their régime. This, rather than as is so widely believed in the West, because the masses of the Russian people willingly accept the Soviet rule.

The Kremlin, no doubt, knows better.

It is impossible that a personality of Prime Minister Joseph Stalin's caliber can be taken in by the daily eulogies of the Soviet press, the flatterings of subordinates or the mass demonstrations of enthusiasm for his régime. He knows only too well how these things can be commandeered and made to look spontaneous.

Nor can Stalin have forgotten the conviction he himself expressed as a young man during his years of underground fight against the czars. "Nothing," he said then — in 1901 — "can be more dangerous to tyrannical authority than the people's curiosity."

Forty years later, in a conversation with Harry Hopkins, he gave evidence that he still kept thinking about the "dangers to tyrannical authority," though this time he was on the other side of the fence. Speaking about the cracks in the Nazi armor, he told Mr. Hopkins in July 1941, that he saw Hitler's greatest weakness in "the vast number of oppressed people who hate Hitler and his immoral government."

Stalin's reference to the "oppressed people" is most significant, since this term hardly applied to the Germany of 1941 where the vast majority of the people were proud of their "Führer" who had conquered half of Europe at practically no cost to themselves. It therefore is probably correct to infer that Stalin's opinion on the Germans reflected what he actually suspected of the Soviet people.

Everything indicates that only in their dreams can the Soviet people think of a change of government. As soon as they are awake, they have no choice but to submit — and they probably try to persuade themselves that they never dreamed.

In this attitude they are assisted by everything they see and hear in their daily activities. And even those things they cannot see and hear, because they are withheld from them by their government, help condition the Soviet citizens in a subtle manner to unquestioning submission.

For a citizen of the western democracies, it is easy to ask: "Why do the Russians put up with their tyrants?" But this question is unfair to the Soviet people. It implies that they fail to do something within their reach. To be fair — and realistic as well — the question should read: "What keeps the Russian people from overthrowing their régime?" The answer is: Force, ignorance and illusions. Force is the most obvious obstacle — the force of the Soviet executive. It is in the hands of the members of the Politburo. They wield it through the laws they issue. These laws are enforced by the bureaucracy, the Party and the secret police—three groups deliberately set apart from the rest of the population by their preferential treatment with regard to social standing, income, food, housing, and so on.

The army—a fourth potential arm of the executive, to be used only in an emergency—also has been lifted above the masses. It appears to be less reliable than the other three, but it has been so interlaced with Party members and secret police officials that the chances for an army putsch on the lines of the July 1944 putsch against Hitler, seem extremely remote.

Ignorance is another obstacle for the Soviet citizen. Every channel of information is under the Kremlin's strict supervision. People can only know what they are intended and allowed to know. They see the outside world only through the distorting mirror of their controlled press.

They have hardly any idea of the true nature of their rulers. They even cannot form a valid judgment on events that affect them personally. Press, radio and party lectures keep them in a constant state of confusion, befuddlement, doubt and expectation. In the end they grow so despondent and tired that they give up any attempt to understand what is happening to and around them.

Then there is the uncertainty. The Soviet Union is huge. Stalin is far. Few of the people know more than the district they live in. Few ever travel. How are they to know whether abuses they see in their own town or village are not only local in character?

If work is too hard, taxes too high, the police too rude—couldn't that be the fault of local officials? There is a sting as well as solace in the thought that in the next district—or, at any rate, in the next province—plant managers may be considerate, officials understanding, party members helpful, stores well-stocked.

That they are badly off need not be the fault of the "system" and certainly not of Stalin. "If Stalin knew, things would be different here," people say; just as so many Germans said, "If Hitler only knew…" when they saw corruption rampant or heard of concentration camps.

In addition to the effects of ignorance and uncertainty, there are the promises with which the Kremlin lures the people, and the government's appeals to their emotions and idealism. Their days are dark. But the promises are bright. Leisure and comfort shine on the horizon of the next five-year plan. Despite all their disappointments, hope keeps whispering: "One more push, Ivan. This may be the last stretch."

So they trudge on and slave on. Only a few of them are materially better off than before the Revolution. They probably were unable to read then. But they could say what they thought. And they could talk freely in their homes and to their friends. Now they can read, but only what the government wants them to. And they have to hide their thoughts. They cannot share them with their friends; not even with their children.

This is why the Soviet people cannot rise against their régime.

Soviet Bear Wears Three-Faced Mask [9/3/52]

"Russia has only one opponent: the explosive power of democratic ideas and the inherent urge of the human race in the direction of freedom."—Karl Marx

Sovietism is a system with a mask.

The mask shows the eyes of Lenin, the mouth of Engels and the beard of Marx. But behind the mask is the face of the absolute ruler of the Soviet Union, Prime Minister Joseph Stalin.

Wherever one looks in the Soviet Union, there are masks. Nothing can be taken at face value in the original sense of this term.

There is a difference between what things pretend to be and what they really are. Soviet statistics wear masks. So do Soviet laws and Soviet rules for education, family life, writing books, composing music, research in natural and social sciences, and the rights and duties of industrial workers and peasants.

If it were different, there would be no need to seal the Soviet Union off so completely from the outer world. The country's isolation is the régime's only means of upholding the deception—the gigantic hoax—which the Politburo under Stalin's leadership has played on the Soviet people and the entire world.

Under Stalin's régime, words have been hollowed out and filled with new meanings which contrast grotesquely with what the words meant originally. Freedom western-style now stands for "slavery," and slavery Soviet-style is called "freedom." Soviet dictatorship is defined as democracy, labor exploitation as "Socialist competition," aggression as "peace campaign," and Sovietism as "Communism."

Actually, with the single exception of the agricultural program, Sovietism has hardly anything in common with either Communism or Socialism or with the doctrines evolved some hundred years ago by Marx.

It is deeply significant that in this single instance in which Stalin has not deviated from Marxism he has run into the greatest difficulties, has met the most determined opposition and still is further from victory than in any other field.

In the 27 years since he assumed supreme power, Stalin has demonstrated on countless occasions that he does not mind deviating from Marx. He has put labor in a straitjacket; he has built up a class state with rigidly enforced rules and graded privileges for the various classes; he has scrapped all concepts of freedom, equality and human dignity which Marx put into his dream edifice of a Communist society; and finally, he has embarked on an expansionist policy anchored in the strength of the Soviet Army.

The available evidence suggests that Stalin discarded Marxism in the 1920s. After that he became not only a non-Marxist but an anti-Marxist — the most consistent and ruthless anti-Marxist of all. He probably finds it highly amusing to see how economists and politicians outside the Soviet Union have attacked him to this day for being the protector and propagator of Communism.

He has, however, not been completely successful in deceiving all the people of the Soviet Union despite almost three decades of rigid isolation and constant indoctrination.

This can be seen from the answer a Soviet soldier who recently deserted to the West gave to his interrogator. When asked to define Capitalism and Communism, the soldier said: "Capitalism is a system that allows workers to strike," and "Communism is what does not exist in the Soviet Union." There certainly are many more Soviet citizens who think this way but who either dare not or, more likely, cannot escape.

It is strange that outside the Soviet Union communism and Sovietism are generally considered identical. This may have something to do with the fact that nowadays the terms "Communism" and "Communist" are favorite weapons in the fights between competing political parties. As a result, many persons are reluctant to say that Stalin is no Communist and the Soviet system is not Communism lest they be suspected of secret sympathy with the Kremlin.

But to differentiate between the two "isms" does not mean that one advocates the adoption of either. The Marxist doctrine was, from the very beginning, full of demonstrable fallacies and misconceptions.

Today it is an anachronism, a museum piece of the mid-Victorian era. Its philosophical foundation is easily refutable; most of its economic theories have either

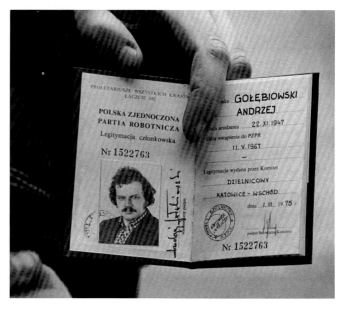

Top, life-sized figure of Stalin in facade of museum in Tbilisi, Georgia. Above, Polish Communist Party membership identification. Next page, top left and bottom, May Day 1989 in Moscow. Top right, make shift shrines commemorating hereos of the Revolution in Romania, February 1990.

fallen by the wayside or have lost their challenging character; and its demands for improving the living standards of the workers have largely been fulfilled—not in the Soviet Union, but in the Capitalist democracies. The only element of the doctrine that has remained alive is its fairy-tale part, the alluring picture of a society unencumbered by laws, unmolested by economic problems, free in the choice of work, and enjoying an abundance of leisure.

In order to be able to utilize these utopian promises for his own ends, Stalin has retained the name of Communism. Under the slogan of social progress he has engineered the greatest social regress in modern history.

He has, as it were, wafted the smell of roast duck under the noses of people to whom he fed water soup with potato peels. By accepting his claim to Communism, the non-Soviet world has enabled him to get away with his hoax and not only keep the Soviet people in bondage but also enslave a large section of Europe and direct so-called Communist Parties in all five continents.

The obvious first step, therefore, in the fight against Sovietism should be to call things by their correct names. Instead of speaking of Marxism, of which there is none now in the Soviet Union, it might help to speak of Sovietism, or Stalinism, or Kremlinism. Communist Parties outside the Soviet bloc might well be compelled by law to change their names to Sovietist, or Kremlinist, or Stalinist party. In this manner, the so-called Communists would be plainly marked as followers of a foreign power. They also would be prevented from hiding under the cloak of Marx, who, despite the grave mistakes of the system he evolved, did see the need for improving the conditions under which the poorer classes labored in the mid-19th century.

Shift in Moscow Régime
May Cut Soviet Influence   [3/5/53]

By Joseph C. Harsch

Much of the speculative uncertainty of the moment about the meaning of Prime Minister Joseph Stalin's departure from the driver's seat in Moscow can be dispelled, I think, by an analytical separation of those elements of Stalin's power which can be transferred easily to a successor from those which cannot be easily transferred or bequeathed, if at all.

The transferable powers begin with the physical power of the Russian state. Russia is governed by an immense bureaucracy bolstered by the mechanism of the Communist Party and by the pervasive apparatus of the secret police. This machinery takes its orders blindly from the Kremlin and undoubtedly will continue to take its orders from the new master, or masters, there, whoever they may be. This has been the pattern of Russian history for centuries and there is no substantial reason to expect any significant change.

Next is the power of the armed forces of Russia. The control of the Kremlin over these forces was maintained during the war and tested and reaffirmed after the war. To the best of our knowledge there is no serious present reason for doubting the continued strength of these armed forces and their subordination to the will of the Kremlin.

Next is control of the Russian propaganda apparatus. This is a weapon of power over the Russian people. It is part of the machinery of government. There is no reason to doubt that it will obey the new masters.

These were all elements of Stalin's power. They are all elements which in any big country are relatively impersonal. They must always be presumed to be transferable.

But while these elements were the background of the power machine which Stalin controlled, they were not the whole of it. He also exercised power by means of his enormous personal prestige within the world Communist movement. He was the senior Communist leader of the oldest Communist country. This is a position which was built gradually over a period of 20 years. Stalin did not enjoy it when he came to power. During his 20 years he became the final authority of Communist doctrine, but it took him the first 14 of those 20 years to establish authority.

When Stalin first seized the reins of power in Moscow there were many authorities in the Communist world. A Communist could disagree with Stalin and cite acceptable authority, such as Lenin, Trotsky, Engels or Marx. Of late years the older "prophets" of the Communist movement became usable only through Stalin's interpretations.

This personal prestige of Stalin's is not transferable as is control over the Red Army, the secret police or the bureaucracy. And this element was particularly important in the area of Stalin's power outside the borders of the Russian state itself. Stalin's personal prestige has had much to do with holding the satellite system together. Stalin's position as the only true expounder of Communist gospel was an important tie holding together the many elements of the Communist parties in the free world.

Budapest, Hungary in 1956 after the revolution.

In time, many years probably, a successor to Stalin may be able to regain a position as strong in world Communist eyes as Stalin enjoyed in recent years. But such power cannot be bequeathed or transferred by *ukase* (imperial order having the force of law). It is an intangible and a personal form of power.

The fact, which, above all others, must be troubling the men in the Kremlin now is that the most powerful, most successful, and most respected (by Communists) leader in the Communist world today is not even a Russian. He is Mao Tse-tung of China. And they must reflect with anxiety also that another strong and well-known Communist with considerable personal prestige, President Tito of Yugoslavia, is not even allied with Moscow in the power struggle.

That is, a Russian no longer towers over the Communist world movement demanding, and receiving, the respectful homage of all Communists except those in Yugoslavia. There is no Russian Communist who could today challenge Mao either in temporal or in ideological matters. Thus there is no certainty that the Kremlin can continue to dominate either the great satellite of China or the thoughts of Communists outside of the Iron Curtain. Both political and doctrinal schism is suddenly possible beyond the borders of the Russian state.

Thus, while it is probably foolish and idle to think that a struggle for the succession to Stalin's power can weaken the control of the Kremlin over the Russian people and the Russian state, it is almost certain that the Kremlin has lost, and may never regain, the special power it possessed through the person of Joseph Stalin to control the satellite countries and the outside Communist parties.

After Khrushchev — What?   [3/3/64]

By Paul Wohl

Moscow was getting ready for Christmas just when I was about to leave. In my room sat Akiki, an African student, asking me to get him a fellowship in the US. He had taken part in the "mourning procession" for the Ghanaian who passed on mysteriously on the eve of what was to be his wedding to a Russian girl.

There was a shadow on the face of this prosperous-looking young man. He was earnest, intelligent, alert — too alert for the kind of ideological processing to which he was exposed.

"I accepted many of their tenets when I arrived," he said. "But my Soviet fellow students themselves look for a new way. They are disappointed with what they have, but too fettered by the need to conform to strike out in different directions. One has a feeling of imprisonment."

"Why? Are you not free to leave?" I asked, "Surely, your embassy will pay for your return."

"This is not the kind of imprisonment I mean. Judging by what they tell me, there never has been more freedom in Russia than there is today. Freedom to travel, freedom even to talk in small groups."

I felt sorry for Akiki. This young intellectual reminded me of myself 30 years ago. These could have been my words then.

I, too, had gone to Moscow with great hope. My field then was transport coordination, and in the Soviet Union there seemed to be vast perspectives.

What made me leave Moscow in the spring of 1935 was a feeling of imprisonment, of being walled in amid a lively, lovable people. But still walled in.

The Stalin purge then was only in its beginning. The vast majority were apathetic. "Let the rats devour each other," a railway track man cracked as he saw me looking aghast at a banner headline about "slimy traitors," who only yesterday had been heroes.

But there also was the genuine fervor of fresh Revolutionary realism. And here I was in the Moscow of today — the second visit within the last two years — with my African alter ego sitting in front of me.

When I came here in October 1961, the 22nd Party Congress, in a characteristically Russian outburst of inchoate violence, had just decreed that Stalin's body no longer could lie in state next to that of Lenin.

The public was barred from flood-lit Red Square. All around groups talked excitedly. What did it mean? Where would "they" bury "him"?

Former inmates of concentration camps stood silently. Their children and grandchildren saw a great light. "These were not mistakes," I heard a young factory worker say — his Adam's apple jerking wildly — "these were crimes."

During the night, Stalin's name disappeared from the mausoleum. His body had been removed to a nearby place off the Kremlin wall under a big stone slab bearing his name and chronology.

Everything must have been prepared in advance. This shattering drama had been prearranged, timed and planned.

Soviet intellectuals raised in the cult of Stalin paled when questioned about it. Yet there was hope. Something new had started.

Khrushchev visiting a turkey farm in Maryland on October 10, 1960 during his tour of the US. Two days later he was banging his shoe on a table at the United Nations.

"Za Rabotu, Tovarishchi! Let's Get Down to Work, Comrades!" was the slogan with which Premier Nikita S. Khrushchev had closed the 22nd Congress on October 31. His words echoed through the Soviet Union. This was to be an era of practicality, a break with the past.

Last November, I returned again to Moscow. What has happened to the Khrushchev era?

Outwardly the Soviet Union never looked more prosperous. Signs of progress are everywhere. People still are public spirited. They try to appear businesslike. They are strong and sturdy as always. Yet something has changed. It is hard to pinpoint.

I looked up old acquaintances, listened endlessly and traveled more than 4,000 miles by rail—part of the way hard (lowest) class—from Moscow to Tbilisi, Georgia, and Yerivan, Armenia, and back.

People are better dressed. Shops look well supplied. Urban transportation is superb. Proceedings of the Supreme Soviet, or legislature, were businesslike, albeit noncontroversial, as expected under a one-party system; the deputies keen, prosperous, respectable.

Yet something has gone wrong. Akiki had put it in the right words. Mr. Khrushchev's clarion call to action, his endlessly repeated slogan "Za Rabotu, Tovarishchi!" lit a short-lived spark.

People are disappointed. There is a feeling of emptiness, of frustration. The farm calamity has something to do with it. The steep rise of prices for clothing, household gadgets, motorcycles and motorcars is another factor.

"The rich are getting richer; the poor, poorer," said a charwoman in the eastern Ukraine.

This is something new and deeply saddening in today's Soviet Union. It affects many more people than ever before, because of the increased number of educated men and women everywhere.

Before going to the station, I visited Russian friends in a rather gloomy industrial district south of the Kremlin. It was a sad leave-taking.

"Well, goodbye, Pavl Ludvigovich. Don't forget us. God knows what is going to become of us."

In many ways this sums up, it seems to me, the intangibles of the present situation.

In Brest, the last Soviet station before the train adjusted to Western European and American gauge enters Poland, there was an hour's stop.

On one side of the waiting room, a bust of Lenin; on the other side, where Stalin's bust had stood, an empty spot.

In the waiting room there were peasants and local workers, who could have been there 30 years ago. Only then Brest was called Brzeso, and was Polish.

Khrushchev — And His Critics [3/13/64]

Both in 1962 and last year this writer has heard Soviet people express concern over the Premier's "galloping tempo." He is criticized for putting over, and convincingly promoting, one sweeping reform after another without giving it a chance to take root.

Obviously Mr. Khrushchev has felt a need to defend himself publicly against this reproach. He apologetically referred to his "restless mind." On at least one occasion he publicly admitted that he "clearly had been foolishly hasty."

Some Soviet citizens find these admissions appealing. Others, with the Russians' developed sense of decorum, dislike his frankness just as they resent his clowning and occasional cavalier manners. These are surface matters, however.

More serious are certain patent errors in judgment. Thoughtful Soviets have not forgotten the Premier's remark that it would have been better not to build at Bratsk, eastern Siberia, a water power giant more than three times the capacity of Grand Coulee, but to set up instead three or four power stations in the warm climate of central Asia.

"One cannot always think of everything at the right time," Mr. Khrushchev later told a central committee plenum.

Billions of rubles were sunk into Bratsk. Tens of thousands of young Communists were recruited for the grueling venture. Not all of them survived. Others returned maimed or bitter.

Mr. Khrushchev's handling of the Cuban affair is not usually interpreted as the brilliant success it is officially made out to be. The thwarting of the Premier's proposal to set up a joint planning board for the Soviet bloc's Council for Mutual Economic Aid also is remembered.

There is discontent about his "liberality" in extending assistance and credits to underdeveloped countries. "They are bad business; they cannot pay," one foreign trade official commented.

Others complain about the many students from exotic countries. "The government pampers these people. They receive enormous stipends and get into all institutes into which our children cannot get," is a line one frequently hears in the Soviet capital.

Agriculture is Mr. Khrushchev's weakest point. Yet he is supposedly the party's agricultural specialist in contrast to Stalin who "understood nothing of agriculture" and the men of the 1957 "anti-party group," especially former Premier Georgi M. Malenkov.

Mr. Khrushchev's latest panacea—chemicalization—enthusiastically promoted by the party, privately has caused some shaking of heads.

Again, thoughtful people feel that the pace is too fast, that too much is expected from the farm officialdom and that it is unwise to put all the reserves of the country's admittedly overtaxed capital resources into one venture.

Another major mistake, it was pointed out to me, is the careless handling of the country's water reserve.

Last fall, Mr. Khrushchev started a big campaign for irrigation, which together with chemicalization and better and more farm machinery was to bring about agricultural abundance. Yet he neglected the tenuous water budget of the Volga, the greatest of Russia's European rivers and the Caspian Sea's only major source of water.

As the level of the huge inland lake drops, the "tongue of the desert" moves westward and spells drought in the Soviet Union's most fertile lands.

As early as the 1930s the Academy of Sciences, on the basis of research started under the Czar, warned that the projected "Volga cascade" of giant power stations with reservoirs so large that they were dubbed "inland seas," demanded too much from the mighty river.

Evaporation would sharply reduce its flow. Unless the Volga water was replenished, the scientists forecast a rapid shrinking of the Caspian Sea and the ultimate loss of more land to the desert than all the virgin lands which since 1955 have been reclaimed at great cost and with doubtful success along the Chinese border.

As a remedy, the academy proposed the southward diversion of two rivers now flowing into the Arctic Sea—the Pechora and the Vychegda. The watershed between these two rivers and the Kama, the Volga's only major tributary, is very low and the project technically and financially feasible. But it would take a few years.

The project was publicized throughout the Soviet Union in the late 1930s and hailed as an example of planned economy and Communist wisdom. It was to be started shortly before the war.

Eight years ago American electrical engineers were told by Mr. Malenkov, then Minister of Power Stations,

that the Pechora-Vychegda project was "in the works." It now has become general knowledge among Soviet economists and technicians that the project has never been started.

The same thing happened with several other projects which are indispensable complements of spectacular works undertaken elsewhere.

"In some of our most developed economic regions we have even today a sharp water shortage," stated I.S. Senin, chairman of one of the legislature's budget committees in his report to the December session of the Supreme Soviet.

People remember with bitterness the bubble of hope which was launched four years ago about an immense underground freshwater lake, another veritable "inland sea," below the virgin lands of Kazakhstan, and which only had to be tapped.

Seen against this background the Premier's stature in the eyes of his more informed countrymen has diminished. Like a circus magician he continues to pull one rabbit after another out of his hat, but some Soviet people have begun to wonder what happens to the rabbits after they have been shown.

Soviets Promote Honesty [3/25/64]

One morning, as I jotted down some notes in my Moscow hotel room, the telephone rang and the caller said: "You have left your wallet on the table. Come and get it." It was the coffee shop of the hotel where I had had breakfast about an hour ago.

I thanked him effusively, but did not want to believe my ears. In the wallet were several hundred dollars and a lot of papers difficult to replace.

Outwardly quiet, I walked back to the coffee shop as fast as I could.

There was the table at which I sat with old Mr. Byelo'usov, a Russian who before the war had worked in the United States as a confectioner but who had returned to his homeland, where he now was a bookkeeper on a large state farm east of the Volga. Mr. Byelo'usov had disappeared.

The waitress directed me to the matronly manager who took the wallet out of a drawer.

"This is yours, isn't it?" she asked in a matter-of-fact manner.

I accepted the wallet, thanked her, and returned to my room.

Intact, in the inner pocket, were all my dollar bills. At the black-market rate of 3.50 rubles to the dollar, the contents of my wallet would have equaled six months' average earnings. Yet not a single dollar bill, not a single paper was missing. It would have been different 30 years ago.

Was it Mr. Byelo'usov's doing? Maybe the spare little fellow was a man of importance.

I may never know who Mr. Byelo'usov was. He spoke soberly and freely, admitting that the crop on his farm had been bad that year and that the farm might be too large for efficient management.

He also admitted that Soviet bookkeeping often is complicated. Its purpose, he said, is to educate people to be thrifty, to instill orderliness, and to drive home a sense of gains and losses.

What he said about educating people to honesty and of making them conscious of gains and losses reminded me of a conversation I had in 1935 with a member of the board of what today would be called the Ministry of Transportation.

I had suggested a simplified method of collecting operating costs of the new subway, a method originally recommended in Prussia and tried out successfully in Russia under the Czar.

The Soviet transportation expert had smiled. "You have a point there," he said. "It would be cheaper, but first we have to bring home to our people that you get nothing for nothing."

In other words, what mattered was to demonstrate the economic principle to a precapitalist people.

Now the objective is to teach orderliness and honesty.

The way the slippers, which I had forgotten in the train on my arrival, were returned to the militia and now the return of my wallet intact showed that something had changed in the Soviet mentality. Incessant teaching, buttressed by severe discipline, had left a noticeable mark.

My wallet may have been returned by order of Mr. Byelo'usov, but Mr. Byelo'usov was not alone.

Education to honesty had brought about astonishing changes. A Frenchman, temporarily employed in a Moscow factory, told me about a new experiment. Pay envelopes now are stacked up on payday, and everyone takes his envelope without checking or making out a receipt. The pay envelopes contain bank bills not checks. So far never has an envelope been missing. If it were stolen, the police would have a hard time finding the thief.

The success of the experiment is said to be based on the fact that the workers know each other and have a sense of identification with their enterprise. "Mutual vigilance" also plays a part.

Recently Moscow introduced another experiment in social honesty. Buses no longer have conductors who collect or check the fare.

Each bus has a box at the rear and at the front door into which passengers are supposed to drop their fare (five kopeks on a bus, four kopeks on a trolleybus—at the official rate of exchange a little less than five cents). There is no controller.

The people do the checking themselves and seem to enjoy it. Little groups usually form around the coin boxes. One passenger may have only a 20-kopek piece. Another has a ruble. Another one, in a trolleybus, may have a five-kopek piece and two single kopeks. Deals must be made in the packed bus, precisely and fast so that everyone pays his fare and that the transit authority gets its money.

People are very serious about these transactions, which may strike an outsider as funny. When someone cannot drum up the appropriate change he needs, a fellow passenger usually helps out by providing the missing kopek.

"The main thing is that the bus is not cheated," I heard an old lady say. "It belongs to the people."

In all my bus rides through Moscow I only once met a man who refused to help out a fellow passenger with the needed change. Judging by his dress and figure, he belonged to the managerial upper crust. His haughty indifference irked the other passengers.

"He's the kind of man," one passenger remarked, "who would address his associates, regardless of age, in the second person (the familiar "ty") and expects to be talked to in the official plural ("vy"—which corresponds to the French "vous").

This sort of education to honesty is something Soviets are proud of. Sometimes it is done heavy-handedly and is accompanied by solemn hectoring which Westerners would find hard to take. But the results are visible and commendable.

How does this education to honesty jibe with "blat," the under-the-counter practices which have spread widely in the past few years?

Both are part of the Soviet pattern. "Blat" shows its face when the wheels get stuck. Where the system works smoothly there is no "blat."

The system gets stuck very often, but more frequently it works, and that is why, despite everything, education to honesty in the Soviet Union has made progress.

The Soviet Family of Nations   [4/2/64]

Today's USSR, as was the Czar's empire, is a multi-national state. Great Russians account for little more than half of the people.

When I first visited Moscow 30 years ago, I was reminded of Chicago and New York. Faces were represented from all over the world. Only dark-skinned Africans were missing.

One had to be ethnographically trained to distinguish Buryat-Mongolians from Chinese, Uzbeks from Persians, blond Leningraders from Swedes or Finns, or Transcaucasians from Levantines. Anyone could have taken the old Kirgizian watchman next to my friend's home for an American Indian.

And then there was the mass of Slavs — Great Russians, Byelorussians, and Ukrainians. How similar they seemed to Poles, Czechs or East Elbian Germans. Traveling in the Soviet Union, one heard as many languages as one saw racial physiognomies.

Today, after 40 years of Soviet nationality policy, one hears more Russian, although with many national inflections.

In Kiev and Kharkov in the Ukraine, Russian is spoken in the streets rather than Ukrainian. It is the same thing in Minsk, Byelorussia, and, I was told, in the cities of the Chuvash and Tartar republics along the Volga.

One of my traveling companions on a train ride last December was a lovely blond Tartar woman on her way to a Black Sea resort. Her Russian was indistinguishable from that of the other Soviet citizens. When she casually remarked that she was a Tartar, the Russians among us were genuinely pleased. She gladly explained particularities of her national tongue.

The older people, she said, did not speak "educated Tartar," as she did. "It was only in the last 40 years that the Tartar language became literary and cultured."

In Moscow, a Chuvash and a Karelian had said similar things about their languages. Yet they all behaved and moved more or less like Russians.

The picture changes only when one enters one of the larger non-Slav "sovereign" republics such as Armenia or Georgia.

In Georgia even simple farmhouses have porches or verandas. Cities are built according to a different pattern and have a peculiar Byzantine-influenced architecture, half Romanesque, half Persian. There is a distinct national cuisine reminiscent of food served along the eastern Mediterranean.

Gait, gestures and habits of the people are different. Georgian-born Russians and Ukrainians speak Russian with Georgian gestures and intonation, but Georgians born in Russia never speak Georgian with a Russian accent.

As one sits in one of Tbilisi's many cafes — a few of them resembling modern cafes in Italy or Spain — listening to the lively talk in Georgian one might imagine oneself among Catalans or Basques.

Culturally, Georgians feel superior to Russians. Their nation has an older history and civilization.

Economically Georgia had it good under Stalin, people say. Their attitude toward him is ambivalent. The combination Stalin mustache and haircut, which was quite frequent among Georgians two years ago, has almost completely disappeared.

Russians as a nation are accepted in an aloof way. The great majority of children and young people attend Georgian (not Russian) high schools and colleges. The choice, as in all national republics, is open.

The people's attitude toward the Soviet system varies. I met some of the most fervent Communist ideologists among Georgian intellectuals. But there were others who, like their Russian counterparts, paid lip service to the party and took advantage of the cultural leeway offered them as Georgians to study ancient history, folk art and Caucasian philology.

Only the lowest types seemed to have assimilated the crude features of Russian-style Communism. Every morning early on Tbilisi's main boulevard, hundreds of women, snow and rain notwithstanding, queued up for French-type white bread and rolls. The bread was sold out after 20 minutes and most of the women returned empty-handed.

When I questioned a Georgian acquaintance about the rudeness of the man who controlled the entrance to the bakery, he suggested that this was "our type of corporal … who copies the Russians." He probably was only half right.

Georgians, like the Corsicans of France, whom so many of them resemble, have a reputation of tending to bureaucratic and police careers.

The other side of their nature, which draws them toward their Armenian neighbors and toward the equally Transcaucasian Moslem Azerbaijani, is their penchant for private independence and trade.

At the Rustaveli Theater, named after Georgia's greatest poet, I saw a comedy whose main figure, a soft, comfort- and leisure-loving Papa — speculator or parasite by Soviet standards — was sympathetically pictured.

Just as in a "bourgeois" comedy, Papa's beautiful student daughter eloped with a romantic student-poet, aided by a philosophizing cobbler who stood for the Georgian Communist version of the proletariat. The theater was crowded and the audience visibly enjoyed the show.

Armenia, much less fertile than Georgia, also is strictly non-Russian and even more given to "Capitalist survivals."

If Georgia's favorite color is pink, Armenia's is pale purple, the color of the volcanic tufa stone of Yerevan's modern buildings.

Armenia, too, has its distinct style, and Armenians, who have an even older history than their Georgian neighbors, are deeply conscious of it.

Armenians from all over the world flocked to Yerevan in several waves of remigration before and after World War II. However, one meets more people of other nationalities there than in more homogeneous Tbilisi.

In Yerevan, people know better than anywhere else in the USSR how poorly their material existence compares with that of the West.

The many American and French Armenian families who returned to this stony remnant of their homeland after the war, brought several hundred children of their own along with them, who at the time of their "return" were old enough to remember the Capitalist way of life.

Most of these foreign-born "returnees" have a deep nostalgia for the West, maintain an active correspondence with relatives abroad, speak English or French at home, and still hope to return to the country of their birth.

Their condition is harder than that of the Armenian-born because they must hold down two or three jobs in order to have their families enjoy at least some of the comforts to which they were accustomed. Parcels from "the old country" also help; their contents are actively traded in the gray market.

All Armenians I met were proud of the way in which their ancient city has been rebuilt. Whereas Tbilisi always was a fairly rich town, Yerevan and Soviet Armenia, where originally only a fraction of the Armenian nation lived (the majority lived in Turkey), were very poor.

Nearly half of the population of Yerevan still lives in earth huts below ground level which one can see behind the beautiful street fronts of the new town. But not so long ago this was how all of Yerevan looked. Econom-

ically, Soviet Armenia has a split personality. Under Communism there is no rational explanation of how an ordinary worker can afford a two-room cooperative apartment or house for which he has to pay down 1,233 rubles ($1,355), or 30 percent of the price. The balance is paid off in 10 years.

Monthly earnings, even if a man holds two jobs, are only around 110 rubles. Without the gray or black market it would take a family of two many, many years to save enough money for the down payment. Yet these down payments are made and all around Yerevan new cooperative houses are going up.

The mood in Yerevan did not seem to be a happy one. Armenians lack their Georgian neighbors' aloof attitude toward the Russians. More Armenians than Georgians go to Russian schools and colleges in preference to their own. "It is more useful to them in their careers," I was told.

People are national minded but bored by narrow folk culture, the only one permitted or encouraged under Communism.

When I was in Yerevan the Armenian Folk Dance Ensemble happened to give a performance in the opera house. The costumes were fabulous, the musical instruments fine and authentic, but the big hall was almost empty.

I asked an Armenian intellectual about the insignificant attendance.

"It is always the same thing," he complained. "When you have seen it once or twice, you do not go any more."

Armenians, like Balts, know that the world beyond the Soviet border is so much more variegated, colorful free and exciting. For most of them the present Soviet system, while they accept it for the time being, is not the last word.

Apart from the foreign-born, they feel at one with the Soviet family of nations with whom they have been linked for so long and where they are so prominently represented by outstanding scholars and artists, engineers, not to forget their own Anastas Ivanovich Mikoyan, even though he infrequently visits his national homeland.

As the Moscow express train pulled out of one of the last Armenian stations, a boy of about 17, carrying a big loaf of bread, leaped out of the crowd and ran for the train. It was his dash for escape from provincial narrowness. A group of older men caught him and then let him go.

I still see him walking out into the stony field, his head bowed.

Soviet Pressures
Against Dissent Accepted   [4/3/64]

"Why must you always have unanimity?" I asked my companion, a beautiful young woman who worked for the Soviet tourist office.

"Oh, we also have dissenting voices now," she replied. "One woman complained to our television station about the barrenness of atheistic programs," she told me, "and this was publicly discussed. We are against monotony."

My companion—let's call her Tonia—was a history graduate and a convinced atheist.

Last week her point was made by *Izvestia*, which quoted a letter of a self-styled atheist, Mrs. Smirnov.

"The problem of life worries people," wrote Mrs. Smirnov. "The usual formula that life expresses movement of matter is hard to understand and offers neither consolation nor joy.

"Human nature is imperfect and has many vices. Above all, man should understand that two things are true: that his neighbor is a brother and that work is a point of honor. "It is not the believers who obstruct the building of Communism but the absence of moral qualities in the masses of the people."

Izvestia, a government organ, disagreed with Mrs. Smirnov. It admitted, however, that "the same questions were raised in other letters so that it became necessary to bring Mrs. Smirnov's letter to the attention of the readers."

Tonia had said more or less the same thing. Yet she insisted on the need for unanimity. Dissenting voices should be aired only "to make people think more clearly. In major matters with us there can be no dissent."

I asked: "Would Stalin's repressions have been possible if you had public criticism? Injustices happen elsewhere, too, but they can be corrected and kept down if there is a protest movement." I quoted examples.

Tears welled in Tonia's eyes. "No, no," she said impassionately. "We have to believe in one truth. We could not live with your skepticism."

Among the young this passion for unanimity is the emotional basis of Communism. Occasional voices of dissent now are allowed for reasons of expediency.

Behind this passion lies fear that suddenly "everything might go to pieces."

This insecurity is drowned out by party and state bombast, but it is there as in prerevolutionary Russia.

Greater prosperity, growing sophistication, and youthful optimism are steadying factors, but still deep down there is the feeling of insecurity.

Lenin, Stalin, and after them, Khrushchev, have tried to overcome this Russian sense of doubt in the continuity and solidity of things. To an extent they have succeeded. A new generation with technical know-how has gained self-respect and a modicum of security. But the doubt continues.

Fear that "everything might go to pieces" also explains why the struggle behind tightly drawn curtains in the upper party echelons cannot be aired publicly.

Yet there is evidence of disagreement. Consumerism is one such issue on which the leadership is divided, as shown by contradictory public statements. The expediency of downgrading Stalin is another issue.

In this connection differences of opinion were voiced on Stalin's role during the battle of Stalingrad and at the beginning of the war. Chief of Staff Marshal Sergei S. Biryuzov took one side and Defense Minister Rodion Y. Malinovsky took the other. The leading party newspapers of the Ukraine, Byelorussia and Kazakhstan never published Marshal Biryuzov's scathing critique of Stalin with concomitant praise of Premier Nikita S. Khrushchev.

Another example: the date of the arrest of rehabilitated victims of the purge recently has been quoted differently in different newspapers. Earlier dates make it appear that Premier Khrushchev, at the time of the arrests, did not yet belong to the Politburo. Other dates implicate him.

Soviet intellectuals are acquainted with the Premier's dramatic confrontation at the Central Committee meeting of June 1957, with the men later branded as "the anti-party group." There Mr. Khrushchev, according to western Communist correspondents in Moscow, shouted at Messrs. Molotov and Kaganovich, "Your hands are stained with the blood of our party leaders and of innumerable innocent Bolsheviks."

"So are yours," Molotov and Kaganovich shouted back.

"Yes, so are mine," Mr. Khrushchev is reported to have replied, "but during the purges I was merely carrying out your orders. I was not then a member of the Politburo and bear no responsibility for its decisions. You do!" According to some Soviet sources it now appears that Mr. Khrushchev was a member of the Politburo when certain recently rehabilitated purge victims were arrested. Such differences are closely watched by Soviet intellectuals. As usual, they find an

The Christian Science Monitor **from April 2, 1964.**

expression in current jokes. The following joke was brought back from Moscow a few weeks ago:

"Two men chat in a correction camp. 'How many years did you get and for what?' asks one.

'Five years for one pair of shoes.'

'How come?'

'I worked in a shoe factory and took a few scraps of leather home to make a pair of boots for my daughter. And you?'

'Ten years for one word.'

'Why?'

'I had a picture of Stalin in my room. Last year I put up one of Khrushchev. Comes the party man and shouts: "Take that scoundrel down."

'All I said was: Which?'"

Behind these veiled differences and jokes close observers sense an uneasiness lest the leaders clash, and terror once again come to the fore. Terror did not completely disappear.

I remember a talk in a train with a young soldier who questioned me about America. As we talked, a small, somber-looking civilian appeared in the corridor looking at us. When the soldier noticed this man, he rose brusquely without saying goodbye. Later I passed through his car on my way to the restaurant. I waved. He looked away.

The Soviet Union and its People [1/12/81]

By David K. Willis

The sound was immense, a shattering, guttural growl, filling the midnight air. As we ran toward Gorky Street where it joins Moscow's inner ring road, prehistoric gray-green silhouettes loomed into view.

Heavy metal treads sliced into the road surface, scattering tiny pieces like chaff. Exhaust pipes spat out clouds of diesel fumes that stung the back of the throat.

Four abreast they rumbled down the hill to Karl Marx Prospekt, massively incongruous on the wide city street, long narrow gun barrels thrusting forward beneath the trolley-bus wires, the drivers' heads helmeted like the flying aces of World War I. Khaki canvasswathed machine guns stuck out at the rear.

A pause. Engines idled. A soldier marched to the center of the road, held up a red flag, then ran for his life. The commander's jeep shot off in the lead. And the T-72 battle tanks, on display for the first time in Moscow as they rehearsed for the November 7 parade in 1977 (the 60th anniversary of the Soviet state), roared up the hill and into Red Square.

Each machine, 38 tons of polished and painted metal, vanished into the distance beneath the striped, brilliantly lit onion domes of St. Basil's Cathedral at the far end of the square. The domes towered, unearthly, against the black sky, like the backdrop to a Russian opera at the Bolshoi Theater.

That moment, as my wife and I stood there, ears ringing, the taste of fumes in our mouths, watching plainclothes KGB agents watching western military attachés who had been watching the tanks … that moment summed up the menace, and the basic challenge, that the Soviet Union presents to the rest of the world today, almost 6 1/2 decades after Lenin seized power in 1917.

That challenge is materialism—the constant claim that material force is what counts in the world; that Soviet armor can support Soviet ideology in a way that is superior to the ideals and ideas of the West, the worth of the individual, man's right to live and pray unoppressed by the state.

The Kremlin represents a form of government that believes might makes right. Its Marxist-Leninist-Stalinist ideology seeks to justify Soviet force and material appeal by arguing that they are the "inevitable" historical conquerors over all other ideas and forms of government and social order.

Man is put at the center of the universe. Religion is dismissed as a mere outgrowth of economic forces. There are no eternal verities.

The challenge needs to be faced rather than feared. It is the antithesis of the concept that ideas are mightier than military metal and brute force.

For it is force and fear that today's Kremlin uses to keep order at home and to expand influence abroad. To the huge geographical entity created by the czars, the Communists have added the imported, western ideology of Marx and refined it to local conditions so that it both forces an expansionist world view and justifies that view. The old religious icons have given way to the new: ballistic missiles and T-72 tanks.

Materialism shows up in the Soviet preoccupation with force here at home, even on "festive" occasions.

Every time I left Red Square after a November 7 or May 1 (May Day) parade, I would look to my left through a tall door in the Kremlin wall just before starting down the slope from the square proper to Karl Marx Prospekt beyond.

Through the half-open wooden door, in the shadows, out of sight but on the alert, was a squad of young Red Army soldiers, well-fed and red-cheeked, Kalashnikov automatic rifles ready in their hands. A hitch in the organized spontaneity outside and they would be ready.

On November 7, 1980, walking to my last parade, I passed more soldiers, armed and outfitted, in the long pedestrian underpass that leads to the square.

Nothing is left to chance. The mammoth parades themselves, with their massed ranks of people, red flags, banners, paper flowers, portraits of Politburo leaders on rubber-tired floats, are meticulously rehearsed. Even the crowd cheers are on a prerecorded tape blasting from loudspeakers high on the Kremlin wall.

The instinctive way the Kremlin coped with 100,000 non-Communist visitors here for the Olympic Games in August 1980 was to use a show of force. Not since a World Youth Conference in 1957 had so many foreigners come to Soviet cities. Party officials wanted to limit their contact with local people, to control the impact of outside ideas.

So hundreds of thousands of militia (police) militia trainees, soldiers and officers patrolled the streets of Moscow (and the other Olympic cities: Tallinn, Leningrad, Minsk, Kiev). Out-of-town traffic and Soviet visitors were simply turned away at the outer ring road. Many westerners were astonished to find so little traffic, so few local people, so many uniforms, so little vivacity or joy.

Leaving Lenin Stadium each night, I felt as though I was in an armed camp. Platoons of militia marched to bus pickup points. Squads of soldiers moved away into the darkness. Messenger boys in green windbreakers were drilled in double file. Truck convoys coming in to take the men away for the night consisted of as many as 97 ten-wheeled vehicles each.

Of course, the Soviet Union is not just force and fear. It is many other things besides: people and families, ballet and opera, cosmonauts and chess players, ice-skating and cross-country skiing, dachas and mushroom picking, cities and farms, hopes and dreams (the latter will be discussed later in this series).

But central control, ensured by force, is the hallmark of the Communist system. The thinking behind it, the intense rivalry the system sees itself locked into with the rest of the world, the adversary relationship the Kremlin believes to be inevitable, is the main challenge to President-elect Ronald Reagan and all other non-Communist leaders as well.

The other Communist superpower, China, lacks superpower weapons or a history of aggressiveness abroad. Moscow has both.

The Kremlin's materialism shows in its view of Soviet citizens themselves. They are deemed to possess only those rights conferred by the state, which means by the Communist Party, which in turn means a handful of men at the top of the hierarchy. The entire country is the party's domain, to be ruled as the party thinks fit. The western concept of man as an individual possessing inherent rights is alien here.

The 1977 Constitution has 174 articles, laying out what the party allows its citizens to have, from housing to health to public catering to marriage.

Article 62 says, "Citizens of the USSR are obliged to safeguard the interests of the Soviet state and to enhance its power and prestige." Soviet people tend to be extremely patriotic, emotionally so. But the party doesn't feel able to rely on innate patriotism: It has to spell it out.

Surveillance and suspicion are part of the system, part of Lenin's and Stalin's materialist legacy, part of Russian history itself.

"Every apartment building has its 'watcher,' often someone elderly, who stays around the building all day, sees people come and go, makes a note of anything unusual, and tells local microregion officials," one Moscow man told me in his apartment late one night, lowering his voice as Russians habitually do when making a critical statement.

He picked up his phone, dialed "2," and put a pencil in the hole to the left of the metal finger-stop to prevent the dial returning to normal. Many Russians are convinced the state listens in through the phone lines, so if they interfere with the line, sometimes putting the phone itself into a drawer, they feel safer.

Memories of the Stalin years die hard.

"If I come home with a new stereo set, for instance, and the 'watcher' suspects I could not have afforded it on my salary, I am likely to have a stranger knock at my door and start asking questions. No threats. No Siberia. But the message is clear enough ...." Said another man, also late at night, as we walked along deserted, dimly lighted streets in the bitter cold: "Step out of line in your factory or office, and you'll be visited by a trade union official, or called in 'for a chat.' In the bigger establishments it's the *Pervii Otdel* [First Department] that will see you, the personnel people, except that they're either KGB or internal police.

"You'll soon realize what you might lose if you don't get back in line—the right to buy a car, or a pass to a resort hotel in Sochi [on the Black Sea], or the right to buy food in bulk from the canteen once a week. Ninety-nine times out of a hundred, you decide to behave. It's fear."

The Soviet Union itself is an empire, the last 19th-century empire on earth. The Czar's armies marched into Azerbaijan, on the southern border and adjoining what is now Iran, in 1723, but were unable to consolidate control until a century later—about the same time Britain was taking Ceylon (now Sri Lanka).

The Czar overran Turkmenistan as the British conquered the Gold Coast (now Ghana)—about 1840; and he took what is now Uzbekistan about the same time the British took Nigeria (about 1860).

Ceylon became independent in 1948, Ghana in 1957, Nigeria in 1960. But no one ever seems even to suggest that Moscow give up what the Czar took.

In this century, the Communists have added the Baltic states and part of Poland. Even now their forces are struggling to cement control over Afghanistan. Meanwhile, Soviet leaders repeat endlessly that the Western world alone is "colonialist."

What holds the internal empire of 15 Soviet socialist republics together is force. Article 72 of the 1977 Constitution says each republic "shall retain the right freely to secede from the USSR."

But no one that tried to do so would get very far.

Huge resources go into maintaining a 4 million-man army and internal police force, including border guards.

Filled as the huge country is with Slavic inefficiencies, the party has done two things well: It has infiltrated every power base and controlled it; and it has created nuclear, strategic, and conventional armaments equal to those of the United States, whose gross national product is about twice that of the Soviet Union. The Soviets rule with an iron hand over their immediate empire—Eastern Europe, and now Afghanistan. The crisis with Poland shows clearly that force, size and proximity are all the Kremlin has to rely on. Without them, both Eastern Europe and Afghanistan would thankfully go their own ways.

Moscow also uses proximity (Finland) or a mixture of proximity and force (Mongolia) to keep its neighbors quiet. Where it fails—with China, Iran, Turkey—the Kremlin feels constantly threatened. It has no internal dynamism, no vibrant self-made example, on which to fall back.

This reliance on material force rather than the attraction and vitality of ideas means fewer consumer goods for Soviet citizens than western countries provide—though the Soviet system does not look so economically inadequate when compared with the rest of Asia: China, Pakistan, India, Afghanistan, Iran.

The party blames the tragic loss of 20 million people in World War II for most shortcomings today, 35 years later. Mammoth arms spending is, however, the real reason shoppers still stand in long lines to get into dirty, badly lighted shops to buy basic necessities such as potatoes and meat.

This winter, meat is in such short supply that even in Moscow, the best-stocked city in the country, open complaints are often heard. Westerners report Russian friends asking, with embarrassment, if potatoes and rice could be bought for them in hard-currency stores open only to foreigners.

The average person here lacks color, variety, diversion in his daily life. The Soviet Union remains an underdeveloped country with overdeveloped arms: a Bolivia with the bomb.

The party does have achievements to its credit. It has provided many new apartment blocks, better clothes, color television sets, imported shoes. It has sunk massive sums into agriculture. It has provided its people with genuine superpower status through the force of its arms. It has maintained the Russian tradition in ballet and opera and music. Health services and education are free. Housing rents are very low.

But the costs in human freedom are enormous.

When I came to the Soviet Union in August 1976 it was still the era of détente—despite the Kremlin's successful support (mainly with black Cuban soldiers) of the Popular Movement for the Liberation of Angola, and the tying of more trade to Jewish emigration from the USSR.

But détente has changed. So has the United States. So have I. Gone is the concept that being "nice" to materialism will make it nice to you. It is plain, instead, that being nice encourages it to believe you are weak.

True, the West needs always to be courteous in personal dealings and upright in sticking to agreements. But the relationship with the Kremlin must always, at bottom, be an adversary one.

It's not a case of us deciding arbitrarily to be nasty to them. It is that their way of thinking is implacably opposed to us.

Kremlin thinking is more single-minded than that of western leaders. The Kremlin does have a kind of public opinion at home to cope with—within the party. It will have even more trouble if it doesn't provide more meat, and soon. Already trade union officials here have

confirmed in private talks with western diplomats that there were, indeed, "work stoppages" in various parts of the country in 1980, though they gave no details. Yet the Kremlin permits no significant internal political opposition.

That said, it is worth remembering that materialism has its weaknesses as well.

For all its might, Moscow remains insecure, thin-skinned, an outsider in the world community. Finland might watch its step in foreign policy, but that doesn't prevent the overwhelming majority of Finnish individuals from being passionately anti-Soviet. By relying on force, the Kremlin ceases to appeal with its ideas. It constantly demands that the US treat it as "an equal."

The journal *Voprosy Istorii KPSS* (Questions of History of the Communist Party) claims wildfire successes: Communist parties working in more than 90 countries now, compared with 37 countries in 1922, and "already more than 75 million Communists in the world."

"It becomes increasingly more difficult to outline and carry out an effective national policy" in Italy, France, Japan, Portugal, Greece and Cyprus without working with local Communists, the journal argues in its November 1980 issue—failing to mention that Communism in those countries is not always the Soviet brand, and that the current general trend in the western world is to the right, not to the left.

Marxism-Leninism-Stalinism still fights the battles of a century ago. It still talks in the language of the 19th century, when Marx added an economic dimension to history and saw (correctly) how industrialization was turning workers into victims. Now the West is racing into the era of microchips and wall television and word processors, while the Kremlin's only step away from nib pens and inkwells is inside its military establishment.

In many fields, Soviet policy is essentially to react to what the West and China do. Often, the Kremlin's fortunes depend more on how the United States and China are doing rather than on the appeal of its own ideas. Where the US does well (Camp David in the Mideast for a while, for example), the Soviets do badly. Where the US does poorly, the Soviets come up again.

Soviet foreign policy remains a mixture of superpower rhetoric and bombast, expansionism, target-of-opportunity maneuvering, and meticulously planned ventures all backed by force.

There are unlikely to be quick changes internally. The Soviet people have little history of internal revolt, no tradition of democracy to which to return, no tradition of successfully challenging central authority.

Russian and Soviet history combines Oriental secrecy, despotism, isolation and rural poverty with an overlay of western arms, technology and ideas.

The West has to find ways to face this challenge in a spirit of confidence in the vitality of western ideas, liberties and religious ideals. And it needs to do this without flagging or fear—and without hatred for the Soviet leaders or people as individuals; they can be as warm, gregarious and outgoing as any other people in the world.

Tass: All the Propaganda That's Fit to Print
[1/12/81]

By David K. Willis

MOSCOW—The Kremlin challenge comes not only in tanks and rockets, but also in words—the kind that clack endlessly from the small gray teleprinter that stands beside a battered gas stove and a small and ancient refrigerator in the back room of *The Christian Science Monitor* office here.

The room was built as a kitchen; the office, like all others in our building, was originally a small apartment.

The kitchen setting is apt, though. The little gray machine serves up dish after dish of propaganda prepared by the Soviet news agency Tass (the Russian initials for the Telegraph Agency of the Soviet Union) according to recipes set forth by the Kremlin.

The material is hard to read, harder to digest. No spontaneity, no fun, no liveliness. But after standing by the machine for 4 1/2 years, starting and ending the day with its gray view of the world, I find myself wishing all Americans and their allies also had to read it for at least a few days.

They would find the broadest and crudest of challenges: their own world turned on its head, all ideals and assumptions reversed, all items subordinated to the destructive view that everything good in the world is Soviet or pro-Soviet, and everything bad is American or pro-American.

Tass sends its basic service around the world. It reads all major overseas wire agencies and countless western journals, taking advantage of western freedom to play back criticisms of the West and ignore positive developments.

(Senior members of the Communist Party here are not given such heavily censored material. Some get *White Tass*, which is a fuller compendium of Associated Press, United Press International, Reuters and others.

Clockwise from top left: Farmers in Georgia, USSR. Contemporary street scenes in Leningrad and Moscow. Factory worker in Tashkent.

Top people get *Red Tass*, which appears to be an almost complete version of daily news. In short, what anyone can read abroad, only the top Communist Party people can see here.)

Tass is not a "news" agency at all, except that it does relay Soviet speeches and announcements. Every now and then it inserts a lighter note (the walrus population rising, the discovery of the bones of mammoths on which man may have beaten out primitive music), but even then the basic aim of Tass is preserved: to boost the Soviet system.

When it comes to the United States, no slander is bad enough. Here is one complete item, which indicates its lack of normal western standards of reporting:

Bonn February 9 Tass — During exercises in the FRG (West Germany), an American tank ran into a fence around a residential house in the city of Alzev, knocking down a West German policeman. The tank drove away from the accident scene. The policeman died. Item ends.

No other details. No explanations. Nothing except the barest details rewritten from local reports to make the US look as bad as possible. Have there been accidents involving Soviet troops in Eastern Europe? Don't read Tass to find out.

The Russian service is translated into other languages. The English version is awkward, since translation must be word for word to ensure political correctness.

The last man to see the material before it is handed to teleprinter punchers is the political editor, who sees that nothing untoward creeps in.

Tass is a nonstop Government circular and a relentless propagandist. And it uses words familiar to outside readers—"peace," "détente," and so on—but on Tass they have very different meanings.

The world of Tass is worth looking at closely. It gives insights into the heavy hand of Kremlin thought and action, the ideology in whose name all actions are taken and justified. Many people openly disbelieve the ideology by now, but its hold on power is still great.

If we let Tass words bounce around the world without knowing what they are and what they want to do, we simply make the Kremlin's job easier.

So here (below) is a minidictionary of Tass terms. It is offered in the tradition of the Marquis de Custine, a wise French nobleman who toured czarist Russia for five months in 1839.

"I do not blame the Russians for being what they are," he wrote later, "I blame them for pretending to be what we are."

At first sight the words look the same as the ones we use. But they are not—whether on Tass or in the Soviet speeches. They are the channels of Soviet ideology, and should be read as such.

'Dictionary' of Tass Words and Phrases

Across the ocean: code-phrase for the US, as in, "Those across the ocean who want...."

Aggravated: what the arms race is, because of "those across the ocean."

Aggression: the foreign policy of the US, China, Egypt, South Africa, Britain, Australia. Usually "naked" or "unrestrained."

Bases: what Americans have around the world. The Soviet Union in Cuba, Aden, Vietnam and elsewhere has only "friends."

Champions: those who support peace, Soviet-style (see "peace" below). As in, Helsinki peace champions held a rally today...".

Consistent: Soviet policies. American ones are inconsistent.

Counterrevolutionary: anyone who favors a government Moscow doesn't. Western equivalent: "rebel," "guerrilla."

Democracy: one-party rule. Party selection of candidates for office, followed by ratification by the citizenry by "voting" for one preselected candidate per post.

Détente: an easing of the prospect of a global shooting war, so that Moscow can get on with fighting Capitalist states for influence by all other means (see "peace" below).

Don't you see?: parenthetical phrase to denote irony. As in, "The United States, don't you see, thinks it can lecture the USSR ..."

Facts are stubborn things: favorite Tass headline on its own version of events.

Farce: event "staged" by the West to criticize Moscow or its allies.

Good neighborliness: Soviet relations with its friends. The US only exploits.

Gunsights: what the imperialists have trained on peace.

Helsinki Final Act: document signed in 1975 to approve the postwar Soviet sphere in Europe. Also used by US and others to "interfere" in Soviet internal affairs.

Heroic: Soviet actions.

Hopeless: trying to threaten the Soviet Union. Suggesting Soviet troops leave Afghanistan.

Hullabaloo: much-loved Tass word. Any statement in the West construed to be anti-Soviet (Tass does a lot of

**Police cars in Red Square with Lenin's
Tomb and Kremlin wall in the background.**

construing). As in, "…The supporters of Bangkok raised a hullabaloo over these actions…".(Vietnamese troops had just attacked Thailand from Cambodia.)

Independence: freedom from US influence, thus openness to Soviet influence.

Instigator: the US, also Egypt, China, etc.

Interference: any statement criticizing the Soviet Union or its friends. Anti-American statements by Moscow are the wise pronouncements of a great power.

Irreversible: what "détente" is (see above).

Liberation: freedom from US influence (see "independence"). It is predetermined by historical "laws."

Lies have short legs: favorite Tass headline attacking the West.

Nobody: the USSR, as in, "Nobody threatens Japan [or Yugoslavia, or Western Europe, or détente]."

Nonaligned: anti-US, potentially pro-Moscow, as in Cuba.

Outrage: any action opposed to Soviet interests.

Peace: the absence of shooting war, in which Moscow can use all other means to dominate other countries.

Principled: a favorite word. Refers to all actions of the USSR, but none of the US.

Quill drivers: the western press.

Racism: how the US treats blacks and South Africa as well. Only found outside the Soviet Union.

Reaction: as in, "forces of imperialism and reaction." (Also, what Tass spends a lot of time doing; some westerners call Moscow the "reaction capital of the world" for the way it reacts to even the smallest events abroad.)

Rebuff: administered by Moscow or its friends to any critic. Usually verbal. Almost always "resolute" or "firm."

Revolutionary: Soviet ideas, and others based on them.

Righteous: Soviet, Marxist, Leninist. Formerly also: Stalinist.

Rights: what the 1977 Soviet Constitution guarantees. What the US tramples underfoot.

Slander: criticism of Moscow or its friends.

Telegram: method of Tass propaganda. Separate items are devoted to even the most routine telegrams to other governments—and to the replies, no matter how formal or meaningless. As in: "A telegram has come in to Andrei Gromyko, minister of foreign affairs of the USSR, from Hans Dietrich Genscher, who express grattitude for the congratulations on the occasion of …"

Threat: what the US is to the world.

Vital interests: what the Soviets have around the world. What the US does not have in the Persian Gulf or in Cuba.

An Isolated Giant; Suspicious, Insecure, Cunning   [1/13/81]

Word flashed into the compound where we lived: Large crowds had defied police in emotional scenes outside the avant-garde Taganka Theater, just two miles from Red Square. Thousands had jeered and shaken their fists.

That such a scene could happen at all in a tightly controlled Moscow was news. That it happened during the Olympic Games (it was the end of July 1980), when the city was swarming with tens of thousands of extra police and soldiers to keep order, was remarkable.

Craig Whitney of the *New York Times* and I jumped into a car. The main protest was over by the time we parked near the drab two-story building; crowds had rebelled when police tried to clear people from the road as they listened to funeral rites inside for a revered actor and balladeer, Vladimir Vysotsky.

It was late afternoon, hot. Emotion was still tangible in the air as crowds, mainly young people, spilled into the road. Red fire trucks stood nearby. Police asked everyone to step back and let trolley buses through.

We were wearing old clothes, no ties. But as we began talking to bystanders, a middle-aged woman instantly recognized us as *innostrantsi*, foreigners. She glared.

"Foreigners," she said sharply. "We don't need you. We can solve our own problems by ourselves." I shivered.

A few hours later I told another Russian about the incident, a woman who knew a number of westerners. She said firmly, "I agree with her."

Outwardly, Russians look and act much like people in the West. But they remain a race apart. This is today, as it has been for 1,000 years, an isolated country, suspicious of outsiders, unexpectedly emotional beneath its uniform and patrolled surface. It is rigidly controlled from the center, Asian and rural in tradition, insecure, as shrewd and cunning as a 19th-century *muzhik*, or peasant, largely ignorant of the outside world.

The Soviet Union spans two continents, Europe and Asia, embracing 8 1/2 million square miles of land. It is three times the size of the United States, seven times the size of India, twice as big as China, one-sixth of the land surface of the globe, stretching across 11 time zones. When families are eating their evening meals in Minsk in the west, others are getting up the next morning in Khabarovsk on the far east coast, not far from Japan.

Church vs. State: Statue of Lenin and churches in the Kremlin.

Most of it is cold, more Canadian than American in latitude: Moscow is way north of Edmonton; Yakutsk is as far north as Greenland; sunny Tashkent in Soviet Central Asia is actually farther north than Denver.

It is remote. My wife and I found out the hard way when we drove back from London in August 1978. Dover to Bavaria was an easy two days; on to Warsaw took another two, driving on two-lane Czech and Polish roads behind ramshackle trucks; and on to Moscow took yet another two, across the vastness that never seems to end. Before the car and the jet, the journey took weeks.

This goes back to a cataclysm that shook medieval Russia six centuries ago, the most important event in the country's history before 1917: the 250-year occupation by the Golden Horde of the Mongol Empire beginning in 1237.

Led by Mongols but consisting mainly of Tatars, the horde swept across Russia like an avalanche from the east. It burned the central city-state of Kiev, pillaged its way farther west, and could have taken all of Europe but for the death of the Mongol *khan*, or emperor, in 1242. Back streamed the horde from camps in what is now Hungary. Never again did it penetrate farther west than the edge of modern Russia; if it had, Europe might look and feel more like Russia today.

The Mongols' iron occupation meant brutal, central control. Small Russian city-states stayed alive by currying favor, and Moscow was best — or worst — at it. Moscow princes learned how to terrorize; they learned the importance of efficient communications between center and circumference of empire, and how to extract taxes and men for the army from the *boyars* (nobles).

The man who learned the lessons best was Ivan IV (Ivan the Terrible), who lived from 1530 to 1584 and was the first ruler to take the permanent title of "czar" ("caesar"). Until then it had been reserved for the Mongol rulers. Ivan shattered the boyars by seizing their lands, and set the stage for wildly emotional, Oriental oppression, which continued into the 19th century.

For Russians this meant no Magna Carta. No Renaissance. No Reformation. No successful challenging of royal authority by the men of the towns (bourgeoisie), of the land (boyars), or of the church. (The Russian Orthodox Church, conservative and respectful of authority, was as much under the czars' control as everything else.) So the flow, the pattern of history here, just didn't happen in the same way as it did in England, Spain and France.

The Russian heritage is more Asian than the West commonly supposes. The Russians' ancestors knew oppression, totalitarianism, poverty, rural conditions, and other influences from the east (largely from the Mongols). Today, the Russian words for money (*dengi*) and customs (*tamozhnaya*) are rooted in Mongol terms. Since Peter the Great at the end of the 17th century, a thin layer of western ideas has been adopted by the tiny governing elite. But the old ways have persisted underneath.

The situation is the same today: imported Marxism at the top, with western influences in the elite's life style; but relative poverty below.

Intellectuals in Moscow and Leningrad rarely refer to the Asian heritage, locked as they are in confrontation with China. "You're not even European," university students can be heard remarking to other students from Siberia or Central Asia.

Soviet bathrooms are Asian in their primitiveness and dirt. Apartments are mostly cluttered and chaotic. The Slav is light-years away from Scandinavians in hygiene, order, efficiency. Big-city shops bear an Asian, rural stamp in their lack of bright light or comfort.

Such influences linger. Few average Russians ever see other countries, even East Europe (where living standards are higher). In most of the country people watch, hear, read and know only what the Communist Party decrees. Glimpses of the West are seen and heard in Moscow and Leningrad; elsewhere not much is known of western life styles.

Another set of influences is also at work, this time from the south: a Levantine sense of barter and trade. Cities did not develop in Russia until the end of the 19th century. Under the czars they were places to trade and to pay taxes. Most people lived outside them. Today many cities remain too hot for comfort in summer and too cold in winter, cut off by snow and then mud. Only autumn is balmy.

The GUM department store, which forms one side of Moscow's Red Square, is, in fact, a Middle Eastern bazaar filled with small separate shops. The Moscow pet market, unofficial but tolerated, is another bazaar. Sellers stand side by side, holding a tiny glass jar containing two bright fish, or a bag of birdseed, or a puppy buried in the folds of a voluminous and shabby coat.

Farmers' markets, allowed in most cities, are echoes of the pre-1917 past as rural workers sell the fruit, vegetables, and meat they have raised on their tiny private plots. They water down peeled carrots to make them shine, offer a sliver of cheese or a taste of honey, providing what the state stores do not: a choice. Prices are high, often outrageously so, but people pay.

If the Soviet Union is compared with the rest of Asia (except for Japan), its industrial achievements look much better. Soviet Central Asia is far ahead of Iran, Afghanistan and Pakistan in electric power, water supplies, literacy, transportation. Tashkent, the biggest Soviet city in Central Asia, is used as a showcase for visiting delegations. It is even building a subway.

But Moscow constantly compares itself with the West, not the East. It insists it is better than the United States in every significant way.

Its own propaganda is so far from reality in such areas as basic consumer services that many intellectuals grow cynical. They stop reading the controlled press and occupy themselves with personal and family matters rather than politics. Workers, too, are nonpolitical. It is hard to find time for revolution when you have to stand in line for hours every day to buy basic necessities like potatoes.

"We aim to survive," one Latvian told me calmly, "just to survive." On the other hand, workers in heavy industry plants live and eat relatively well.

Russians are intensely emotional about their families, their close friends, their Motherland. Officials of the Ukrainian Communist Party had tears in their eyes as they sang to a group of western reporters some romantic folk songs over lunch near Lvov. In a land where Stalinist control and historic suspicion of strangers still linger, people live, by order and by choice, in their own circles—workers with workers, painters with painters, ballet dancers with ballet dancers, even composers with composers.

I once asked Dmitri Kabalevsky, last of the great Russian composers of the 1930s, where he lived; he waved toward a tall apartment block not far from Tchaikovsky Hall on Herzen Street. "Over there," he said. "Shostakovich was next door and Khachaturian upstairs...."

Within these circles, bonds are close. I remember one night, on the outskirts of the city, snow and ice thick outside, sitting shoulder to shoulder in a warm, cheerful kitchen with nine Muscovites, eating slices of cheese, dark bread, boiled potatoes, cabbage and chopped beetroot (beets), watching my friends toss back small glasses of vodka while I drank tea, and listening to them gossip.

They talked about who was having an affair with whom; what store sold good fish (sometimes); how "they" said Moscow traffic police were involved with a gang of car thieves; how life was harder these days; how meat was in short supply; how people spouted party slogans just to get ahead, not because they believed in them; how they were planning holidays and children's events; how imported lipstick had appeared in one shop, only to disappear the next day; how the system didn't need librarians or linguists or the humanities, but only steelworkers and managers and soldiers....

Soviet borders are the longest in the world: 37,000 miles, nine times the length of US borders. Unlike the US, Russia has been invaded many times—by Mongols, Swedes, Teutonic and Livonian knights, by Napoleon, by Hilter. Outsiders remain strange, alien.

"Shpioni," young boys call to each other in Ukrainian cities when they see the white license plate of a foreign car. "Spies." Communist suspicions reinforce historical ones. The Kremlin has a legitimate concern with security. Its ideology makes it not just defensive, but also aggressive. It has armed force to lend weight to its words. But it often acts as though it is still insecure, still an outsider.

Whenever Brezhnev makes a speech or the Communist Party holds a meeting or greets a foreign leader, the press and television collect quotations from the European and US presses and broadcast them—as if no achievement really counts unless approved abroad.

Citizens make far fewer decisions affecting their own lives than westerners do. I have talked to Soviet diplomats and scientists abroad who were alarmed at the personal responsibilities the West takes for granted.

"Say a man is a good engineer but he wants to play the guitar," one diplomat said to me. "What a waste to the state." I said I called it freedom. He shook his head.

Young people here are assigned their first job out of school, university or institute. They can switch after three years, but even if the first job is thousands of miles away from home, many stay.

The average person has little or no control over where he goes to school or what factory he works in. Most don't want such control: Let the state decide. The Soviet Union is the ultimate example of what happens when the state runs everything, when individuals agree to the right of others to decide what is best for them. Endless red tape and a lack of incentive are just two of the results.

With rewards not related to work done, productivity is low here—much lower than in Europe, the US or Japan. But the people know only their own system. They cannot read widely about others. They have no tradition of democratic action or individual thought.

An individual is defined more by his relationship with others than by his own nature.

"Yes, you have better consumer services than we do," one Soviet scientist told me. "You'll always have better hotels and railroads and airlines. But look at what we have: jobs, homes, free education, free health care, low food prices. You have unemployment, drugs, crime, insecurity...."

No official I met acknowledged the existence of unemployment benefits, or any of the social-welfare support systems the West has erected.

Ethnically, this is a far more diverse country than many Westerners realize. More than 100 nationalities, at least 37 of them Turkic and Muslim, crowd in, from Balts and Byelorussians in the west to Uzbeks, Kazakhs, Nogays and Tungans in the south and east. There is no real prospect of any of them breaking loose, but Moscow must be constantly on the alert for trouble.

The 137,397,000 Russians as of January 1979 (52.4 percent of the population) have a solid grip on power. Armenians (4.1 million) and Georgians (3.5 million) have carved out degrees of cultural and religious and social autonomy; they leave political and economic matters largely to Moscow. The most active minority is Jews, but their main desire seems to be to emigrate rather than to undermine the party.

The fastest-growing group is in Central Asia, but, despite three representatives on the 14-man Politburo, they wield little decisive, political influence at the top.

This is a far more rural country than figures show. By 1979 the population was two-thirds urban, one-third rural. Soviet control has seen a massive flight to the cities, as rural people have looked for new opportunities for themselves and their children, and the state has funneled manpower into arms production, heavy industry and factories.

Yet this shift has taken place in less than 40 years. As late as 1940, two-thirds of the people still lived in the countryside; in remote and backward villages little changed since the last century, except for electricity and an occasional car. This means cities here are largely made up of people fresh off the farm or only one generation removed.

Yet this remains not only a rural-rooted society, but a blue-collar one, blunt in speech and manner as well. Even in the big cities, telephones are answered with a curt "Yes?" or "I am listening." Life is lived without cars; much time is spent standing in lines, shoving, pushing.

Naturally, one encounters people who are extremely polite and considerate. But even the Soviet press prints articles asking for a book like Emily Post's to improve manners. When I wrote about one such article, the author (clearly under pressure from his superiors to rescue the Soviet reputation) wrote to *The Christian Science Monitor* in Boston alleging I was guilty of poor manners in even mentioning his article. He could criticize, apparently; a Westerner could not.

A Russian obeys the police, and other authority, with alacrity—but, on the other hand, untold millions steal from the state all the time. The system cannot fill the shops with attractive, useful goods, so people use every way they can to extract the good-quality dresses and suits, rugs, stylish shoes, and other items they want.

Many are law-abiding citizens—and the party is quick to point out the extent of crime in the West. All true. But the press here is also filled with accounts of theft and bribery, even though the system is supposed to have removed the "social cause" of crime.

Russians use their jobs as ways to do favors for others, to get favors in return. Among the most coveted jobs: working behind a meat counter (meat is always in short supply); or in a factory with access to tools that can be used for after-hour repair work; or in a theater box office (tickets to good shows, reserved for those with power or influence, can always be exchanged for good shoes or a tube of lipstick or a tip that the local department store has just received some of the wall units many Russians thirst after these days for their apartments).

So great is the shortage of quality goods that Russians who come into contact with westerners constantly ask for pens, watches, jewelry, jeans, winter coats, books, records, boots, vodka, stylish jackets, well-cut summer clothes and other goods. My heart went out to many of them: good people, wanting to be honest, beset by temptation. We have so much; they have so little.

The materialistic system encourages illegality by failing to provide the right goods at the right places at the right times. Soviet citizens are not, like many in the West, worried about what to do in their leisure time. Nor do they heed party exhortations to beware of becoming too fond of consumer goods.

That's fine for party officials to say, a common attitude goes. They have their privileges and their cars and their special food and clothing shops. As for us, we want better food and clothes and we ought to get them.

"It's all those other countries we have to support that drain us," said one Muscovite with irritation. He

Food and gas shortages around the USSR create long waiting lines.

meant Cuba, Angola, Ethiopia, South Yemen, Vietnam, Laos, Cambodia.

"One benefit of foreign aid is that we get sugar and coffee in our shops," a party lecturer, billed as an external economic expert, told a Moscow audience.

"Then why can't I find coffee or sugar in the shops?" demanded a questioner.

"That's an internal economic question," replied the lecturer. "I am an external economic expert, so I can't answer. Next?"

The currency system here also encourages abuses. There are no fewer than five kinds. First, there is western currency, used in certain shops by westerners and some residents. Then there are "D" coupons, sold only through the foreign-trade bank for western currency and used by foreigners in certain stores, such as supermarkets.

There are also "certificate rubles," coupons Russians who have worked abroad can buy with hard currency. (A few years ago these were also divided into "soft" and "hard" varieties. European currencies bought "hard" coupons, Arab and Asian bought "soft" ones.) These certificates can be redeemed in yet another system of special (though anonymous) shops. Finally, there are also "soft rubles," and, for the ordinary citizen, plain rubles.

"Soft rubles" are bought by third-world embassies in Geneva and Vienna for about four to the dollar (Americans in Moscow get only 66 kopecks, or two-thirds of a ruble, for a dollar). Diplomats then bring the rubles back here and pay bills with them, according to informed diplomatic sources. It is an accepted but under-the-counter way of helping potential third-world allies.

It adds up to an attitude to law that might suprise westerners, but not people in developing countries.

Currents of Nationalism, Dissent
Beneath Crust of Communist Conformity [1/15/81]

Between gilt mirrors and the glowing colors of priceless icons hung painting after oil painting of the czars: Catherine II looking like a latter-day Queen Victoria, beshawled and plump...a stern Alexander I in resplendent uniform...Paul I, Catherine's son, whose sensitive, wide-eyed look belied a passion for precise military drill by his army...Empress Elizabeth, daughter of Peter the Great....

Down they stared from ornate frames topped by imperial crowns at a scene that itself looked like a painting: the drawing room of a Russian nobleman of the 19th century, perhaps, rich, disheveled, emotionally charged.

The room was crowded with French empire-style furniture fashioned in mottled birchwood from Karelia, on the Finnish border, embossed and decorated in brass. Antiques stood everywhere, from tall-legged occasional tables to massive sideboards.

There was hardly room for four people, let alone the eight squeezed around the circular table dominating the center of the room; the table was supported by a single pedestal adorned with Egyptian-like goddesses with brass wings.

Death masks of two Russian heroes—Gogol and Pushkin—hung like icons. A life-size marble bust of Pushkin stood on an inlaid chest. Across the room was an oil painting of his predecessor, Gavrila Romanovich Derzhavin, Russia's greatest 18th-century poet, who wept when hearing the younger man's verse for the first time. Candelabra glittered. Metal icons in gold and silver reflected their light in a hundred facets. Bronze eagles, frozen in the moment of landing, spread their wings on the armrests of a huge empire couch.

All the room needed to complete the sense of Russian history and tradition was a black-robed Russian Orthodox priest...and lo, in he came, his wife dressed in black a few paces behind. His name: Fr. Giorgy, from a city in the Urals. His robe, his long beard and shoulder-length gray hair, the heavy metal-and-glass cross dangling from his neck, blended into the outpouring of Russian cultural identity around him.

To a westerner like me, to sit at that table, to listen to the priest expound on his family tree (he claimed to trace it back through 600 years of Russian nobility to Prince Dmitri Donskoi in the 14th century), to watch the owner of the apartment, the nonstop and controversially successful painter, Ilya Sergeyevich Glazunov, hurry in and out as he juggled three separate groups of guests in different rooms—all this was to feel that Russian, Slavic history and tradition still lived amid the atheism and totalitarianism of the Soviet Union today.

Glazunov sees himself, his art, his supporters in and out of the Communist Party, and men like Alexander Solzhenitsyn who share his messianic belief in Russian, as opposed to Soviet ideals, as cutting edges of a revival of Slav patriotism and culture.

"Millions think as I do, and I speak for them," he says. While he may be exaggerating, he does seem to represent a growing phenomenon in the Soviet Union as it has evolved 63 years after the revolution of 1917: a search by Russians for Russian roots—a search that rejects the cold, angular brand of materialism represented by the Communist Party.

His own career is full of twists and turns, of both acceptance and rejection by the party, of valleys of despair and peaks of triumph. It is a nonstop roller coaster of tension, travel and hard work. It mirrors the challenge he and his ideas pose to the ruling party Politburo, which is torn between its own pride in Russianness (10 of its 14 members are Russian nationals) and its recognition that the powerful emotions unloosed by the pre-1917 past must be strictly controlled if they are not to lead to an undermining of the Party and its monopoly on political, economic and military power.

The Politburo moves first this way, then that, as it tries to harness pride in the Russian past to its own strategems. Its aim is to use the pride as a way of conferring legitimacy on itself to present the Party and its sterile ideology as the heir to all that was good and progressive in the past.

It is a tricky business; Glazunov's brand of Russianness inextricably links nationalism with religion. "Dostoevsky once said that if a man is not Russian Orthodox, he is not Russian," Glazunov has told me, "and I believe that."

The Russian search for prerevolutionary roots stands out as one of a number of intellectual and emotional currents in the Soviet Union today, circulating beneath the frozen surface of Communist conformity.

From abroad, this vast country looks like a monolith, forbidding, austere, primitive. From up close, the monolithic features are also evident—but so is the life that teems below. It is repressed, politically powerless, but vital nonetheless.

The other currents include the human-rights, religious, and nationalist dissidence that sprang into prominence worldwide with the Daniel-Sinyavsky trial in the late 1960s, gained new impetus from the Helsinki Final Act 1975, and has been ruthlessly attacked and put down by the Kremlin since then. Among their witnesses:

1. Dr. Andrei Sakharov, winner of the 1975 Nobel Peace Prize, exiled from Moscow to a drab apartment hundreds of miles east in Gorky, a KGB official stationed at his door to watch all comers, his shortwave radio jammed so that he is forced to walk with his wife in a nearby park to catch static-filled snatches of the outside world.

2. Anatoly Shcharansky, jailed amid worldwide headlines in the summer of 1978, and the founder of the dissidents' Helsinki human-rights group, Dr. Yuri Orlov.

3. Burly Estonian Mart Niklus, just sentenced to between eight and 10 years in labor camps followed by five years' exile in Siberia. A lifelong nationalist, he has already served eight years for sending photographs of Estonian slums to the West.

4. Fellow Estonian Dr. Yuri Kukk, quiet, intense, and soft-spoken, who resigned from the Communist Party in the university city of Tartu after spending a year in Paris and seeing how the people in the West live. He was tried with Niklus and sentenced to two years in labor camps after doctors had failed to show he was mentally unbalanced.

5. Russian Orthodox priest Gleb Yakunin, sentenced in August 1980 to five years in a labor camp and five more in internal exile for founding the Christian Committee for the Defense of Believers' Rights.

6. The brave, dogged Pentecostalists known as the "Siberian Seven," who dashed into the US Embassy 2 1/2 years ago past Soviet guards in a desperate attempt to win the right to emigrate to freedom of worship in the US. Pyotr and Augustine Vashchenko and their three adult daughters, and Maria Chymkhalova and her teen-age son Timofei, live, eat, study, crochet and pray in one small room whose barred window looks out at the street inches from the stout black boots of the guards outside on round-the-clock duty.

7. Writers Yuri Grimm and Valery Abramkin, in jail for three years for daring to edit an underground journal called *Poiski* (Searches).

These are inheritors of a tradition of western ideas that goes back to the Decembrist uprising of army officers in 1825, and, indirectly, even further back to the time when Peter the Great seized books full of western concepts and imposed them on a rural, backward, mostly Asian landmass and dragged it by the ears into a more modern world.

They are justly celebrated in the West and at the Madrid Conference on European Cooperation and Security for opposing the oppressive central government here. Best known among them tend to be Jewish activits who have organized skillful and influential Jews abroad to help them.

All of them are, however, but a fragment of the population as a whole. True, Jews argue that almost 230,000 of their number left the Soviet Union between 1968 and 1978, and 370,000 others have sought invitations from Israel—a total of almost 20 percent of the present Jewish population of the USSR.

Pentecostal believers say tens of thousands among their congregations would leave if they could. Armenians, Germans and others are all going in small numbers.

The forces of religion and freedom and nationalism are still potent, and the party has had to adapt to them.

Yet the Sakharovs and the Shcharanskys and the others are essentially using outside, non-Russian ideas either to change the Soviet system (with little success) or to gain the right for themselves and others to emigrate. The significance of men like Glazunov, and his supporters in the party and the intellectual elite, is that they work here, within the system, refusing emigration.

They stand for an alternative, no matter how remote from power it might seem at the moment. Their influence is limited. Their currents remain under the surface, the ice above them unbroken. But they also symbolize another basic issue: how any change in the current frozen system might emerge.

Since Peter the Great at the end of the 17th century, two conflicting groups have clashed in Russian history: the prowesterners, who claim that outside ideas must be engrafted on Russian society; and Slavophiles, who say the genius of the Russian people is what counts, a mystic messianic blend of autocracy and Orthodox church.

Today the party rules in the name of a westerner (Karl Marx) and of a Russian intellectual who imported his ideas and molded them to local conditions (Lenin). Marxism-Leninism is alien to the old Russia of peasants, piety and imperial panoply. Dissidents like Sakharov and Shcharansky are fired with the more enlightened western tradition of individual rights.

Mr. Glazunov, his friends, and the men he admires—Solzhenitsyn, dissident mathematician Igor Schafarevich, nationalists Igor Ogurtsov and Vladimir Ossipov (both now in Siberian jails)—base their dissent on what they perceive to be purely Russian ideals. They are opposed by Sakharov, who denounces their "patriarchal romanticism."

Some of their ideas are distasteful to western ears: running through the Russianness of the last century was an ugly streak of anti-Semitism and a mixture of indifference and paternalism toward other minority groups and nations. Many in the West have been disappointed to find the towering moral stature of Solzhenitsyn combined with the author's own Russianness, and his advocacy, not of democracy, but of a kind of benevolent Orthodox theocracy.

The tall, spare, ascetic Sakharov insists that only outside ideas, support, and publicity can change the Soviet Union and liberalize it. A fellow dissident and opponent, Roy Medvedev, ruddy-faced and voluble, says change can come only from within; he stays here, writing history, keeping in touch with his party friends and with western correspondents as well.

Glazunov sees salvation from modern atheism in a return to Russian ideals alone. From the canvases in his top floor studio on Moscow's Kalashny Pereulok, from the pages of thick books of his own art printed abroad (sold only in hard-currency shops here), tumble the images of czardom and the church: knights, princes, generals, monasteries and onion domes.

The party still doesn't quite know how to handle him. He has powerful friends. He also has powerful enemies. The party hierarchy appears divided on how far Russian nationalism can be allowed to go—and bound up in that issue is yet another: how best to maintain control of the Russian internal empire itself, the 15 Soviet republics, of which the Russian Republic is the largest.

Stalin built his power on the Russian Republic, wiping out the short-lived independence of his native Georgia in the early 1920s. When the Nazis attacked in World War II, he appealed not to Marxism or Leninism in his efforts to arouse the people to resist, but to the "Motherland"—based on Russia. Today, as then, the party itself is dominated by Russians, not by Ukrainians or Georgians or Armenians. The Russian tongue is the *lingua franca*, the language of ideology, of technology, of power, of ambition.

Russians hold the real power in the officer corps of the armed forces, in the KGB, in the MVD (internal police). Each Soviet republic is allowed one of its own people as party first secretary; but the key post of second secretary is held by a Russian, and it is he who runs and maintains party patronage as well as law and order.

Some Western scholars believe that Khrushchev, by denouncing Stalin in 1956 and ecouraging minority groups, caused a backlash of Russian nationalism that in turn has led to much internal dissent to this day by Ukrainians, Germans, Poles, Moldavians, Georgians and Armenians, and by the militant Sufi (Muslim) brotherhoods of the Caucasus and Central Asia.

Many minority groups resent the growing stress by Moscow on spreading the Russian language and culture through the country. The stress grows as the percentage of Russians here (52.4 percent in 1979, down from 53.4 percent in 1970) falls slowly toward the 50 percent mark.

Russian birthrates in the crowded, cold, housing-short western areas (where 80 percent of the Soviet population lives) continue to drop; Muslim birthrates in Central Asia, while themselves falling, nonetheless far outstrip Russian ones. The Soviet Muslim population has risen from 24.2 million (11.6 percent of the population) in 1959 to 43.1 million (16.5 percent) in 1979. If current trends continue, Muslims in Central Asia will approach one-third of the population by the year 2000.

Some in the West predict trouble for the Russian Politburo. For example, every third recruit into the armed forces by the year 2000 could well be a Central Asian who speaks imperfect Russian and who may not face the Chinese or other potential enemies as reliably as Russian Slavic soldiers would.

Yet after 4 1/2 years here, and visits to all Central Asian Republics, I see this thinking as more wishful than realistic. Russians will keep on giving the orders, and Central Asians will keep on taking them. Very few Central Asians make top-level decisions. Asian recruits will keep on being sent for national service thousands of miles away from their homes.

Prolonged food shortages might arouse the people, but in Central Asia, warm weather and local conditions generally mean more food available than in the colder north and west.

Yet the party must, and does, remain alert to all nationalist movements, Central Asian included. It worries that the Muslim nationalist upsurge in Iran and Afghanistan might affect local Soviet Muslims across the border—though there is almost no sign at all that any such thing has happened. The party stays flexible, suppressing nationalism where it can, accommodating it where it must.

When thousands of Georgians marched down the main street of Tbilisi to protest a new draft constitution that retained Russian as an "official" language in Georgia but omitted the Georgian tongue, Moscow gave in quickly. One telephone call from Tbilisi by an armed-forces commander, and Georgian was restored. Local constitutions were also altered to restore Armenian and Azerbaijani in neighboring republics—all this after a new countrywide Constitution had been introduced in 1977.

Party control stays solid in the Baltic states on the western frontier. But Russian nationalism requires even more careful handling. And that is what makes Glazunov and the ideas he supports so interesting.

The party permitted Glazunov no exhibitions at all for many years, then let him have one in Moscow in 1978 and another in Leningrad in 1979. Half a million people stood in wind and rain in Moscow during a three-week period to get in; 600,000 stayed in line up to eight hours to see the Leningrad showing.

Glazunov was allowed to paint a gigantic mural for the UNESCO headquarters in Paris in mid-1980, which was accepted despite the Soviet invasion of Afghanistan. He was then bestowed the title of "People's Artist of the USSR."

But the Soviet Academy of Arts still blackballs him, denouncing him in closed party meetings as anti-Soviet, religious, and mystical. When in late 1980 he was presented with an emblem of one of the two Spanish art academies to invite him to membership (at a Moscow reception ostensibly called by the outgoing Spanish ambassador to say farewell to Soviet leaders), Academy Vice President Vladimir Semenovich Kemenov and other officials walked out in protest.

Glazunov paints portraits of western leaders (Indira Gandhi, UN Secretary-General Kurt Waldheim) and travels widely; he could not do so without party friends (reported to include veteran Politburo ideologist Mikhail Suslov and Minister of Culture Pyotr Demichev).

The party permitted the 600th anniversary of the Russian victory of Prince Dmitri Donskoi over Mongol general Mamay at Kulikovo Field south of Moscow in 1380 amid pomp and an outburst of Russian military pride. The occasion also reminded Russians of the danger lurking in the east—China. It allowed the making of the first full-length feature film about Fyodor Dostoevsky to celebrate the 100th anniversary of Dostoevsky's death (February 1981). The writer is a hero to modern Slavophiles, a champion of Russian Orthodoxy. It permits Slavophiles to open Russian museums of folk art, documents, and history in Moscow, Novgorod, Suzdal, and Yaroslavl—all monuments of Russian antiquity.

Yet the party also cracked down sharply on Russian nationalist dissidents such as Igor Ogurtsov and Vladimir Ossipov, punished after publishing their own journal in the 1960s.

What kind of a man is Ilya Glazunov? He is a nonstop worker and chain-smoker; a man who wears Western suits and defiantly favors a dark-blue tie with the double-headed eagle of the Romanoff czars on it; a man who seems to be a success within a system he dislikes, but who sees his own life as a constant struggle to use the leverage represented by his successes in the

West to extract privilege and freedom in his own country. He refuses to emigrate. "The struggle," he says, "is here."

In a car with me in Leningrad in 1979, driving away from his exhibition, he stared out at some of the 600,000 who attended as they stood patiently in snow and ice outside the hall. "They are my people," he said vehemently, "and I work for them."

Many of my western friends in Moscow would scoff at such a remark. They see him as a charlatan, a poor painter, a KGB agent ("how else could he travel and mix with westerners here?"), and an anti-Semite. Indeed, he is a mixture of many qualities.

I found him a man driven by his own cause, trying to appease the party hierarchy by painting in Vietnam and in Siberia, and by painting party leaders and family members. "Opportunism," say his critics. "Buying time to paint what he wants to paint," reply his friends.

Outwardly successful, he was inwardly and constantly worried by the steady refusal of the Arts Academy and the Union of Artists to support him. Friends say he feared what they might do to him. Strongly behind him was the Union of Writers of the Russian Republic, ostensibly for the 250 illustrations he has done for the works of Dostoevsky, Alexander Blok, and many others, but also because he was such a passionate upholder of Russian nationality.

Not all the people who attended his exhibitions liked his work. Comment books in Moscow and in Leningrad contain entries from hundreds of people who rhapsodized, but also from many who regarded it as anti-Communist.

His large canvas, "The Prodigal Son," arouses a storm of comment; the party tried to stop it being shown in Leningrad but finally backed down, since it had already been on display in Moscow.

In the foreground are the snouts and jaws of huge hogs at a trough; behind them are signs of the debauchery of modern life, from alcoholism to churches being burned; to the left a young man clad only in a pair of jeans (symbol of modernity) kneels at the feet of a Christ-figure (the soul of Russia) while the Glazunov pantheon of Russian heroes looks on: Gogol, Pushkin, Dostoevsky, Tchaikovsky.

Party officials object to it on religious and ideological grounds, suspecting the hogs represent communist materialism. To them he shrugs and says the canvas must be interpreted by each viewer.

His bigger painting, "Mystery of the Twentieth Century," has never been shown. Some accuse him of painting it only to gain publicity abroad. (It was banned from a planned show in 1977 in Moscow and Glazunov canceled the show in protest.)

It contains figures anathema to current Communist ideology, from Christ Jesus to Pope John XXIII to Stalin on a bier of blood to Solzhenitsyn in Gulag prison clothes.

Some notes from a conversation with him in Leningrad:

"The Kremlin is not an extension of the old Russia under the czars. (This point was also made passionately by Solzhenitsyn, who once told a Stanford University audience, that 'the Soviet development…is…a completely new, unnatural direction, inimical to the Russian people…')"

Glazunov continued: "Old Russia was based on three principles, the Orthodox Church, the autocracy, and Russian nationhood. The Soviet Union is against religion. It believes in the dictatorship of the proletariat [the party], and it takes an internationalist view, not a nationalist one… the Soviet Union is the flowering of the Communist system, not of the Russian people….

"The Czar didn't want colonies… Russia had enough people and enough wealth… the Ukraine asked to join Russia, and the Baltic states as well" (points emphatically refuted by Ukrainian and Baltic nationalists). "Armenia begged to be protected against the Turks… Czar Alexander I revived the Finnish language banned by the Swedes….

"Diplomats and foreigners who come here think dissidents are mostly Jewish and that they want to leave. Another kind of dissident wants to stay."

Born in Leningrad, Glazunov spent his early years in Novgorod, capital of medieval Rus, when the Nazis laid siege to his city in World War II. "He is something of a puzzle for us," said an intellectual woman waiting to enter the Leningrad exhibition. "He paints in so many styles. Which is his own? To me his pictures of the blockade [the Nazi siege] are the most interesting. I was a little girl then…. His portrait of Dostoevksy has depth. …He has a sense of the spectacular, of the dramatic…. Perhaps he is best suited to theatrical design…." Even as she spoke, you could hardly move inside the hall because of the crowds. Scalpers were photographing tickets and selling the prints for 5 rubles ($7.50 each) to those willing to take the risk to try to get in.

Yet no Glazunov pictures hung in any Leningrad museum. None were in the Hermitage. A mere two had appeared in the Tretyakov in Moscow, and then only for six months.

In Glazunov's living room, I asked Fr. Giorgy if he could foresee a return to the old days when the church was privileged and a different kind of autocracy ruled.

"Oh, yes," he replied at once, his eyes alight. "Oh, yes." He paused. "But we have to wait. It is necessary to wait, you see."

The wait will be a long one. Glazunov once described himself to me as a "heroic pessimist" fighting to retain the collective memory of his own ideals.

"I am also a pessimistic optimist," he added—a wry comment in a land where, for all his own commitment, and for all the history of the Russian people both good and bad, the prospect of political change any time soon is slight, indeed.

Yet he pushes on, rushing from project to project, never fully secure. He sees no other course. Fr. Giorgy waits. Solzhenitsyn, exiled, thunders his own concept of Russian cultural and religious ideals and unity and strength.

Beneath the ice, the currents flow. There will be no early thaw, but the currents do not stop.

Kremlin in Transition: Can New Generations Break with Rigid Past? [1/16/81]

We sat in a car at midnight, a Russian friend and I, talking about the future of his country—a future so important to the rest of the world.

Snow fell steadily, theatrical and glittering flakes turning the grimy winter street outside into a stage setting of black and white. Dim streetlights barely pierced the gloom. We had stopped near the main entrance of a hotel. Inebriated men and women occasionally rattled the door handles and tapped on the window, trying to find a ride home.

My friend's words were as somber as the scene. He was an intellectual who had served his compulsory military training in Siberia. "It was terrible," he said. "So much drunkenness among the people, so much ignorance about the world outside."

He simply did not see changes in the future welling up from the ordinary people. Their education and their history were against it. "Never in our history have we had the kind of democracy you in the West have had," he remarked. "Our tradition is rule from the center, from the top, and that is the way it will continue."

He fell silent for a moment, staring out at the snow and at a man and woman lurching toward our car, mistaking it for a taxi.

"There is only one hope for the future," he said at last, as the couple turned away after shouting at us through the window.

"That is, that our next set of leaders will be more enlightened, better educated, more liberal. They're the ones that will dictate the changes ahead. The people themselves can't do it. The new leaders will be Slavs, because Slavs have all the power in this country. I only hope that they will make life better for us."

His assessment, so soberly realistic, leads to more questions: What kind of new leaders will the next set be? And what kind of changes might they be able to engineer?

Answers are necessarily speculative, since so little is known about the mysterious inner workings of the Kremlin.

But some points can be made about the social forces that shape Soviet leaders these days, and about the pressures working for—and against—change.

This has become a slow-moving society. Since the 1917 Revolution the country has had only four leaders, against 13 presidents in the United States from Wilson to Reagan. Lenin seized power, Stalin consolidated it for 30 years, Khrushchev tried to tinker with the machinery, and Brezhnev has maintained the status quo, refusing to try the kind of internal party changes that landed Khrushchev in trouble and eventually cost him his job.

Leonid Brezhnev has led the Communist Party for 16 years now: years of glacially slow movement inside the party. Officials associated with him since the late 1930s in the Ukraine dominate the ruling Politburo, the Council of Ministers, key areas of the Central Committee, the Ministry of Internal Affairs and the KGB. If Brezhnev retired or passed on tomorrow, his basic thinking would undoubtedly continue for a year or so at least—and his shoes would likely be filled by the silver-haired Andrei Kirilenko, currently Number 4 man in the Politburo.

Kirilenko is three months older than Brezhnev but in much better physical health, yet he would probably be only a stopgap leader, for several years at the most. Behind him dozens of younger men are stacked up, members of the Central Committee (whose average age of about 62 is almost a whole decade younger than the Politburo itself). In theory, at least, they will help select the top Politburo leaders of the future.

Men like Brezhnev, Kirilenko, and Defense Minister Dmitri Ustinov, born between 1900 and 1910, shot to prominence when Stalin purged many of the older men above them in the 1930s. The late Alexei Kosygin and the veteran foreign minister, Andrei Gromyko, found themselves holding big government jobs while still in their 30s. Brezhnev was moving up through the party bureaucracy; so was Kirilenko.

Men born in the next decade, 1910 to 1920, were between 20 and 30 years of age when World War II broke out. The younger they were, the more likely they were to have been killed; war losses amounted to about 20 million in the Soviet Union all told. Survivors now in their middle or late 60s include KGB chief Yuri Andropov, Ukrainian party chief Vladimir Shcherbitsky, Moscow party leader Viktor Grishin.

Significant changes inside the Soviet Union are not likely to come from men like Kirilenko or Ustinov, whose most traumatic experiences came fighting the Nazis in World War II and who belong to the Brezhnev group.

Some changes might come from slightly younger men like Andropov or Shcherbitsky, who received fairly good educations in the 1930s and may be more flexible than Brezhnev.

The most likely age group to produce change, however, could be in the next two generations—symbolized by the two youngest men in the Politburo: Leningrad party leader Grigory Romanov, born in 1923, and Mikhail Gorbachev, born in 1931, who was elevated to full voting status in the Politburo only in 1980 and put in charge of agriculture.

Mr. Romanov's generation is perhaps the most tragic of all, decimated as it was by World War II. His generation was in its late teen-age years when the war broke out. It bore the brunt of the losses. Statistics worked out by Dr. Jerry Hough, a US scholar, show huge losses in the generation born between 1919 and 1926. It is also the generation whose college education was interrupted most by the fighting. Its survivors tend to be pragmatic men, educated on the job after the war.

Mr. Gorbachev's generation is by far the best educated, since it was too young to fight in the war and completed college later. The difficulty in speculating about it, though, is that so few westerners have even met Mr. Romanov or Mr. Gorbachev, let alone studied their thinking up close.

Will they and their peers be more liberal than the Brezhnev elite, less afraid of the West and of China, more open to loosening party control at home, to decentralize industry and agriculture, ready to let Soviet people travel more freely, to have greater access to western consumer goods?

Or will they be even more rigid than their elders, more chauvinistic, more xenophobic, more determined to defend and enhance the Soviet Union's superpower status in the world, to hold on to its empire in Eastern Europe and its allies in Cuba, Africa and Asia?

Much will depend on what happens in the rest of the world—whether, for instance, the United States, Moscow's main rival, continues to build arms, to see Moscow as aggressive and threatening, to worry about protecting the sources of its imported oil. Perhaps the United States will develop more alternative sources of energy, become more self-confident, work out better ways of containing the Soviet threat, divert arms budgets into more peaceful pursuits.

At this writing, with Soviet troops in Afghanistan and on the alert around Poland, and Ronald Reagan about to take over the White House, the former US course seems more likely than the second. But much could change between now and the year 2000, especially in the third world, where most flare-ups now seem to start. Much also depends on China. A significant increase in Chinese offensive arms, or a US policy to provide such offensive arms, would greatly alarm the Kremlin and lead to a risk of desperate Soviet actions. Such a US policy would seem unwise, given the emotional and primitive way the Kremlin thinks of its own security. Does the West really want to goad the Soviets into actions everyone might regret?

Those few Westerners who have met Mr. Romanov find him acerbic, volatile, sharply intelligent. At one dinner with a visiting group of US senators, he kept interrupting his interpreter and issuing orders from his place at the table. He also has imperial tastes: A widely circulated story has it that he once used imperial china from a museum for a wedding reception for his daughter—and incurred Kremlin wrath in the process.

A man like Romanov was shaped by World War II as Brezhnev was, and especially by the impact and aftermath of Leningrad's 900-day siege by the Nazis. Romanov could hardly be indifferent to the Soviet perception that both West and East Germans must be contained forever. He cannot but recognize the key strategic value in holding sway over the three Soviet Baltic states. He is likely to be apprehensive about external enemies everywhere.

A man of his generation might choose to try some internal decentralizing in both industry and agriculture. But he is not likely to adopt a sudden softer tone toward the West—or China. He may not be as committed to Marxist-Leninist ideology as his elders, but he has

The struggle for democracy can be seen
in open religious worship and in
dissidents such as the late Dr. Andrei
Sakharov [above right].

to be a strong patriot, both suspicious and ignorant of the outside world.

Given the Russian phobia about the East, stemming from the Mongol invasion nine centuries ago, he is also bound to be apprehensive about the sight of China determined to throw off the confusion and chaos of Mao Tse-tung and to rearm with the latest weapons it can find.

To a westerner, Russia looks far stronger in firepower along the Sino-Soviet borders. But the Russian fear was summed up by one official who took a US visitor to a map of the world and said:

"No, we are not afraid of China. We're not afraid of anyone. But how would you feel if a neighboring country of yours, say, Mexico, had 1 billion people, possessed nuclear weapons and preached that a third world war was inevitable and that only it would survive?"

Mr. Romanov has never visited the United States. In fact, now that Mr. Kosygin has passed on, only Brezhnev and Gromyko among top leaders have firsthand experience of the United States, and that only fleeting. It has been 40 years since Gromyko lived in Washington as a young diplomat and then ambassador during World War II.

As for Mr. Gorbachev's generation, we just don't know enough about it. Its education was uninterrupted by war. Its teen years were spent under Stalin; it experienced Khrushchev's attempted thaw in the late 1950s, and his clampdown again. It has known the privations that followed the war and the slowly rising standards of living in the last three decades.

Does all this make it more pragmatic, less ideological? Or vice versa?

The Brezhnev generation knows very well the nuclear strength of the United States. Though the Kremlin never admits it now, the same generation knows that American trucks and airplanes provided crucial help to Stalin in defeating the Germans. And wartime US Ambassador W. Averell Harriman says Stalin told him so on several occasions.

Do the Romanov and the Gorbachev generations have the same healthy apprehension of US power? Or do they see the United States as a power in decline since the 1960s, defeated in Vietnam, humbled in Iran, unable to free hostages from Tehran for more than a year, unable to mobilize a united western front against Soviet troops in Afghanistan?

Among the forces that might cause rapid change within the country, one would have to include popular revolt in Eastern Europe—the classic example right now being Poland. The speed with which Moscow put its troops around Poland on alert in November, just three months after the concessions made to the Solidarity union in Gdansk by former Polish party leader Edward Gierek, indicates the vital strategic and political importance of all of Eastern Europe to the Kremlin.

If popular unrest boiled over in Warsaw and Gdansk…if Soviet troops could not quickly put that rebellion down…if pent-up emotions in Czechoslovakia and Hungary also burst out…if significant elements of the Soviet Central Committee saw their leaders facing the virtual loss of the buffer zones between Soviet borders and West Germany and the breakup of the Warsaw Pact…then change, indeed, might come quickly here.

But what kind of change? A new Kremlin leader might prove even sterner than Brezhnev or Khrushchev. A swing back to Stalinist days could follow—an even greater arms buildup as the Kremlin vowed to conquer Eastern Europe all over again. There is no guarantee that the Kremlin answer would be to loosen the reins, to ease central control.

Other forces for change could include violence by minority nationalities.

On June 29, 1978, a prison administrator shot and killed the interior minister (the top policeman) and two of his subordinates in the Azerbaijani capital of Baku, on the Caspian Sea, close to the Iranian border. A spokesman for the minister's deputy confirmed to Western correspondents on the telephone that Lt. Gen. Arif Geidarov had been shot by a man named Muratov, who was said also to have shot himself. General Geidarov had worked in the Azerbaijani KGB for a quarter-century; his obituary in Bakinski Rabochi, Baku's party newspaper, was signed by the first deputy chief of the KGB in Moscow, Semyon Tsvigun.

On December 4, 1980, someone shot and killed the prime minister of the tiny republic of Kirghizia on the Chinese border as the official lay asleep in a sanatorium on Lake Issyk-Kul, east of the capital city of Frunze. An official of the party newspaper in Frunze told a western correspondent by telephone it was a "political murder" designed as a "provocation" on the eve of the 26th Party Congress in Moscow in February 1981.

Some have speculated here that terrorism by minority groups could conceivably gain momentum and force concessions from a frightened Kremlin. But it is a long, long way from two incidents to a national wave of dissent. The Kremlin possesses ample armed force to put down local uprisings and to keep them down.

Then there is the possible threat of food shortages causing popular revolt. At the end of 1980, meat was in short supply in many Soviet cities. Reports of strikes in the cities of Gorky and Togliatti persisted; while emphatically denied by various sources (some of whom had an interest in affirming them), trade union officials did confirm in private conversations with western diplomats toward the end of the year that there had indeed been some "work stoppages." They did not say where.

Despite the reports, it seems wishful to assume that some food shortages in some places can add up to a grass-roots drive against the government in a country where the party has the monopoly on firearms, and possesses huge internal police and arm- ed forces to use them. The US ambassador to Moscow, Thomas J. Watson, believed Americans consistently underestimated the capacity of the Russian people to "take it." They were still way above "the bread line," he observed, and even when they had sunk down so close to it in World War II, they had survived. He was right.

It could also be argued that the country might run short of oil, since production has already almost peaked, and a severe energy shortage might conceivably cause leadership changes in the Kremlin. That remains to be seen. Moscow already courts the Arab world persistently. The Soviet Union is still, for the moment, the world's largest oil producer (though the second-largest exporter, behind Saudi Arabia).

Barring upheavals in Eastern Europe, the forces working against rapid change seem to outweigh those operating in favor of it. These forces include:

1. Party control: The Communist Party so thoroughly dominates all levels of society and of the armed forces that prospects of a popular or military uprising against the Kremlin are more remote than in many developing countries. The force that makes the Soviets a threat abroad is turned against its own people at home.

This was, and remains, a country of conspiracy and surveillance. The Communists are the most dedicated conspirators, the most relentless surveillants.

Control of the Army, based on a network of political officers at all levels, permeates the officer corps. The rank and file consists of young men whose parents lack the *blat* (influence) to get them out of compulsory service by enrolling them in overcrowded and sought-after universities and institutes.

The Party controls internal police and the border guards stationed at the foot of every ramp to every plane coming from or leaving for overseas, and guarding all train and road exits and entrances.

2. Party achievements: Lenin inherited a country shattered by winter, famine, and war—a somnolent rural giant that had nonetheless industrialized rapidly, reaching impressive growth rates (especially between 1909 and 1913) in oil, railroad and transport sectors. The country's growth was uneven but definite, ranking it in the world's top 10 in coal and copper production and the smelting of cast iron and steel. The Communist Party has stamped the seal of an authentic superpower on the new Soviet Union, expanding the frontiers of czarist Russia (parts of Poland, the three Baltic states, Mongolia) and holding intact the rest (Azerbaijan, Central Asia, the Ukraine). This is a great deal to achieve in just 63 years. It is a cause for party and nonparty pride alike.

Supporting Poland today costs a small fortune. Supporting Cuba, Angola, Ethiopia, Vietnam, Laos, Cambodia, etc., costs even more. Yet it all serves political ends—and everything in this country is ultimately designed for political ends, as defined by the party hierarchy. Those ends are considered vital for security as well as prestige.

Eastern Europe is the buffer zone between the western USSR and Central Europe. Mongolia, whose flat veldt is now a gigantic Soviet tank exercise ground and fighter-bomber runway, is the buffer against China. Traveling southward by train across Mongolia from Moscow to Peking in the summer of 1979, my wife and I counted Soviet jets by the score in reinforced hangars on a huge airfield east of the trainline after leaving Ulan Bator.

Any serious move toward loosening the party's central control from Moscow would—as the Kremlin well knows—also loosen the armed hold Moscow has on Eastern Europe, the three Baltic states, and Mongolia. It might well encourage the Sunni Muslims of Soviet Central Asia to pay more attention to the Islamic nationalism in neighboring Afghanistan and Iran. Many of the Russian Slavs who hold the levers of power in the Soviet Union would support the party's strong fight to retain not only its own power but the sway over its own empire. If Eastern Europe threatens to break away, what would third-world allies like Angola and Ethiopia think? All of Moscow's carefully wrought status around the world could start to unravel.

The party has created a military-industrial base comparable to that of the United States, on an economy only half the size, and against the rigors of climatic extremes. Industry is turning out better consumer goods than it has in the past (though they are still below those of other developing countries).

Living standards have risen, especially when compared with the Mideast and Asia. The party has built millions of new apartments. Demand still outpaces supply, but the party can claim to have provided many people with new places to live.

It ceaselessly proclaims that it led the people to victory in World War II—which is not called World War II here, but the "Great Patriotic War." The war, to Russians, was the war against Germany, fought on their own soil, and ultimately victorious, though at dreadful cost.

3. Geography: Any new leaders in the Kremlin will inherit the longest borders of any country in the world. They will be preoccupied with the threat of invasion. They will have studied an ideology that preaches that the outside world is poised and ready to undermine the world's first Socialist state.

4. History: New leaders will take over a country with no tradition of individual rights, no grass-roots democracy, no political power shared among government, courts, industry, farmers, aristocracy, cities, managers and professionals.

When I once asked a party supporter why there was only one candidate on each ballot for "elections" to the country's Supreme Soviet, or rubber-stamp parliament, she replied, "Why not? The party chooses the candidates and the party knows what it is doing."

How did she know? Had she attended any selection meetings?

"No, I don't have to. The party knows more than we ordinary people do. Of course it does. It has to, it is the party." It was all quite clear to her. She became increasingly surprised—even irritated—that it was not clear to me.

"What do you mean, the party runs the country?" she asked. "The government runs the country. The party is quite separate." So citizens here are taught; so most of them believe. I suggested that the party controlled the government, that all key officials belong to the party. I pointed out that the chief official in the country was always the party leader, not the chief of state (though Leonid Brezhnev became the first Soviet leader in history to take both posts).

But she couldn't see it. As we talked, her eyes narrowed. I could imagine her thinking: "This man is a foreigner. He knows nothing of how our country is really run. He is trying to undermine my beliefs and my

country's legitimacy." She dismissed Americans as people ignorant of her country's customs and literature (she had a good point there), but denied Russians were ignorant of America. "Everything it is necessary for us to know about your country, we know," she said loftily. That was that.

5. Patriotism: When the Nazis attacked in World War II, Stalin did not appeal to the people to fight in the name of the party. He urged them to fight for their "Motherland." The party skillfully identifies itself today with "Mother Russia."

Russians I talked to might criticize aspects of Communism under their breath—but they were fiercely loyal patriots.

6. The social system: It is a system of rank and privilege orchestrated and arranged from the party headquarters in Moscow. Those with status fight to preserve the system that gave it to them. Those without it want it. They don't think of upsetting the system. The resulting chaos would end all privileges. The very thought is abhorrent to most Russians.

The few average people I met in 4 1/2 years had an ingrained passion for order, for stability, for letting the government handle foreign and economic and social and all other policy issues, while they themselves looked inward, concentrating on family and friends and the endless search for better consumer goods in a system generally unable to produce them.

What Americans see as individual liberty appears to Russians as a babel of conflicting voices and ideas. Russians tend to be genuinely repelled by the America as presented in Soviet propaganda. They will never be able to travel and see for themselves. Even if they could, chances are high that the Capitalist system would be too hard, too demanding, too sophisticated, for them.

Even those here who know the propaganda about the US is false say that listening to it and reading it every day has a cumulative effect. Abe Stolar was born in Chicago and moved here in 1931 at the age of 11, when his émigré Russian parents decided to answer Stalin's call for Russians abroad to help build the Motherland. He still speaks English with a Chicago accent. He has been trying to emigrate for several years.

Why, I once asked him, had he waited so long to try to leave? The answer was complicated, but part of it was: "... And you know, when you hear and read every single day that America is filled with violence and crime, drugs and unemployment, exploitation and racial violence, you wonder about it. Of course, I would say to myself. It isn't all like that. America isn't as bad as the

Top left and right, recent demonstrations in the USSR and Poland. Above, a display of victims of Stalin's repressions was held during the Week of Conscience in the House of Culture, Moscow, 1988.

Soviets paint it. But I found myself saying, well, maybe some of it's true.... Maybe it isn't the place for me after all, I would argue with myself."

A Russian with no firsthand knowledge of America must be convinced that it is hell on earth.

The Marquis de Custine, traveling in the Soviet Union for five months in 1839, observed in his journal that the Table of Ranks instituted by Peter the Great at the end of the 17th century, by which society was divided up into 14 layers corresponding to ranks in the armed forces, bred in Russian people a "fever of envy ... [and] ambition...."

The Communist Party today has taken over the job of the czar in allocating rank, each rank carrying its own defined privileges. The "fever of envy" is a hallmark of Soviet life. It is a deterrent to change, not a producer of it.

7. Social mobility: The five social ranks outlined in the third article of this series allow for a good deal of movement between ranks and within them—though not much from the rising rank (professionals and managers and frontier workers) up to the top rank, which runs the country. The way up there is through the 17 million-member Communist Party itself.

But the rush from country to cities in the last 40 years, an immense transformation turning a rural country into a two-thirds urban one, has meant an upward push for many a peasant family, as both parents and then children joined factories and began elbowing up through the ranks of skilled workers.

Industrialization itself has opened up millions of new factory jobs at all levels in the last 50 years. The really ambitious join the party, whether they believe in it or not.

A family can boost its earning power by "going east" to Siberia to work in frontier boomtowns on the oil and gas fields. Many do. An entire underclass of speculators, many of them in Georgia and Armenia, earns small fortunes by supplying people and enterprises with the goods and raw materials the system itself, hopelessly clogged in red tape, cannot deliver.

So the forces for the status quo outweigh the forces for change. Yet, it would be wrong to assume that no changes at all will come. In 1952 the system looked stable and set in its ways. But Joseph Stalin died March 5, 1953, and Nikita Khrushchev, shouldering his way to the top, let more westerners in (for instance, for the 1957 World Youth Festival). He also indirectly laid the foundations of the dissident movement that flowered in the Daniel-Sinyavsky trial a decade later and in Yuri

Orlov's dissident Helsinki committee on human rights a decade after that.

Mr. Khrushchev tried a number of experiments, including changes in the party's own structure, to bring about more specialist control of industry and agriculture.

Then reaction set in. He was ousted. The hallmark of the Brezhnev era has been a return to orthodoxy: not to the atmosphere of Stalin's day—the midnight knock on the door, the banishment to Siberia—but to stability within the party.

Mr. Brezhnev saw the US force Soviet missiles out of Cuba in 1962. Since then he has paid great attention to building up Soviet armed might. He tried to use détente with the US to prevent Americans from building more missiles; he also tried to persuade Washington to allow businessmen to provide Moscow with the sophisticated technology it so badly needs to move its centralized economy ahead.

By 1981 the SALT I treaty had expired, the SALT II treaty was signed but would not be ratified, Soviet troops had gone into Afghanistan and were on alert around Poland, the US had cut off economic and scientific and cultural links because of Afghanistan, and US voters had thrown out Jimmy Carter and installed Ronald Reagan in part because they, too, were alarmed at Soviet expansionism. The world seemed back in the Cold-War days of the early 1960s.

It is entirely possible that a new leader after Mr. Brezhnev could put his own unpredictable stamp on Soviet policies, internally and externally. Yet he will also have to deal with underlying social forces. He will not have complete freedom of action. The party membership, especially the Central Committee, has known so little internal movement for so long that any radical lurches would be risky, indeed.

This is not to say they won't be made. It is to say they will probably come slowly—and that they could be restrictive rather than relaxing.

Many western experts feel the current system will stay in place for 50 years or more. They dismiss liberal thinking in the West that argues that a second Russian Revolution is just around the corner. They see dissidents as a tiny minority in a huge country. They agree with the traditional school of thought that argues that true change inside the Soviet Union must come from inside, not from without. They feel Jimmy Carter's public stress on human rights only forced the Soviet Union to "show its manhood," as former US Ambassador Malcolm Toon once put it to me. It made the

Kremlin crack down more sharply than it otherwise might have.

Early in the next century Soviet Central Asia with its high (though falling) birthrate could be providing one-third of the Soviet work force. But Russian Slavs hold the keys to power and will keep them.

The western world, however, needs to find better ways to confront the Soviet challenge.

The United States needs a closer relationship with Paris and Bonn, in particular, if NATO is to present a coherent shield to Soviet aggression. This is particularly difficult at a time when Western Europe finds it cannot afford the range of social services it erected after World War II. Europe wants to cut back on defense, right at the time Mr. Reagan believes it should be keeping defense spending high.

Moscow knows this full well. Its propaganda tries to widen the split at every turn. Europeans, physically closer to Moscow, want trade and distrust military and economic sanctions as weapons.

The Soviet threat to Poland at the end of 1980 produced more NATO harmony—but as yet no concrete agreement on just what the alliance would do if Moscow did invade.

Living here for 4 1/2 years has made me an advocate of high defense spending in the US and Western Europe—high enough to deter any sudden Soviet moves. Already Moscow is roughly equal to the US in nuclear weaponry and is ahead in some aspects of conventional warfare. Correcting the military balance from the tilt in the US's favor after World War II has clearly lent the Kremlin more confidence to invade an Afghanistan. The need now is to make sure it understands the risks of taking similar actions elsewhere.

The tendency in Washington in has been to exaggerate Soviet capacities to intervene in the third world. Those of us resident in Moscow were more aware of the huge costs to Moscow in supporting Communist régimes in Cuba, Angola, Ethiopia, and Eastern Europe. From Moscow, Soviet policies in the Mideast often looked snarled. Policies toward Japan seemed bungled. A Moscow dinner conversation with a visiting congressman in late 1980 turned into a debate between his own fears that Moscow could strike anywhere at any time and resident correspondents' more restrained views.

The West also needs to watch the tone in which it addresses the Kremlin. Belittling Soviet achievements is hardly likely to make the Soviets listen. Nor is acting as though they had no legitimate world interests. Talking down to Moscow won't work. The Soviets are thin-skinned, but also supreme realists: What a man does is more important to them than what he says. Talking big and acting small is a recipe for disaster in dealing with Moscow.

Diplomatically, Washington, London, Paris and other capitals fall into the Soviet trap of dealing directly with the Soviet ambassador on the spot, instead of making sure that definitive national positions are laid out by their respective ambassadors in Moscow, to the Soviet Foreign Ministry. Not surprisingly, the Soviets like to pit a professional (their own highly trained ambassadors) against "amateurs"—host-country foreign ministers and presidents who are generalists rather than specialists on Soviet relations.

The result is that the Soviets have a daily edge in the business of diplomacy. The Soviets hear a range of nuances of a western country from their ambassadors. But can the West be certain that in every case the ambassador transmits the nuances precisely to Moscow? Maybe, maybe not. Directing ambassadors in Moscow to detail positions in the Soviet Foreign Ministry would give these envoys more access to the Soviet hierarchy.

At the same time, the West must try to avoid trusting that the Soviets are nice fellows after all, and that Communism is somehow just another "ology," harmless, really. Westerners should understand that Marxist-Leninist ideology has manufactured a gigantic military-industrial complex from a relatively weak geographical base, and has provided the rationale for the weapons it produces to be used—if not in war, then as ballast for Soviet diplomacy.

The relationship between the USSR and the West is essentially, and will remain, an adversary one. It should be treated as one—firmly, without illusion. Nothing can be gained by assuming the Kremlin is about to give up and go away.

The West must also realize the Communist challenge is persistent, single-minded. The West can go on vacation, think about social problems, worry about a host of issues. But the Kremlin always keeps its eye fixed on the competition with western ideals and its own hopes of ultimate victory.

Finally, my stay at the heart of the Communist empire has convinced me that the answer to the challenge of materialism lies within each one of us. We cannot leave it to governments or armies, propaganda or pious hope. Each individual has a role to play in countering Soviet and other forms of materialism by emphasizing the spiritual values which can effectively oppose them.

THE CHRISTIAN SCIENCE MONITOR

VOL. 82, NO. 7

ALFRED/SIPA PRESS

SUPERPOWER TALKS

Malta Summit Lays Groundwork for Arms Agreements in June

Meeting not so much about power as lack of it

By Peter Grier
Staff writer of The Christian Science Monitor

VALLETTA, MALTA

AT their wave-tossed meetings in a Malta harbor, President Bush and Soviet leader Mikhail Gorbachev prepared the way for a summit of extraordinary potential in the United States next June.

Backslapping like old pals, the superpower leaders all but promised that major arms pacts would be ready by then. "That summit meeting [in June] will drive the arms control agenda," President Bush said.

This was but one indication of Bush's and Gorbachev's evident intention to personally push their bureaucracies toward better relations. Others included:

• A common desire to avoid insult or recrimination over the changes in Eastern Europe.

• A commitment to work together more closely on economic matters, such as increasing investment by US business in the Soviet economy.

• An unprecedented United States admission that the Soviets can do some good in the Middle East.

"If a meeting can improve relations, I think this one has," said Bush.

In today's increasingly complicated world, summits between superpowers are peculiar institutions. The press descends on summit sites by the thousands and the world watches the two

men as closely as if they were medieval kings who still had power to divide up the world.

But regarding perhaps the most important world political event since the advent of the cold war – the breakup of Eastern Europe – this summit was not about power so much as the lack of it.

There was no Yalta-like agreement on what the face of Europe should look like. There was no conclusion as to the future of West and East Germany.

Instead, President Bush defended his lack of celebration over the falling of the Berlin Wall, saying it would not help the Germans and would only annoy the Soviets. Gorbachev indirectly indicated that East and West Germany should remain separate nations. But in what could almost serve as a superpower lament, he said larger forces than his own preferences were at work.

"History itself decides the processes and fates on the European continent," Gorbachev said.

On things the two leaders still control, namely direct relations between their countries, the Malta meetings showed the importance of direct leadership involvement. If there was no personal commitment by Bush and Gorbachev to new arms agreements, they might not be reached, at least not in the time frame the leaders are talking about.

Bush learned the necessity for prodding the bureaucracy after the now-famous "strategic review" which began his presidency. Thousands of meeting-hours and

See **SUMMIT** next page

LEIPZIG RALLY: *Massive street protests began in Leipzig and Dresden but have since spread to other East German cities. Despite Communist Party resignations, these opposition rallies signal continued disapproval of the party leadership.*

East German Public Protest Sets Pace for Reform

Opposition calls for immediate elections, investigation of corruption

By Francine S. Kiefer
Staff writer of The Christian Science Monitor

WEST BERLIN

IN East Germany these days, people on the street set the political agenda and the timetable – not the politicians.

By forcing the resignation of the Communist Party's Politburo and Central Committee on Sunday, the people voted "no" to Egon Krenz's halfway reforms and "yes" to swifter change.

"The timetable will advance" on such issues as democratic elec-

tions; round-table discussions with the opposition; a real coalition government; and German reunification, says Daniel Hamilton, an expert on East Germany at the Aspin Institute here. "The people are not patient."

Yesterday Berlin's New Forum member Rolf Henrich reportedly called for the immediate creation of new election laws – to be decided by the people, not parliament. Another opposition group, the Social Democratic Party (SDP), said that the government was incapable and demanded elections for early next year.

A report on Communist Party

corruption and privileges delivered in the parliament on Friday drove demonstrators to demand immediate leadership changes over the weekend. The report, also broadcast on television, revealed that party leaders under Erich Honecker used state money to build private hunting reserves and sumptuous villas for themselves and that they lined their pockets with significant amounts of hard currency. The trade official responsible for hard currency has meanwhile fled the country. He allegedly directed an illegal arms-export scheme.

See **E. GERMANY** next page

5. Cracks In The Wall

A series, USSR Grappling with Change, *was written by Ned Temko upon departing his Moscow assignment in 1983. It marks a transition between the height of the Cold War and its end. Temko's* article Finding Islands of Freedom in a Sea of Soviet Authority *describes the early stages of many evolutionary trends in the USSR—not just in its subject matter but in the remarkable number of Soviet senior officials he was able to interview—many of whom had been previously unapproachable by the press. Temko dug deeper to get behind the bromides of the "party line". By soliciting frank comments from senior officials he gave his readers new insight into the changes in the thinking of the leadership which would inevitably lead to reform. These "cracks in the wall" of the ideology of Communism would eventually lead to the events resulting in the fall of the Berlin Wall and the rest of the Iron Curtain in 1989.*

Four articles selected from the magazine World Monitor *on Gorbachev, religion, art and the Security buraucracy examine the power structure as exemplified in the KGB, Gorbachev's reforms, and in artistic and religious undercurrents in the culture. One piece is also included from the television program,* World Monitor, *on the departure of Soviet troops from Prague in 1990.*

Finding Islands of Freedom In a Sea of Soviet Authority [11/15/83]

By Ned Temko

Across the street from where Lenin was born, in Ulyanovsk near a wide and icy Volga, a modern hotel rocks to the beat of an electric band. A young blonde woman near the crowded dance floor confides: "I don't work nowadays. Work is boring. . . .

"I love beautiful things, like gold and crystal."

She is Lena, divorced from a husband who gave her beautiful things but also drank for a living. She is one of dozens of ordinary people—neither officials nor dissidents—who have jolted the stereotypes I toted to Russia three years ago.

Russians since Stalin have reached an oddly comfortable covenant with authority. That is to say: comfortable for them, less so for authority.

Instinctively, they build "islands" on which to live, dream, drink, inform themselves of the world outside, discuss things, acquire goods and services, even prosper, beyond the reach of the powers that be—often in ways their parents would not have contemplated.

In return for Soviet-style "freedom," they work, if sometimes as little or as shoddily as they can get away with. They pay lip service to official campaigns of one sort or another. And they otherwise forswear political activity.

Dissidents are the few who break the rules of the game and refuse to stay within their private "islands."

And the system crushes them. Even the little ones, like Viktor Tomachinsky. . . .

Viktor was a self-styled poet and A-one auto mechanic. He was a stocky leprechaun of a man with unruly hair, faded blue jeans and a seemingly irrepressible urge to smile.

He was 35 when I met him, in late 1981, in the stairwell of the apartment house where reporters and diplomats live. He was handing out "invitations" to Moscow City Court, where he planned to sue the KGB and the Soviet Interior Ministry for $20,000 the next day.

His "case" was that KGB and ministry officials had promised him and his family exit visas, but reneged.

"They should pay me what I could have earned as a mechanic if the visas had been granted as agreed," he said.

I attended his day in court, a snow-chilled afternoon. A panel of judges, headed by a middle-aged woman with red hair, spectacles, and a look of puzzlement, heard the plea and withdrew to an adjacent room. They returned in half an hour or so to declare, with none of Viktor's evident enjoyment of the show, "We do not have jurisdiction."

That night, security police arrested Viktor. Two years later, friends say, he died in prison. His wife was informed the cause of death was pneumonia.

I remember asking him, before his courtroom appearance, whether it might be wiser to give up his suit. He thought otherwise: "I don't know," he said. "I guess it's just a matter of temperament."

"This Tomachinsky was crazy," says Rima, a nondissident friend of mine. It is not so much that he wanted to leave Russia—Rima, too, has felt that way—or that he was angry with the KGB. But, she explains, thinking things is one thing. Going public, challenging the authorities to a fight, is insane. It is pointless.

"*Nado jit*," Russians say: "You have to live." And within limits instinctively felt and observed, living here is a less neatly ordered business than western stereotypes imply.

Yuri Andropov's calls for "discipline" have afforded an example.

In early 1983 sudden spot-checks by police for truants in grocery stores, movie theaters, and other public places sent shock waves through Moscow. People began showing up for work more often and promptly, laboring rather than drinking on the job, leaving work later. Then the authorities called off the spot-checks, deciding against what an official calls "shock" tactics that could not have had a lasting effect without a return to other, darker tools of the Stalin days.

Since then, an official notes, the fresh "discipline" has lost some momentum. Downtown Moscow stores seem as crowded as ever with off-the-job shoppers.

"People do have a greater awareness of discipline since Andropov came to power," adds a factory worker among pedestrians I have stopped to interview.

But on the job, he and others say, there has yet to be lasting change: no mass firings for being late, or for taking an hour or so off to do the family shopping. "There is simply more awareness. We are a bit more careful," a worker says.

And vodka, a prime foe of discipline, is very much alive and well.

Russians drink everywhere: on the job when possible, in restaurants, at home. And on the street, falling-down drunks are a familiar part of the urban landscape.

In 1981 the Brezhnev régime announced the latest in a series of vodka price hikes, linked to an equally familiar campaign against alcoholism. But a few months ago, in a move most Muscovites saw as pleasingly out of sync with the campaign for "labor discipline," a new, cheaper brand was suddenly introduced.

I asked an official why: People simply started buying up subsidized sugar and other ingredients for a home-made firewater. They stopped buying vodka through state stores. "We lost a billion rubles [about $1.3 billion] in revenue. . . . And people were still drinking."

But if many Russians, on their "islands," drink and deaden the mind, others feed the mind, exercise it. They trade bootleg cassettes of music—a practice that is officially proscribed. They inform themselves, in one way or another, of what is happening within the Soviet Union and beyond. They participate in what must be the world's most frenetic joke-and-rumor mill.

One result is that large numbers of Russians are more informed about—and fascinated by—the world outside Soviet borders. This is partly a function of détente, a process declared dead in Washington but having lasting grass-roots effect here. Another factor is domestic: Russians who have grown up since Stalin are better educated and more curious than their forebears.

A Russian I know recounts a lecture tour he gave in Byelorussia in late 1980: "I was amazed by the information they had on Poland, but also on other issues" like the death of John Lennon.

Far more widespread is the fame of a Russian bard named Vladimir Vysotsky, whose death in 1980 briefly overshadowed the Moscow Olympic Games. He was

PHOTOS BY R. NORMAN MATHENY – STAFF

Shopping: a national sport

USSR: GRAPPLING WITH CHANGE PART ONE OF A SERIES

Finding islands of freedom in a sea of Soviet authority

By Ned Temko
Staff writer of The Christian Science Monitor

Ulyanovsk, USSR

Across the street from where Lenin was born, in Ulyanovsk near a wide and icy Volga, a modern hotel rocks to the beat of an electric band. A young blonde woman near the crowded dance floor confides: "I don't work nowadays. Work is boring. . . .

"I love beautiful things, like gold and crystal."

She is Lena, divorced from a husband who gave her beautiful things but also drank for a living. She is one of dozens of ordinary people — neither officials nor dissidents — who have jolted the stereotypes I toted to Russia three years ago.

Russians since Stalin have reached an oddly comfortable convenant with authority. That is to say: comfortable for them, less so for authority.

Instinctively, they build "islands" on which to live, dream, drink, inform themselves of the world outside, discuss things, acquire goods and services, even prosper, beyond the reach of the powers that be — often in ways their parents would not have contemplated.

In return for Soviet-style "freedom," they work, if sometimes as little or as shoddily as they can get away with. They pay lip service to official campaigns of one sort or another. And they otherwise forswear political activity.

Dissidents are the few who break the rules of the game and refuse to stay within their private "islands." And the system crushes them. Even the little ones, like Viktor Tomachinsky. . . .

Viktor was a self-styled poet and A-one auto mechanic. He was a stocky leprechaun of a man with unruly hair, faded blue jeans, and a seemingly irrepressible urge to smile.

He was 35 when I met him, in late 1981, in the stairwell of the apartment house where reporters and diplomats live. He was handing out "invitations" to Moscow city court, where he planned to sue the KGB and the Soviet Interior Ministry for $20,000 the next day.

His "case" was that KGB and ministry officials had promised him and his family exit visas, but reneged.

"They should pay me what I could have earned as a mechanic if the visas had been granted as agreed," he said.

I attended his day in court, a snow-chilled afternoon. A panel of judges, headed by a middle-aged woman with red hair, spectacles, and a look of puzzlement, heard the plea and withdrew to an adjacent room. They returned in half an hour or so to declare, with none of Viktor's evident enjoyment of the show, "We do not have jurisdiction."

That night, security police arrested Viktor. Two years later, friends say, he died in prison. His wife was informed the cause of death was pneumonia.

I remember asking him, before his courtroom appearance, whether it might be wiser to give up his suit. He thought otherwise: "I don't know," he said. "I guess it's just a matter of temperament."

"This Tomachinsky was crazy," says Rima, a nondissident friend of mine. It is not so much that he wanted to leave Russia — Rima, too, has felt that way — or that he was angry with the KGB. But, she explains, thinking things is one thing. Going public, challenging the authorities to a fight, is insane. It is pointless.

"*Nado jit*," Russians say: "You have to live." And within limits instinctively felt and observed, living here is a less neatly ordered business than Western stereotypes imply.

Yuri Andropov's calls for "discipline" have afforded an example.

In early 1983, sudden spot-checks by police for truants in grocery stores, movie theaters, and other public places sent shock waves through Moscow. People began showing up for work more often and promptly, laboring rather than drinking on the job, leaving work later.

Then the authorities called off the spot-checks, deciding against what an official calls "shock" tactics that could not have had a lasting effect without a return to other, darker tools of the Stalin days.

Since then, an official notes, the fresh "discipline" has lost some momentum. Downtown Moscow stores seem as crowded as ever with off-the-job shoppers.

"People do have a greater awareness of discipline since Andropov came to power," adds a factory worker among pedestrians I have stopped to interview.

But on the job, he and others say, there has yet to be lasting change: no mass firings for being late, or for taking an hour or so off to do the family shopping. "There is simply more awareness. We are a bit more careful," a worker says.

And vodka, a prime foe of discipline, is very much alive and well.

Russians drink everywhere: on the job when possible, in restaurants, at home. And on the street, falling-down drunks are a familiar part of the urban landscape.

In 1981, the Brezhnev regime announced the latest in a series of vodka price hikes, linked to an equally familiar campaign against alcoholism. But a few months ago, in a move most Muscovites saw as pleasingly out of sync with the campaign for "labor discipline," a new, cheaper brand was suddenly introduced.

I asked an official why: People simply started buying up subsidized sugar and other ingredients for a homemade firewater. They stopped buying vodka through state stores. "We lost a billion rubles [about $1.3 billion] in revenue. . . . And people were still drinking."

But if many Russians, on their "islands," drink and deaden the mind, others feed the mind, exercise it. They trade bootleg cassettes of music that is officially proscribed. They inform themselves, in one way or another, of what is happening within the Soviet Union and beyond. They participate in what must be the world's most frenetic joke-and-rumor mill.

One result is that large numbers of Russians are more informed about — and fascinated by — the world outside Soviet borders. This is partly a function of détente, a process declared dead in Washington but having lasting grass-roots effect here. Another factor is domestic: Russians who have grown up since Stalin are better educated and more curious than their forebears.

A Russian I know recounts a lecture tour he gave in Byelorussia in late 1980: "I was amazed by the information they had on Poland, but also on other issues" like the death of John Lennon.

Far more widespread is the fame of a Russian bard named Vladimir Vysotsky, whose death in 1980 briefly overshadowed the Moscow Olympic Games. He was part Soviet Bob Dylan, part James Dean. But he was not really a dissident, he did not sing "protest" songs. He sang of the way Russian life is, its sadnesses and joys and hypocrisies, in the language of the street. He laughed with Russians about Russia.

The authorities never allowed him to perform publicly in Moscow. But his songs were taped at private concerts, then retaped countrywide. Although death was not announced, thousands showed up for his funeral. More have been streaming to his grave ever since.

A friend of mine visited the Far Eastern port of Nakhodka last year. Speaking to local kids, he was promptly asked: "How did Volodya Vysotsky die?"

He died, as Russian as he lived, of drink. And before long, the whole country will know every detail, by word of mouth.

In 1982, when Lebanese militiamen killed hundreds in the Palestinian camps of Beirut, the Soviet line was in effect that Israel pulled the trigger. But when I interviewed people on the street, almost none offered this version. Lebanese did the shooting, they said. Some named the militia group responsible.

Some knew from Western radio broadcasts, which are not always perfectly jammed. Another source of unofficial information is the Yugoslav press, which is available to some Soviets at places of work or study.

Even Pravda helps. A surprising number of people scour the paper as closely as any Kremlinologist. In the case of the Beirut killings, a man explained that Pravda had quoted a foreign report charging the killing had occurred "under the very nose of Israelis." So, he said, "We knew Israel didn't actually do the shooting."

An Armenian makes a point

The Soviet news media have increasingly been offering such bits, in tacit acknowledgment that large numbers of people are getting the news anyway.

Similarly, the Kremlin is well aware of the fascination here with the technologies and consumer trappings of the West. The Soviet version of the Korean jet incident stressed the plane was a Boeing jumbo full of space-age Western gadgetry that could not have failed without sinister United States design. The argument, an official noted, was particularly effective.

Nor does "unofficial" knowledge of things Western always stop with the young and well educated, though it is certainly more widespread there.

Spot-checks don't deter many customers

In April 1981, the son and grandson of famed Russian composer Dmitri Shostakovich defected to the West — a fact that went unmentioned by the Soviet media for some weeks.

Days after the defection, I sought pedestrians' views on the successful landing of the first US space shuttle. Near the end of my interview tour, I stopped a rather elderly woman laden down with shopping bags — not, to look at her, a likely listener of Western radio broadcasts.

But after a few words on the shuttle, she asked in a whisper: "Is it true the Shostakoviches are staying in the West?"

For the intelligentsia, compartmentalization of life is a careful, conscious thing. A poet-singer I know works hard to produce softly lyrical ballads about love and nature — of a type that has allowed official release of some of his songs.

In the privacy of a small, disheveled apartment outside town, meanwhile, he paints modernist canvases and strums occasionally more barbish compositions that would never win official OK. These songs he performs only for small circles of friends or fellow artists. That is his island, and he is happy on it.

Even Pravda holds clues to unofficial views

For more ordinary Russians, the process is less conscious, more a function of everyday living.

Depending on what's available in the shops, for instance, many people technically break Soviet law by doing unofficial deals for goods and services "through the back door" of state outlets. They buy state-subsidized gasoline from truck drivers who get it for work, use less than they report, and sell the remainder on the side.

Or they occasionally take an hour or two off work to shop, see a movie, go to the steam baths.

Although this is visibly worrisome for the authorities, none of it necessarily has political implications.

Nor does the ever-present, if generally superficial, fascination with things Western. Or the endless political jokes, the most recent batch of which centers on Andropov's KGB past: They've developed a new apple, named "Androploko," a takeoff on the Russian word for that fruit. "It is so bitter it makes you snap your mouth shut and put your hands behind your back!"

Generally, Russians remain patriotic. And particularly outside Moscow, they seem to absorb a fair bit from the endless spew of official propaganda on things foreign. A typical remark comes from a young Tatar woman who shared a table with the lively blonde Lena in Ulyanovsk:

"All in all, I think our society is humane. The best people are true Communists . . . [although] we have our swine, too. . . ."

A bit later, she offers a familiarly disjointed Russian image of America: "Will Reagan send American soldiers to fight Russians?" she asks. Then, she says:

"I think America was the first defender of freedom. . . . I would like very, very much to go there. But I am almost sure I would not get permission." This is said without rancor, just a statement of fact.

A somewhat older Russian I picked up hitchhiking in the north offers another widespread view: The "haves" in America are far better off than any Russian, but "some others live worse. And you have all that unemployment."

And by and large, Russians really do find life easier in Russia than they suspect it is abroad. As long as one stays within certain political limits, the state virtually manages an individual's life from cradle to grave. Education is free. Work is guaranteed. Initiative is not required.

Ordinary Soviets have, nonetheless, become gradually more outspoken in recent years on all sorts of political questions. An officially encouraged forum for diverse opinion — letters to Soviet newspapers — provides a measure of this.

Even on as politically sensitive an issue as the Korean airliner incident, a major newspaper got what a senior Soviet source calls "a large number" of letters. Most backed the Soviets' downing of the plane. Yet one-third asked for an explanation of why the Soviets had fired.

Still, even young Russians generally tend to be leery of making explicitly political statements beyond either small groups of trusted friends, or officially sanctioned activities.

Still, if, in small groups of trusted friends, Russians who have grown up after Stalin are more outspoken than their elders, both groups tend to steer clear of any public political activity that is not officially sanctioned.

A Moscow joke, too nearly true to be only a joke, sums things up best. It is the story of the "six great paradoxes" of Soviet socialism:

First: There is no unemployment but nobody does any work.

The second: Nobody works, but year after year, state economic plans are "fulfilled or overfulfilled."

The third paradox is that plans are fulfilled religiously, but there is nothing in the shops.

The fourth: There's nothing in the shops. But if you go to the typical Moscow apartment, delicacies that haven't been in the shops for months somehow end up on the dining room table.

Fifth: People find special ways to get goods even when the shops aren't selling them. But people still complain.

And finally: Everyone complains. But when elections roll around, everyone votes: "yes."

Next: the political agenda

The Christian Science Monitor
from November 15, 1983.

part Soviet Bob Dylan, part James Dean. But he was not really a dissident, he did not sing "protest" songs. He sang of the way Russian life is, its sadnesses and joys and hypocrisies, in the language of the street. He laughed with Russians about Russia.

The authorities never allowed him to perform publicly in Moscow. But his songs were taped at private concerts, then retaped countrywide. Although his death was not announced, thousands showed up for his funeral. More have been streaming to his grave ever since.

A friend of mine visited the Far Eastern port of Nakhodka last year. Speaking to local kids, he was promptly asked: "How did Volodya Vysotsky die?"

He died, as Russian as he lived, of drink. And before long, the whole country will know every detail, by word of mouth.

In 1982 when Lebanese militiamen killed hundreds in the Palestinian camps of Beirut, the Soviet line was in effect that Israel pulled the trigger. But when I interviewed people on the street, almost none offered this version. Lebanese did the shooting, they said. Some named the militia group responsible.

Some knew from western radio broadcasts, which are not always perfectly jammed. Another source of unofficial information is the Yugoslav press, which is available to some Soviets at places of work or study.

Even *Pravda* helps. A surprising number of people scour the paper as closely as any Kremlinologist. In the case of the Beirut killings, a man explained that *Pravda* had quoted a foreign report charging the killing had occurred "under the very nose of Israelis." So, he said, "We knew Israel didn't actually do the shooting."

The Soviet news media have increasingly been offering such bits, in tacit acknowledgment that large numbers of people are getting the news anyway.

Similarly, the Kremlin is well aware of the fascination here with the technologies and consumer trappings of the West. The Soviet version of the Korean jet incident stressed the plane was a Boeing jumbo full of space-age western gadgetry that could not have failed without sinister United States design. The argument, an official noted, was particularly effective.

Nor does "unofficial" knowledge of things western always stop with the young and well educated, though it is certainly more widespread there.

In April 1981 the son and grandson of famed Russian composer Dmitri Shostakovich defected to the West—a fact that went unmentioned by the Soviet media for some weeks.

Days after the defection, I sought pedestrians' views on the successful landing of the first US space shuttle. Near the end of my interview tour, I stopped a rather elderly woman laden down with shopping bags—not, to look at her, a likely listener of western radio broadcasts.

But after a few words on the shuttle, she asked in a whisper: "Is it true the Shostakoviches are staying in the West?"

For the intelligentsia, compartmentalization of life is a careful, conscious thing. A poet-singer I know works hard to produce softly lyrical ballads about love and nature—of a type that has allowed official release of some of his songs.

In the privacy of a small, disheveled apartment outside town, meanwhile, he paints modernist canvases and strums occasionally more barbish compositions that would never win official OK. These songs he performs only for small circles of friends or fellow artists. That is his island, and he is happy on it.

For more ordinary Russians, the process is less conscious, more a function of everyday living.

Depending on what's available in the shops, for instance, many people technically break Soviet law by doing unofficial deals for goods and services "through the back door" of state outlets. They buy state-subsidized gasoline from truck drivers who get it for their work, use less than they officially report, and sell the remainder on the side.

Or they occasionally take an hour or two off work to shop, see a movie, go to the steam baths.

Although this is visibly worrisome for the authorities, none of it necessarily has political implications.

Nor does the ever-present, if generally superficial, fascination with things western. Or the endless political jokes, the most recent batch of which centers on Andropov's KGB past: They've developed a new apple, named "Androploko," a takeoff on the Russian word for that fruit. "It is so bitter it makes you snap your mouth shut and put your hands behind your back!"

Generally, Russians remain patriotic. And particularly outside Moscow, they seem to absorb a fair bit from the endless spew of official propaganda on things foreign. A typical remark comes from a young Tatar woman who shared a table with the lively blonde Lena in Ulyanovsk:

"All in all, I think our society is humane. The best people are true Communists . . . [although] we have our swine, too. . . ."

A bit later, she offers a familiarly disjointed Russian image of America: "Will Reagan send American soldiers to fight Russians?" she asks. Then, she says:

"I think America was the first defender of freedom. . . . I would like very, very much to go there. But I am almost sure I would not get permission." This is said without rancor, just a statement of fact.

A somewhat older Russian I picked up hitchhiking in the north offers another widespread view: The "haves" in America are far better off than any Russian, but "some others live worse. And you have all that unemployment." And by and large, Russians really do find life easier in Russia than they suspect it is abroad. As long as one stays within certain political limits, the state virtually manages an individual's life from cradle to grave. Education is free. Work is guaranteed. Initiative is not required.

Ordinary Soviets have, nonetheless, become gradually more outspoken in recent years on all sorts of political questions. An officially encouraged forum for diverse opinion—letters to Soviet newspapers—provides a measure of this.

Even on as politically sensitive an issue as the Korean airliner incident, a major newspaper got what a senior Soviet source calls "a large number" of letters. Most backed the Soviets' downing of the plane. Yet one third asked for an explanation of why the Soviets had fired.

Still, even young Russians generally tend to be leery of making explicitly political statements beyond either small groups of trusted friends, or officially sanctioned activities.

Still, if, in small groups of trusted friends, Russians who have grown up after Stalin are more outspoken than their elders, both groups tend to steer clear of any public political activity that is not officially sanctioned.

A Moscow joke, too nearly true to be only a joke, sums things up best. It is the story of the "six great paradoxes" of Soviet Socialism:

The first: There is no unemployment but nobody does any work.

The second: Nobody works, but year after year, state economic plans are "fulfilled or overfulfilled."

The third: Plans are fulfilled religiously, but there is nothing in the shops.

The fourth: There's nothing in the shops. But if you go to the typical Moscow apartment, delicacies that haven't been in the shops for months somehow end up on the dining room table.

The fifth: People find special ways to get goods even when the shops aren't selling them. But people still complain.

And finally: Everyone complains. But when elections roll around, everyone votes "yes."

Two young, contemporary women in downtown Riga, Latvia.

The Soviet People: Caught In a Tangle of Central Plans [11/16/83]

The joke here goes that a Soviet leader, reviewing the troops on Red Square, is suddenly distracted by the sight of four tough and burly men in gray business suits.

He turns to his KGB chief and, with a hint of admiration, asks: "Are those your boys?"

No, says the secret police chief. "Not mine."

"Not mine, either," says the Soviet defense minister.

Then the head of the Soviet Union's gargantuan state economic planning organization, Gosplan, steps forward and interrupts: "They're my boys . . . and they are an awesome destructive force."

The Soviet economy tops a daunting Kremlin policy agenda for the 1980s, and central planning—that awesome destructive force—is but one in a dense tangle of problems.

The economy is not going to collapse. For one thing, this country is oozing with natural riches—including hard-currency export commodities like energy, gold and diamonds.

And in its own, often incredibly inefficient way, the Soviet Union will, no doubt, continue to ensure at least subsistence levels of food, clothing, housing and other staple goods and services to its roughly 270 million citizens.

The hitch is this: for a leadership facing rising consumer expectations at home and escalating competition with the United States abroad, mere performance as usual is deemed no longer good enough.

Though the Kremlin has gone out of its way in recent months to signal new concern for the Soviet consumer, it is the heightened tension with Washington that most drives Moscow's concern over the economy.

Twice in the past 18 months, the country's top career military man—armed forces Chief of Staff Nikolai Ogarkov—has publicly stated the obvious: A superpower can't be truly strong in the latter half of the 20th century if its economy is weak.

For one thing, Marshal Ogarkov points out, you can't be ready for a war if your economy isn't ready to supply one. "The armed forces can operate successfully only when they can rely on a powerful scientific, technical and economic base and on its steady functioning in wartime."

Yet beyond this, the superpower arms race has more and more become a superpower technology race: "The basic scientific progress in weapons systems is renewed every 10 to 12 years," the marshal notes.

Viktor Afanasyev, editor of Pravda.
**Next page: (top) Making shoes
at a commune factory in Moscow.
(bottom) Lines at a liquor store, Moscow.**

To live in the Soviet Union for three years is to be reminded almost daily of what, by both of Marshal Ogarkov's criteria, is a pervasive Soviet weakness.

Technologically, Russia lags well behind the United States and remains slow to innovate.

Go into a shop or an office here, and you're much more likely to hear the clacking wooden beads of an abacus than the whisper of an electronic calculator.

Personal computers? The Soviets have produced a small batch of imitation US models that might best be called "red Apples," but they're in use virtually nowhere in the economy, and nowhere in the school system.

Recently, I toured a special math and science high school run in concert with Moscow University. There were no "red Apples," only one terminal for the university computer and it was normally open to students two days a week.

Mechanization? One of the achievements of the Soviet system is that there is no unemployment. But one reason—witness the armies of men and women, young and old, sweeping streets, repaving or chipping ice from them—is that a host of tasks throughout the economy are far less mechanized here than in the West.

Miniaturization? Here there has been some progress. But from computers to electric typewriters and from tape recorders to missiles, bulk and bigness remain Soviet trademarks.

A current joke here tells of a Moscow factory's search for the appropriate slogan—of slogans, there is no shortage—to spur Soviet catch-up with the West's production of microchips. After much hemming and hawing, an activist comes up with the perfect answer:

"Soviet microchips: the biggest microchips in the world!"

Moscow planners and political leaders are keenly aware of all these problems—more keenly aware, and for a considerably longer time already, than is often assumed—and they are visibly scurrying to do something about them.

When Yuri Andropov took over, he redoubled efforts begun during Leonid Brezhnev's last years to "give a new technological turn" to the economy. A recent party decree moved to correct one particularly damaging fault in the traditional central planning guidelines in an economy still almost exclusively steered from the center. In the past industries often stood to lose money if they rocked the production boat and risked short-term plan fulfillment with technological innovation. The new decree is designed to compensate costs incurred in the switchover.

Under Brezhnev in 1979 a more general move was made to shift plan targets for many industries away from mere volume. Bigger was no longer automatically better.

In theory.

In fact, at least some of the targeted industries have simply ignored the decree. And the main substitute planning index introduced in the 1979 decision—the amount of value added to a product at each stage in its production—has produced distortions and bottlenecks of its own.

Indeed, a major snag in shoring up this planned economy seems the very fact that it is a planned economy.

Some of the problems with central planning are trivial, if amusing: Moscow commands a huge fleet of trucks that, theoretically, spray water on the streets in warm weather and, with a switch of machinery, plow snow in winter. But central planners' wall calendars, not the weather, determine the precise day of the switchover. So on the inevitable days of unseasonable cold before winter officially punches in, the trucks find themselves spraying not water, but ice, as if at halftime in a citywide hockey game.

Or, there are the repeated instances when factories relentlessly "fulfill plan" for production of consumer products Soviet consumers don't want—like synthetic fabrics, or homely Soviet shoes, or the model of television set that, in Leningrad some time back, took to catching fire when summer weather "slowed air circulation."

Planners' minds, inevitably, work more slowly than consumers'.

A tougher problem is that planning an economy as complex as the Soviet one, in a nation as huge as the Soviet Union, virtually ensures mutually reinforcing inefficiencies.

There are not enough trucks or crate nails, for instance, so vegetables don't get packed and shipped. They rot. A factory gets too little steel, or gets it too late, so its entire production suffers.

Only the distant planners keep the big picture in mind. Go progressively down through levels of management, ending with the individual farm or factory or shop, and there is progressively more single-minded preoccupation with just meeting one's own particular plan target.

The nail manufacturer meets plan by turning out thousands of nails. It is not his worry when, or whether, they get where they're supposed to go.

The truck driver, or train conductor, can meet plan simply by carrying nails or other cargo the requisite distance in the requisite time—for instance, by toting material from the factory to construction sites hundreds of miles distant, rather than to ones a few miles away.

The inevitable result is that individual factory or farm managers take to hoarding all sorts of materials in hopes of having them on hand when needed—thus exacerbating bottlenecks further.

At year's end, everybody blames everybody else.

Which brings us to the main hitch: Soviet people, the way they are ruled and the way they think.

They lack initiative, commitment to quality workmanship, imagination or the urge to innovate. They take the path of least resistance. They fulfill plan—the simpler the plan, the better, no matter how inefficient for the economy as a whole.

Show up at any Moscow shop a minute before lunch break—more often, even five minutes before—and no one will stretch the rules to let you in.

But come back after lunch and you'll find shelves full of consumer products that are at best functional and unattractively finished, at worst not in working order by the time you get them home.

The general nonchalance about product quality leads Soviet consumers of all ages and descriptions to automatically assume that any foreign item is more reliable than its domestic counterpart.

One area in which "quality uncontrol" is especially evident is the distinctly Soviet institution called the "*remont*." Literally, the word means "a repair," and buildings of all sizes and descriptions get it with reassuring regularity, in some cases starting only a few years after construction.

My wife and I "*remonted*" our apartment here: a task that—due to a Soviet work schedule that generally included two hours' talk, one hour's cigarette smoking, two hours' lunch and maybe two hours' work each day—took months. One day, three workers teamed for three hours to remove old kitchen tiles. Having half-finished, they then broke for an equally long lunch. My exasperated wife decided to remove the other half. It took her 58 minutes.

Two of some two dozen *remont* workers—an electrician and a carpenter—displayed initiative and genuine pride in their jobs. They were the exceptions.

As in almost all other spheres of Soviet life, the initial response to any special request—moving a water heater a few feet, for instance, to keep it from spewing hot ash into a bathtub—was "*nelzya*." Impossible.

The Christian Science Monitor
from June 8, 1989.

After varying degrees of dispute, the workers involved would invariably reveal that "impossible" was a relative term, its degree depending on how much extra cash or other bribe was offered.

Defy these rules, and work suddenly goes more slowly. Workers suddenly find themselves needed by another, presumably more lucrative customer. The Soviet press indicates factory managers have much the same problem. As a ranking official puts it privately, "There are many instances when managers pay 'bonuses' just to get people to work."

After our *remont* was technically over, I stopped in at an official labor placement agency for an article I was researching. The woman in charge let me leaf through her file of jobs on offer, which, as it happened, included these:

"Construction work on apartments for foreign representatives. . .

"Taking into consideration high demands on quality in working on building projects for foreigners, there will be a 25 percent bonus for all workers."

Bonuses can do only so much. They do work sometimes. For example, an increase in state purchase prices for livestock has been one explanation—better weather is the main one—for recent Soviet success in ending the chronic meat and milk shortages of the past few years.

But there are limits to the effects of mere monetary incentive: For one thing, there is the chicken-and-egg problem that extra pocket money is useful only if consumer items that workers want to buy are available. One reason the agricultural "incentives" have had some effect is that they are disbursed, in part, in the form of feed grains and other "in-kind" payments farmers need and want.

Another major problem is this: The aftereffects of world war and domestic purges, and the need to shift energy and other extractive projects to the forbidding expanses of Siberia, have helped create overall labor shortages in many industries. A truly enormous exodus from countryside to city in the past several decades has created a similar effect down on the farm.

Thus if a manager genuinely uses incentives—that is, if he pays people who work better a lot more than people who do not—then he risks losing the offended workers to a less demanding employer. A small-circulation book by a journalist in Soviet Latvia recounts the tribulations of a collective-farm chief there—among them that, with labor short and a plan to be met, he wouldn't dare fire workers even if they did more drink-

ing than working on the job. "The indispensable drunkard," lamented the author.

Finally, and most seriously, is the bias of the entire Soviet system—economic, political, social—against individual initiative. Even senior Soviet officials are beginning slowly, privately to acknowledge the problem, though they tend to trace its causes to czarist and feudal traditions which the Revolution could not instantly overturn.

The very Russian language hints at the enormity of the problem. When people pass a particularly long line in front of a shop here, they inevitably stop and try to find out what is on sale. In Russian, they ask, "*Chto dayut?*"—literally, "What are they giving us?"

Pervading the Soviet style of government is a similar approach: almost of schoolmaster to adolescent. A Soviet policeman has the right to stop a motorist and fine him for not keeping his car clean.

The Soviet Constitution—Article 44—notes that all citizens are guaranteed the "right to [state] housing." The article continues: "Citizens of the USSR shall take good care of the housing allocated to them."

A changing Soviet people does, gradually, seem to be showing more initiative—but within the framework of a comfortable covenant with authority that channels this drive and imagination into improving one's own insular existence.

Thus, a Soviet journalist I know explains how his wife, like most other Russians, has gotten used to making under-the-counter deals for products and services the planned economy imperfectly provides.

Now, he says, she has come up with another solution: leaving a rather well-paying job at a medical research institute to work at a public clinic. The pay is much less. But, he explains, "People will come up to her there and say, 'Next week we will have nice imported boots at the store where I work . . . or tangerines. . . .'

"With this information, my wife will be able to show up and get these products at [state-subsidized] official prices, rather than pay more under the counter."

In a market economy—with its accompanying disciplinary scourges unemployment and competition, and with its more realistic supply-and-demand pricing for inputs at all levels—individual decisions, like the ones taken by this Soviet journalist's wife, are part of what makes the economy work and modernize.

Here, such decisions are planned by men in gray suits—"very well-paid men in gray suits," adds the young Soviet official who first told me the joke about their "awesome destructive force."

And the most pervasive side effect is that the overwhelming majority of Soviet people have got used to the system, its comfortable removal of responsibility from all but the central planners. The western assumption—at least my own assumption when I arrived in the Soviet Union—was that ordinary Soviet workers and farm directors and plant managers were straining for release from the rigidity of a command economy. Give them freedom, and they'll grab at it. They'll show initiative.

This just is not the case. Or, at the very least, the response is far from immediate. Thus, when the Soviets formally unveiled a national Food Program last year that was partly designed to shift decision-making power from central authorities to regional and local ones, the central bureaucrats proved to be but one of the early obstacles. As public statements from various senior officials made clear, newly created regional organizations have often proved reluctant to assume their new powers, for evident fear of the new responsibilities that are part of the package.

Another western assumption—less credible to a foreign resident here the longer he stays—is that the Soviet military is isolated from such problems.

The quality of individual products—from trucks to missiles—may indeed be greater in the large chunk of the economy under military supervision. The best scientists and technicians may, indeed, be claimed by the military as well. A Soviet specialist, in a remarkably straightforward criticism of the economy in *Pravda* last year, went so far as to lament that military products were the only area in which Moscow could truly compete on world markets. But whether the Soviets can fully compete with their main rival, the US, is more problematic.

The men on the factory floor, ordinary Soviets who have worked in the military sector say, are not wildly different from Soviet men anywhere else in terms of the pride or initiative they are apt to show on the job. They're just more disciplined.

And to judge by one very visible aspect of the "military" economy—the crews of uniformed youths called on to help pave roads or lay water pipes in Moscow and other cities—the men in khaki are every bit as fond of the chatty, intermittent approach to work.

Technologically, the Soviets are still playing catch-up in the military sphere as well. True, their rocket firepower is awesome. And guidance systems are improving. Moscow also seems to be approaching an equivalent of the radar-dodging US cruise missile, with its miniaturized direction apparatus, more quickly than the Americans had hoped. But the first step was American.

One reason the Soviets are so reluctant to deal away their huge land-based ballistic missiles—inefficient overkill, military style—is an abiding sense here that security depends on matching superiority in size and numbers with the US advantage in the technology race. This may not always be true. But for the foreseeable future, it seems unlikely you'll find US spies stealing Soviet microchips instead of the other way around.

Most important—and disturbing, for the West—the Soviet military seems not greatly better off than the civilians in making quick, considered decisions of the type impossible without a sense of individual responsibility and initiative.

The Keystone-Kop nature of the Soviets' handling of the Korean airline tragedy from Minute 1 to Day 6—when Moscow finally and unequivocally admitted it had shot down the plane—seems ample indication of this.

The Ripening of Soviet Policy: Straight Party Line Adopts Nuances   [11/17/83]

Central Casting goofed. Alexander Bovin, Kremlin foreign policy analyst, isn't what a Soviet official is supposed to be.

His huge girth, imperfectly restrained by bulging suspenders, and his amused eyes suggest some Soviet Socialist Pillsbury Doughboy. His intellect, wit and cool crisis-manager's vocabulary—his sense of limits of power in a nuclear age—suggest a Soviet Socialist Henry Kissinger.

He speaks with nuance: whether on potential for compromise at arms talks where each side's public positions seem irreconcilable; on balancing each superpower's "understandable" national interests in areas like the Middle East; or on the intricacies of internal United States politics.

"Nixon for President," proclaims one of dozens of political buttons decorating the entryway of Bovin's downtown apartment. "Black Power," cries another. On his living room bookshelf sit Nixon's "Memoirs," and Kissinger's, a photo of controversial Russian balladeer Vladimir Vysotsky, and a collection of the speeches and writings of Yuri V. Andropov.

Once, when Bovin was out of the room, I could not help opening the Andropov volume. "With respect," it was inscribed by the author.

Alexander Bovin is part of a "transition" process in the Soviet political system that really began not one year ago, with Yuri Andropov's accession, but decades earlier with the end of the one-man "rule by paranoia" of Joseph Stalin.

Bovin is one of dozens of analysts, specialists, and advisers with whose help the Kremlin has slowly altered the way this country is run. The process is by no means complete. It has its limits and potential pitfalls—not the least of which is the fact that, in some ways, Russians have changed *how* they think more slowly than what they think.

Yet the shift has by the early 1980s allowed a widening tendency within the political elite to view domestic and world problems through a prism of informed, relatively objective analysis, rather than force their bends and angles into the perfect circle of Marxist-Leninist rhetoric.

One myth about present-day Russia is that its rulers think their system—notably, their economy—works fine, and that the idea of a "reformist" loosening of some of the chains of command planning is profoundly controversial.

Or that the Soviets see crises like the upheaval next door in Poland as mere dastardly plots of "US imperialism" with no lessons for the way East-bloc states run.

Or that Moscow, as *Pravda* likes ominously to imply, seriously contemplates "giving up" on dealings with the Americans because it finds President Reagan distasteful and because it sees the basing of new US missiles in western Europe as inevitable in any case.

Yuri Andropov—says a ranking official with a refreshingly tentative air—"is an important page, maybe even a chapter" in this transition process that has begun undermining such assumptions about the Soviet Union.

"Andropov himself is not the only factor," says the official. "I see him as a continuation of a trend that took form in the late 1970s under [Leonid] Brezhnev. . . . Its main aspect is the sense that Socialism needs improvement in all directions—above all, as regards our economy."

In a political vacuum, something for which the Kremlin no doubt often fervently wishes, the goals and limits sought in the Soviet system's long march of change are already fairly evident.

A full free-market economy is no presently on the agenda. Nor is anything resembling western-style democracy. On the international front, continued emphasis on nuclear arms production and development is a given.

Yet the slowly solidifying consensus in the corridors of Moscow power, as three years of interviews with ranking officials of various ages and backgrounds suggest, includes the following:

1. Economic "reform." Some form of gradual, measured decentralization of authority is essential to make the Soviet economy keep pace in a modern age.

Details remain to be worked out—subject to political considerations, officials make clear, and to the outcome of debate on some elements of a "reform" package.

And even in the smoothest of circumstances, officials make clear, the task is sufficiently complex to ensure that western pundits' persistent predictions in the past year of an "economic reform" session of the full party Central Committee will be moot until at least next spring. But major elements are essentially agreed upon.

Central planners will remain ultimately in charge, stresses Oleg Bogomolov, a prominent economist who worked under Andropov in the 1960s, and has been involved since the tail end of the Brezhnev era in Kremlin research and evaluation of other East-bloc states' experience in economic reform.

Indeed, in some senses, the idea is to "strengthen" central planning by eventually trimming the number of competing decision-makers and bureaucrats between Moscow and the local farm or factory floor.

But within this framework, the energies of central planners will be focused on working out overall targets and coordinating larger projects, with "maximum autonomy for local initiative in how these plans are implemented."

Market forces also must be strengthened. "The long-term aim," says another ranking official, "is to make economic levers, like salaries and incentives, work better than verbal exhortations, administrative pressure, sanctions or reprimands do."

And the system of grossly inefficient subsidized prices, wholesale and retail, must be entirely revamped. Again, gradually. Prices will still be set centrally, but, as Bogomolov and various other officials see it, in closer accord with true market value. Similarly, the practice of continuing to finance the many state enterprises that are either inefficient or outmoded will gradually stop.

2. Social policy. Although under an umbrella of Marxist theory, the policy machine must be supplied with far more data on just how the Soviet system works—or doesn't work—and on how Soviet people think.

The Christian Science Monitor
from July 6, 1989.

As with economic "reform," there are clear limits. Various senior officials make clear there will be no return to the brief Khrushchev-era heyday of something approaching true western-style sociological study and theory. Marxist ideology will remain the one sanctioned explanation for social phenomena.

But one official foresees a genuine invigoration of opinion polling, for instance, tracing this to a sense in the Kremlin that "especially after the Polish events, it is necessary to know true public opinion."

And the Kremlin wants more active "sociological study, on a micro level" with the aim of seeing how various economic reform levers, like incentives, might best be used to correct profound weaknesses in the economy. "In the long run," the official says, "this [kind of research] is a serious aspect in insuring the stability and development of society."

Part of this bid to activate economic- and social-policy inquiry is spilling into the official Soviet news media. In the past year, for instance, something approximating debate on approaches to economic reform has spilled into major newspapers. One editor in chief says that, early in the process, all major editors convened to discuss whether the back-and-forth should perhaps be reined in. Ultimately, he implied, that could happen. But the decision, for now, "was that the difference of views was natural and indeed better than if everyone says the same thing."

3. Foreign policy. Internationally, there is the primary need for a stable, working relationship with the United States.

Particularly during the past few years' run-up to planned deployment of new US cruise and Pershing II missiles in western Europe, the Soviets have publicly tried to emphasize their separate relations with key West European states like West Germany and France, and generally to encourage divisions between Washington and its NATO partners.

This, senior officials make clear, will continue. Moscow would be foolish, they say in so many words, not to make use of the vulnerability of western rulers to internal political pressures.

But equally, they view any all-out split within NATO as highly unlikely and stress that the inevitably crucial foreign-policy relationship for the Kremlin is that with the US.

In a nuclear age, Soviet options are limited. Thus, early in the Lebanon war of 1982, Alexander Bovin smiled when asked about western predictions of a superpower showdown.

Yes, he recalled, in the 1973 Mideast war, the superpowers had gone on nuclear alert in the run-up to its negotiated finale. But in 1982, for one thing, Israel had quickly thundered all the way to Beirut with no serious resistance.

The Arabs were in no shape to reverse that situation without direct, large-scale intervention by Moscow. "This is not a realistic possibility. . . . We are realists," Bovin remarked.

Similarly, Soviet options in replying to eventual deployment of new US missiles are constrained. Yes, various senior officials say, a "counterdeployment" of Soviet weapons is definite—first in East Germany and Czechoslovakia (a move they revealed privately before its formal announcement in October), and then "within roughly 10 minutes' striking distance of US territory."

But the counterdeployment will not go so far as basing missiles on Cuba, since this would be an obvious violation of the 1962 accord ending the Kennedy-Khrushchev showdown.

The Geneva talks on European nuclear arms are virtually sure to be cut off. But, says Valentin Falin, arms expert and former longtime ambassador to West Germany, "sooner or later" talks on Euromissiles will, of course, resume.

Mikhail Nenashev, prominent Central Committee member and editor of the official party newspaper for the Russian Republic, adds that even if the specific Euromissile negotiating format is not revived, Moscow is not about to shelve the arms negotiating process with the US.

Another official, speaking after a formal Andropov "statement" in late September that implied Moscow had "given up" on serious dealings with Washington under Mr. Reagan, cautioned against taking the words too literally.

"Reagan may manage to stay for a second term. We may have him for some years to come," the official explained. "The Andropov statement was meant to convey genuine disappointment, genuine alarm. But of course it is also a part of our pressure on each other."

Generally, three decades of post-Stalin evolution have produced an establishment of policy analysis that reflects more sophistication.

During the intermittent East European upheavals of the 1950s, the then-Yugoslavian ambassador to Moscow later suggested in his inside account of the period, no senior Soviet official expressed the slightest doubt that the trouble was completely due to western instigation.

In the Polish crisis of the early 1980s, a newer breed of ranking official, including ideological specialist Richard Kosolapov, offered a much more nuanced view.

But the Solidarity movement, he and others freely acknowledged, was clearly no mere creature of western intelligence agencies. Ten million Poles can't be subverted by the CIA.

The officials did feel strongly that Washington was stirring the pot, and that large numbers of Solidarity members were being duped by "extremists." But Lech Walesa was not included among the radicals.

And after imposition of martial law, these officials have added the obvious: that notwithstanding public Soviet and Polish statements, true "normalization" is a long way off.

On one point, even older Soviet officials joined the newer breed throughout: Direct Soviet intervention must be avoided under any circumstance short of a genuine threat of "losing" Poland to the West.

Pravda editor Viktor Afanasyev remarked at one point that intervention, after all, would mean "feeding 36 million Poles." Besides, another official said, it very likely wouldn't work. Days after martial law, he added: "Everyone on the Politburo knew there were some problems tanks wouldn't solve. . . . They realized such a step should be avoided under any—*almost* any, I should say—circumstances."

A parallel addition of nuance has occurred among domestic policy specialists. If tanks won't solve some problems, senior officials make abundantly clear, mere fine tuning of the "planning mechanism" has similar limitations on the home front.

An official recounts various moves over the past 15 years or so to resolve Soviet economic inefficiencies by "magically" coming up with a new "index" for use in setting central targets. "But each one has its problems," he says.

Another official notes that any long-term solution to Soviet economic problems must necessarily address fundamental aspects of Soviet *society*—and that, inevitably, deciding on change could prove easier than implementing it.

"In 1965 [when an earlier economic reform ultimately bogged down in bureaucracy and inertia], we spent a long time preparing, only to find out those reforms were not fully practical, or worked through.

"We still don't even have a science of political economy for Socialism. We have a system, but no laws for it. No models. And nothing to extrapolate from.

"To say we can extrapolate from the different situation of a Hungary [the main East-bloc exponent of economic reform] is not serious," the official argued. "Our country is not taught to work as in the West . . . to show initiative. This country has, historically, usually worked only under the stick."

Economist Oleg Bogomolov adds the obvious corollary: "It seems to me we find ourselves today at the very *beginning* of serious changes. While it is hard to foresee precisely what form they will take, undoubtedly the turnaround has begun."

Much the same might be said about the Soviet political system as a whole.

The Soviet-style best and brightest—the Arbatovs, Bogomolovs, Bovins, Kosolapovs, Nenashevs, Afanasyevs, and men like US affairs expert Georgi Arbatov and international relations commentator Fyodor Burlatsky—represent a major sense in which the system has already modernized. Various of these figures, as it happens, started their careers in Jacuzzi-size think tanks attached to the party Secretariat under Khrushchev—this, at the very time a younger Yuri Andropov worked there.

But interviews with them and many other, older senior officials on how the system operates serve to put the development in better perspective:

Decision-making—as opposed to the overall policy process—remains the province of a very few: the Politburo, the Central Committee's inner Secretariat and dependent staff or "apparatus," the military, and a smattering of other senior figures.

The so-called *aparatchiki*—not to mention the full members of the Politburo, Secretariat, and military command—tend more often than such policy analysts and specialists to be products of a technical or party-school education.

Mr. Andropov may be something of a special case. He did work closely with men like Arbatov, Bovine, Burlatsky and Bogomolov earlier in his career. He seems to maintain a working relationship with them based on genuine mutual respect. But he is not one of them. And as in all political systems, the leadership bases decisions only partly on objective analysis. Subjective considerations—how a decision will look to internal rivals, external foes or to the Soviet people—are very much a part of the process.

And an abiding, sometimes aggressive Russian sense of insecurity—over change at home, and "threats" from abroad—still pervades the entire system.

On most major policy decisions, in any case, there is substantial input from a greatly modernized Soviet policy-analysis machine. Mostly, the input comes in written form, or via policy-specific committees, officials say. Sometimes, individual analysts will be summoned to Secretariat or Politburo sessions.

Yet on questions of crisis, when time is short, consultation often seems to go no further than the "apparatus" of the party leadership, generally party careerists with much less of the knack for nuance than the specialized policy analysts outside.

Interestingly, and unencouragingly, the Soviet system seems often to bungle such crisis decisions. One example came in 1981 when dissident physicist Andrei Sakharov went on hunger strike to press the authorities to give his daughter-in-law an exit visa. The gut response was: "No." Only with the foreseeable buildup of western support for Sakharov, and an equally foreseeable decline in his health, did the issue get fuller airing in the Soviet policy establishment. The result: an embarrassing reversal as Moscow gave in.

Similar, but of a more serious order, was Moscow's handling of the recent Korean airliner tragedy.

If the shoot-down itself ensured a time of difficult decisions for Moscow, the public handling of the affair greatly compounded the crisis. Charted by a relatively closed circle of figures in the party leadership, the military, and the Secretariat apparatus, the initial decision was to say as little as possible.

Only later—when, officials make clear, other cogs in the policy machine were brought into play—did the Kremlin acknowledge having shot down the jet.

Alexander Bovin refuses comment on the plane episode—as did a few other officials clearly uninclined to risk too high a profile on an issue of controversy within the political elite. But another ranking official said that a day or so after the plane was downed, Bovin refused to address the issue on one of his periodic Soviet television appearances, saying he would do so only after Moscow had publicly aired a full version of the incident.

I asked one of various senior officials who were evidently unhappy with Moscow's delay why it had occurred—only weeks after top-level statements on the need to make Soviet propaganda more prompt and "convincing." The official spoke of abiding rigidities in the system and added that saying they should be corrected is not the same as being able to correct them.

There's a joke here about an elderly professor who goes to a specialist and cries: "You've got to help me! I used to be an athlete. But I can no longer run even a mile."

The specialist, puzzled, says: "Come on! You are, after all, in your 70s."

"Yes. But I have a neighbor who is in his 80s. And he says he can still run a mile. . . . "

"OK," says the specialist. "I've got the solution: You do the same: Say you can still run a mile."

How Soviets Think: The Unknown Factor in the Superpower Equation [11/18/83]

"What worries me most," says a puzzled Moscow pedestrian I asked for his thoughts on Ronald Reagan a few weeks ago, "is how little you Americans know of how we Russians think." Not just *what* the Russians think.

To understand the Soviet Union of the 1980s is, in large part, to resolve how a nation with an ever more sophisticated, subtle, and aware political elite still shoots down a civilian jumbo jet and takes six days to admit having done so.

From sidewalk to Central Committee, Russians' image of themselves differs strikingly from Americans' image of Russians.

Where Americans see strength, Russians — senior officials included — sense weakness and vulnerability.

Where the outside world sees brashness and aggressiveness, the Soviets convey a profound sense of insecurity, even fear.

The "Soviet threat" of which President Reagan speaks so often owes at least as much to weakness as to strength.

It has less to do with ballistic missiles than with a potentially destabilizing mixture of the Soviet mind-set, American rhetoric and very real problems confronting the Kremlin at home in the 1980s.

The Soviet economy does not work right — a problem for which, the leadership knows, there is simply no easy remedy.

The Soviet people are increasingly difficult to manage for a political system still not quite sure how best to rule without the extremes of the *gulag* (labor camp) or the unifying cement of world war.

The Soviet decision-making apparatus, whether civilian or military, is slowed and confused in times of crisis by abiding rigidities.

And Yuri Andropov's startling no-show at last week's Revolution Day parade in Red Square is at the least a reminder of his mortality — and at worst, a warning bell for a second possible Kremlin power transition in as many years.

At least as important as who follows Mr. Andropov, if he should pass from the scene any time soon, will be

Clockwise from top far left:
Demonstrations in Manyezh Square,
Moscow, 1990. Police in Moscow
wrestle with protesters, 1989.
Protesters in Wenceslas Square,
Prague, 1989. Demonstration for
independence, Tallinn, Estonia, 1990.

how smoothly the changeover goes. That is hard to predict. But this second, unwanted transition would benefit from far less thorough preparation than the long-awaited passing of Leonid Brezhnev a year ago.

United States assertiveness makes for potential instability. It is not so much Ronald Reagan's policies that matter in this equation—just as it is not really the Soviet military machine alone that is most threatening.

As Soviet foreign-policy specialist Alexander Bovin said at the time of last year's Israel-Lebanon crisis, the men who run Moscow are "realists." They understand—and respect—strength. They have a keen sense of lines that should not be crossed.

And the Kremlin has entered a stage in its long post-Stalin transition where, as a ranking official puts it, both domestic and international considerations have dictated a "long overdue" focus on putting the Soviets' own house in order.

For all the talk in the news media, on both sides of the Atlantic, of a "new Cold War," the first years of superpower politics under Mr. Reagan have been remarkably serene.

There has been no Cuban missile crisis. No Berlin blockade. Nor, to draw on more recent comparisons, have Cuban troops shown up in a new Angola, much less Soviet troops in a new Afghanistan.

And the Middle East showdown of a year ago involved nowhere near the level of superpower brinkmanship of the Arab-Israeli war a decade earlier.

If there are unsettling signals, they have flashed in brief crisis episodes either ignored or soon forgotten by the world outside. And to the extent that a "US factor" has entered into the equation, it has had less to do with Mr. Reagan's policies than with his vocabulary.

When Israel thundered into Lebanon in the summer of last year mere logic promptly convinced Soviet officials of their depressingly limited options. Moscow could, and did, spew invective. The Soviets could, and did, resupply a battered Syrian military. They could, and did, shift "blame" for the sorry state of affairs to crippling disarray within the Arab world.

But late in the game, irrationality took over. It is the most worrisome of responses in an age where no sane superpower would risk head-on confrontation.

It was a little, and ultimately harmless thing—a public warning to the Americans from then-President Leonid Brezhnev—but it was important for what it conveys about how Soviet leaders think and react.

What was surprising about the warning—which said that if the US sent marines to Lebanon, Moscow would "build its policy with due consideration of this fact"—was that it occurred at a time when the dispatch of marines was a clear possibility about which the Soviets knew full well they could and would do nothing.

"If it were up to me, I wouldn't have written this Brezhnev note," was the frank, morning-after remark of a ranking official who, colleagues suggested, had indeed been consulted. "If we know we can't do anything, the less words, the better.

"But there was a feeling we had to show the image of a superpower."

He and other officials later suggested this feeling was particularly acute at a time of clear "pretransition" in the Kremlin, and of almost "gloatingly anti-Soviet" rhetoric from the White House.

The Korean airliner crisis is another, and more disturbing, illustration of the complex factors at work on the Soviet mind.

For one thing, the same systemic problems that so unsettle the Kremlin about its national economy proved to work, or perhaps not work, on the Soviet Far Eastern Anti-Air Defense Command.

Even from updated US accounts it seems likely that the fighter pilots who chased and downed the crowded civilian jet had no idea what plane they were rocketing. They appear to have assumed they were after the US spy plane that had turned back toward US territory more than two hours earlier.

The same rigid centralization and disincentives for individual initiative that plague the civilian sector conspired to ensure the tragic outcome.

The Far East commander, senior officials make clear privately, contacted Moscow relatively early in the affair. Notwithstanding the public Soviet version, an official says that the local chief would not ordinarily have had the authority to order the downing of the Korean plane.

The system, it appears, simply didn't work.

Though Moscow was consulted, the Korean plane subsequently left, then reentered Soviet air space. It was not until the plane was about to leave for good, both Soviet and US accounts indicate, that its fighter-jet pursuers were in position to do anything about the "intruder."

Here, with the plane's imminent "escape" apparently ruling out full consultation with the top brass, what two senior officials separately term the "military mentality" took over. Which is worse, the local commander seems to have asked himself, downing an "enemy" plane—the natural reaction in a nation primed to assume the worst of the outside world—or taking the responsibility for letting one go?

The answer is virtually automatic in the Soviet Union—whether you are a shopkeeper, airline reservations clerk, traffic cop, construction worker or anti-air defense commander. Play it safe. Don't risk taking the initiative.

And the automatic impulse, after the fact, was to play for time, avoid any suggestion of error, then go on the propaganda offensive.

It took nearly a week for the Soviets to give their full version of events—at an unprecedented news conference by armed forces Chief of Staff Nikolai Ogarkov.

The day after Marshal Ogarkov's news conference, I showed a senior civilian official a transcript of the military chief's remarks and asked for comment.

Better late than never, was the gist of his reply. But on several points, he remained unhappy. "For instance, when Ogarkov was asked whether, if we had known there were 269 people aboard we still would have fired, I would have said flatly, 'No.' "Marshal Ogarkov's reply had been longer and a good deal less explicit.

Another senior official suggested that old Russian insecurity, translating in crisis to something approximating siege mentality, had played a part in the way the Soviets had publicly handled the affair. "Almost immediately, there was this tidal wave of accusations and propaganda from the rest of the world. . . ."

More telling were the comments of another official, a prominent member of the party Central Committee, with whom I talked at length a few days later.

We were trapped, he said in effect. We had two terrible choices: "First, the plane is let through. This would mean the Soviet Union would find itself humiliated—that the Soviet Union will tolerate anything. . . . It would put us in the position of supplicants in the superpower equation.

"Or . . . the plane is not let through. Then you [Americans] shed public tears over the incident and accuse the Soviet Union of inhumanity."

Initially, the official seemed reluctant to discuss the incident at all. When I said my main interest was to understand not so much what had happened but why, what thought processes had operated, his attitude changed. "I will tell you," he remarked, "because from your question, it is clear you see what the main issue is."

The main issue—though senior officials, as part of the issue, would not phrase it so explicitly—is that the Soviet Union senses that only huge ballistic missiles make it a superpower.

Part of this may spring from a history of intermittent invasions by a superior force, organization or civilization. Long before the Bolsheviks took power, for instance, there was the case of the Greek cleric who, on a visit to Russia, was for years barred from leaving lest he carry home tales of Russian backwardness.

But much is of more recent vintage: the West's diplomatic, and at times military, bid to isolate the Soviet régime in its first years, for instance. Or, the sense here that only a desperation of convenience produced the brief World War II alliance of the West with Soviet Russia.

A greater impulse is of even later manufacture. The immediate postwar years were ones of true Cold War. The Soviet state had, inevitably, won world recognition as a great power. But this was a nuclear age, and a rival, greater power—the US—held first a nuclear monopoly and, for a long time thereafter, commanding nuclear superiority.

The 1970s, in many ways, began ever so slowly to dent the Soviet sense of not quite being a superpower. Huge-scale rearmament produced at least "parity" with the American nuclear arsenal. Richard Nixon inaugurated a process of summitry and arms talks that—in ways more important to the Soviet psyche than a westerner might assume—formally and publicly established the Kremlin as an "equal" partner with the US on the world diplomatic stage.

True, Soviet officials knew, the Americans remained fundamentally stronger. Their economy worked better. Their military-industrial complex maintained a technology gap that Moscow finessed by reliance on enormous land-based ballistic missiles.

This sense of compensation for technology with brute muscle is one reason Moscow has so far rebuffed Reagan strategic-arms proposals that would, in one official's words, "force" Soviet modernization.

Still, time would even out the US-Soviet superpower equation, officials here supposed during détente.

But as the Soviets see it, the "psychological" gains of the postwar years have nearly evaporated.

When the Brezhnev warning on the Mideast came last year, officials suggested a catalyst that, to the American eye, seems oddly trivial: Ronald Reagan's rhetoric. Particularly galling for the Soviets had been Mr. Reagan's remark, before the British Parliament, that Marxism-Leninism would inevitably find itself on the "ash heap of history."

Trade sanctions, or efforts to that end, also played a part. But it was not so much the sanctions themselves.

These, from an economic point of view, could be circumvented. What hit home was the sense that the world's truly secure superpower felt it could treat Moscow in such a cavalier fashion.

"We are not El Salvador or Panama," a senior official remarked at one point.

Another, a few weeks ago, digressed in an interview on arms control issues: "I don't think the proper comparison in our relations with the Americans is the Cold War. . . . We have regressed even further, to a point where the very question of acceptance, recognition, of the Soviet Union is called into play."

Domestic factors are at least equally important in fueling Kremlin insecurities. Brezhnev's Mideast warning came at a time of pretransition in Moscow — or, as one official put it in the closest thing to informed local confirmation of a power struggle one is likely to get here, "a time of personal differences" within the leadership.

The Korean plane incident, similarly, seems to have occurred at a time when Yuri Andropov was not only out of Moscow for his annual vacation, but also ill.

Such junctures tend to create in Soviet officials a much keener awareness of what one of them terms "our public opinion" — a reference not to voters, obviously, but to that shared sense within the political elite of the necessity to maintain, or credibly establish, Soviet superpowerdom.

A more fundamental domestic reinforcement of superpower insecurity, meanwhile, is the Soviet people itself.

That there is no visible threat from that quarter is immaterial. The powers that be are sensitive nonetheless.

The Kremlin fundamentally mistrusts the Soviet people. Indeed, sometimes Soviet people seem to mistrust themselves. Raised in a system where authority, not the individual, makes most key decisions, Soviet citizens, particularly older ones, can more than occasionally be heard to hanker for the more "orderly" times of Stalin.

The Korean jet affair offered examples of the insecurity of the Soviet powers that be about the people over whom they have power. The delay in going public derived partly from the perceived need first to explain the incident in terms that would best play at home: the time-tested idea of a threat from foreign quarters that Moscow had no choice but to counter.

Yet even after airing the full details, the Soviet media's main thrust seemed to reflect a deep sense of uncertainty. The emphasis was on excerpting, as selectively as the Soviet version required, bits from western, and particularly American, newspapers. The tacit assumption was that the Soviet people might not take their own leadership's word at face value — but that if the *New York Times* or *Washington Post* weighed in, well, that was a different matter.

By the same token, a particularly effective and energetically pressed element in the Soviet version was to point out that the downed airplane had the most sophisticated of western guidance equipment. Translation: western technology, unlike ours, just doesn't break down.

The policy implications of abiding Soviet insecurities are not perfectly predictable.

Considered decisions — those that fully work through a modernized policy machine — may prove largely immune. A senior official argues that "economic reform" might be slowed as a result of "psychological barriers" created by Reagan-era "anti-Sovietism." But even in a political vacuum, that process would be a drawn-out affair, to say the least.

Yet also likely to come into play — indeed, already coming into play — is the leadership's approach to cultural, intellectual and artistic life. To speak of a "crack down" on artistic experimentation is a little difficult when literary, musical, dramatic or other cultural ventures are already so constrained. But the authorities can, and recently have begun to, turn the screws yet tighter.

Perhaps the most worrisome of potential effects on the home front, to go by private remarks of various officials of the post-Stalin era, involves intellectual "freedom" within the power elite. This is a key element in the overall process of "transition" from Stalinism for the Soviet system.

And at least some officials express concern that the more Kremlin insecurity is encouraged, the narrower will be the bounds of permissible inquiry and discussion for the younger analysts, specialists and advisers who have been brought into the policy machine in recent years.

Internationally, the main effects of reinforced insecurities are likely to be felt on issues of crisis, where time considerations severely limit the extent to which decisions are filtered through the policy machine.

Marshal Ogarkov was careful, in his news conference, to discourage western suggestions that the Korean airliner incident raised the possibility of similar foul-ups on a nuclear scale.

Lech Walensa (top left) speaks at
Solidarity rallies in Gdansk and Gadania,
Poland, 1989.

A prominent Party Central Committee member added privately that the Kremlin's failure to use the hot line or other channels to get in touch with the Americans before shooting at the "spy plane" would not apply should a nuclear crisis arise.

But he did note: "Without doubt, I think that what the present US administration says and does makes for much higher tension. It creates a hair-trigger atmosphere. . . . Some accidents, whether such as the plane incident or others, become inevitable."

For some Soviet officials, particularly the professional propagandists, such remarks are the transparent preface to a charge that, much to the dismay of a peace-loving Kremlin, a "madman" named Ronald Reagan has shredded détente and nudged the world toward a nuclear abyss.

The officials do not explain why, without Ronald Reagan but with a peculiarly Russian mind-set that seems to have survived détente largely intact, the Soviets both positively identified, and opened fire upon, another Korean civilian airliner over Soviet territory in 1978.

More interesting are the remarks of those ranking officials who view the "decline of détente" as no simple creature of Mr. Reagan and acknowledge that Soviet actions, like the invasion of Afghanistan, have played a part.

Their argument is not so much that it is time to oust Mr. Reagan and magically resurrect the embryo stage of the Nixon-Kissinger era, although that would certainly please them.

"What I think is necessary, above all," says one such official, "is a return to the idea of equality . . . of acceptance of the idea that the Soviet Union is not a country to be dictated to by the Americans."

"This factor of acceptance is vitally important," argues another official. "Reagan, in this sense, really knows how to hit the sensitive psychological button here. . . .

"I would not speak in terms of restoring détente with the Americans. I would use the word 'normalization,' in the sense that it is abnormal for two nuclear powers to have the relationship we now do. . . . Maybe for Israel and the Arabs it is normal, but not for the US and the Soviet Union."

I asked one official in effect how Moscow had expected US officials to view moves like the dispatch of Cuban troops to Angola in 1975—for the Americans, one of the first big cracks in the structure of détente.

For the Soviets, in fact, the "crack" had come earlier —with the Americans' bid explicitly and publicly to link most-favored-nation status in trade to freer emigration rights for Soviet Jews.

But the official said the Angola crisis was not, as some in the West have suggested, a conscious Kremlin reaction to the emigration dispute. "I would say only that if Soviet-American relations had been stronger, it is possible, probable, there would have been no Cubans in Angola. . . .

"There is no direct link. But generally, bad relations between the superpowers contribute to an environment where critical options, like the Cubans in Angola or us in Afghanistan, are used."

In the fall of 1988, The Christian Science Monitor *launched both a monthly magazine and a nightly television news program. The following articles from the magazine provided insight into some of the richer cultural dimensions in the Soviet Union.*

Marshall Goldman is Professor of Economics, Wellesley College, Associate Director of the Russian Research Center, Harvard University, and author of Gorbachev's Challenge: Economic Reform in the Age of High Technology. *Professor Goldman's article appeared in the prototype issue of the magazine.*

The Amazing Gorbachev and His High-Risk Reforms

By Marshall I. Goldman

When I was last in Moscow a typically sardonic Russian story was making the rounds: A foreign visitor is standing next to a Muscovite watching the annual November 7 parade pass through Red Square. The tanks clank by. Then the giant missiles. Then goose-stepping elite soldiers. Suddenly a platoon of men in business suits with briefcases marches past the reviewing stand.

"Who are they?" asks the visitor.

"Those," replies Ivan Ivanovich, "those are our most destructive weapon of all. They're bureaucrats from GOSPLAN. They can destroy the entire economy without firing a shot."

And they could destroy the celebrated economic reform program of Soviet leader Mikhail Gorbachev.

After all, it is those briefcase-carriers—actually several hundred thousand bureaucrats in Moscow ministries and GOSPLAN (the central planning agency)—who have thwarted the reform plans of previous Soviet leaders since Stalin. It was Stalin, in his long reign, who established the massive central planning system.

Why should anyone care, besides Gorbachev?

Because Gorbachev is the kind of forward-looking executive who holds the key to an optimistic scenario for Soviet-American relations during the coming months and years. If the bureaucrats beat him, his agreement with President Reagan to blow up their countries' mid-range nuclear weapons could be a bang followed by a whimper in terms of progress toward peace, trade, and lowered distrust.

Allies become enemies. Enemies become allies. Down through the centuries many such realignments have occurred.

Sometimes the enemies-turned-allies are the super-powers of their day. Napoleonic France and Britain, for example. Or Germany and Britain. Thrice-warring Germany and France. The United States and Germany. The US and Japan.

Can it be that a switch from opponent to relatively friendly competitor will occur between the United States and the Soviet Union?

That blockbuster question is really the sum of a lot of other questions. Answers will affect the lives of almost everyone reading this. They will do so more extensively than all but a few other global matters.

So let's take a look at the promise and the pitfalls in the way the Soviet leader operates. On this depends much of what will happen after those first missiles have been blown up.

Gorbachev's strategy, since he took power three years ago, has included a series of daring moves to outflank resistance. Even before he came to office, he and his mentor, former KGB head Yuri Andropov, began getting rid of deadwood from the era of Leonid Brezhnev's leadership. The old guard was replaced by Gorbachev loyalists. But even some of these have come to value their perks and to argue for going slow on his reforms.

Gorbachev has also used his skill as Great Communicator, Eastern Model, to win the backing of intellectuals and news media leaders for his restructuring of the Soviet system. And he has used that communicator skill abroad to generate pride and momentum at home.

The trouble is such popularity abroad does not always translate into honor for the prophet at home. His restructuring program poses a threat to housing, food, and transport subsidies of many blue-collar workers. Worse, it threatens the jobs of tens of thousands of those workers, in addition to the jobs of the Moscow

bureaucrats. Pride in a dynamic leader on the world stage doesn't count for much when it runs up against worry about job security.

But Gorbachev plunges on—even when his opponents score points against his protégés or erode his reforms. No matter what historians ultimately say about Mikhail Gorbachev, one thing is clear: this is a man who is determined to do it his way. Moreover, in large part he did it his way at least through his first three years as General Secretary. Almost single-handedly, he imposed the concept of *glasnost* (openness to disclose and debate shortcomings) on Soviet society. Indeed this was one of those rare occasions when a purely national phenomenon became a worldwide event. *Glasnost* has now entered almost every one of the world's languages.

Similarly Gorbachev deserves a significant share of the credit for reducing world tensions between the United States and the Soviet Union. His mentor, Yuri Andropov, had ordered Soviet negotiators to leave the US/Soviet bargaining table in Geneva. While officially it was Konstantin Chernenko who ordered the Soviet negotiators back to the Geneva arms talks in January 1985, in fact (or at least as far as we can tell) the decision to return was Gorbachev's, since by late 1984 Chernenko already had become bedridden. This reversal of tactics subsequently led to a remarkable relaxation of tension and ultimately the signing of the historic Intermediate-Range Nuclear Forces (INF) Treaty to eliminate mid-range nuclear weapons.

Thus both within the Soviet Union and in the world at large, Gorbachev's Soviet Union has become a more tolerant and compliant society. This is in marked contrast to the rigid and disruptive force it was before.

Just as there are those who doubt that Gorbachev is for real, there are those who have always insisted that the Soviet Union was a model society and that we on the outside have been the troublemakers. But *glasnost* undermines this rosy view. Now more and more Soviet officials (even those who formerly led the propaganda campaign) are beginning to concede openly that, more often than not, the Soviet Union has been the one at fault. Nonetheless, in this new candid era, these Soviet officials continue to remind us that the Soviet leadership, including Gorbachev, has no intention of rejecting everything the Soviet Union has stood for in the past. Thus the Communist Party is to retain its monopoly, the Soviet police their control, and agencies like GOSPLAN and the ministries much of their influence.

Yet even if Gorbachev's reforms fall short of turning the Soviet Union into a competitor that plays by the

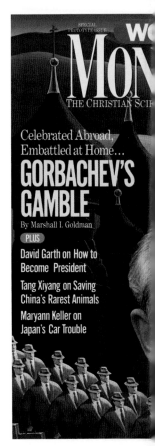

Clockwise from top left:
Latvian parliament in session. Anti-Communist, pro-democracy demonstration in Manyezh Square, Moscow 1990. Prototype edition of World Monitor, The Christian Science Monitor **monthly magazine. Posters for peace at May Day parade in Red Square, May 1989. Election rally with candidates for Congress of People's Deputies.**

rules, the changes he is ordaining have the potential for creating a very new international situation. There is now at least a fair chance that the nuclear arms race which has burdened the world for more than 40 years may be reversed. The actual destruction of shorter- and medium-range missile launchers that President Reagan and Gorbachev agreed to under the INF agreement is, as noted before, a historic breakthrough. There is even the possibility that, once begun, the process will continue.

Given the level of distrust that has been built up over the decades, neither of the world powers is likely to enter into an all-out embrace of the other based on the INF Treaty alone. But now that INF has been agreed to, the path toward other arms control agreements becomes a smoother one. Two of the biggest hurdles to any American-Soviet agreement have been addressed: 1. Gorbachev has agreed to very far-reaching verification measures. 2. He has openly acknowledged that there are asymmetrical balances between the two sides, more often than not in the Soviet Union's favor.

Thus the INF agreement calls for the US and the Soviet Union to exchange vast amounts of detailed data that heretofore spies would gladly have given their lives to steal. Now the Soviet Union has even willingly turned material over to *The New York Times* to publish.

Similarly, the Soviets have agreed to destroy missiles carrying a total of three to four times as many warheads as those on missiles to be destroyed by the US. While nothing in the American-Soviet relationship follows inevitably, the progress in verification and the precedent of uneven cuts significantly improve the process of reaching agreements about the reduction of long-range missiles (ICBMs) and conventional weapons. That progress should also make it easier to limit underground testing. As we begin to move toward agreement on these treaties, the momentum seems to be building. Conceivably, this may also increase the incentive for the Soviet Union to follow through on the pledge to withdraw its troops from Afghanistan, despite delays. That, at least, is the hopeful scenario.

Admittedly, much of this still is wishful thinking. But there is a sense of movement that did not exist before. It is not perfect. But at Gorbachev's level, at least, there is a degree of openness that we did not see even in the days when the ebullient Nikita Khrushchev was at the Soviet helm.

As recently as two years ago, who would have thought that a Gorbachev would have permitted a widely known dissident like Andrei Sakharov to read a critical statement about human rights in the Kremlin itself? Or, for that matter, have allowed Armenians emboldened by *glasnost* to demand, however unsuccessfully, the return of territory now included in the Soviet Republic of Azerbaijan? Or have tolerated demonstrations by Latvians, Lithuanians and Estonians in the capitals of Riga, Vilnius and Talinin protesting Soviet annexation of their nations? And even have allowed Tatars to demonstrate in Red Square to complain about their displacement from their homeland?

During a visit to Moscow in June 1987, I personally was asked to sign a petition protesting a plan to cut down a 200-year-old elm tree. According to the demonstrators, this was a tree that had shaded some of the Soviet Union's most revered poets and writers. Thinking for a moment that I was back in Harvard Square, I signed immediately. Only later did I come to appreciate what a change such citizen protest represents for Moscow.

Similarly, who would have dreamed that the Soviets would begin to allow an outflow of young and presumably still somewhat impressionable undergraduates, so that they might enroll for the year as regular students in colleges like Wellesley, Sarah Lawrence and Middlebury? There is no immediate likelihood that the number of Soviet undergraduate and graduate students enrolled in American colleges will in any way approach the 20,000 students in the US from China. Nonetheless it is undoubtedly the case that a major decision has been made to permit increased, although not completely free, access by Soviet students and officials to the West.

Abel Aganbegyan, the bold economist who is one of Gorbachev's main advisers on semi-Capitalist economic reform, was rarely allowed to leave the Soviet Union during the Brezhnev years. But in 1987 he visited, among other places, the United States, Britain and Austria. Already this year Aganbegyan has finished another trip to the US. This time, however, his arrangements were made by an avant-garde educational organization, the Esalen Institute in California, and included a stop as far from Esalen as the venerable Council on Foreign Relations in New York.

Aganbegyan's access to the Soviet leader tells us something about Gorbachev and how he tackles a problem. When Gorbachev was called to Moscow and put in charge of Soviet agriculture by the Central Committee of the Communist Party, he found that the situation was much more serious than he had imagined. Like John F. Kennedy, with his widespread use of scholars, Gorbachev sought to find a new approach by calling in some academic specialists, including Tatyania Zaslavs-

kaia who had written about Soviet agriculture. She in turn included some of her colleagues from the Siberian Division of the Soviet Academy of Sciences.

Aganbegyan was one of those invited. As Gorbachev's responsibilities were enlarged by Yuri Andropov, so was the scope of Gorbachev's seminars. Aganbegyan was finally asked to move to Moscow in 1985 and head an Economic Commission of the Academy of Sciences. From this base he meets frequently with Gorbachev and other members of the Politburo. Aganbegyan was called on in particular to provide advice about a series of key reforms such as the Law of the Enterprise which was adopted in mid-1987. He was also asked to accompany Gorbachev to the United States for the December 1987 summit meeting. Gorbachev wanted Aganbegyan to do some preliminary scouting to see what American businessmen were thinking and what they might ask Gorbachev at a subsequent meeting at the Soviet Embassy.

There is also stirring in the field of US-Soviet trade. The sums involved are still modest. But, after a sharp drop in trade following the invasion of Afghanistan, American-Soviet trade negotiators are once again beginning to seek each other out.

Washington's grain embargo and boycott of Soviet imports at the time was costly to both sides. So neither party wants to move too fast for fear of a similar loss in the future.

Now the Soviet Union has begun to authorize joint ventures with Capitalist firms on Soviet territory. The Capitalist partner can hold as much as 49 percent of the equity. So far, there are relatively few such ventures (about 20 as of the beginning of 1988). Only two firms are American; one, Combustion Engineering of Stamford, Connecticut. CE will hold 49 percent interest in an enterprise that will assemble advanced factory control systems for 210 Soviet petroleum product plants. CE will be compensated for its efforts with a share of the increased petroleum output. It will then sell the petrol products outside the Soviet Union.

Other proposed American joint ventures include partnerships that would produce herbicides, diesel engines and pizza. Madison Avenue ad agencies have also sought contracts to do Soviet TV commercials.

While modest in comparison to the several thousand joint and wholly owned foreign ventures that exist in China, Moscow's joint venture program does reflect improved Soviet relations not only with the United States but with the world at large.

The decision to allow Capitalists to operate within the Soviet Union represents a major reversal of the

Marxist-Stalinist ideology. More important, to achieve a payoff, the Soviets have to commit themselves to an extended period of relative tranquility and stability. At the first sign of overseas adventurism or major domestic repression by Soviet authorities, American firms are likely to curb not only the flow of capital investment but the flow of technology. Much of the rationale for the formation of such ventures thus would be lost. Their whole purpose is to permit continuous upgrading of technology and skills.

Such constant modernization has not occurred when complete western factories were bought outright. The vast majority of past Soviet purchases of foreign equipment quickly became obsolete—in effect, museum pieces. For example, a Soviet factory recently bought some much-needed American computer equipment, only to leave it unused in boxes for lack of trained installers and maintenance workers. The Soviet system does not provide an incentive to upgrade such equipment. The Soviets therefore hope that their foreign partners will provide that incentive. If these foreign ventures were to be aborted in midstream because of tension the Soviets cause, they obviously would suffer.

Such agreements and investments constitute a potentially powerful force toward improvements in international relations. If signed and honored, they could lead to further relaxation and increases in trade, and additional cutbacks in military expenditures. Gorbachev's team in the Soviet Union and the current majority in the United States Congress would divert resources that now go for military expenditures to the civilian sector and to budget reductions. It is even possible that if tensions between the United States and the Soviet Union subside enough, both countries might jointly begin to redirect their foreign policy frustrations at some third party or parties—such as Iran.

But the US-Soviet relationship is hardly the same as the current French-German military and commercial cooperation between old enemies. After all, even though France and Germany have often fought over a common border, for the last 43 years they have also shared a common economic and political system. In contrast, despite Soviet *glasnost* and debate over "democratization," the Soviet Union still has a long way to go before its system resembles a western democracy. Soviet police are still very much in control, which means there are still fixed limits to what is and is not permitted.

The sudden uncorking of *glasnost* may actually increase political instability inside the Soviet Union. If carried to extremes, it could even set off some second thoughts in the West about the wisdom of closer ties with the Soviet Union. The problem is that more openness or less censorship does not necessarily mean that only Soviet liberals will speak out.

After an initial period of hesitation, *glasnost* has been marked by a darker and more threatening phenomenon. Some spokesmen for groups like Pamyat—extremist Russian nationalists—have now begun to call for a turning away from the West. They argue for a return to what they see as their roots. That usually means the adaptation of values represented by Russian peasants, and some form of Russian orthodoxy. Some, even further to the right, go so far as to reject Russian orthodoxy because of what they see as the Judaic influence in the early church. To the extent that the Soviet leadership is seen to share or even tolerate such views, American-Soviet relations will undoubtedly be adversely affected.

Even liberalization, if carried to the extreme, could serve to complicate the way to closer US-Soviet relations. Too much liberalization coming too fast is likely to cause backlash and reaction in the Soviet Union just as the Solidarity labor movement did in Poland. Americans are unlikely to be quite as eager for US-Soviet rapprochement if the authorities decide to launch a massive crackdown on dissidents and refuseniks.

What will happen if Gorbachev's economic reforms, which made him so attractive to the West in the first place, are rejected or if they spark riots at home? Just as he has been widely praised for his determination to seek such reforms, so Gorbachev will be criticized for any failures that occur.

To the extent that the reforms set off inflation and shortages, there are likely to be massive protests. If those protesting what they regard as political slights (such as a prohibition against speaking their non-Russian language, or a failure to curb pollution) are joined by those suddenly unemployed or convulsed by soaring prices, Gorbachev may find himself having to deal with real social disintegration. This would be certain to precipitate a political crackdown as well as a move away from the West, which would inevitably be accused of seeking to undermine Soviet authority. Given the magnitude of the varied difficulties facing Soviet economic reformers, it is hard to see how the reforms can be successfully implemented.

Another likely source of tension between the Soviet Union and the United States is Eastern Europe. Gorbachev's call for *glasnost* and *perestroika* (restructuring) has not been confined to the Soviet Union. What happens if some of the Eastern Europeans take him at his word? This could also cause political turmoil, particularly among some of the more conservative members of the bloc, such as the German Democratic Republic and Czechoslovakia.

Already there has been a protest by 10,000 citizens in Hungary, and a more violent protest by as many as 20,000 in Romania. What if the local authorities suddenly find themselves unable to control such unrest? What will it mean, not only for Gorbachev's reform efforts, but his credibility and his relations with the West if he finds it necessary to send in Soviet troops? Yet if he fails to act decisively, would this serve to spark similar unrest throughout other East European countries? In the same way, will he dare to tear down the Berlin Wall? This would ultimately be the true test of a change in Soviet and East European political control. But if the Wall were to go, there would be a flood of refugees again.

It would seem very probable therefore that there must be some limit to the fruits of *glasnost*, an in turn to a fully developed relationship between the United States and the Soviet Union. The enemies may move toward more normal big-power rivalry—but not to anything approaching alliance.

Finally, even if the Soviet Union should manage to accommodate itself to a continuing process of benevolent *glasnost*, not only within its own borders but in Eastern Europe as well, there are still likely to be continuing tensions with the US.

Much of the past trouble between the two countries has arisen because of their mutual suspicion of each other's intentions in the Third World.

Often as not, these conflicts arose not because of any scheming or ideological crusading by one side or the other but because a purely local feud grew to threaten a change in the status quo. Such balance-of-power conflicts arise even when both superpowers are trying to cooperate—when neither side is looking for aggravation. The US and USSR are simply sucked into the struggle.

Because of these hazards American-Soviet relations still have a long way to go before they become as routine as US-European or US-Japanese relations. But there is no doubt that they have moved a long way since 1985. Should the positive trends continue—particularly the Soviet move to economic and political liberalization—we are indeed likely to see more arms control efforts and more trade, even if that trade must be financed with more credits. Already we have begun to see what

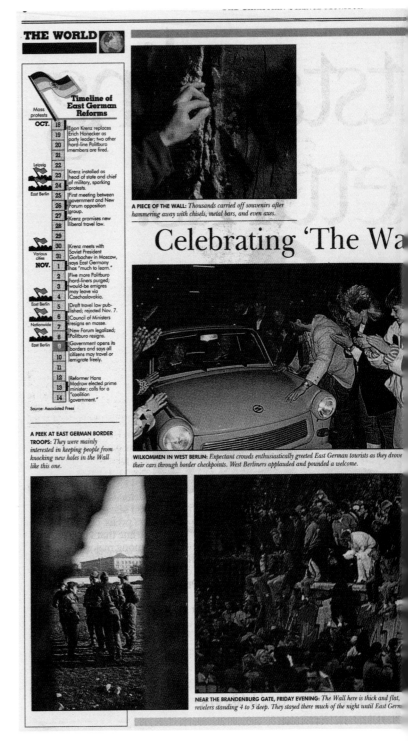

THE WORLD

Timeline of East German Reforms

Mass protests

OCT. 18
19 Egon Krenz replaces Erich Honecker as party leader; two other hard-line Politburo members are fired.
20
21
22
Leipzig 23 Krenz installed as head of state and chief of military, sparking protests.
24
East Berlin 25 First meeting between government and New Forum opposition group.
26
27 Krenz promises new liberal travel law.
28
29
Various cities 30 Krenz meets with Soviet President Gorbachev in Moscow, says East Germany has "much to learn."
31
NOV. 1
2 Five more Politburo hard-liners purged; would-be emigres may leave via Czechoslovakia.
3
4
East Berlin 5 Draft travel law published; rejected Nov. 7.
6 Council of Ministers resigns en masse.
Nationwide 7 New Forum legalized; Politburo resigns.
8
East Berlin 9 Government opens its borders and says all citizens may travel or emigrate freely.
10
11
12 Reformer Hans Modrow elected prime minister; calls for a "coalition government."
13
14

Source: Associated Press

A PEEK AT EAST GERMAN BORDER TROOPS: *They were mainly interested in keeping people from knocking new holes in the Wall like this one.*

A PIECE OF THE WALL: *Thousands carried off souvenirs after hammering away with chisels, metal bars, and even axes.*

Celebrating 'The Wa

WILKOMMEN IN WEST BERLIN: *Expectant crowds enthusiastically greeted East German tourists as they drove their cars through border checkpoints. West Berliners applauded and pounded a welcome.*

NEAR THE BRANDENBURG GATE, FRIDAY EVENING: *The Wall here is thick and flat, revelers standing 4 to 5 deep. They stayed there much of the night until East Germ*

The Christian Science Monitor
from November 16, 1989.

Berliners from both East and West spent the weekend at the world's largest block party, reveling in the end of a 28-year separation. More than one million attended.

's' Demise

By Mark M. Sheehan
Special to The Christian Science Monitor

— WEST BERLIN —

THE woman looked down and brushed self-consciously at tears she could not stop. She didn't see that her husband and many of the other East Germans walking ahead and in back of her were doing the same thing.

The couple had just stepped across Sandkrug ridge into West Berlin and a crowd of hundreds was cheering them on as they continued to walk west. They laughed because it was so easy and then they waved to the West Berliners who had come to welcome them.

"I just want to see it," said the young grandmother, getting at best only a blurry view of West Berlin. A grown daughter guided the weeping woman by the elbow while pushing her own daughter ahead in a stroller.

"We want to take a ride in a taxi!" said the daughter.

"We waited 28 years for a ride in a taxi," said

it a perfect platform for West and East German e sprayed them – lightly – with water cannon.

Photos by
R. Norman Matheny,
Staff photographer

the grandmother. By now she was laughing.

"First, I just want to look," said a young man when asked what he wanted to do first. He and his girlfriend had crossed through the checkpoint several minutes before, but were still hugging each other.

"I want to see the Brandenburg Gate," he finally decided.

"What for? We've seen that plenty of times," said his girlfriend.

"Not from this side," he answered.

The celebration of East Germany's newly opened border began Thursday night at the Brandenburg Gate. Symbolically it was the perfect place for East and West Berliners to meet. The gate is the symbol of a city and the Wall, the symbol of the cold war and a divided Europe.

For practical considerations, too, it was the best place to celebrate. With the exception of the semicircle around the Brandenburg Gate, most of the Berlin Wall has a rounded concrete top. It's difficult to stand on. But at the Brandenburg the wall is wide and flat.

From Thursday night until Saturday morning, thousands of people climbed onto the Wall. The carnival of singing, chanting, and smashing at concrete with hammers was the perfect media event. Even after East German border troops drove the crowds from the top of the Wall early Saturday morning, huge numbers of people flocked to the gate.

Oblivious to the stares of the 200 border troops standing above them, people hammered away at the wall throughout the day. They pulled out small chunks with their hands, or used rocks and metal bars to loosen larger chunks. Especially prized were chunks with paint on them.

South of the Brandenburg Gate at Potsdamer Platz, a new checkpoint was being made. The East Germans planned the opening for early Sunday morning, but that didn't stop a large crowd from gathering at the spot Saturday afternoon.

One young man straddled the round-topped Wall like a horse. He waved to the crowd and laughed as police from both sides of Berlin used bullhorns to ask him to get down. Finally he raised his right hand, shouted "Freiheit" (freedom), and climbed back down.

Rattling, smoky Trabants rolled slowly through the border crossing, impeded less by red tape than by a cheering mass of West Berliners and off-duty US servicemen.

Last weekend Berlin welcomed over a million guests to an East-West freedom party.

'FREIHEIT' (FREEDOM): *This young West Berliner at the Potsdamer Platz finally agreed to come down after gentle persuasion by both East German border guards and West German police. In his hands are the hammer and chisel he used to make his own mark on the Wall.*

Cracks in the Wall

was once considered to be unattainable flexibility by the Soviets in some cultural exchanges.

From my personal perspective, it is particularly astonishing to see the sudden eagerness of senior Soviet scholars to visit or work at Harvard's Russian Research Center. At one time most Soviet officials would routinely refuse to have anything to do with the center. We were regarded as an outpost of the CIA. Now, recognizing not only that those charges were never true but that scholars at the center have had some interesting insights into Soviet problems, more Soviet officials have asked specifically to visit us. One recent week we had as many as three different sets of visitors. The center has become a Niagara Falls for Soviet scholars.

The case of Boris Yeltsin raises one last warning flag. Yeltsin is the Gorbachev protégé who was ousted from his post on the ruling Politburo last fall. He was the equivalent Mayor of Moscow—a vocal supporter of Gorbachev reform, a Mayor Koch-like figure riding the subways and popping up everywhere to chat with citizens in the manner of his mentor. Yeltsin's expulsion and humiliation show that Gorbachev's road to reform is not a smooth one at the top leadership level. There are many who are convinced that the attack on Yeltsin was a thinly disguised attack on Gorbachev himself. How many Yeltsin-like setbacks can Gorbachev absorb before he himself is threatened?

US-Soviet tensions have been reduced much more quickly, and the relationship extended much further, than almost anyone could have predicted. Yet the inescapable fact is that this is largely the initiative of one man. As the two countries reach more understandings and sign more treaties, they should be able to create a basis for a more durable relationship independent of any single personality, but until that happens we must continue to depend on the fate and abilities of Gorbachev. That may be more than enough, and it is certainly better than anything we have had for some while. But it does suggest that for the time being, at least, the association remains a fragile one.

Harvey Cox's books range from The Secular City *(1965) to* Religion in the Secular City *(1984). Mr. Cox is a professor of divinity at the Harvard Divinity School, he is also an ordained American Baptist minister. He has lectured in many countries. He writes further about religion in the Soviet Union in his forthcoming book,* Many Mansions: A Christian's Encounters with Other Faiths *(Beacon Press).*

By Harvey Cox

During the early summer of last year I found myself living in Moscow with time on my hands and an unexpected question on my mind. Was a new representation of Jesus—a "Soviet Christ"—emerging among the people in the atheistic state around me? The question had been raised by reports of a "return to religion" among Russian intellectuals — and by a sensational new novel with a Christlike hero. I didn't know that my search for answers would begin quite as it did.

I had come to the Soviet Union with my wife, a historian of Russia, who was here as an exchange scholar. Since I had little to do myself, I visited historical sites and museums, walking through the streets and markets and exploring the endless reaches of the subway system.

One day I decided to stroll through the inner court of the Kremlin grounds — which are open to the public — to see the splendid churches, now museums, which date far back into the imperial period.

I spent several hours in the Uspensky (Assumption) Cathedral, the Blagoveshchensky (Annunciation) Cathedral, and the Cathedral of the Archangel. I was stunned, overwhelmed by the sense of an interrupted but still living history, and by the brooding dignity of the icons, especially the severe renditions of Jesus. I understood how these images of religious figures — so often simple paintings on wood — could themselves be considered sacred by Russian believers. Here was a living tradition entwined with the Russian Orthodox Church, a branch of that Eastern Orthodox Church which officially separated from the Roman Catholic Church more than a thousand years ago and remains, along with it and Protestantism, one of the world's three main streams of Christianity.

Eventually I walked out into the bright sunlight of the courtyard. As I did, a young Russian man who appeared to be about 30 introduced himself to me in excellent English. He said he had noticed that I was a foreigner, probably an American, and that, instead of rushing past the "holy icons," as he called them, I seemed to be absorbed in them. Was I by any chance a believer?

At first I did not know how to respond. Was this the beginning of a KGB entrapment? Did he want to buy my running shoes? I hesitated. But something in his straightforward manner and earnest smile put me at ease. I told him I was in fact a believer, and that I had indeed sensed something compelling about the icons.

We started to stroll as we talked, first past the statue of Lenin, then out the gate, into Red Square, and on to the Arbat, the picturesque old quarter of Moscow. He was a television writer, he told me, and he'd come to the Kremlin to prepare a show. With an hour free he had wandered into the Uspensky and noticed me. After we chatted a while, I ventured my question. What did he know about the widely reported "return to religion" among Russian intellectuals? Was it really going on? Was it widespread? What did it mean?

He stopped walking to answer. "I suspect," he said, "that I would have to be counted among them." I told him I was very much interested, not just objectively but personally. I said that I wanted not just to talk with people about this phenomenon but to speak mainly with those for whom the quest for a new spirituality had become in some way their own. Could he help?

My new acquaintance, whom I'll call "Yuri," told me he had to get back to work then (he was already an hour late, he said), but he made a date to meet me at the Novodevichy Convent the following day, which was Sunday, for vespers. At that time, he said, he would introduce me to a friend of his who was exactly the right person to help me.

For a moment I felt like a character in a novel instead of an inquirer about the theme of a very controversial one: Soviet writer Chingiz Aitmatov's *The Executioner's Block*. In it a pious Russian Orthodox seminarian named Abdias Kallistratov, the son of a priest, is expelled from the theological school because he asks too many questions. Deprived of his original vocation, Abdias begins to work for a Komsomol (Communist youth) newspaper. After a series of adventures he is arrested when he declines to join a campaign to exterminate excess antelopes. He is tried in Stalinist style as an "enemy of the state." He is finally put to death at 33. Through it all Abdias retains a kind of moral simplicity and purity. He never loses what the author calls "his interior flame."

Aitmatov's book caused something of a sensation in the Soviet Union, and the debate it touched off has tested the limits of *glasnost*, the openness of discussion proclaimed by Soviet leader Mikhail Gorbachev.

Some critics compared Abdias to Prince Myshkin in Dostoevsky's *The Idiot* — a traditional Russian Christ figure but this time one of Soviet vintage. He is mercilessly squeezed between a rigid church and an atheistic state, institutions that Aitmatov characterizes as twin "mastodons." Other critics called the book jumbled and derivative. Still others saw it as proof positive that

the current generation of writers has gone soft on religion.

But no one denied that Aitmatov's question was becoming unavoidable: Is the whole idea of a "Soviet Christ" an oxymoron, as contradictory as "hot ice" or "cold heat"? Or is a new representation of Jesus emerging here, as it has elsewhere, one combining the classic features of the Russian Christ that we know through the Orthodox icons and through Dostoevsky with the experience of 70 years of Soviet history?

I thought Yuri's friend might help me understand. And on Sunday I decided I would go to the Novodevichy vespers, though without any real hope of seeing Yuri. But when I climbed out of my taxi, he was there, standing with his friend, a slightly younger man. He introduced me, and right away whatever doubts I had harbored about whether people would want to talk with me about this topic began to melt. I spent my remaining weeks in Moscow doing little else.

By the time I left I had met poets, editors, translators, screenwriters and musicians — enough different people to persuade me that the search for a Soviet Christ was neither ephemeral nor faddish. It was real, though amorphous, sometimes tentative and still very fragile. It meant different things to different people.

Perhaps the best way to convey a feel for it all is to introduce some of the seekers and believers I talked with. I have changed their names not to protect them from official harassment, which none of them thought likely, but to respect the privacy of people who were willing to speak quite openly about what is after all a very personal matter.

I stayed clear of both official interpreters and official church leaders. I didn't want either the government or the ecclesial line. Though my Russian is weak, the mainly well-educated people I talked with either knew some English or had a friend who could translate.

I started with Ivan, whom I met through Yuri's friends. Along with Ivan's wife, a teenage son, and a daughter of eight years, we met in Ivan's apartment where he invited me to share a late supper.

Ivan was a professional translator of poetry from modern European languages into Russian. A square, handsome man in his middle 40s with a sprinkling of gray hair around the temples, he had an intense expression in his eyes but a warm and ready smile. He told me he had been raised in a completely nonreligious family with a Jewish ethnic background. When he became personally concerned about a religious quest, he found himself attracted to Russian Orthodoxy, in part because there seemed to be little else available, and also because it suited his aesthetic temperament. Even as a boy, he told me, he had always loved the icons.

You could see he still did. There were icons on the walls of every room in the apartment, but with a special cluster in the corner of the main living room where, as is often the case in Moscow apartments, we gathered around the table for supper. Ivan invited me to join the entire family in standing to face the icons while they repeated the Lord's Prayer in Russian, crossing themselves in the Orthodox right-to-left style as they said "amen." After the meal of soup, ground meat cakes, fresh radishes, and savory black bread with butter and sour cream (there was no alcohol), Ivan and I talked about his pilgrimage.

Ivan still loved the icons, but as our conversation unfolded it became clear to me that his faith was part and parcel of a wider affection for "tradition" that he believed was an indispensable component in a truly human life. For example, when we talked about the religious denominations in the West, with which he was somewhat familiar, he asked me with a puzzled look if it was true that there was really a debate going on about the ordination of women to the priesthood. When I told him there was, and that in fact some churches already ordained women, he shook his head. He did not agree with such "departures."

After we'd been talking for a few minutes I began to sense a certain awkwardness in Ivan. Perhaps he recognized how often a traditional Orthodox believer can sound intransigent and even condescending to religious believers from other traditions. There was an uneasy pause.

The conversation turned to American jazz, and Ivan brightened. Leaning back in his chair, he plunged into an animated discussion of his early love affair with Duke Ellington and Charlie Parker and of his continuing enjoyment of American big band music. He told me that he had understood completely when a prominent Russian poet told him that the most memorable moment of a visit to America was when he met saxophonist Gerry Mulligan in a nightclub in New York.

After the discussion about jazz had run its course I asked Ivan whether he thought the "return" of Soviet intellectuals to religion was real. He told me that, although part of it certainly bore the marks of a fad, there was also something deeper and longer lasting going on. He added in slightly regretful tones that he was not at all sure the Russian Orthodox church was in any position to respond to this interest.

I listened carefully. It was the first time he had voiced even a hint of criticism about his church. Why, he wondered, was there not something to supplement the liturgy and the music that would inform people about the history and theology of Orthodoxy?

"What the priest told me," he said, "was 'the icons teach us all we need to know.'" He punctuated the sentence with his hands thrown up in a gesture that could have meant either that he wished the priest had said more, or that the statement revealed something of the mystery and genius of Orthodoxy.

The day after my conversation with Ivan I met Elena, an acquaintance he had called on my behalf, at a restaurant in downtown Moscow. A tall woman in her early 50s, she wore a tailored suit, white blouse, and had her graying auburn hair in a ponytail. Seated at a comfortable table in the wooden-beamed dining room, Elena thoughtfully ordered what turned out to be the best meal I ate in Moscow — borsch, salad and pork chops with broccoli and potatoes.

Elena wanted to talk about the philosophical and moral question of "betrayal." She told me that she and many other writers from the Stalin years became painfully aware that tyranny is possible only if people are willing to inform on each other, sometimes in large ways but often in small ones. Repression relies on such informers.

This was the reason, she said, that she was drawn time and again to the story of Peter's denial of Jesus, about which she had recently written a short play. She smiled and said the director told her "that he was aware of the need to use the new liberty of *glasnost* but was not sure that the Moscow theater public was ready for a play drawn directly from the Bible."

By the time I spoke with Elena I had discovered that Aitmatov's novel and his question about the possibility of a Soviet Christ functioned as something of an inkblot test in my conversations with Moscow intellectuals. Everyone had read it, and everyone had a strong opinion about it. It seemed to allow them to speak about themselves and issues of faith in a more relaxed way, since they did not have to focus on their own personal quest so directly.

When I asked Elena she leaned back and frowned ever so slightly. I could tell by her tone that she was not favorably disposed toward *The Executioner's Block* but that she wanted to phrase her criticism in a measured way. The trouble with Aitmatov, she finally said, was that he wrote as though he had just discovered the Bible last week and was suddenly inspired to use it for his novel.

**Tiny evangilist with traditionally
decorated Easter eggs.**

The Executioner's Block contains a long flashback to a conversation between Jesus and Pontius Pilate, and I asked Elena if this was what she meant. She pointed out that this was hardly an original device. Bulgakov had used it in his famous novel *The Master and Margarita.*

I pressed a bit more. I told her that some religious believers had told me they were outraged by Aitmatov's use of the Gospel since he continued to describe himself as an atheist. She shrugged briefly, shook her head, and seemed to dismiss the issue. Still, she added, for many Russians the Aitmatov novel was an example of a superficial, even racy way of responding to the current upsurge of interest in theology. She thought something much more serious and engaging was needed and that we could confidently expect it in the future, maybe quite soon.

If Elena represented the seeker, Dmitri, whom I met two evenings later, stood at the opposite end of the spectrum: He had found. An energetic man in his middle 30s, Dmitri had been raised in a strict Communist family, had belonged to the Komsomol, and had only begun to have his doubts about Leninist dogma during his years at the university. There, in part because of conversations with other students but also because he began to read 19th-century European philosophy, he found himself drifting out of the ideological stockade. He told me that his first "conversion" took him toward a kind of 19th-century German idealism. From there he said he moved toward Orthodoxy, because he believed that Russian history had churned up all of the basic and besetting issues of human life and that the religious tradition of his homeland had answered them in the most satisfactory way. More recently he had gone on to a stricter version of Orthodoxy, a congregation of Old Believers.

At first I was astonished to be talking to a living Old Believer. I knew the Old Believers' movement was the product of the "great schism" of the 17th century that erupted in response to the effort of Patriarch Nikon to rid the Russian Orthodox Church of local accretions and to bring it more in line with the other Orthodox churches. The Old Believers would have none of it. Eventually many of their leaders were exiled to the most remote regions of the Russian Empire, but this only served, inadvertently, to spread their ideas further.

Today the Old Believers movement is still alive but is divided between those with duly ordained Orthodox priests who have chosen to serve Old Believers' congregations, and a more sectarian group that has no priests and interprets the defection of the regular Orthodox priesthood as a sign of the Last Days. Dmitri belonged to the first, the more moderate branch. But he insisted that for him it was the only "true church," the one which has preserved unchanged and "unedited" the revelation of God in Christ and the authentic tradition that has flowered from it.

As we continued to talk, I slowly discovered that Dmitri was the best informed and most widely read of my respondents. He was the only Orthodox believer I met who was familiar with German philosopher Martin Heidegger, whose writings he said he prized. Dmitri seemed positively impressed when he learned that I had studied with Paul Tillich, since Tillich was himself influenced by Heidegger.

When I asked Dmitri why he felt sympathetic to Heidegger he explained to me expansively. Heidegger, he said, had seen more clearly than any other European philosopher the gross error of modern technology and of modernity itself; he had called for a return to the original sources and had believed that most if not all of modern thought, including its theology, was a nest of mistakes.

Later I discovered that Dmitri had organized a circle of discussants who met regularly in their Moscow apartments to argue about theological and philosophical themes in a kind of symposium atmosphere. Just before we parted, Dmitri smiled and assured me that, although it was clear we agreed on some things, there were still many others on which he was equally sure we disagreed, and that we should start right away with them the next time we met.

When I asked him what he thought the principal issue of disagreement might be, he shook his head and told me that I probably would have a lot of difficulty understanding the messianic role to which God had called the Russian people. I told him I might but that I wanted to hear more. He told me that he firmly believed God had chosen Russia both to continue the suffering that Christ had borne on earth and also to preserve intact the Gospel in all its richness and with all its traditional embellishments "unedited."

Dmitri had used the word "unedited" before, and it now occurred to me that the fact that he worked in a publishing house might have influenced his choice of words. He also told me his reddish medium-length beard (unusual among present-day Muscovites) was an example of not "editing," of letting things, including a religious tradition, grow in a natural way. He assured me that this special calling of his own people did not reflect on the character, morality or worth of any other nation. It was, in fact, a kind of burden that God had laid on Russians, like God's choosing the Jews.

If Dmitri was the best informed and the most articulate of the new Christian intellectuals I met in Moscow, Masha was perhaps the most touching. Far from being a well-read or highly informed believer, Masha knew virtually nothing about the history and theology of Orthodoxy. Yet, in a society that still disapproves of and sometimes makes life difficult for those who declare themselves to be believers, she did so openly.

A young poet, still largely unpublished at 35, Masha met me in a friend's *dacha* just outside Moscow where she lived with her young daughter during the week and was joined by her husband on weekends.

In her tiny unpainted hut equipped with a table and rough-hewn chairs, she also had an icon corner. The icons, however, were of the cheapest paper variety available for a ruble in any monastery gift shop. As we talked I began to surmise that her having them on the wall was not meant to say much about them but to say something about the tradition they represented and to which she felt drawn.

Masha did not think of herself as an institutionally affiliated believer at all. She was desperately curious to find out from me all she could about the various religious traditions of the world and of the United States. What about Buddhists, Quakers, Baptists? What did Muslims believe about Christ? Unlike Dmitri she voiced no criticisms and made no claims. For her the Orthodox tradition was simply there. It was the one she turned to naturally as the principal resource for her spiritual life.

Masha told me she worried constantly about the religious formation of her five-year-old daughter. She said that children learned nothing about God in the public schools, and seemed surprised when in response to her questions I told her that there was also no religious teaching in the public schools of America. She asked about the availability of religious literature for children in the United States, and I told her we had a lot, almost a surfeit of it, and the problem was not finding it but selecting what was valuable out of all the junk.

She looked incredulous. She had, she said, tried for years to get her hands on a Russian Bible, but they were virtually unavailable. She had rarely been able even to see one, let alone have one to read.

Masha wanted to continue to talk, but her daughter and a friend appeared at the door in their bathing suits carrying inflated inner tubes and demanding that she keep her promise to take them swimming. Still she wanted my advice on how one could possibly raise these children to become believing Christians.

I had only a moment or two to answer but told her I thought the most important thing was to tell them the stories. Make sure they knew about David and Ruth and Miriam and Jeremiah. Tell them about Jesus and his various encounters. These stories, I told her, would ultimately be more important for her children than the theological doctrines she might teach them. She nodded vigorously and seemed to agree but still looked at me in a puzzled way. As she disappeared down the path on the way to the pond, I began to understand her perplexity. How could she tell them the stories when she didn't know them herself?

The one non-Muscovite I talked with in my series of conversations was Ana, a Leningrader who had just finished her comprehensive exam in classical archaeology and was in Moscow to vacation and visit friends. Some of my new acquaintances told me she was terribly bright, so much so that she had gotten into the university without ever belonging to the Young Pioneers or the Komsomol. They also thought it would be important for me to talk to her, since Ana was only 26 and would be the youngest of all my respondents.

I phoned. Ana gladly agreed to talk, suggesting that we meet one morning at the gigantic statue of Lenin in Octyabrskaya Square. She said she was tall, had auburn hair, and she described the clothes she would be wearing: faded blue jeans (almost *de rigueur* for Soviet young people today) and a maroon blouse.

Ana arrived a few minutes after I did and needed no encouragement to leap into the conversation. She was one of those young people at an exploratory stage who are forming opinions on everything and do not mind sharing them with anyone who will listen.

Ana came from a family of Orthodox believers who had never abandoned the faith but had become less open about it during the worst years of religious persecution. Only recently had they gone more public in their religious practice. She was not "returning" to anything: She'd always been there.

I asked Ana about her friends in the university and whether many of them were religious in any serious way. She told me that there was such a trend but that in her view most people who followed it were "not serious." As it turned out, the phrase "not serious" was one Ana used often. She obviously wanted both to be a serious person and to be considered one, and she was predictably severe toward people who didn't — in her view —

share that proclivity. For example, she could summon only a certain kind of disgust for the major animating passion of her fellow students at the university, which she claimed was devotion to different rock music groups.

Ana had heard about Aitmatov's book but told me she had absolutely no intention of reading it. "Aitmatov," she said, "is not really serious." Lifting her eyebrows she told me that in the novel, she had heard, "Aitmatov has Pilate's wife refer to him as 'Pontie.' " Apparently for Ana this represented the height of bad taste and was further evidence of Aitmatov's lack of seriousness.

I asked if her main objection was that Aitmatov was not a believer. Yes, she said, it was. She told me she thought Aitmatov had little business in fooling around with Jesus and the Apostles when he did not believe in God and could have no real feeling for what these figures meant to believers such as herself.

Ana and I walked by the northern wall of the Kremlin and stopped to look at the towers of its churches with their bulbous golden domes glittering in the late afternoon sun. I told her I found it a beautiful sight, but Ana was not impressed. She could not, she said, appreciate the Kremlin anymore. It had become "a toy."

I was glad my friends had suggested that I talk with Ana. She was no Slavophile. At one point she looked at me directly and said that her most urgent hope in life was some day to be able to emigrate from the Soviet Union. Her Orthodox religious faith was in no sense interchangeable with a deep affection for Russian culture. But she also resented, as any serious religious person does, the transformation of churches and sacred architecture into tourist displays, museums and folklore. She, of course, blamed the trivialization of these monuments on Communism. I felt I should tell her that the same sad fate had overtaken many religious buildings and paintings in the West as well, and that emigration, though it might solve some of her problems, would hardly solve that one. But I did not.

Two nights before I left Moscow I had a conversation with Piotr, a 40-year-old performing musician. A handsome man with a full beard, heavy mane of hair, and sparkling eyes, Piotr would have been a central casting dream for a 19th-century Russian peasant if it weren't for the modern western suit coat and open throated shirt he — like most other Moscow professionals — wore.

Piotr was the son of an Orthodox priest. He told me that he still strongly identified himself as an Orthodox believer but that he had come to have many questions. In reminiscing about his childhood he remembered that the hardest part about growing up in a strict Orthodox home in the Soviet Union was not that he felt discriminated against by official policies but that the spiritual régime enforced on the whole family by his father's vocation was so severe and difficult for a child to understand.

The family had observed at least part of the monastic discipline of early morning prayers, prayers at eventide, and more prayers before going to bed, on a daily basis. Piotr was also steered sternly away from such childhood pleasures as movies and card playing. As a young man he had gone through a period of rebellion against his father's tutelage and had ceased practicing his faith. But he had never given up the core of Eastern Orthodox religiosity he had inherited from his parents. Yes, he said, he was a part of the return to religion among Russian artists and intellectuals, but unlike most of them he had something to return to, and he was glad.

Piotr was an instrumental performer, but he also liked to sing and had a fine though untrained tenor voice. He told me he enjoyed singing in the choir of a small Orthodox church in the southern part of Moscow almost more than anything else. He harbored no regrets that in Orthodox services the choir sings unaccompanied. He felt that it was one of the few places where the purity of the human voice could reach the heart unimpeded and unembellished by organs or other artificial elements. Since we were sitting in the privacy of my apartment, I asked him if he wanted to sing. At first he declined, but later he belted out a part of last week's liturgy. I could see why he loved it.

Like Masha, Piotr wanted to talk about the difficulty he and his wife felt in raising their children as believers in Soviet society. He did not believe that official sanctions or administrative harassment provided the main problem. Rather, as in the West, parents had to watch their children absorb values and attitudes that seemed in direct conflict with Christianity. He talked about the fascination Soviet young people have with rock music, transistor radios, tape recorders and the latest baggy blouses. He was afraid that both Soviet and western societies were turning in a more materialistic direction and that this was making it difficult for the parents of young people to nurture them in the kind of Christian religious direction he and his wife wanted them to have.

I asked Piotr about Aitmatov's novel with a certain amount of apprehensiveness. I was afraid he might feel, like the other believers, that it represented an intrusion

The Christian Science Monitor
from November 20, 1989.

---

on or misuse of his faith. This was not the case. He told me that the biblical imagery and stories were the patrimony of a much larger group of people than those contained within any particular religious community, and that a novelist should feel perfectly free to draw on them in telling his story.

Piotr seemed glad that the very existence of Aitmatov's book extended the boundaries of the current freedom of debate a little more. He insisted it was important to use every opportunity to broaden and deepen the range of topics and opinions so that something like a genuine exchange of ideas, including ideas about religion, might eventually become possible.

Recalling the question I had asked him earlier in the evening, about what Orthodoxy meant to him personally, he reached outward and upward to trace a large semicircle in the air. "It's ample," he said. "It's large. It can include everything. It gives us the widest imaginable horizon. It's not like the tiny, petty little ideas and theories and ideologies we're supposed to settle for." With these last words he returned his arms from their extended position and hunched over to indicate minuscule little things with his fingertips.

On my last day in Moscow I decided to pay a farewell visit to what had become my favorite spot, the small and somewhat overlooked chapel inside the Kremlin walls called the Church of the Deposition of the Robe. As in all Orthodox churches, the main altar is shielded by an iconostasis, a screen covered with ranks of icons. On this particular screen, however, there is an unusual feature: One whole rank is devoted to the life of Jesus beginning with the Annunciation and Nativity and ending with the Resurrection and the scene on the road to Emmaus.

In looking at this iconostasis I noticed that there was only one event in the adult life of Jesus between the Dedication at the Temple and the Triumphal Entry which seemed worthy of depiction to those who painted it. This was the episode of Jesus raising Lazarus from the dead. There were no teaching scenes, no Sermon on the Mount, no miracles; only the powerful image of the Saviour calling forth life from death. The raising of Lazarus plays a powerful role in the history of Russian religious faith. For Dostoevsky it represented the miracle of faith itself. In *Crime and Punishment* he pictures Sonia reading about it to Raskolnikov:

"She was trembling in a real physical fever.... She was getting near the story of the greatest miracle, and a feeling of immense triumph came over her. Her voice rang out like a bell."

Sonia's quivering anticipation as she read the story sprang from the hope that its sheer power and beauty would surely touch the heart even of the unbeliever. He, too, by the power of this Russian Christ, should be called from the death of skepticism and contempt into the joyful life of faith.

As I stepped out of the darkness and silence into the brick Kremlin square next to the mammoth Czar Bell, surrounded by clumps of chattering tourists from the Soviet hinterlands, it occurred to me that the Church of the Deposition of the Robe had helped me understand my conversations with my new friends. Ivan's priest was at least partly right. Though they may not teach us all we need to know, "the icons teach us." I could also understand Masha's and Elena's feeling that the music and liturgy of Orthodoxy bring something to the human spirit that penetrates deeper than ideas. I could understand Dmitri's reluctance to allow any of this to be watered down by relativism or adaptation. Mostly I could almost hear Ana's voice when, thinking of that overwhelming iconostasis depicting the raising of Lazarus, I said to myself, "This is serious."

The search for a Soviet Christ is surely underway. I have no wisdom on whether it will succeed, even on what success in such a quest would be. I doubt that Masha or Dmitri or Ivan even think much about the success of their venture. Their search for Mystery and Meaning — for God — is shaped to some extent, as it is for anyone, by the contours of the society they live in. But the search also leads to something that is, to use Piotr's words and gestures, larger and more ample.

But I did decide one thing: The search for a Soviet Christ will never go anywhere unless it deals with the Russian Christ, that resolute figure who gazes mournfully but serenely from the icons. To know him would not be easy in any society, and although *glasnost* may now make the quest more possible, it will not make it any less difficult.

John Simpson, foreign affairs editor for the British Broadcast Corporation (BBC) television news, travels around the globe for insight and information. Visits to the Soviet Union, a decade apart, gave him a remarkable opportunity to check on the fortunes of Ilya Sergeyevich Glazunov, one of that country's most famous contemporary artists.

He has written for World Monitor: The Christian Science Monitor Monthly *from many parts of the globe including South Africa and Iraq.*

'Perestroika' and the Painter [12/88]

By John Simpson

In the hot Moscow sunshine, the one remarkable thing about the line of people was its incredible length. Otherwise, they could have been waiting for anything: a consignment of Polish shoes, of Hungarian sausage, of Czech glassware. Many of them even carried the symbol of Soviet Man's eternal optimism, the string bags that Russians call "Just-in-case" — just in case they pass a shop that has something worthwhile to sell.

But they weren't there to buy anything. They were lining up to share in an experience which, in this summer of 1978, still had a guilty, illicit air about it. Religion, royalism, a nostalgia for the imperial past were dangerous things, which Russians had learned for sixty years to bury deep in themselves. And yet in the very center of Leonid Brezhnev's Moscow the largest exhibition hall in the capital was featuring an exhibition of paintings by an artist who verged on the politically unacceptable, and whose works were celebrations of czarism and the Russian Orthodox Church.

A political system demonstrates that it's in a state of decay by becoming confused about its symbolism. Here, in the final years of the Brezhnev reign — which nowadays, under Gorbachev, is known as the period of stagnation — confusion was piled on confusion. The Manege, originally the Imperial stables, is a splendid neoclassical rectangle just outside the walls of the Kremlin. Brezhnev and the other old men in his Politburo (of which Gorbachev was very soon about to become a much younger member) often drove past the structure on their way to and from their offices. It is immense — 150 yards long and 40 yards wide. And yet the queue waiting to see the exhibition of paintings by Ilya Sergeyevich Glazunov went three times around the outside of the building. As the people shuffled slowly in through the splendid double doors at the front, the line was continually being added to at the remote far end.

From the outside it was hard to see what all the fuss was about. An enormous placard covered the front of the Manege, announcing that an exhibition of modern Bulgarian painting (than which few things could have been more boring) was taking place there. So it was — in one corner of the hall. The Bulgarian Communist Party newspaper published a photograph of the queue around the Manege and claimed quite fraudulently that it showed how popular Bulgarian art was in Moscow. In the photograph you couldn't even spot the small poster, a couple of feet across, which bore the name of the real attraction: Glazunov, whose paintings filled three-quarters of the hall.

It all represented an official compromise: A risky artist was being allowed to show his work under the pretense that the exhibition was too insignificant to really matter. But in a closed society like the Soviet Union, it's not the loudness of the official trumpetings that counts, it's the private information network that anyone can access.

Inside, the Manege was redolent with that unmistakable, sickly sweet smell — composed of sweat, perfume and Soviet tobacco — which clings to public buildings in the Soviet Union. There was also an intensity of intelligent interest. People moved from one Glazunov painting to the next only when the pressure of the crowd forced them to.

And what paintings they were! Haunted, starved peasants with huge suffering eyes trek across the snow; savants and writers hang in the air like wraiths while Jesus comforts a child of modern industrial society and dead bodies litter a pig-infested banquet; anxiety-wracked figures from Dostoevsky move through elegant St. Petersburg streets; czars in gorgeous, jewel-like collages order executions or stand victorious on mounds of corpses; and everywhere there are churches, priests, crowns, angels, saints, icons, crosses.

There is something else, too, something almost unthinkable in an exhibition which, in order to take place, required official approval, no matter how muted. There is a sense of guilt and shame for the 1917 Revolution and the murder of Czar Nicholas II and his family. An angel crowns a young boy in an icon, while a threatening hand brandishes a dripping dagger from a flaming sun. Most harrowing of all, the body of the Czarevitch, the young Crown Prince, lies sprawled across the canvas, his toy horse and wooden cart poignantly abandoned behind him. His eyes are open, sorrowfully and accusingly, but his throat is cut. The crowd in front of that painting was the largest and quietest in the entire Manege.

In the middle of the whole event — sweating slightly in the heat and surrounded by admirers, hangers-on, seekers after favors, and a few personal friends — was the artist himself. He didn't look much like an artist. You might have taken this man in his late 40s for an Italian tenor who was just beginning to hit the big time: effusive, dapper, smiling, his hair fashionably long, signing autographs in exhibition catalogs with a flourish and a friendly inscription, even to people he was meeting for the first time. I too came away with my signed catalog,

dully illustrated in black and white. Looking at it afterwards, I could hardly recall the brilliance of the golds, the blood reds, the emerald greens; but that evening a mutual friend got me an invitation to dinner at the Glazunovs', and the colors returned with a vengeance.

At nine o'clock my friend and I found ourselves in a dingy street near the Arbat, lighted only by the faint rays from the weird street signs of Moscow, which even then were being phased out and have now been entirely replaced: each a white disc of enamel, the shape and size of a large chafing dish, inscribed with the name of the street and topped by a blue metal roof with a single light bulb inside. We found the front door, old, ill-fitting, and noisy, pushed it open, and took the unsteady elevator to the seventh floor. A large padded door opened to our knock and Glazunov himself, in a magnificent dark blue silk dinner jacket, invited us in.

In Mikhail Bulgakov's fantastical, daring novel *The Master and Margarita*, the Devil comes to Stalin's Moscow and establishes himself in some style in a flat not far from where we now found ourselves. The contrast between the Stalinist grimness outside and the Devil's headquarters was scarcely greater than that between the Brezhnevian decay of the street and the brilliance of the room we were ushered into. Glazunov's studio was a large, high room with a wooden gallery along one side of it. A refectory table lit by candles a foot high was set out with food, and people were sitting around it, laughing and eating. Russian Orthodox Church music was playing on an invisible sound system, filling the darkened room as thick as incense.

But what I found overwhelming was that the walls of the studio, 14 feet or more high, were covered from floor to ceiling with icons, carvings and brass crosses. Along one side of the gallery were 20 church bells; another wall was completely taken up with the huge painted doors from a 16th-century monastery. Saints and demons, kings and knights, glimmered faintly in the light from the candles. Even when we were sitting on benches like monks at the table, within the warmth and gaiety of the conversation, it was hard to prevent myself from continually turning to look at the richness which surrounded us in the gloom.

I took little part in the conversation, since I spoke only the most rudimentary Russian, and the others were too animated to want to slow the conversation down by continual translation. To my right sat Glazunov's wife, Nina, a delicate-featured woman some years younger than her husband, with the blue eyes, dark hair, and white skin that characterize many Russian women. She, too, said little, smiling gently when someone spoke to her or asked her a question. Otherwise she would sit quietly, eating little and looking down at her long hands, occasionally turning the rings very slowly and thoughtfully on her fingers.

Glazunov, for his part, was witty, challenging, and powerful by turns. Even now he didn't seem like an artist so much as a polemicist, explaining how the authorities were pulling down churches or allowing them to decay. He would point to some object on the walls around him and explain how this or that marvelous work of art had been saved from the iconoclasts (literally, the destroyers of religious images). Sometimes he would describe — acting it out and giving us the gestures and voices of everyone concerned — how he'd bought these things from drunken workmen or stupid local officials. It was a bravura performance, and his guests, those who could understand him, shrieked with laughter. I laughed too, occasionally glancing across at Nina Glazunov, who would be watching her husband and smiling her quiet smile.

When it was all over, my friend and I found ourselves back in the silent, dreary street. As we walked to the Arbat Metro station, I still couldn't work out in my own mind how Glazunov — whose opinions and enthusiasms ran counter to every form of political orthodoxy — could not only survive in Brezhnev's Russia but also, apparently, flourish.

From our conversation:

"Everything in this country is to do with influence. Glazunov knows all the right people."

"But how can he get an exhibition in the Manege, with all those religious pictures? And the one with the Czarevitch?"

"If you're in with Brezhnev's crowd, then, believe me, there's nothing you can't do."

"And he really is in with Brezhnev's crowd?"

"So everyone says. I'm only passing on the gossip."

Ilya Glazunov is the kind of man who attracts gossip. Compared with the drab uniformity of the Soviet Union, his life is lived in a riot of primary colors. Everything about him, from his artistic talent to his political opinions, is larger and more striking than the circumstances of ordinary people — even of ordinary artists. But it was ten years before I had the opportunity to question him and find out whether the gossip surrounding the Manege exhibition had any foundation in fact. During that time Brezhnev had died, and his successor, and his successor as well. The fourth General Secretary within four years, Mikhail Gorbachev, set out to change every-

thing that had happened during the Brezhnevian period. It became possible to talk about subjects that had been buried deep within the consciousness of every Russian.

People who had been treated like criminals and traitors when I had seen them in 1978 were now officially encouraged to speak their minds. For example, Andrei Sakharov, the distinguished physicist who was the main voice of dissent within the Soviet Union, had been watched and followed everywhere by the KGB when I had last met him. Now he was free to give a press conference at the Foreign Ministry, and he supported — with reservations — the new orthodoxies of *glasnost* and *perestroika*.

The degree of criticism of the workings of the Soviet system in the official press was extraordinary. Suddenly it was possible to criticize virtually everything, except *glasnost* and *perestroika* themselves. One senior figure in the Communist Party attacked another in an interview on a western television program — something that would have been unthinkable even a matter of months before. The most secret crimes of the past started to be brought to public attention.

For artists and intellectuals, it was the most exciting time of their lives. No one had had this much freedom in the Soviet Union since the early days of the Revolution, and they were determined to use it to the full. In a park on the edge of Moscow, which from the early days of Gorbachev had been a place where artists could show works with a certain amount of daring and yet feel safe from the police, I strolled along in the hot sunshine, examining the kind of thing that was on show. Religious themes were popular. The quality was not particularly good, and just about every major western artist from Gauguin to Hockney was imitated in uninspired and diluted form. But it was clear that the kind of thing which Glazunov had barely managed to get away with in 1978 was a matter of course in 1988. The past could be brought into the open.

It was even possible to be a royalist once again. As I reached the gates of the park where the artists were showing their work, a man and a woman in Tolstoyan clothes were offering for sale imperial genealogies, portraits of the czars, and engravings of long-destroyed churches and monasteries. They, it appeared, were members of *Pamyat*, or Memory — a curious coalition of traditionalists and outright reactionaries, some of whom were active in preserving buildings that belonged to the Russian national heritage, while others were virtual fascists, deeply anti-Semitic, illiberal, and anti-

PERESTROIKA AND THE PAINTER

Amid glory and gossip, Ilya Glazunov presides over an incredible Moscow lair and tries to push Marxist Moscow back to its Russian roots.

By John Simpson

N THE HOT MOSCOW SUNSHINE, THE ONE REMARKABLE THING ABOUT the line of people was its incredible length. Otherwise, they could have been waiting for anything: a consignment of Polish shoes, of Hungarian sausage, of Czech glassware. Many of them even carried the symbol of Soviet Man's eternal optimism, the string bags that Russians call "Just-in-case"—just in case they pass a shop that has something worthwhile to sell.

But they weren't there to buy anything. They were lining up to share in an experience which, in this summer of 1978, still had a guilty, illicit air about it. Religion, royalism, a nostalgia for the imperial past were dangerous things, which Russians had learned for sixty years to bury deep in themselves. And yet in the very center of Leonid Brezhnev's Moscow the largest exhibition hall in the capital was featuring an exhibition of paintings by an artist who verged on the politically unacceptable, and whose works were celebrations of czarism and the Russian Orthodox Church.

A political system demonstrates that it's in a state of decay by becoming confused about its symbolism. Here, in the final years of the Brezhnev reign—which nowadays, under Gorbachev, is known as the period of stagnation—confusion was piled on confusion. The Manege, originally the Imperial stables, is a splendid neoclassical rectangle just outside the walls of the Kremlin. Brezhnev and the other old men in his Politburo (of which Gorbachev was very soon about to become a much younger member) often drove past the structure on their way to and from their offices. It is immense—150 yards long and 40 yards wide. And yet the queue waiting to see the exhibition of paintings by Ilya Sergeyevich Glazunov went three times around the outside of the building. As the people shuffled slowly in through the splendid double

John Simpson, diplomatic editor of BBC television news, travels around the globe for insight and information. Visits to the Soviet Union, a decade apart, gave him a remarkable opportunity to check on the fortunes of Ilya Glazunov.

Photographs by Rais Mukharamov

Inside spread from the December 1988 edition of the World Monitor **magazine.**

western. The new freedoms, Mr. Gorbachev was discovering, could release destructive energies as well as creative ones. Pamyat demonstrations were small and mostly peaceful, but they occasionally turned nasty when the police tried to break them up or prevent them from demanding the expulsion of Jews from the Soviet Union. At one stage, while some western friends of mine and I stood watching, Ilya Glazunov's name cropped up in the conversation.

"Oh, Glazunov. He's the kind of person that turns up at this sort of thing, you know."

"What, Pamyat?"

"Sure. And then the next day you'll see him at an anti-Pamyat rally. He seems to like playing both ends against the middle."

"Have you ever seen him at them?"

"Well, no, not personally. But that's what people say."

A few days later I went to see the organizers of the first art auction to be held in the Soviet Union by a western company — Sotheby's of London. The sale was entitled "Russian Avant-Garde and Soviet Contemporary Art," and four of the works in it were by Glazunov, including his powerful study "Ivan the Terrible." One of the organizers of the sale was showing me around, and we stopped in front of the painting.

"We've had a lot of complaints about including Glazunov in this exhibition," she said.

"But he's much better than some of the people you're showing here."

I looked at the paintings on the walls, some good, some insipid, some downright derivative.

"It's not that," she said. "People have been saying he's too closely connected with Brezhnev and the — what do they call that time?"

"The period of stagnation," I said.

All the while I had been trying to get hold of Glazunov, but he was remarkably elusive. Once, together with a friend, I went to his flat on the top floor of the rickety building near the Arbat which I remembered so clearly. But no one answered his doorbell. "He's off in Leningrad," said a middle-aged man who was lounging in the hot sunshine near the entrance to the apartment block. "He spends a lot of time in Leningrad nowadays."

"How do you know?"

The man shrugged. Plainly, everyone in the area knew Ilya Glazunov: He wasn't the kind of person one could easily ignore.

And yet even that piece of gossip turned out to be untrue. Glazunov wasn't in Leningrad, he was in Mos-

cow. And he agreed, over the phone, to see me at 11 o'clock the following morning.

Entrance hall, elevator and front door were all as I remembered them from ten years before. But the artist himself, when I came face to face with him, seemed indefinably changed. At 58, he seemed to have energy as considerable as ever, and he remembered, unprompted, that we had met at his Manege exhibition of 1978. He was as well dressed as ever, in his slightly flashy way. The bright sunlight that streamed into his flat glinted on the silvery suit he was wearing in preparation for a visit to the Ministry of Culture. The carefully combed hair, the handsome, jowly face still gave him the operatic touch I had previously noticed, only nowadays he seemed like an Italian tenor at the very peak of his abilities and earning power, about five years away from the big announcement of a retirement from the stage. But there was something different about him, all the same: Something seemed to have gone out of him, and only later did I find out what it might be.

There was a deeply satisfying atmosphere of Russian disorder in the flat. Glazunov was racing around trying to organize a dozen things simultaneously, while the telephone rang continually; a stream of friends and acquaintances came to the door asking for tickets to his latest exhibition; one or the other of the two old women in headscarves who were working away in the kitchen would ask him what food he wanted; and he kept breaking off from everyone to rush into his studio to find another painting of his which would illustrate some point he wanted to make to me.

As for the flat itself, ten additional years of collecting had made it a stunning place. It was big enough even by western standards; by Soviet standards, five different families could have lived there. Every available surface was covered with splendid objects: busts of 19th-century noblemen; bronze double-headed imperial eagles, collections of engraved seals; miniatures; spurs; gilded knickknacks; an entire suit of armor; death masks; snuffboxes; plaster casts of noses, mouths, and foreheads; photographs of the last Czar and Czarina; and shelves sagging under the weight of magnificent old books. Paintings were everywhere: vast 16th- and 17th-century canvases, Spanish, Italian, and Russian, with fleshy nymphs and horsemen and Old Testament prophets pursuing each other through classical landscapes. But on the elaborate marble mantelpiece in his drawing room one modern picture stood out from the rest — a large framed photograph of Raisa Gorbachev, with a long scribbled inscription registering her admiration for Glazunov's works. It was a contemporary icon, imbued with special powers for warding off political demons.

At last the phone calls and the urgent demands for advice and help died away, and we retreated into his studio — the holy of holies. There, among the genuine icons and the incomparable carvings, Glazunov put on a record of church music, and something of the atmosphere I remembered was created. We sat down at the familiar refectory table, and his formidable energies were condensed into conversation: witty, angry, and powerful by turns, with the words "sabotage" and "conspiracy" cropping up at regular intervals.

"Millions come to my exhibitions," Glazunov says. "At my last one in the Manege, in 1986, two million people visited it, and that included six members of the Politburo. And yet five months ago the Soviet Academy of Painters turned down my application for membership for the sixth time. They said I wasn't helping the construction of Socialism. Who wants all this stuff of mine about czars and history? they said. Who wants my illustrations to Dostoevsky? Dostoevsky is a pessimist. Away with him.

"But although everything else is changing in our country, politically and culturally, the painters' mafia stays the same. They don't like me, because I'm more popular than they are. All they want is to get as much money out of the government as they can and divide it up among themselves. They don't want to have to share it with an outsider."

I point to the marvelous collection of icons that covers the walls around us, and ask about the connection between his love of the Russian tradition and the political nationalism of movements like Pamyat.

"First, let me say that I'm not a collector. Many painters collect icons for their value. I've saved all these from destruction. (His gesture took in a 16th-century icon of St. Nicholas to which the great museums of the West would give an honored place. He'd found it in a church which had been turned to other uses, propping up an electrical generator, and the engineer had demanded three rubles for it — the price of a bottle of vodka — plus another piece of wood to take its place.) But I want them for atmosphere, not for profit. Ten years ago, people used to say I was a religious fanatic because I collected icons. Now they say I must be a millionaire.

"As for this question of Pamyat, I must say at once that I have nothing to do with it. I know that foreign journalists, people who don't actually come and speak to me, say that I do. Some have even written that I finance and organize that kind of group. Six months ago, when I was in Paris, a pseudo-intellectual magazine said I ran an anti-Semitic group here, and I sued the editor.

"It's certainly true that I want to revive Russian national traditions; that's what my paintings are about. But I'm not a Russian nationalist, if by that you mean a chauvinist who says his country is better than everyone else's in every way. Art, for instance, is a bouquet of many national cultures, and I appreciate the diversity of it. But I believe in the fatherland, and in patriotism.

"The painters' union, which is my biggest enemy, accuses me of nationalism and says my works are kitsch. There've been ten major articles written against me by Soviet critics, saying that I have anti-Soviet opinions, that I'm a monarchist, and so on. They can say what they like; it doesn't affect the truth."

Glazunov, whose nervous energy fills the place, showing itself in everything from his clarity of expression to his incessant cigarette smoking, seems to draw strength from the opposition his views arouse. He has a witty, antithetical way of expressing the accusations against him. Now, as he deals with the hostility which he regards as widespread and implacable, the flow of his conversation becomes faster and the ironies stronger.

"One of the leaders of Pamyat, a man called Vassilyev, said that I was a Freemason, and that the Freemasons were the ones who'd tried to destroy Russia by introducing liquor here. You see, my enemies sow the seeds of disinformation against me, but they contradict one another. The magazine *Soviet Culture* said I judged Russia by American standards; and then a magazine in West Germany said I was a KGB agent. I sued them for that, and I won. If a club of drug addicts started up here, someone would say I was the founder of it. That's the way they get back at me."

But what, I ask him, is the secret of his ability to continue working in spite of the dislike of his unorthodox opinions?

"People talk about my imaginary privileges. I have none. I don't receive a pension from the government, and as I told you I'm not allowed to be a member of the Soviet Academy. I was, and remain, a Russian painter, Ilya Glazunov, who wants to bring change to Soviet society. This is why I am in favor of *perestroika*."

He pauses, anxious to let the point settle in. Glazunov may fight the artistic establishment — the mafia, as he rightly terms them — and he may have religious and political opinions that the Soviet system finds dubious; but he has always been careful not to run counter to the political orthodoxy at the top of the Soviet state. He did not oppose Brezhnev, and he doesn't now oppose Gorbachev; he finds the concepts of *perestroika* and *glasnost* very much to his taste. Indeed, his masterpiece, "The Mystery of the 20th Century," which is an enormous, politically daring group portrait of the leading figures who have affected life in Russia this century, from the Czar to Stalin and beyond, has finally been accept-ed for public showing as a result of *glasnost*. But how given the opposition which he constantly referred to, has he been able to show his paintings? Is it true that he had Brezhnev's personal blessing, which made it possible for him to hold his 1978 exhibition in the Manege?

The response is long and circumstantial. No, the stories about his having painted portraits of Brezhnev's powerful, corrupt daughter Galina are untrue. And he wasn't, as some had suggested, the court painter to Brezhnev. But among the well-known international figures whose portraits he had been invited to paint was Indira Gandhi of India; and Brezhnev, who presented the portrait to Mrs. Gandhi, had taken a fancy to Glazunov's style.

One of Brezhnev's aides approached Glazunov, who naturally agreed to paint Brezhnev's portrait. But in spite of his request to paint Brezhnev from life, he had to be content with a photograph. Brezhnev apparently liked the result, and it caused a sensation when the portrait was published — not least because Glazunov had included the church domes of the Kremlin in the painting but had left out the rows of decorations which Brezhnev habitually wore on his chest. The whole thing had brought him great notoriety, he says, yet had also given him the reputation of being a hanger-on at the Brezhnev court. Nevertheless, he insists that Brezhnev never paid him for the portrait.

And now? What about the photograph of Raisa Gorbachev which I had seen in his drawing room?

"I haven't been asked to paint her portrait. But when I held my exhibition in the Manege two years ago, she came to see it. The organizers offered to clear the place of visitors, so that she could see it on her own, but she told them no, she wanted to be like everyone else. She spent two-and-a-half hours there, looking at my paintings very attentively, and she asked me some impressive questions. Three days afterwards, a policeman came to the door with a large envelope. In it was her photograph, with an inscription. It was a great honor for me."

Two paintings by Ilya Glazunov titled (top) "Mystery of the 20th Century" and (bottom) "One Hundred Centuries of Russia". (below) Walls filled with sacred images known as icons in Ilya Glazunov's home.

Cracks in the Wall

The Russian Revolution overthrew the monarchy, but it has created one of its own, and the Gorbachevs are the new royal family of the Soviet Union. It seems to me, listening to Ilya Glazunov, that his own sense of the imperial past had given him the skills of a successful court politician, even though he wasn't, and never had been, a court painter. But he knew how to keep the favors of the great, while fighting off the envy of lesser talents around him. He has never, therefore, been a dissident painter, in the sense that Solzhenitsyn was a dissident novelist or Sakharov a dissident intellectual. He hasn't set out to challenge the Soviet system, he has managed to find a way of coexisting with it while doing and saying what he wants. The opposition has come from lesser artists who resent his tactical skills as much as his talent.

Glazunov maintains that the opposition has gone to extraordinary lengths. I catch a reference, for instance, to "my late wife," and sitting at the table where I had seen her sad, quiet presence ten years before, I ask when she died. It had been a few days before the 1986 exhibition which Raisa Gorbachev had visited. The official verdict was that she had thrown herself out of the window of the flat. Glazunov refuses to accept this, saying that she was too religious to commit suicide, and too fond of her children, who were playing in the yard outside and saw her fall.

Perhaps such experience accounts for the impression he makes a decade after our first meeting: that he has been in some way diminished, that he has lost some of his resilience. Characteristically, he saw the death of his wife as as work of his enemies — rival artists who wanted to stop his exhibition from going ahead. He adduces as corroboration a strange incident that happened soon afterwards.

His son was standing at the front door of their apartment block when a passer-by plunged a knife into his chest, nearly killing him. There is no doubt that the son was knifed. I saw the scar myself. There is no doubt either that Moscow has a sophisticated and violent underworld which closely resembles the mafia of the West. Glazunov is convinced that the artistic mafia of the Soviet Union uses the same methods.

Glazunov's own past tends to incline him to such views. It is not a comfortable background. The haunted, harrowing figures of his paintings are not drawn from imagination but from memory. As a boy he lived through the long blockade of Leningrad by the Germans, in which hundreds of thousands of people died of hunger. His own parents died before his eyes, and he lost many other relatives as well. He survived because his grandmother had him evacuated across the frozen Lake Lagoda. It was a determination to build up the destroyed beauties of Leningrad (which he insists on calling St. Petersburg) that led him to do what he could to preserve other aspects of the Russian heritage.

Glazunov's friend and ally, the painter Piotr Litvinski, has joined us at the refectory table, and he interrupts the memories to say that Glazunov is the most courageous man he has ever met, that anyone else would have broken down under the blows which he had endured. Glazunov listens to him, smoking nervously, and then breaks in himself:

"I have to be strong, I have to be the victor, because I have a great aim: to save Russian culture. The three principles of Russia under the monarchy were autocracy, orthodoxy and nationalism — in the good sense. Now the principles are the dictatorship of the proletariat, atheism and internationalism. I say we must preserve the traditions of the Russian people. They must not be allowed to fade. So many adverse winds are blowing against the Russian candle that someone has to protect it. That is the task I have set myself. I cannot be weak."

The interview was over, ending on a high emotional note. He put his arm round my shoulder as we left the holy of holies, headed through his workshop with the brass crosses, the plaster masks, and the suit of armor, and entered the living quarters of the flat.

Once there, we were back in the everyday Russian world, where people were still ringing urgently about tasks that had not been done, and favors that were wanted. The women in the headscarves called out from the kitchen:

"Ilya Sergeyevich, what do you want to eat for lunch?"

But there was no time for lunch. Glazunov had to go to the Ministry, and he had mislaid his smart jacket, and a search was instituted in every room in the flat while the phone rang unanswered and three more people came to the door. Once the jacket was found, he seized a beautifully produced book of his paintings, with a portrait of his wife on the cover, and in the magnificent scribble I remembered from the dull black-and-white catalog of the Manege exhibition ten years before, he wrote out a splendid dedication. I glanced through it quickly, to see the czars and the peasants and the barbarians, and the Czarevitch lying dead with his toy horse abandoned in the dark birch forest behind him. And the candles that appear in painting after painting, representing the Russian tradition, threatened by the adverse winds.

Victor Sheymov is a former KGB officer who was granted political asylum in the United States. This article was originally published with Mr. Sheymov's pseudonym, Victor Orlov. At the time, after his defection to the West, he still needed to maintain this "cover."

When Spies Fool Themselves [3/89]

By Victor Sheymov

Recently by sheer accident I saw in a magazine a funny mistranslated recipe. "Chicken soup" was translated into Russian as "chicken juice." So what? Mistranslations are common when any two languages are involved. As a rule, the mistakes stand out in the context with no harm done. Besides, the translator has to be given credit for being open-minded. Who knows what they do to chickens over there in Russia?

Misinterpretations of the language are a more serious matter. They are less noticeable but much costlier than mistranslations. Costliest of all are misinterpretations of another party's ways, means and goals.

Such misinterpretations are not necessarily related to the language barrier. More often they originate in the difference between two cultures, two societies, and they are made most often by well-educated and intelligent experts. These misinterpretations frequently harm one party. Sometimes they harm both parties. But practically never do they benefit them both.

The Soviet Union, where I spent most of my life, is a classic example of an entity riddled with misinterpretations of the West and, in particular, of the United States. Easy to understand, for the general population suffocates from lack of objective information about the outside world. Glasnost has done little to change this situation. It has made official much information about the Soviet Union itself that the intellectual elite knew unofficially; it has not done much for the general public, especially in regard to knowledge about the West.

For example, with the selective reporting by the Soviet media, the vast majority of the people do not suspect at all the existence of a middle class in the United States. All they get in their media are numerous pictures of the slums, quotations of sensationalized newsmaking crime stories, and glimpses of glamorized Hollywood-type parties. (I always wondered what Hollywood was really like.)

The Soviet people base their interpretations on their experience with how their own media portray their own country. How can one blame these people? They make the only logical conclusion: If that is what the American media are reporting, the real situation there must be much worse.

The very few people who have been to the US are not much help to the others. Saying anything good about the "Capitalist" society is a major ideological offense. So the well-traveled ones say something like this even to their close friends: "Sure, quite a few workers in America have their own cars, but..." and there it goes, some sort of dutiful blood-chilling horror story. The farthest one can go is to refer with tongue in cheek to Karl Marx's famous line about "rotting Capitalism": "Well, they are still rotting — and not badly, I must admit."

The real misinterpretation in the USSR starts with the KGB and GRU espionage agencies. Their interest in the United States and all aspects of its life is very definite, professional, and not exactly humane, as opposed to the general and human interest in America of the common people in the Soviet Union.

Those figuratively red-bannered platoons of spies, quietly marching in American streets and partially funded by the US taxpayer through the United Nations, are well aware of the existence of the American middle class. They are also well aware of many aspects of life in the United States. And still all too often they commit misinterpretations. No matter what the Communist Party does to educate them, these people cannot comprehend a lot of things just because of their background.

For instance, Soviet intelligence officers cannot comprehend the abundance of an extremely important — from their standpoint — source of information: public records. They disbelieve that this kind of information can be genuine. That disbelief is supported by their performance evaluation system, largely based on how impressively the information they obtain is classified as secret. Sometimes, in fact, a case officer persuades his agent to put a classification stamp on an otherwise nonclassified document "for the common good." It is a common good indeed. The agent gets paid better, the case officer gets a good evaluation eventually leading to a promotion, his boss gets a "good boy" remark from the Central Committee in Moscow, and the customer is happy with "reliable information."

Incidentally, the cheating takes a slightly modified form in the KGB's political intelligence in the third world. Under this scenario, the case officer recruits somebody who is as worth recruiting as Morris the Cat. A problem? Not to worry. After every meeting — mainly a friendly chat with quite generous allowances — the officer just files his own or somebody else's analysis of the political situation along with newspaper reports for "local flavor" — stating his "star" agent as the source. The effect is the same.

Everyone involved is happy. Works very reliably; that is, until the officer goes back home and another case officer takes over the agent. Then the new guy, having discovered the scheme, has a choice. He can continue the game or he can foreclose. In the latter case, he most likely would be accused of not being able to find a good approach to the "asset" and thus not performing well. As a rule, the buck does not stop and the game goes on. Such rollover can continue until the agent's retirement.

Given all this, still the most interesting phenomenon of Soviet misinterpretation lies with the Central Committee and its top leadership. Having virtually all the information they want and definitely not having any illusions, these people misinterpret some major matters concerning the West and the United States in particular. The most likely explanation is that they have fallen victim to their own propaganda. Indeed, when one repeats lies all of his life, after a while he is bound to start subconsciously believing in them himself. Some sort of self-hypnotic side effect of one's hypnotic efforts.

Strange as it may seem, the Soviet leadership definitely does not understand the American political structure. To start with, they dismiss the system of checks and balances as the cover for a "real" political structure, a cover made up just to help it look democratic. The roots of this misinterpretation rest with the Soviet leaders' own experience within their own system.

Surprisingly to many, the superficial similarity between the "cover" Soviet system and the actual American system is striking. For instance, the Soviet constitution looks incredibly democratic, with all the freedoms "guaranteed." In some instances, the protection of justice and civil rights goes even further — on paper, of course — than in the United States.

Note the following examples of Soviet "paper liberties":

During police and KGB undercover operations related to corruption and counterespionage, it is prohibited to "provoke" or "tempt" the suspect. In other words, the undercover officer cannot offer a bribe to the suspect; the bribe must be solicited by the suspect.

Or any search in somebody's dwelling must be authorized and performed with two independent representatives of the general public, such as the suspect's neighbors, present to guarantee against any setup by the police.

Clips taken from World Monitor TV as Soviet Tanks and soldiers leave Frenstat, Czechoslovakia in February 1990

Or no actions of any sort can be taken against anybody before the suspect is proven guilty by the court, and no action can be taken against anybody based on his or her relative's guilt in any crime. And so on. Of course, everybody knows that all this is just on paper. But for various reasons these "paper liberties" do exist.

The Soviet leaders are the product of their society as much as anybody else in the country. They do not come straight from Yale, and they have to work their way up in the Soviet system not only with all its "paper liberties" but with all its Communist realities. On the way they become immune to the official status quo. A deep disbelief in the reality of any official political structure becomes their nature and is implanted in their minds on the subconscious level.

That is why these leaders cannot understand the nature of the relationship between Congress and the Executive Branch in the US. This becomes especially noticeable during the negotiation of treaties. The Soviet leaders genuinely do not understand how Congress could refuse to ratify a treaty signed by the President — other than by a prearranged plot. And they invariably take the warnings by American negotiators of possible difficulties (even in timing) in the ratification as merely a negotiating trick.

Such attitudes are not likely to change quickly even though Mr. Gorbachev is "democratizing" the Soviet Union's own government. Strange as it may sound, deep inside, these leaders are still searching for a mysterious center of the ultimate power in the United States. Not totally satisfying but still tempting to the Soviet leaders was the once popular myth that the United States is ruled by the "wealthiest 200 families" of the country, with the power delegated to some sort of "Committee." The trouble was that the KGB failed to locate the "Committee."

Nevertheless, the Soviet leadership still seems to believe in the myth. In the last political dance during the INF treaty negotiations Mr. Gorbachev's reference to Moscow's own "conservatives" who could have "objections" to the ratification of the treaty on the Soviet side looked like especially clumsy and amateurish negotiating. However, it just reflected his understanding of the Americans' uncertainty about ratification as a pure negotiating trick and his attempt to counter it. The fact that he made it look "clumsy" simply shows his conviction that the Americans were "negotiating," not really doubting the possibility of the ratification. It also shows his irritation with such a "cheap shot" in the negotia-

President Vaclav Havel (top) being interviewed by Simon Marks, World Monitor TV.

tions. He is too good to be clumsy, and, of course, there was no conservative opposition in Moscow.

Another example of the Soviet leaders' misinterpretation on the highest level was their total dismissal of the reasons for Watergate. They firmly believed that the underlying actual reason for the magnitude of the scandal was that President Nixon displeased the "real power holders" by becoming too independent in his decisions — for instance, by going too far in improving relations with the Soviet Union.

Misinterpretations on the US side also take their toll. These are somewhat understandable because of the closed nature of the Soviet society.

A classic example came in the late '70s and early '80s, when a lot of people were guessing the successor of ailing Leonid Brezhnev. Somehow somebody in the United States started the cute idea that Yuri Andropov could not be a serious contender because of his KGB background and thus inability to have popular support in the Soviet Union. The idea quickly caught on, and Andropov was swiftly removed from the list by many, if not most, western observers.

Nobody can blame these observers for not knowing such details of Soviet politics as Dmitri Polyansky's false start in the race for the helm, provoked by Andropov and Brezhnev himself, which cost Polyansky his career.

But the fundamentals should have been known. The simple fundamental principle of Soviet society is that popularity in the USSR comes with the office, not vice versa. Soviet politicians who tried to do it the other way around, invariably failed: Leon Trotsky, Sergei Kirov, Grigory Ordzhonikidze, Vasily Tolstikov, Dmitri Polyansky.... The first three of them paid with their lives for the mistake.

This sort of misinterpretation could lead to serious misjudgments even by the experts. For example, the CIA was apparently enchanted with the idea that a KGB man could not replace Brezhnev. It seemed to disregard a strong signal from Moscow at the time. Starting in about 1978, the whole mood of the KGB began to change — with Andropov's blessing. After a long "mild" period in its history, new tunes were being heard but not outside the KGB. Obeying orders of the direct superior without hesitation or questions was stressed as never before.

Traditionally, for all of the KGB headquarters staff, the only weapon had been the pistol. All of a sudden a lot of officers were required to take submachine gun training and were introduced to street battle techniques. After Lavrenti Beria's reign ended in 1953 the KGB was stripped of all military units except the lightly armed guards located at the borders. Under Andropov — surprisingly for those who knew KGB history — very quietly the border guards were given their own air force and armored units. Furthermore, since 1979 and until Brezhnev's death, at any given point in time a large number of KGB pilots and armored-unit officers were stationed in Moscow for "training." Of course, the heart and soul of all that quiet activity in the KGB was Yuri Andropov. For inside observers there was no question: Andropov was getting ready. Carefully.

But under the influence of the "no popularity" doctrine the CIA apparently dismissed the information on the spot and did not even seem to report it as a "raw intelligence." That was an unfortunate misinterpretation, as proved when Andropov did succeed Brezhnev at the pinnacle of Soviet power.

Another example of some American observers' misinterpretation is the attempt to forecast changes in Soviet strategy based on such purely tactical moves as *glasnost* and *perestroika*. The amazing thing is that this hunt for strategic hints looks like a mirror image of the KGB hunt for classification labels. In fact, all the information on Soviet strategy is openly available in the form of fundamental party documents that have never really changed since Lenin's time. The current campaigns in the Soviet Union represent strictly tactics and by no means reflect any change in the Communist strategy.

The best acknowledgment of that distinction was given by then Foreign Minister Andrei Gromyko and, of course, was not intended for the outside world. Answering in private the question of the largest weakness of the American policy toward the Soviet Union, he is quoted by his former aide Arkady Shevchenko as saying: "They don't comprehend our final goals. And they mistake tactics for strategy." This truly brilliant observation has to be taken very seriously.

To correct those misinterpretations it is important not to just disregard the fundamentals of Communism as "old, boring stuff" but to view them as the strategic manual that they really are. The best way to make the Communists happy is to try to find hints of Soviet strategy in their erratic PR stunts.

So, to avoid giving the Soviet Union an unearned advantage, it is important for the West to avoid basic misinterpretation as well as "chicken juice" mistranslations — to make a proper distinction between Soviet strategic and tactical moves and to keep in mind the fundamental differences between the two societies.

Powerful pictures can sometimes convey more than just words. The following television segment combines the visual impact of tanks leaving Prague with the perspective of Czechoslovakia's President Havel's wise words.

Soviet Troop Withdrawal From Czechoslovakia.   [2/26/90]

As Reported By Simon Marks for *World Monitor TV*

SM: They are the tanks that overthrew a government and today they finally went home. Years after they crushed the reforming Prague Spring, they were loaded and made ready for the trip back to Moscow.

It was a dusty, slow procedure, but in some ways, quicker than expected. The Communists have only been out of power here for three months.

The sixty soldiers selected to join the tanks on their journey were drilled one last time on Czechoslovakian soil, in the yard at Frenstat station. The atmosphere was informal, even commanding officers said they were happy to be pulling out.

[The camera is on Viacheslav Tretiak, Deputy Commanding Officer, and he says, "In Russia we say it is good to be a guest, but it's always better to be at home." The scene then switches to something else.]

SM: They may have been guests once, but now they've overstayed their welcome. Their political masters in Moscow know they've no choice but to begin bringing their men home.

[The camera now goes to Simon Marks and he says, "All two and a half thousand Soviet troops based here in Frenstat should be out within two weeks. But this is just the start of a full-scale national withdrawal. The new Czechoslovakian government has made it clear it wants to close the chapter opened when the Soviets invaded this country in 1968.]

SM: Then Frenstat was one of the main points of arrival for the Soviet invasion force—tanks appearing in the town square.

To commemorate today's events, a ceremony was held at the Frenstat Soviet army base. The world's press were invited in. "We have nothing to hide," the Soviets said.

The soldiers who will be on the next trains home were told the withdrawal was the result of changed political thinking in Moscow, rather than the changed political situation in Czechoslovakia. When news of the imminent pull-out broke ten days ago, the new non-Communist local officials say, everyone was thrilled.

[Dalibor Norsky, Civic Forum, says, "We had a meeting with the representatives of the Soviet army base, the local council, and Civic Forum. I ran out and told everybody. Everyone was very happy and they congratulated me."]

SM: The Soviets spent most of the weekend packing—loading the few sticks of army furniture worth transporting onto army trucks. Their future in the Soviet Union is dubious. The Russians say they don't have enough housing for the 75,000 troops who will return from Czechoslovakia over the next few months.

Some items they leave behind, remnants of an invasion the purpose of which was completed long ago. But a used Czechoslovakian car could ease life back home, so some fevered last-minute bargaining has been done with local drivers.

The Russian base is off limits to the local people, and as recently as this weekend to our cameras as well. From a hill overlooking the town we could see tanks still under wraps awaiting this morning's movements.

The countryside around the base has traditionally attracted tourists. Local politicians with the Soviet problem resolved, have a chance to develop that side of the region's economy.

The Soviet issue has dominated local and national politics here. Negotiations about the Russian withdrawal have continued since the pro-democracy government was propelled to power by last November's bloodless revolution.

Last week President Vaclev Havel told World Monitor the troop pull-out is just the beginning of a new relationship with Moscow and Prague.

[Vaclev Havel is interviewed by Simon Marks in Havel's apartment. These are Havel's words: "We were a Soviet satellite, a Soviet colony, and it's difficult for a slave to be a friend to his master. Now we will be masters in our own country, and we can establish a real friendship."]

SM: In Moscow today, President Havel and President Gorbachev settled the argument over the timetable for complete withdrawal. All Soviet troops will now be out of Czechoslovakia by July 1st next year.

By early this afternoon the first 30 tanks were loaded onto the train. Food and other provisions were also brought for the long train ride ahead.

At precisely 2:40 local time the Frenstat-to-Moscow express sounded its horn. The journey was soon under way. The moment the people of Czechoslovakia had waited 20 years to see was happening. The Red Army had begun its withdrawal from Czechoslovakia.

For World Monitor, I'm Simon Marks in Frenstat.

The Christian Science Monitor
from December 7, 1989.

Gorbachev Hands His Ace to Kohl [7/20/90]

By Joseph C. Harsch

Moscow has "played the German card" and the power world will be different now, as it always is when a major move is made on the great stage of world politics.

This is the move long foreseen, long dreaded by many, and long sought by others. It is the second such major move since World War II. The first was in 1972 when Richard Nixon went to Beijing, released China from the Soviet embrace, and thus redressed the military balance of the world.

The arrangements made on July 16 at an obscure little resort in southern Russia between the leaders of the Russian and German peoples releases the Germans from the division and servitude imposed upon them by the victors of World War II, and allows them to resume a major and independent role in world affairs.

Before July 16 two thirds of Germany was controlled from Washington and London, the other third from Moscow. Beginning on July 16 Germany is again what it was under Bismarck, Kaiser Wilhelm II, and Adolf Hitler—a rich, powerful and independent force able to direct its own course and destiny.

Moscow has had the ability to do this from the day Stalin seized upon the Eastern part of Germany and made it a separate state under his control backed by a half million Soviet soldiers. What Moscow took in 1945, Moscow alone had the power to give back.

Mikhail Gorbachev chose July 16 of this year to play the "German card," his ace of trumps. He chose a moment when the German mark was the world's strongest unit of currency and the West German economy one of the two soundest and most productive in the world. He handed the greatest prize possible, independence, to a Germany which is financially and economically capable of giving him the help he needs to revive his own failing economy. And he gives it when that Germany is willing as well as able to offer that economic support.

It is a balanced deal between the Russians and the Germans. The Russians get both needed economic support and also a promise that the new and independent Germany will sign the nuclear nonproliferation treaty. Germany, being independent, will be free to remain in the NATO alliance if it chooses to do so. But, for how long? Germany is perfectly free under this deal to choose to remain in or withdraw from NATO, to remain in and later pull out, or more probably, gradually attenuate its membership until it becomes meaningless.

It is a deal of mutual interest concluded exclusively between Russians and Germans. Americans, British, French, and other western countries had nothing to do with this deal. They were not consulted, or advised in advance.

They were spectators, and that fact causes every senior diplomat the world around instantly to remember the previous place and occasion. Rapallo, in Italy, in April of 1922, when the Russians and the Germans met together without consulting or advising any of the others and signed a treaty of mutual convenience the main visible feature of which was arrangement for substantial improvement in the flow of trade between the two. The two pariahs of the world joined in a mutual escape from the semi-ostracism of the rest of the world and helped each other mightily to regain economic health.

Rapallo has another implication. There were secret military clauses. The Germans had been forbidden to train armored units and a military air force by the terms of the Treaty of Versailles. Under the secret clauses the Germans were allowed to send their tanks and their aircraft into Soviet territory and train in collaboration with Soviet armor and aircraft. The armed forces with which Hitler later invaded the Soviet Union had their original training in modern weapons inside Russia with Russian consent.

There is no evidence of secret military clauses in the July 16 deal. But there is no reason this time for any secret military clauses. An independent Germany is automatically free to do whatever it likes within self-imposed and willingly accepted limits. There are now new limits on German military power set by the terms of this new agreement. They are set by the Russians. They are accepted willingly by the Germans. The obligation to observe them is owed exclusively by the Germans to the Russians.

One of the more interesting comments on these events of July 16 was that "there are no longer any superpowers." More precisely, this is an increasingly pluralistic world which is no longer dominated by two superpowers, the US and Soviet Union. The two rivals of the Cold-War era have still the largest economies in sheer size. But both are tired, sluggish, and relatively lower in the scale of productivity. The US was once rich enough to be able to finance the economic recovery of western Europe. Today Japan and Germany are the only two economies with enough surplus wealth and energy to be able to undertake the burden of reviving the economies of Eastern Europe and the Soviet Union.

It is merely a fact that when Moscow started looking around for economic help it found both limited ability and definite reluctance in both Washington and London. Neither was eager to do even what it could do. And what it could do was limited.

The power of initiative now has passed from the hands of Washington and London to the Germans.

Chancellor Helmut Kohl of Germany is today the most influential and powerful national leader in the world and his country is potentially the most important and influential in the world.

Where will all this lead?

The future is a blank page to be written upon. The Germans will do much of the writing. The Japanese will also be of high importance. Will Japan find in China the same outlet for its energies and resources that Germany is likely to find in Eastern Europe and the Soviet Union? Will the Soviets invite Japan into the task of developing Siberia, while the Germans are content with Europe to the Ural mountains?

There are many questions. We must wait for the answers.

Photo Credits